MODERN SOUTH WALES: ESSAYS IN ECONOMIC HISTORY

Modern South Wales:
Essays in Economic History

edited by
COLIN BABER
and
L.J. WILLIAMS

CARDIFF
UNIVERSITY OF WALES PRESS
1986

British Library Cataloguing in Publication Data.

Modern South Wales: essays in economic history.
1. Wales, South — Economic conditions
I. Baber, Colin   II. Williams, L.J.
330.9429'4085   HC257.S/

ISBN 0-7083-0943-7

Typeset in Great Britain by Quality Phototypesetting Ltd., Bristol
Printed in Great Britain by J.W. Arrowsmith Ltd., Bristol

Contents

Section C Twentieth Century

Tables, Figures, Maps and Appendices

List of Abbreviations

CG	*Colliery Guardian*
GRO	Glamorgan Record Office
H. of C.	House of Commons
H. of L.	House of Lords
HLRO	House of Lords Records Office
MSWCA	Monmouthshire and South Wales Coalowners Association
NLW	National Library of Wales
PP	Parliamentary Papers
PRO	Public Records Office
RC	Royal Commission
SC	Select Committee

In addition, when reading R.O. Roberts's 'Banks and the Economic Development of South Wales before 1914' see list of abbreviations on pp.288–9.

Preface

In December 1972, a colloquium was held at Gregynog Hall, near Newtown, Powys, the Conference Centre of the University of Wales. This was the first annual meeting of the staff and students, respectively teaching and studying economic history in the constituent colleges of the University of Wales. These meetings have concentrated on a variety of themes, ranging from 'Business History' and 'Entrepreneurial History' to 'The History of Economic Thought and Policy' and 'European Economic History'. To celebrate the tenth anniversary, it was decided to hold a special conference on the theme 'The Economic Development of South Wales 1780–1945' at which a number of leading academics working in the field would present papers. This volume is the result of that conference held in 1983. Gregynog Hall provided both a highly conducive and most appropriate setting with its close association with the family of David Davies from nearby Llandinam – the entrepreneur who successfully broke the port of Cardiff's coal export monopoly, by building Barry Dock by 1889 and linking it by railway to the Rhondda valleys: an example which aptly symbolizes the economic evolution of south Wales.

In addition to the contributors, the conference profited from the helpful comments and insights of a number of distinguished academics including Professor Glanmor Williams, Professor Sir Bryan Hopkin, Professor Eric Kerridge, Professor W.A. Cole, and Dr John Latham. Mr Harold Prescott, Professor Christopher Griffiths, Mr John Rhys, and undergraduate students of economic history from the colleges of the University of Wales also greatly enhanced the opportunity of analysing major features of south Wales's economic past. The Board of Celtic Studies and the Pantyfedwen Trust together provided the finance without which the conference could not have taken place. The editors wish to accord both bodies their grateful thanks. Finally, we wish to acknowledge the support of the University of Wales's Gregynog conference scheme which made the whole project possible.

Contributors

Brinley Thomas, formerly professor and head of Department of Economics, University College Cardiff (1946–73)

Colin Baber, senior lecturer in economic history, University College Cardiff

Michael Atkinson, WEA tutor/organizer, West Somerset

M.V. Symons, lecturer in civil engineering, UWIST

R.O. Roberts, honorary college research fellow in economic history, University College Swansea

David Howell, senior lecturer in history, University College Swansea

Tom Taylor, senior lecturer in economics, UWIST

A.G. Kenwood, senior lecturer and head of Department of Economics, University of Queensland

Hamish Richards, Director of Operations, Population Policies Branch, International Labour Organization, Geneva

M.J. Daunton, reader in history, University College London

Trevor Boyns, lecturer in economics, University College Cardiff

Robin Craig, formerly senior lecturer in history, University College London

L.J. Williams, senior lecturer in economic history and head of Department of Economic and Social History and Sociology, University College of Wales, Aberystwyth

Graeme Holmes, senior lecturer in economic history, UWIST

R.H. Morgan, senior lecturer in economics, Polytechnic of Wales

Brian Staines, careers officer, Argyllshire County Council

D.A. Thomas, lecturer in economics, University College of Wales, Aberystwyth

Introduction

Despite its active economic past the south Wales region has not proved to be a rich source of research for economic historians, and compared to the other major industrial regions in Britain the study of the economic development of south Wales is characterized by the paucity of the detailed scholarship which has been bestowed upon it. This is somewhat surprising as the region has spawned more than its fair share of eminent academic economic historians, including Brinley Thomas, John Habakkuk, Arthur John, and David Joslin. Although in 1950 Professor John's pioneering *Industrial Development of South Wales*[1] promised the start of a rich vein of academic achievement, the lead was not followed, and it was not until thirty years later that the next major step in chronicling the economic history of south Wales occurred when Professor Glanmor Williams, due to the untimely death of Professor John, assumed the editorship of the fifth volume of the Glamorgan County History and published *Industrial Glamorgan* in 1980.[2] Certainly, articles and a few books, such as J.H. Morris and L.J. Williams's *The South Wales Coal Industry, 1841–1875*[3], were written in the interim about various aspects of the economic history of south Wales, but there was little momentum created, and limited follow-up. Studies were few, sporadic and 'individual' with little or no attempt at bringing them together in meaningful order.

The basic economic development of south Wales since the early beginnings of industrialization is broadly known, but scant detailed analysis exists. Much of the story of south Wales's economic past is to be found implicitly in studies and research that are essentially social or political history. Economic explanations of the implications of social and political change have often found their way into the scholarship as accepted economic pronouncements, when they have, in fact, been marginal to the main emphasis of the work, be it social or political. In the past, economic history in Wales has often found itself, because of its limited independent development, in an academic no man's land. The conference gave an opportunity for economic historians rather than their social or political counterparts to present a view of south Wales's economic past as a contribution to the region's history.

This is not to say, however, that the collection of papers presented in this volume are efforts at reinterpreting the economic development of south Wales in what amounts to the approach of the 'new economic history'. Over the past two decades or so, a veritable revolution has occurred in the approach and therefore the type of scholarship which has characterized economic history, commencing perhaps in 1958 with Alfred Conrad and Joseph Meyer's study of the economic viability of slavery in the southern states of the USA before the Civil War,[4] and by the early 1980s the 'new' approach had been fully accepted into the main body of economic history's scholarship. It would, however, largely because of the paucity of the data, be both inappropriate and extremely difficult at this stage to consider such an approach to the economic history of south Wales. This volume should therefore be seen simply as a means of bringing together the research of academics who are working in this field and thus of effecting an exchange of their ideas, findings and approaches. The editors have, however, attempted to achieve a degree of balance in the contents and so it could be argued that, while not presenting a comprehensive economic history of south Wales, the volume does provide a skeletal framework of the economic development of the area between 1780 and 1945.

We were particularly pleased to welcome as one of the participants Professor Brinley Thomas who was for many years Professor of Economics at University College, Cardiff, who has since 1975 occupied a post as visiting professor in the School of Demography at the University of California in Berkeley, and was one of the founding fathers of the 'Gregynog tradition' of the University of Wales. Professor Thomas, although perhaps best known for his contributions to our understanding of the economics of capital and population migration,[5] has also written widely on the economic history of south Wales, with much of his early work in the 1920s and 1930s contributing to a better understanding of the populating of south Wales during the nineteenth century, and the movement of people from south Wales between the two world wars.[6] In 1962, Professor Thomas edited a major work, *The Welsh Economy, Studies in Expansion,*[7] and in it he reiterated a conclusion which he originally expounded in article form a few years before.[8] In this, Professor Thomas speculated upon the idea that the industrialization which rapidly transformed the valleys of south Wales during the nineteenth and early twentieth centuries assured a future for both the Welsh language and Welsh culture. The Welsh-speaking population, unsettled in the rural parts of south Wales and mid Wales by changes in agricultural organization were attracted by the high wages which the industrialization of the south Wales coalfield generated, and thus poured into small urban concentrations such as Treorchy or Brynmawr, retaining their language and their way of living. The alternative, the wide distribution of Welsh men and women over the English industrial map, would almost certainly have meant a loss of both. Since the idea was first propounded in the late 1950s, it has proved to be a rich vein for subsequent research, as was evidenced by the number of visiting academics and postgraduate students who came to the conference simply to listen to 'Brinley' speak. In the first paper presented below, Professor Thomas revisits his early findings, and, in the light of all the subsequent work in the field, argues that his thesis has adequately stood the test of time. It was thought both appropriate and pertinent to commence with Professor Thomas's essay. Here is a major academic returning to a piece of work which has provided a starting-point for so much subsequent research and which, in becoming one of the major 'topics' in Welsh history, in many ways highlights the contribution which the economic historian can make.

The 'Old Order', as Arthur John has described it,[9] gave way around the middle of the eighteenth century to the beginning of a new economic order which became increasingly based upon industrial activity. While we would not exaggerate the divisions, the whole period of industrialization in south Wales seems to lend itself to three phases, which help us to arrange the papers presented in a meaningful order. The first phase lasted from the middle of the eighteenth century to around 1840. During this period, in addition to small-scale, scattered industrial activities springing up in many parts of south Wales in response to the region's growing population and including wool-making, flour-milling, stone-quarrying and beer-brewing, two areas of distinct industrial concentration emerged. The first of these saw iron-smelting stretch along the northern rim of the coalfield as ample supplies of ironstone and good coking coal were found in close proximity. The only constraint upon the exploitation of the juxtaposition of the two minerals was logistic, and Colin Baber shows in his paper the impact which the building of a few canals had upon the industry's expansion. By linking the coalfield to the coast, the canals made possible in particular a commercially viable iron-smelting industry, and in general the dawning of real industrial development both along the valleys through which they ran and in the towns along the coast where they met the sea.

As the first half of the nineteenth century progressed, iron-smelting rapidly expanded, and by 1840 south Wales boasted the most significant iron industry, not merely in Britain, but in the world. This position was, however, short-lived, and in his essay Dr Atkinson argues that even before the inventions of the Bessemer Converter and the Open Hearth furnace occasioned the advent of cheap, bulk steel manufacture which in its turn necessitated the importation of haematite iron ore especially from Cumbria into south Wales, the pendulum had already begun to swing away from the region's mineral advantages. This, Dr Atkinson explains, occurred as a result of a combination of the 'qualitative' advantages of imported haematite compared to local ironstone, and the increasing costs of raising Welsh 'mine'.

The other industrial area to emerge in south Wales during the eighteenth century was the south-western part of the coalfield comprising the south-eastern parts of Carmarthenshire and south-west Glamorgan. In his paper, Dr Symons analyses the exploitation of the bituminous coal measures in and around Llanelli, and shows how, by the middle of the nineteenth century, the mining of coal in the district had brought the south-west corner of the coalfield into the mainstream of industrial expansion. The mining of coal close to the sea saw not only the early development of an export coal trade but also the attraction of non-ferrous metal smelting, particularly of imported copper ore, to the area.[10] Although the mining of coal existed in many parts of south Wales during this period, it was generally sporadic, and the only other concentrations of activity were along the northern rim of the coalfield where coking coal was mined for the iron industry, and in the Monmouthshire valleys where mining expanded rapidly due largely to the exporting advantages enjoyed by the port of Newport.[11] R.O. Roberts shows how the industrial activities in this first phase occasioned the establishment of banking institutions which in turn enhanced the process of industrialization and provided the short-term capital so necessary in a region with a limited industrial tradition.

From the 1840s, the industrial development of south Wales accelerated, and its geographic extent widened as the growth of coal-mining successively blackened the green rural valleys, and a second phase in the region's industrial history was witnessed. By the end of the nineteenth century, south Wales had become narrowly dependent upon the 'sale' coal industry and had emerged as the world's major coal exporting region. This achievement brought a number of significant implications for the region's economy, and Dr David Howell describes how, as in other parts of Britain, industrial expansion resulted in increased pressure upon the farming sector, which occasioned the emergence of a more intensive agricultural supply; of 'high farming'. Increasing industrialization also necessitated the creation of a more suitable infrastructure, particularly conducive to what was rapidly becoming the region's major economic activity, the export of coal. Tom Taylor examines the formation of fixed capital in the major sphere of infrastructure building in south Wales — railway construction, and this is complemented by George Kenwood's analysis of dock construction in the south Wales ports. Hamish Richards considers the responses made in certain parts of the region to the increasing need for public health and sanitation provision created by the rapid growth of population — a sphere of activity which was so important, yet so often overlooked by historians. Robin Craig in analysing the growth of one of south Wales's major shipping companies during the later nineteenth century reminds us that economic growth was not limited to the actual coalfield and that the ports, in particular Cardiff and Swansea, fully shared in the prosperity created.

In his analysis of the interaction between technological change and the labour force, Dr Martin Daunton presents a detailed view of the productive activities of a number of individual industries, and Dr Trevor Boyns examines the structure of the coal-mining industry, particularly focusing on the varying experiences of two of the major producers, the Powell Duffryn and the Ocean Coal Companies. By the end of the nineteenth century, the British economy had reached a mature stage, which was marked by a decline in the rate of industrial growth, and L.J. Williams examines the south Wales economy during the period and assesses the extent to which the region shared in the British 'climacteric'.

Although the First World War was not in itself the immediate 'cause' of all the region's economic ills thereafter, it did nevertheless mark a reversal in the fortunes of south Wales and the emergence of a third phase of industrial change. Graeme Holmes examines the environment within which the coal industry came under Government control during the war and the implications of the changes which were generated. Despite the revisionism which has largely rewritten the economic history of Britain between the two world wars, it is still possible to see that the period was one of secular decline for south Wales. Whereas the creation of an effective electricity supply went a long way to help provide a base for economic prosperity in the country as a whole, Bob Morgan shows that its effect upon south Wales was limited. Little else occurred within the region to relieve the monotony of the economic hopelessness which was engendered, and one of the few measures which Government did introduce was the Industrial Transference Scheme in 1928. Brian Staines evaluates its role as a means of alleviating the incidence of unemployment, which was the single most pernicious manifestation of the economic malaise affecting south Wales between the Wars. Despite rearmament, it was not until the Second World War that the region's economy was jogged out of the state into which it had fallen, and Dennis Thomas shows how the war succeeded where the Government and the free market system had failed. The Second World War thus marks the commencement of a fourth phase of south Wales's economic development.

The Industrial Revolution and the Welsh Language

BRINLEY THOMAS

In 1959 I wrote an article, 'Wales and the Atlantic Economy', which was published in the *Scottish Journal of Political Economy*.[1] It contained a section entitled 'Industrialization and the Welsh Language', in which I argued that the high rate of economic growth in Wales in the second half of the nineteenth century, far from having been a disaster to the Welsh language, had in fact given it a new lease of life. In the sixty years up to 1911 most of the Welsh-speaking people who had to leave the countryside migrated into the expanding industrial areas of south and north Wales. They raised large families and the majority were brought up to speak Welsh. How else would it have been possible for 633,000 of the population of Glamorgan, Carmarthenshire, Monmouthshire and Denbighshire to be Welsh-speaking in 1911? According to the census of that year no less than 65 per cent of the people speaking Welsh in Wales were living in these four industrialized counties. My analysis of the census figures led me to conclude as follows:

> Instead of bemoaning the rural exodus, the Welsh patriot should sing the praises of industrial development. In that tremendous half-century before the First World War, economic growth in Wales was so vigorous that her net loss of people was a mere 4 per cent of her bountiful natural increase over the period. Few countries in Europe came anywhere near to that. The unrighteous Mammon in opening up the coalfields at such a pace unwittingly gave the Welsh language a new lease of life and Welsh nonconformity a glorious high noon.[2]

At first this maverick line of argument was received rather coldly in certain quarters of Wales. It departed too abruptly from the received wisdom enshrined in the standard Welsh history textbooks, and it ran counter to the orthodox beliefs of most supporters of Plaid Cymru. However, as the years rolled on, the intellectual climate changed and the idea became respectable enough to appear as a question in an A-level Welsh History examination paper. This was partly because several writers had taken up the subject as an area of study, and my statistical argument, when properly defined, came to be accepted as plausible. After more than two decades, it is now a good time to take another look at the topic in the light of recent research.

As originally stated, the argument concerning the Welsh language dealt with the second half of the nineteenth century. It was clear from the migration statistics that in the first decade of the twentieth century the great increase in English immigration into Wales was a potent anglicizing influence. The significance of this watershed will be dealt with later in this paper. To attain the right perspective, one must take the entire nineteenth century and ask what would have happened to the Welsh language if Wales had not had an industrial revolution. The clearest way to pose the question is to set up a counterfactual. What would have been the fate of the Welsh language if Wales had been like Ireland, a predominantly agricultural country without coal or iron? In order to answer this question we must first define the phases of the industrial revolution.

The Industrial Revolution — a drama in three acts

The industrial revolution was Britain's response to the energy crisis which she experienced in the second half of the eighteenth century.[3] Between 1750 and 1800 the population of Britain increased by 47 per cent as compared with only 9 per cent between 1700 and 1750. This population explosion intensified the necessity to change the energy base from wood fuel to fossilized fuel, i.e., from the flow of solar energy to the stock. The crisis expressed itself in a variety of pressures on land use — land for bread grains, pasture for animal products, timber for shipbuilding and housing, oak for the Royal Navy, charcoal for the iron industry, wood ash for alkalies for textiles. Moreover, additional land was required to meet the needs of urban growth, manufacturing, and transport networks. It was Malthusian pressure on a very small land area. England had to rely increasingly on her Celtic periphery for essential foodstuffs. Between 1760 and 1790 the value of Ireland's exports to the mainland went up two and a half times, from £1,451,000 to £3,696,000; imports of Irish beef rose threefold, butter sixfold, and pork sevenfold. In 1794–6 no less than 44 per cent of Britain's imports of grain, butter and meat came from Ireland. Irish land was being called in to alleviate the mounting pressures on English land.[4]

The most pressing problem was the increasing shortage of timber and especially charcoal. Britain was heavily dependent on Sweden, Norway and Russia for bar iron, timber and naval stores. An estimate for 1788 shows that two-thirds of total British iron consumption was dependent on charcoal iron, of which about 75 per cent had to be imported. Between the 1740s and the 1770s the price of charcoal rose 30 per cent in relation to the average price of producer goods, and the price of imported Swedish bar iron doubled between 1750 and 1795.[5] Imports of fir timber went up from 40,000 to 313,000 tons between 1752 and 1792,[6] and reports from all over the country indicated that these supplies from abroad were essential to make up for inadequate quantities of native timber for construction.[7] Even by the early 1750s timber cargoes accounted for as much as one half the total tonnage of ships entering British ports.[8] On the eve of the War of American Independence one third of the British merchant ships had been built in the American colonies. The symptoms of a deep-seated energy crisis were evident in the divergent course of market prices. Between 1750 and the 1780s the trend of the price of charcoal was sharply upward and that of the price of coal was downward in relation to the average price of producer goods. During the 1700s the level of real investment in coal-mining and manufacturing actually fell by as much as one third,[9] a clear sign of the deterioration of investment incentives as a result of the energy crisis. This paralysing structural imbalance could be resolved only by a total switch from charcoal to coal in the iron industry, and this could not be achieved until a fundamental innovation had been made.

After many inventors had struggled with the problem over a long period of time, the solution came in 1784 when Henry Cort invented his puddling and rolling process which overcame satisfactorily all the problems of substituting coal or coke for charcoal in refining pig iron into bar iron in a reverberatory furnace.[10] The energy crisis was over and the era of fossilized fuels had begun. It was the type of bar iron produced by this new process, together with James Watt's steam engine, which made possible the world of railroads, steamships and machine tools. 'Without these discoveries we could never have had such fundamentally important pieces of metal as a railway iron or a ship's plate. The unaided hammer could not have achieved them. The puddle and the grooved roll closed the era of the blacksmith's supremacy and opened the era of machine production.'[11] In the first fifteen years there was a 45 per cent increase in coal output, and in the first half of the nineteenth century it grew from 11 million to 64 million tons per annum. Pig iron production rose from 62,000 tons in the early 1780s to 154,000 in 1796–1800 and reached 3,070,000 tons by 1854.[12]

The solution of Britain's energy crisis meant a release from the Malthusian pressure on her small land area. Thanks to being the first to switch from wood fuel to fossilized fuel, she became the workshop of the world and exchanged the industrial fruits of her new technology for abundant cheap food from land-rich continents of new settlement. This was in effect the equivalent of a vast importation of land; from Britain's point of view this was what the Atlantic economy of the nineteenth century was all about.[13] It was in the second half of the century that most of the harvest of the industrial revolution was reaped because it took several decades of transition (1790–1850) to prepare the foundations of the new economy (machine tools, railroads and steamships). The world-wide network made possible by coal, iron and steel, the transport revolution, new technology, capital exports, international migration, and free trade resulted in a substantial rural exodus and a running down of British agriculture to less than 5 per cent of national income. This extreme specialization, while highly profitable, entailed great hazards for Britain and in the long run was destined to be a short-lived bonanza. The great economist Jevons warned about this as early as 1865 even before Britain reached her prime. 'For the present', he declared, 'our cheap supplies of coal and our skill in its employment, and the freedom of our commerce with other wider lands, render us independent of the limited agricultural area of these islands, and apparently take us out of the scope of Malthus' doctrine.'[14]

To summarize, Britain's industrial revolution was a drama in three acts:

Act I   1760–1790   Malthusian pressure and energy shortage. *Solution* through fundamental innovations by Henry Cort and James Watt.

Act II   1790–1850   *Transition.* The new technology applied to the building of machine tools, railroads and steamships — the prerequisites for a

modern economy based on coal, iron and steel and an
international transport revolution.

Act III   1850–1900   *Fulfilment.* Britain the workshop of the world and the centre of
the Atlantic economy. By 1870 she was producing one third of
the world's manufacturing output. Abundant imports of cheap
food from 1870 on. Four-fifths of Britain's wheat supply came
from abroad at the end of the century. The population doubled
and its overall standard of living doubled.

The Industrial Revolution and the language, 1790–1850

During what I have called Act II of the industrial revolution, the ironmasters of south
Wales took a leading part in adopting Henry Cort's puddling and rolling process.
Richard Crawshay of Cyfarthfa ironworks was one of the first to take out a licence and his
furnaces were producing bar iron with the new technique as early as November 1787. The
Penydarren works also adopted puddling in the same year. The innovation spread rapidly
and by 1815 the output of puddled bar iron in south Wales was about 60,000 tons which
was almost twice the total production in the whole of the British iron industry in 1788.
The growth of pig iron output in Wales in the first half of the nineteenth century was as
follows:

Output of Pig Iron[15]

Year	South Wales (000 tons)	North Wales (000 tons)	Welsh output as % of U.K. output
1806	71	3	30
1847	707	16	36

During the forty years ending in 1847 pig iron production in south Wales grew tenfold
from 71,000 to 707,000 tons per annum and in north Wales fivefold from 3,000 to 16,000
tons per annum. By 1847 Wales accounted for 36 per cent of total United Kingdom
output. The same spectacular expansion was seen in the coal industry.

Coal Output[16]

Year	South Wales (000 tons)	North Wales (000 tons)	Wales (000 tons)	Welsh output as % of G.B. output
1801–6[a]	1,200	350	1,550	12.0
1854	8,500	1,430	9,930	15.4

[a]Annual averages.

The annual output of coal in south Wales went up sevenfold to 8,500,000 tons and in north Wales fourfold to 1,430,000 tons between 1801–6 and 1854, and in the latter year Wales contributed 15.4 per cent of total output in Great Britain.

Rapid industrialization in the first half of the nineteenth century entailed considerable in-migration from the countryside as well as a high rate of natural increase in the areas transformed by the booming coal and iron industries. By examining these demographic movements we can estimate the effects on the Welsh-speaking population. Between the first census of 1801 and that of 1851 the population of south Wales grew from 315,000 to 726,000. Of this increase of 411,000 people, no less than 272,000, or about two-thirds, were living in Monmouthshire and Glamorgan. Table 1 gives the figures for the six counties.

Table 1
Population of south Wales by county, 1801–1851 (nearest 1000)

County	1801 (000)	1851 (000)
Monmouthshire	46	157
Glamorgan	71	232
Brecknockshire	32	61
Pembrokeshire	56	94
Carmarthenshire	67	111
Cardiganshire	43	71
South Wales	315	726

Source: *Population Census,* 1801 and 1851.

With the exception of certain parts of Monmouthshire, the spectacular increase in the population of the two major south Wales counties was almost entirely Welsh in character. This was demonstrated by the late Arthur John in his authoritative work published in 1950.[17] 'Attracted by high wages, the agricultural labourers moved into the industrial areas in large numbers from Pembrokeshire, Carmarthenshire, Brecknockshire and Cardiganshire, and in lesser numbers from the English counties . . . The effect of this demand for labour upon the hill country of west Wales was such that between 1821–41 there commenced a long and continuous depopulation which cannot be explained by agricultural reorganisation. In the forties the depopulation spread to parishes in the coastal plain of Carmarthenshire and Pembrokeshire, but never as strikingly as in the mountainous region.'[18]

The Welshness of the cradle of the industrial revolution in Wales was documented in a statistical survey of Merthyr Tydfil in 1841 published in the *Journal of the Statistical Society*

Table 2
An analysis of the population of Merthyr Tydfil,
made in the spring of 1841

Total Population	32,968	Exclusive of Coedycymmer, Hamlet of Vaynor, Taff, and Cynon, and Forest-hill.
Houses..............................	6,145	5½ persons to a house nearly.
Sleeping rooms........................	10,835	Three persons to a room.
Children under three years of age...	3,203	
Children from three to twelve years	6,857	Age for education, full one-fifth of the population.
Lodgers..............................	6,140	One for each house.
English people........................	4,181	13 per cent. of the population.
Welsh................................	27,802	84 per cent. of the population.
Irish.................................	985	3 per cent. of the population.
Persons who can speak English intelligibly...........................	10,917	
Children who go to day-schools, by report of their parents.............	1,272	Less than a fifth of those who ought to go.
Ditto, by report of teachers..........	1,313	
Pupils attending nineteen Sunday-schools at Dissenting chapels.....	4,581	Average attendance.
Ditto at Church Sunday-schools....	350	Average attendance.
Can read..............................	11,774	
Can write..............................	5,709	
Persons among the labouring classes who have other books beside religious books......................	445	
Do not go to a place of worship.....	11,759	
Workmen occasionally intoxicated.	2,587	
Workmen who have houses being their own property................	91	
Lodging-houses	59	
Children working and living with their parents........................	2,940	
Females working......................	404	
Churches 2, will contain.......... } Chapels 26, will contain.......... }	15,182	

Source: G.S. Kenrick, 'Statistics of Merthyr Tydfil', *Journal of the Statistical Society of London*, IX (March 1846), p.14.

of London in 1846 by G.S. Kenrick of the Varteg ironworks.[19] A summary is set out in Table 2. Of the population of 32,968, as many as 27,802, or 84 per cent, were Welsh, 4,181, or 13 per cent, were English, and the remaining 3 per cent Irish. There were 26 Nonconformist chapels with accommodation for 13,350; they were entirely Welsh and the attendance was described as 'full' or 'tolerably full'. The two Church of England churches had sittings for 1,500 and the attendance was estimated at 850. Over a third of the population did not go to a place of worship. Only 1,272 children went to day schools ('less than a fifth of those who ought to go'),[20] but 4,581 pupils attended the Nonconformist Sunday schools. The survey estimated that one in five of the workmen in Merthyr were 'occasionally intoxicated'.[21] As a result of the heavy in-migration of men from the countryside, there were as many lodgers (6,140) as there were houses. The author of the survey commented that '. . . it is surprising that a large village so near the boundary of an English county as Merthyr is, and having such frequent communication with it, should have so small a number of Saxons, as the English are called, among the population — only about 4,000 out of a population of 33,000'.[22]

As a proxy for the Welsh-speaking population at mid-century, figures produced by the Religious Census of 1851, summarized in Table 3, are worth noting.

Table 3
Wales 1851: places of worship, sittings and attendances by denomination

Denomination	Places of worship	Sittings	Attendances		
			Morning	*Afternoon*	*Evening*
Church of England	1,180	279,113	100,953	49,091	39,662
Nonconformists	2,770	610,734	268,612	139,209	369,494
Other Churches[a]	56	8,595	7,451	3,714	4,086
Totals	4,006	898,442	377,016	192,014	413,442

[a] Roman Catholics, Catholic Apostolic, Mormons and Jews.
Source: *Census of Great Britain, 1851, Religious Worship –England and Wales, Report and Tables,* PP (1690), Vol. LXXXIX, Table B.

It is generally agreed that the count of sittings was reasonably accurate. The 4,006 places of worship in Wales in 1851 could accommodate 898,442 people or 75 per cent of the population, easily the highest proportion for any region in Britain. The share of the Nonconformists was 610,734, or 70 per cent, and the vast majority of these sittings were in Welsh chapels.[23]

The statistics on attendances are very difficult to interpret; it is clear that the propensity to worship in the evening was high in the Nonconformist chapels and low in the Church of England. Instead of making guesses about the probable attendance rates, it is best to stay with the accommodation rates and compare the industrial areas with the rural. The figures in Table 4 reflect the redistribution of population in south Wales in the first half of the nineteenth century; the average ratio of sittings to population in 1851 was 61 per cent in the industrial areas compared with 87 per cent in the rural areas.

Table 4
Ratio of sittings to population in urban and rural districts, 1851

District	Population	Sittings	Accommodation Rate %
Neath	46,471	28,285	61
Swansea	46,907	33,618	72
Newport	43,472	24,636	57
Cardiff	46,491	29,944	64
Merthyr	76,804	41,763	54
Monmouth	27,379	18,532	68
Total	287,524	176,778	61
Lampeter	9,874	8,874	90
Cardigan	20,186	18,918	94
Newcastle-in-Emlyn	20,173	16,364	94
Rhayader	6,796	6,323	93
Narberth	22,130	18,897	85
Aberaeron	13,224	11,353	85
Total	92,383	80,729	87

Source: Ieuan Gwynedd Jones and David Williams, eds., *The Religious Census of 1851. A Calendar of the Returns relating to Wales,* Vol. I (University of Wales Press, 1976), Appendix B.

Because of the rural exodus, 1801–51, there was in 1851 an excess demand for chapels in the industrialized districts (Neath, Swansea, Cardiff, Merthyr and Monmouth) and an excess supply in the rural districts (Lampeter, Cardigan, Newcastle-in-Emlyn, Rhayader, Narberth, and Aberaeron): Wales had become predominantly Nonconformist and the areas undergoing industrialization were mainly Welsh-speaking. Even before the railways had transformed the means of mobility,[24] the centre of gravity had moved from the rural sector to the urban with profound implications for the future.

As a counterpart to our analysis of Glamorgan, it is instructive to examine the demography of the north Wales coalfield. A detailed survey of population changes and linguistic areas in north-east Wales in the nineteenth century has been carried out by Dr W.T.R. Pryce.[25] The population of north-east Wales increased from 79,500 in 1801 to 166,500 in 1891. According to Dr Pryce's analysis,[26] the distribution of the 1891 population by type area was as follows:

North-east Wales	Per cent
Coalfield	16.4
Lead-mining	11.4
Agricultural	12.2
Agricultural parishes with market towns	12.0

Population had more than doubled as a result of industrialization. What was the effect on the Welsh language? Thanks to Dr Pryce's thorough analysis of language zones, it is possible to give a quantitative answer to this question for the period 1801–51. The results are given in Table 5.

Table 5
North-east Wales: distribution of population by language zones, 1801 and 1851

Language zones	1801		1851	
	Number (nearest 100)	%	Number (nearest 100)	%
E Consistently English	7,600	9.5	10,300	7.7
BE Bilingual becoming virtually English	9,800	12.3	15,200	11.4
B Consistently bilingual	19,700	24.9	41,600	31.2
W Consistently Welsh	25,400	32.2	38,000	28.5
aW Slightly anglicized but reverting to Welsh	3,200	3.9	5,100	3.8
WB Welsh becoming virtually bilingual	13,500	17.2	23,200	17.4
North-east Wales[a]	79,200	100.0	133,400	100.0

[a] Excluding five parishes with no clear evidence on which to establish long-term linguistic trends.

Source: W.T.R. Pryce, 'Migration and the evolution of culture areas: cultural and linguistic frontiers in north-east Wales, 1750 and 1851', *Transactions of the Institute of British Geographers* (June 1975), Table 2, p. 92.

In Table 5 all persons classified in zones other than E (consistently English), and BE (bilingual becoming virtually English), were able to speak Welsh. From the standpoint of this paper, the interesting fact is that the number of Welsh speakers in north-east Wales rose from 61,800 in 1801 to 118,200 in 1851. This is an important contribution towards an answer to the basic question which I posed originally, namely, the effect of the industrial revolution in Wales on the *absolute number* of people speaking Welsh not on the *relative numbers* of Welsh speakers in areas where English immigration became heavy. Dr Pryce is more interested in the long-run significance of bilingual zones; in his view, '. . . the bilingual zone was an agent of socialization and, therefore, of anglicization . . .'[27] This may well have been so in certain areas and I do not underestimate the importance of this aspect of the subject. Nevertheless, it cannot alter the fact that by the middle of the nineteenth century the *absolute number* of people speaking Welsh had reached a total which would have been impossible if Wales had not had an industrial revolution based on coal, iron, steel and ample capital resources.

The Industrial Revolution and the language, 1851–1911

In the second half of the nineteenth century, which I have called Act III of the industrial revolution, south Wales again played a pivotal role as a result of the enormous expansion of the steam-coal export trade. The annual output of coal in south Wales rose sevenfold — from 8.5 million tons to 56.8 million tons between 1854 and 1913. My original analysis was based on the demographic history of this period and particularly on the statistics of the number of persons speaking Welsh which began in the 1891 population census. A thorough statistical scrutiny of my results was carried out by Philip N. Jones in 1969.

Table 6
Lifetime in-migrants enumerated in Glamorgan in 1891 and 1911 by nationality and district of residence

Nationality	1891			1911		
	Coalfield	Non-coalfield	Total	Coalfield	Non-coalfield	Total
Welsh	98,569	24,396	122,965	126,169	24,963	151,132
Non-Welsh	71,687	57,597	129,284	141,464	68,033	209,497
Total	170,256	81,993	252,249	267,633	92,996	360,629

Source: Philip N. Jones, 'Some Aspects of Immigration into the Glamorgan Coalfield between 1881 and 1911', *Transactions of the Honourable Society of Cymmrodorion* (1969, Part 1), p. 87 and 89.

Taking the county of Glamorgan between 1881 and 1911, he rightly pointed out the need to divide the county into two parts, the coalfield and the coastal areas (non-coalfield), and to examine the flow of migrants, Welsh and non-Welsh, into these two sections of the county. The figures for 1891 and 1911 are shown in Table 6.

According to Philip Jones, the analysis of the population census figures demonstrates that '. . . in 1891, at the end of many decades of persistent migration gain, the orientation of the vast majority of *Welsh* migration was to the Coalfield part of Glamorgan and not to the coastal centres of Cardiff and Swansea. For English migration the position was, generally speaking, reversed . . .'[28] He went on to conclude that '. . . this migration situation does not appear to support, perhaps, the view of Professor Thomas, since the selectivity exhibited by Welsh migration into Glamorgan resulted in a "massing of reserves" — their strength was not dissipated by being evenly spread through the county'.[29]

It is well-known that the final phase of the expansion of the south Wales coalfield, 1901–11, attracted a record volume of immigration from England.[30] Table 6 shows clearly how this flood of non-Welsh migrants penetrated the largely Welsh coal-mining valleys of Glamorgan; the number of non-Welsh lifetime immigrants enumerated in the coal-mining area of the county doubled between 1891 and 1911 (from 71,687 to 141,464), whereas the number of Welsh immigrants enumerated there went up by only one third (from 95,569 to 126,169). Between 1891 and 1911 the proportion of Welsh people in the stock of lifetime immigrants in the coal-mining districts fell from 56 per cent to 47 per cent and in the county as a whole from 49 per cent to 42 per cent. The watershed revealed in Table 6 must be regarded as significant in that it threatened the *future* of the Welsh language. This point was emphasized by R.I. Aaron in the following comment:

> There is clearly much to be said for Professor Thomas' thesis that 'the Welsh language was saved by the redistribution of a growing population brought about by industrialism'. But the immigrants to the south Wales industrial areas did not come solely from the Welsh rural areas. Up to the beginning of the century the big majority were Welsh-speaking, and they absorbed with comparative ease the few non-Welsh who joined them. The figures for the decade 1901–11, however, tell a different story; they show that immigration from outside Wales in this decade was exceedingly large . . . The linguistic balance was upset and instead of absorbing the English-speaking immigrants the Welsh speakers themselves were in danger of being absorbed. The most significant figure in the 1911 Census Report was not the 50,000 increase in the number speaking Welsh but the decline in the percentage of Welsh speakers in Wales from 49.9 per cent in 1901 to 43.5 per cent in 1911.[31]

Richard Aaron is right in emphasizing that the linguistic balance was upset in the first decade of this century. The following conclusion by Philip Jones must be read in the same light:

> The redistribution of the Welsh language prompted by industrialization was not sufficient to counter the vast flood of outside immigration which was essential to meet the demands which that industrialization, by its scale and intensity, had created. Wales had admitted a Trojan horse.[32]

This statement is valid not for the nineteenth century but for the first decade of the twentieth century. This is confirmed when the author goes on to suggest that his analysis is nowhere more aptly summarized than by the Commission of Inquiry into Industrial Unrest of 1917:

> Until some 15 to 20 years ago (i.e., about 1895–1900) the native inhabitants, in many respects, showed a marked capacity for stamping their own impress on all newcomers, and communicating to them a large measure of all their own characteristics; in more recent years the process of assimilation had been unable to keep pace with the continuing influx of immigrants.[33]

My thesis concerning industrialization and the Welsh language rests on developments during the nineteenth century, and it cannot be refuted by citing the strong build-up of anglicizing forces after the turn of the century. Philip Jones makes this quite clear in the following conclusion:

> Nevertheless, seen in the wider perspective of the economic history of the Celtic countries from the late eighteenth century forward, Professor Thomas's argument is a very valid one. During the eighty or so years after 1800 Welsh rural emigration was diverted to an industrial region within Wales, where it immensely strengthened the fabric of Welsh cultural life in the *nineteenth century,* rather than being dissipated in the alien culture realms of England, America or Australasia.[34]

This statement contains the essence of my argument and later in this paper I shall amplify it in the light of the contrast with Ireland. But before coming to that, I wish to stress that the diversion of Welsh rural emigration into the industrial sector of Wales is only part of the demographic story in the nineteenth century. The Welsh-speaking population was reinforced not only by immigration into the industrial areas from the Welsh countryside but also to a considerable extent by the natural increase (excess of births over deaths) in the industrial areas. Let us leave out the decade 1901–11 and concentrate on the period 1861–1901 when, it is generally agreed, the community life of most of the expanding coal-mining areas was strongly Welsh and '. . . the native inhabitants, in many respects, showed a marked capacity for stamping their own impress on all newcomers . . .'[35] The birth-rate in Glamorgan was substantially higher than the average for England and Wales, as shown in Table 7.

In the forty years 1861–1901 the population of Glamorgan increased by more than half a million, and of this a little over two-thirds (367,000) was due to excess of births over deaths and just under a third (167,000) to net immigration.[36] The bountiful number of children raised in the Welsh atmosphere of the coal-mining communities was quantitatively a more significant factor than the volume of net immigration. Both factors, of course, were the result of the industrial revolution. The valuable researches of Philip Jones and W.T.R. Pryce on the historical demography of the coalfields of south and north Wales respectively have added greatly to the validity of the thesis of this paper.

Table 7

Decennial natural increase as % of the population at the beginning of each decade

	1861–71 % Increase	1871–81 % Increase	1881–91 % Increase	1891–1901 % Increase
Glamorgan	18.6	20.3	18.8	19.2
England & Wales	13.6	15.1	14.0	12.4

Source: *Census of England and Wales* (1911), PP (1912-13), CXI, Cd. 6258, p.11.

Information about the number of people able to speak Welsh has rested mainly on the population census statistics which started in 1891. There are several reasons for thinking that this source gave an under-estimate, particularly for 1891. First, there is evidence that the administration of the census was inefficient. John E. Southall, in his book, *Wales and her Language,* written at the time, reported as follows:

A material help towards elucidating the geographical distribution of Welsh in Wales, and the proportion of inhabitants speaking it, would have been afforded by the Census of 1891, had the resolution of the British House of Commons, which virtually required a return of all persons in the principality who spoke the language, been carried into effect. Instead of honestly endeavouring to ascertain this by sending Census papers with the column to be filled up with the required information, *to every household* in the principality, the authorities took it upon themselves, to some extent, to decide where to send papers with this column; such a course did much, if not entirely, to vitiate in some bilingual districts the trustworthiness of the returns which at the moment of writing are not yet published. . . . Whether the bungling that attended the Welsh Census was the result of ignorance, or whether the authorities were unwilling that the total number of persons who might fairly be credited with ability to speak Welsh should be known, I will not attempt to decide.[37]

If the bungling which Southall observed in Newport, Monmouthshire, was any indication of the performance of census officials in other parts of Wales, there was probably a good deal of under-counting.

Another cause for concern is the fact that in areas where Welsh became a minority language some people were ashamed of admitting that they could speak Welsh and may have given a negative reply to the census question. For example, early in the nineteenth century in the Vale of Glamorgan Welsh was the language of everyday life, literature and religion.[38] In 1884 Thomas Powell, Professor of Welsh at the newly created University College in Cardiff, persuaded the Cymmrodorion to survey the 'use of the Welsh language in elementary schools in Welsh-speaking districts'. They found that of the 123 schools questioned in Glamorgan, 77 were for the introduction of Welsh but 48 were firmly against. The opponents argued that the exclusion of Welsh was the surest means of promoting facility in English; and one of the reasons put forward by those who wanted Welsh in the schools was significant — it would help to eradicate the sense of shame felt by many Welsh children.[39] There can be no doubt that many who had been brought up in Welsh homes became indifferent and even opposed to their children speaking the mother tongue. This attitude was deplored and denounced by Welsh leaders such as D. Isaac Davies, whose remarkable open letters published in *Baner ac Amserau Cymru* in 1885 sounded a sombre note of warning about the future. He was saddened by the fact that many Welsh people, particularly women and teenage girls, were ashamed to acknowledge that they could understand Welsh; and he was afraid that a census count would be misleading unless those who did not care for the language could be persuaded to be proud of being bilingual.[40]

In view of the apparently dubious figures produced by the bureaucrats who ran the 1891 census, it may be preferable to take the results of a private survey relating to 1871 by the famous geographer, E.G. Ravenstein, author of the well-known 'laws of migration'.[41] He obtained his information by sending out '. . . no less than 1200 circulars addressed to registrars of births, clergymen, schoolmasters and others likely to be intimately acquainted with the linguistic condition of their neighbourhood, besides carrying on a voluminous correspondence with gentlemen whom, in the course of my inquiry, I found to take a special interest in the subject I proposed to deal with'.[42] The response rate was 50 per cent, and this was supplemented by his 'voluminous correspondence' (some of it with well-informed innkeepers). Ravenstein had no axe to grind; he was highly skilled in the handling of statistics and was satisfied that his results were '. . . a close approximation to the truth'.[43]

According to Ravenstein's estimates in Tables 8 and 9, there were 934,530 persons able to speak Welsh at the beginning of the 1870s, or 66 per cent of the population of Wales.

Table 8
Welsh-speaking population of Wales, 1871

	Total Population	%	Persons speaking Welsh	%
Districts in which Welsh is spoken by a majority	1,025,573	78.1	887,870	94.9
Districts in which Welsh is spoken by 25 to 50 per cent	113,030	8.7	38,046	4.1
Districts in which Welsh is spoken by less than 25 per cent	174,080	13.2	8,614	1.0
Total	1,312,683	100.0	934,530	100.0

Source: E.G. Ravenstein, 'On the Celtic Languages in the British Isles: a Statistical Survey', *Journal of the Statistical Society*, XLII, Part III (September 1879), 620.

Table 9
Welsh-speaking population of Wales, by county, 1871

County	Population 1871	Persons able to speak Welsh only	Persons able to speak Welsh and English	Welsh speakers as % of population
Anglesey	51,040	31,650	15,850	93.1
Caernarfon	106,121	60,000	38,600	92.9
Denbigh	105,102	39,500	41,500	77.1
Flint	76,312	5,420	47,890	70.0
Merioneth	46,598	17,000	27,000	94.4
Montgomery	67,623	6,600	23,100	43.9
Radnor	25,430	20	1,000	4.0
Cardigan	73,441	34,500	35,600	95.5
Pembroke	91,998	5,430	27,320	35.6
Carmarthen	115,710	37,800	70,920	94.0
Brecknock	59,901	6,340	33,530	66.6
Glamorgan	397,859	48,350	223,100	68.2
Monmouth	195,448	1,500	55,000	28.9
Wales	1,412,583	294,110	640,420	66.2

Source: E.G. Ravenstein, op. cit., p. 636

Of these, about three-quarters (709,000) were in counties directly affected to a large or small extent by the industrial revolution and the remainder (224,000) were in the purely rural areas of Anglesey, Merionethshire, Montgomeryshire, Cardiganshire and north Pembrokeshire. Radnorshire was almost entirely anglicized, and so was south Pembrokeshire (little England beyond Wales), and large parts of Monmouthshire. If Ravenstein's figure of 934,530 Welsh speakers in 1871 was anywhere near the truth, the corresponding total in 1891 would be well over a million instead of 910,289 as reported in the census of that year.

I began by posing a counterfactual question: what would have been the fate of the Welsh language if Wales had been a predominantly agricultural country like Ireland, with no coal or iron or adequate capital resources? The answer is clear. Since Ireland did not have an industrial revolution, her rural exodus, which reached crisis proportions because of the potato famine, could not be absorbed within her borders. There was no alternative to the vicious circle of mass emigration. The population of Ireland fell from 8,175,000 in 1841 to 4,390,000 in 1911: the population of Wales more than doubled in the same period. During the 1880s no less than 655,500 left Ireland for the United States, an annual emigration rate of 13.3 per 1000, whereas the outflow from Wales was only 12,640, or an annual rate of 0.8 per 1000.[44] If Wales had lacked an industrial sector, her surplus rural population, Welsh to the core, would have had to emigrate to England or overseas, and these people together with their children and grandchildren would have been lost to the land of their birth forever. This would have been a disaster to the Welsh language.

Conclusion

The majority of the Welsh-speaking population of over one million at the end of the nineteenth century had been born and bred in the industrial areas. In the words of Ieuan Gwynedd Jones, 'the industrial areas, said one acute observer in 1861, were one grand laboratory. They were experimental places, crucibles in which a new culture was being forged'.[45] And it was a genuine democratic Welsh culture. In the 1890s there were published in the Welsh language two quarterly journals, two bi-monthlies, 28 monthlies and 25 newspapers, making a total of 32 magazines and 25 newspapers.[46] The main publishing centres were in the counties of Glamorgan and Carmarthenshire in south Wales and in the counties of Caernarfonshire, Merionethshire and Denbighshire in north Wales. Beriah Gwynfe Evans estimated in 1887 that the total circulation of Welsh weekly periodicals exceeded 120,000 and that of Welsh monthly magazines was 150,000. One of the leading Welsh firms put the annual value of all Welsh literature of all kinds published at £200,000.[47] Both the demand for and the supply of this Welsh literature depended mainly on the population of the industrial areas. That tired old cliché about the northern and western rural areas as the heartland of Welsh culture should be given a well-earned rest.

The evidence reviewed confirms the proposition that the industrial revolution gave the Welsh language a new lease of life. The cultural foundations had been laid in the eighteenth century through the outstanding achievements of such pioneers as Gruffydd Jones and Thomas Charles. In the nineteenth century this Welsh inheritance was considerably enlarged by the population explosion which accompanied the industrial revolution in Wales. D. Isaac Davies, writing in 1885, was optimistic enough to imagine a bilingual population of 3 million in Wales by 1985![48] He could not have foreseen that in the twentieth century the unprecedented scale of English immigration, the decline of Nonconformity, the impact of industrial depression, the mass media and contraception would turn his dream into a nightmare for the Welsh language. The large and complex question why and how the wonderful legacy of the nineteenth century, a real windfall, was frittered away remains a challenge to historians.

Section A
c.1790–*c*.1840

Canals and the Economic Development of South Wales

COLIN BABER

Although the observation of Phyllis Deane that 'if Britain had to depend upon her roads to carry her heavy goods traffic, the effective impact of the industrial revolution might well have been delayed until the railway age',[1] might seem to be something of an over-simplification, it does pin-point the critical role which canals played in the dawning of the modern economic era. It also provides us with a pertinent context within which to consider the impact of canals upon the economic development of south Wales. Canals made it economically viable to carry heavy, bulky materials to a wider market, thus increasing the possibility of a greater concentration of industrial activity on a regional basis. In many areas, therefore, canals made industrialization possible. Given the state of existing technology, nothing else could do the job of carrying the heavy raw materials and finished goods being demanded at the start of the industrial revolution at a sufficiently low price, and the successful use of water as the basis for a man-made transport service indelibly marked out the early framework of industrial location in Britain. It is recognized that some recent works, see especially W. Albert, *The Turnpike Road System of England: 1663–1844* (Cambridge, 1972) and E. Pawson, *Transport and Economy: The Turnpike Roads of Eighteenth Century Britain* (London, 1977), have questioned the indispensability of the canals to the industrial revolution in England. However, it is here contended that the peculiar topography of south Wales, with deep, narrow valleys providing the conduits for the carriage of heavy, bulky goods from the northern rim of the coalfield to the coast, precluded the emergence of a transport network. Thus a few canals could best provide the simple logistical links which the region's economy required.

Whereas on the main through-routes 'general merchandise' tended to be the main category of goods carried, more than half of the Acts passed by Parliament setting up canals during the second half of the eighteenth century were to promote enterprises the major intention of which was to carry coal; while every self-respecting student of economic history knows that one of the first canals, completed by the Duke of Bridgewater from his colliery at Worseley in 1761, had the immediate effect of halving the price of coal in Manchester.[2] The supply of fuel was one of the critical bottle-necks constraining the start of the industrial revolution, and indeed the need to improve the movement of coal, as Britain became increasingly aware of the diverse range of its uses, did much to expose the limitations of existing transport facilities. It was not merely, as Sir

John Clapham reflected, that people were saved from cow dung fires,[3] but that a vast range of activities were now able to achieve substantial improvements in their production functions, from sugar-refining to iron-smelting, from beer-brewing to brass-founding.

If the canals were an important factor in the early stages of economic growth in Britain, they were essential to the beginning of the industrial revolution in south Wales. The provision of transport facilities in south Wales at the middle of the eighteenth century was limited by the region's slow economic advancement, thus creating a vicious circle of retardation, which in turn did not augur well for the prospective growth of industrial activities. Unlike England, south Wales had little experience of inland navigation,[4] and the rivers of south Wales which traversed the upland coal measures from north to south were seldom navigable beyond the coastal plain. Thus boats could go up the Tawe only as far as Morriston, while the Taff was not used for commercial purposes for much more than half a mile inland. The Neath River was the only one that had had sufficient improvement carried out on it by the mid-eighteenth century to make it of any real economic significance. It was navigable for almost six miles as far as Ynys-y-gerwyn, and had by 1750 emerged as a commercial route for the various metalliferous trades of the lower Neath valley.

Thus south Wales was largely dependent on her roads for the movement of people and goods within the region. These were generally inadequate, of poor quality and seldom maintained to a standard capable of withstanding persistent heavy loads. Bad roads provided a kind of sterility to economic progress. In 1799 Archdeacon Coxe, during his tour of Monmouthshire, was reminded by the appalling state of the roads of an anecdote related in the House of Commons a few decades earlier. In a debate over a turnpike act Morris of Piercefield being asked what roads there were in Monmouthshire replied 'none'. Asked how then they travelled, he replied 'in ditches'.[5] The second half of the eighteenth century did however witness an improvement in the standard of roads.[6] Public interest centred on the poor state of road provision, and the emergence of turnpike trusts began to have an effect on the provision of better quality roads. The first major Act setting up a trust in the region was passed in 1764[7] turnpiking a complete through-route from Cardiff to Swansea, via Cowbridge, Bridgend and Neath, and a number followed in the succeeding decades.

Although the turnpike trusts seem to have served the limited demands of south Wales whilst it remained an essentially agrarian economy, the beginnings of industrialization imposed pressures which the roads soon proved totally inadequate in meeting. Thus in 1767, under the inspiration of Anthony Bacon, a fund was raised by the ironmasters of Merthyr Tydfil to construct a road along the Taff valley to Cardiff, wide enough to take wheeled traffic. Although this certainly seems to have been an improvement over the existing system of carrying the finished iron down to Cardiff on the back of horses or mules along tortuous mountain ridgeways, there were soon encountered serious problems of road surfacing, caused by the excessive wear of heavy wagon loads. As a contemporary opinion put it 'the constant and expensive land carriage necessary to bring those ponderous articles within reach of shipping would be the ruin of the roads as well as of the parishes they pass through'.[8] Quite simply the roads were not capable of providing the sort of transport system which the industrializing economy of south Wales in the later decades of the eighteenth century was increasingly requiring. While the roads of south Wales left much to be desired, road links between south Wales and southern England were little better, and coastal shipping provided the only viable means of inter-regional commerce.

The first canals in south Wales were highly localized and almost without exception built in the south-western part of the coalfield to carry bituminous coal from mining areas a short distance inland to the coast for trans-shipment. The proximity of the coal measures to the coast attracted enterprise to the districts around Neath, Swansea and Llanelli in the first half of the eighteenth century. The first authentic canal in south Wales was built by Thomas Kymmer between 1766 and 1768 to transport the coal of the lower Gwendraeth valley for shipment from his dock at Kidwelly,[9] a distance of three miles. This was followed in the 1770s and 1780s by a number of short canals, none of which penetrated inland for more than five miles, and built for the same purpose of providing a vital logistical link between coal measures and outside markets. Thus Chauncey Townshend, a seemingly[10] active industrialist and promoter in the area, built a canal from his coal-mines just east of Llanelli at Bynea, to Ysbitty Bank on the Burry Inlet in 1770, while his son-in-law, John Smith, built another from Llansamlet to the Birchgrove Wharf at Foxhole on the mouth of the River Tawe in 1784, which served a number of small collieries along its three-mile route.[11] Although their significance might seem limited especially in the light of the major canal developments which were soon to transform the region's economic capacities, these early canals made possible a not insignificant bituminous coal trade in the south-west corner of the coalfield which generated external economies that in turn contributed to the development of the area as a major centre of metalliferous trades.

After the middle of the eighteenth century, a number of entrepreneurs came to the area along the northern rim of the coalfield, drawn by the proximity of easily worked deposits of ironstone, coal and limestone[12], and particularly by the blackband ironstone north of Merthyr Tydfil. The conditions for the rapid expansion of the iron-smelting industry at the heads of the valleys were therefore ideal, except in one respect. The area was a good 20 miles from the seaboard, which in the absence of cheap and reliable transport ensured that these advantages fell short of realizing their potential. By 1790 an arc of iron-smelting works ringed the northern extremities of the coalfield from Hirwaun (1757) in the west to Blaenavon (1789) in the east. These included the four works at Merthyr Tydfil: Dowlais (1759); Cyfarthfa (1765); Penydarren (1784); and Plymouth (1788); and the Monmouthshire works at Ebbw Vale (1789) and Sirhowy (1778). In total there were eleven ironworks in the district, all beginning to prepare themselves for the realization of market expansion. The Seven Years War and the American War of Independence had given an important stimulus to the industry,[13] but the inland location imposed limitations upon the full exploitation of further opportunities for growth. After 1784 the prospect of the introduction of Henry Cort's puddling process,[14] the 'Welsh method', made the question of improved communications with the coast one of urgency, particularly in the

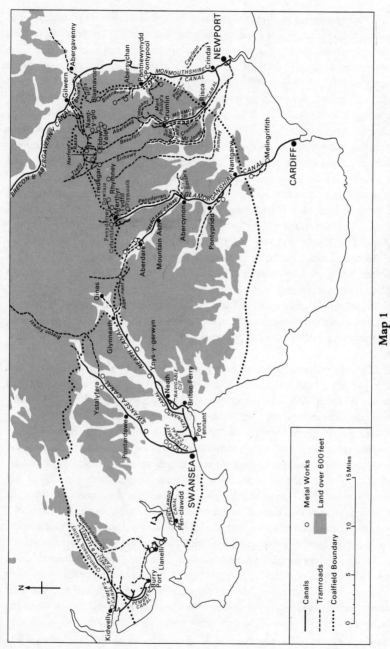

Map 1

The canals and tram-roads of the south Wales coalfield c.1815

Canals
Tramroads
Coalfield Boundary

○ Metal Works
Land over 600 feet

0   5   10   15 Miles

light of the expansion in production which was anticipated. In the north-western part of the coalfield iron-smelting did not emerge as a significant activity until the 1820s. None the less the needs of the main landowners of the upper Neath and Swansea valleys who were beginning to mine both bituminous and anthracite coal, coupled with the requirements of the various metalliferous activities lower down the valleys, made similar demands for an improvement in the means of communication with the coast. That means was provided during the 1790s when four substantial canals were built in south Wales: the Glamorganshire; the Monmouthshire; the Neath; and the Swansea. The decade from 1790 in fact witnessed canal-building in Britain reaching almost epidemic proportions. Canals were seen by the investing class as 'the only form of transport that could accommodate the expansion (industrial growth) and that canals would therefore pay'.[15]

Although the frantic canal-building during the decade did result in some casualties, the four canals built in south Wales during the period of 'canal mania' were to be the basis of the region's infrastructure until the coming of the railways in the 1840s. There were three subsequent additions made to the region's canal facilities in the early nineteenth century. The Aberdare Canal, after being originally authorized in 1793, was finally opened in 1812, extending the Glamorganshire Canal's reach into the Aberdare valley. Also in 1812, the Brecon and Abergavenny Canal connected the area north of the Brecon Beacons with the Monmouthshire Canal at Pontymoile, near Pontypool. Finally, in the early 1820s, George Tennant built a canal from the Neath Canal at Aberdulais, to Port Tennant near Swansea, to secure a better shipping place for the collieries and works of the Neath valley.

In England the main emphasis of canal construction was on the creation of a system radiating from the Midland counties and attempting to link up the different regions of the country. In south Wales the extent of canal-building was limited by the region's topography. The contours of south Wales generally precluded through-routes. There was little economic purpose for a canal along the coastal plain as the Bristol Channel provided an adequate coastal trade. The logistical basis of the canals was thus the provision of a simple linear connection between the coast and the interior. The valleys formed the conduits along which the canals ran. Inter-valley trans-shipments were generally neither feasible nor desirable,[16] and thus the canals became intimately associated with the economic prosperity of a limited geographical area. The canal formed the trunk of a transport system within its valley, with short feeder canals and tram-roads branching out to connect various industrial activities with their lifeline. This was reinforced by a clause included in each of the four major canal Acts which allowed anyone who wished to build a tram-road or wagon-way from up to eight miles to the canal to apply to the Company of the Canal's Proprietors at the Annual General Meeting for their consent, which, if granted, then allowed the applicant to proceed with construction even without the consent of the owners of the land over which the tram-road was to cross.

It may now be helpful to take a brief look at each of the four major canals, and then to make some general observations on the relationship between the coming of the canals, their operation, and the economy of south Wales, which they inextricably altered. The first, and the most famous, was the Glamorganshire Canal. A canal project for the Taff valley, to link Merthyr Tydfil and Cardiff, had first been proposed in 1784 when a bill was introduced to Parliament, but was subsequently delayed by adjournments and prorogations. It finally received the Royal Assent on 9 June 1790.[17] Two months later construction began and in February 1794 the 24½-mile canal was completed between the Cyfarthfa Ironworks Yard in Merthyr and the Bank, a shipping place on the Taff, below the old quay at Cardiff. In 1796 an Act[18] was obtained to build an extension at the Cardiff end where congestion had already begun to cause difficulties, and a sea-lock, which enabled seagoing vessels of up to 200 tons to enter and be loaded from wharves on the canal basin. This was all completed in 1798. Various other improvements were carried out as the volume of traffic subsequently grew, such as the further lengthening of the sea-lock in 1814, but it seems that all too often, necessary improvement was compromised by individual rivalries. In its completed 25½ miles, the Glamorgan Canal had 51 locks to enable it to descend from its elevation of 543 feet at Merthyr down to Cardiff. This often proved to be a source of great frustration as it necessitated a very slow speed of carriage, on average two miles an hour.[19]

The Glamorganshire Canal was built to carry finished wrought-iron from the four works at Merthyr Tydfil to Cardiff, and its history is seen largely in terms of the growth of Merthyr as a major iron-producing centre. From the beginning the Glamorganshire Canal provided a focus for the intense rivalries between the various iron-making interests: especially between the Crawshays of Cyfarthfa and the rest. Although the rivalry took different forms as time progressed, the basic problem was that Richard Crawshay, the canal's main shareholder in the early days, and his successors attempted to operate the canal for the benefit of the Cyfarthfa ironworks and contrary to the interests of the other three works. Indeed, in its early history, the canal played no small part in the dominant position which Cyfarthfa was able to achieve compared to its rivals, as only Cyfarthfa was directly served, the finished iron from the other three works having to be carried along tram-roads to loading wharves along the canal. Crawshay persistently attempted to influence boat-masters to give preference to the carriage of Cyfarthfa iron, and usually succeeded. (Until 1845, it was required by law that canal companies could only provide a transport system, and that the actual carriage of goods should be undertaken by independent shippers).[20] There was constant disagreement between the canal and various industrialists over the canal's tendency to monopolize water supplies. Thus in the late 1790s both Richard Hill of the Plymouth Ironworks and Richard Blakemore of the Melingriffith Tinplate Works were continually accusing the canal of using water that was rightfully theirs. No sooner had the canal been opened than Crawshay attempted, through the Company of Proprietors, to rescind an order which laid down, for purposes of carriage, that a hundredweight should measure 120 pounds, not the customary 112.[21] This caused dissension amongst the other ironmasters, but finally, in 1798 the matter was resolved when the canal brought a case against the Dowlais Company to compel it to adopt 112 pounds as the standard.[22]

There were many areas of disagreement, but the issue of the canal's willingness to reduce the rates of tolls in accordance with an agreement made under the Act of 1790[23] seems to have generated most passion amongst the ironmasters. In the early days, Dowlais, Penydarren and Plymouth were continually demanding that the canal company should reduce tolls, as profits were consistently in excess of 8 per cent, but the matter was not finally resolved until 1808, when the Court of Quarter Sessions granted a reduction in the rates from 5*d*. to 3*d*. per ton per mile on all stone, iron, timber and miscellaneous goods carried, and from 2*d*. to 1½*d*. on all ironstone, coal, lime and all kinds of manure.[24]

From then on, it seems that the canal company fully entered into the spirit of the agreement, and the customers of the canal greatly benefited from lower transport costs. This 'surplus' revenue began to cause an embarrassment in the years immediately following the Napoleonic Wars, and tolls were reduced by 10 per cent. There must obviously have been an elastic demand for transport, however, as this accentuated the problem, and traffic increased to such an extent that for six months in 1816 and 1817 no tolls were charged at all. Tolls were resumed in the spring of 1817, but again at the beginning of 1818, 13/4*d*. in the pound was returned on tolls charged.[25] And so it went on. Obviously the customers of the canal profited greatly from such an arrangement, though the extent of this is perhaps modified by the fact that most of the main customers were also shareholders of the canal.

The disagreements which were to blight the early history of the canal resulted in a number of attempts being made at promoting alternative means of transport between Merthyr and Cardiff. Although these generally proved abortive, the Penydarren tramroad was built from Merthyr to the Glamorganshire Canal at Abercynon by Crawshay's rivals; Dowlais and Penydarren each owning five shares and Plymouth four. The tramroad was completed in 1802, and in 1804 it provided the route for Richard Trevithick's first steam locomotive.

By the 1820s the internal conflicts of the ironmasters seem to have subsided, and in 1824 William Crawshay II was joined on the canal's management committee by his three rivals. This then presented a united front to the canal's main adversary, the Marquis of Bute. In 1830, however, the Marquis decided to build a ship canal in Cardiff, which was completed in 1839, and comprised a waterway 1½ miles long, with a dock basin (the West Bute Dock) and two lateral connections to the Glamorganshire Canal, thus facilitating a substantially improved exit to the Bristol Channel. By this time the canal was operating at something like full capacity, which included night working. In total there were about 200 boats at work and each normally achieved three round trips a fortnight. Despite the competition of the Taff Vale Railway after 1841, the canal traffic continued to increase until the early 1860s. In 1851 the canal carried 190,633 tons of iron and 294,537 tons of coal down to Cardiff, and 96,408 tons of haematite ore, mainly from the Whitehaven area, up to Merthyr. Also in that year, the Taff Vale Railway carried 74,701 tons of iron and 580,000 tons of coal down to Cardiff, and 51,000 tons or iron ore up to Merthyr. From the 1860s on, however, the railway increasingly began to erode the canal trade. In 1898 the section between Merthyr and Abercynon closed, followed seventeen years later by the short section from Abercynon to Pontypridd. The remaining section, from Pontypridd to Cardiff, finally closed in 1942.

The histories of the other three main canals of south Wales were not as colourful nor as tempestuous as the Glamorganshire's. The Monmouthshire Canal was first promoted in 1791, and in June 1792 an Act[26] was passed to allow the construction of a canal from Pontnewynydd, a distance of 11 miles, to join the Usk at Newport, with a branch from Crindai(Malpas) to Crumlin, also 11 miles long. The main line from Pontnewynydd to the canal basin at Newport was opened in February 1796. In July 1797, a further Act was passed which allowed the proprietors to extend the canal through Newport towards Pillgwennlly, where wharves could be built to take seagoing ships. The Act also formalized an existing arrangement that coal shipped from Newport could be delivered duty-free to all ports east of the Holms (Flat and Steep Holm Islands in the Bristol Channel were regarded as the end of the river and the beginning of the sea).[27] Newport was therefore able to enjoy a considerable advantage and largely monopolized the coal trade to the West of England ports, especially Bristol, until all coastwise duties were abolished in 1831. This gave coal exported from Newport in an easterly direction a 5/4d. per ton exemption, and in addition a 1/6d. per ton bounty was paid on all other coal sent coastwise from Newport.

The Monmouthshire Canal greatly benefited from this privilege, and in turn enabled Newport to fully exploit its advantage. Meanwhile the Crumlin Branch line was completed in 1799, and the Brecknock and Abergavenny Canal, projected in 1792, and commenced in 1801, was finally joined to the Monmouthshire at Pontymoile in 1812. The canal and its extensive tram-road network, then became, during the first half of the nineteenth century, the only viable means of transporting the rapidly growing output of coal and iron from the Monmouthshire valleys to continually expanding markets, but from 1853 onwards, when the Newport and Pontypool Railway was opened, the canal's traffic declined.[28]

The Neath Canal was the second of the region's main canals to be constructed, following closely on the heels of the Glamorganshire Canal. It was completed in 1795 along the length of the Vale of Neath from Glynneath to Melin-Crythan Pill near Neath, a distance of 13 miles, for the main purpose of transporting the coal of the upper Neath valley for trans-shipment. Coal remained the predominant traffic until the 1870s when it finally succumbed to the competition of the Vale of Neath Railway which had been opened in 1851.[29]

The Swansea Canal which was completed in 1798 from Swansea (near the present Strand) to Henneuadd, near Ystradgynlais, brought to a close the main phase of canal building in south Wales within the space of a decade. Again the export of coal from the upper reaches of the Swansea valley was the main motivating force behind the canal's construction and operation. However, the prospect of the expansion of the Ynyscedwyn Ironworks, the development of other ironworks, and the growth of the copper-smelting industry also contributed to its early development. The canal was the only means of transporting heavy goods along the Swansea valley until the 1850s when the Swansea Vale Railway was opened, being extended along the whole of the valley to Ystradgynlais by

1861.[30] Although the Swansea Canal, as with the other canals, was unable to weather the competitive advantages of the railways after 1872 when it was purchased by the Great Western Railway, it seems to have been operated profitably until the early 1890s.

The construction of canals required capital outlays which could not normally be accumulated by individuals. In addition, they took a long time to construct and even longer to return a sizeable profit. They were thus largely collectively promoted, though one or two 'interested' individuals usually made the early running.[31] The canals of south Wales were thus initiated mainly by interests requiring an efficient means of transporting heavy goods from the northern parts of the coalfield to the coast and, as with the national pattern, it was those who stood to gain most who met the cost of canal construction and encouraged their development. The two eastern canals, the Monmouthshire and the Glamorganshire both owed their origins to ironmasters, whilst the two in the western half of the coalfield were mainly sponsored by landowners of the upper parts of the Neath and Swansea valleys, anxious to gain effective access to markets.

The Glamorganshire Canal, which provided the 'model' for the canals of south Wales, itself probably owed much to the encouragement and enthusiasm of the three Homfray brothers who came to Merthyr Tydfil in 1782, and two years later established the Penydarren Ironworks. The Homfrays had worked in their father's ironworks at Broseley, on the Severn, and in a forge at Stewponey, which was on the Staffordshire and Worcestershire Canal, and doubtless news of their experiences there had much to do with the decision of the Merthyr ironmasters to proceed with the Glamorganshire Canal.[32] The promotion of the other three canals followed along fairly similar lines, although the Swansea Canal was largely sponsored by commercial interests from the town of Swansea, through the Town's Corporation. Rhys Davies, who seems to have been the main promoter, had extensive mineral properties along the Swansea valley, as did many of the others involved.[33]

All four of the canals were initially sizeable capital projects. Even so, apart from the Swansea Canal, they cost substantially more to build than was originally estimated.[34] The commitment of individuals with direct economic interest in their completion was thus crucial. The most expensive of the four projects, the Monmouthshire, finally cost £220,000, and its elaborate network of tram-roads a further £119,330, compared to the spuriously precise original estimate of £108,476/13/9d.[35] Nevertheless such was the strength of local interest that the promoters seem to have had few problems in securing the necessary funds. The principal subscribers to the Monmouthshire Canal included the Duke of Beaufort and Sir Charles Morgan, substantial landowners on the canal's route, who invested £5,000 and £5,200 respectively; the Harfords, ironmasters of the Melingriffith and Ebbw Vale Works were the largest shareholders with £10,200; Thomas Hill of the Blaenavon Iron Works held £5,000; while many other ironmasters, colliery owners and landowners contributed lesser sums.[36] The supply of capital for the construction of the Glamorganshire Canal was dominated by the Merthyr ironmasters, although there were 17 shareholders in the first issue of £60,000. The Crawshay family held £13,000 worth of the first shares with Richard Crawshay the biggest individual shareholder buying £9,600; William Stevens, an Associate of Crawshays held £5,000; the Harfords of Melingriffith, £6,000; the Homfrays and Richard Forman of Penydarren, £1,500 and £1,000 respectively; the Hills of the Plymouth Works, £1,500; and the Dowlais interest was made up of £1,000 from William Taitt and £500 from Thomas Guest. The shareholding composition of the two western canals followed a similar pattern though they were both more manageable financial projects. The final cost of the Monmouthshire at £220,000; compared to the Glamorganshire, £103,600; the Swansea £53,300 and the Neath Canal £40,000.[37]

The returns on the capital invested varied between the four canals, though a simple assessment of profitability in these terms is not really very meaningful. The Glamorganshire Canal's profits were limited to 8 per cent by statute, but the canal's shareholders as customers benefited substantially from the periodic reductions in tolls charged after 1808. Nevertheless all four canals were successful in providing an acceptable return to their shareholders, though this varied substantially over time. The Swansea Canal paid out 10 per cent or more between 1804 and 1872; the Monmouthshire Canal averaged dividends of 8⅓ per cent from 1799 to 1847; while between 1817 and 1846 Neath Canal dividends averaged 16 per cent.[38] Of greater consequence, however, was the fact that the shareholders made a cheap investment in their own and therefore the region's future.

Much less is known about the provision of short-term capital funds in the promotion of the canals. However, the Wilkins family, who controlled the Old Bank at Brecon, were significant shareholders in all the major canals[39] apart from the Monmouthshire, while William Esdaile, a London banker, invested £3,600 in the Monmouthshire Canal.[40] It would be surprising if these and other banking interests were not sympathetic to the extraneous needs for short-term funds that could not be met out of current revenue.

Two sets of father and son, the ubiquitous Dadfords and the Sheasbys, and all named Thomas, were largely responsible for the building of the region's four main canals. The two older men had gained substantial experience in constructing a number of canals in the Midlands in the 1770s and 1780s and were persuaded, probably by the Homfrays, to leave the Cromford Canal project in Derbyshire, on which they were both employed, to come to south Wales to build the Glamorganshire Canal. Thomas Dadford Snr was however left to complete the project on his own while his son, after commencing the Neath Canal, went on to construct the Monmouthshire Canal, and at the same time was responsible for the building of the Leominster Canal. Thomas Sheasby, after also leaving the Glamorganshire Canal project went on to take over the Neath Canal works from Dadford Jnr and then became engineer of the Swansea Canal where he was succeeded by his own son who later began the construction of the Aberdare Canal. The supply of skilled canal constructors was close-knit — Dadford Snr had at one time been James Brindley's assistant, and although a few other individuals figure as engineers, such as Edward Martin, who worked with the Sheasbys on the Swansea Canal, the Dadfords and the Sheasbys between them can be seen as the architects of the region's canals.[41] Although technically, the canals of south Wales were simpler to build than most of their English counterparts despite the heavy lockage which they entailed, nevertheless their construction was dependent upon simple rudimentary tools and horsepower, and was carried out before the ordnance survey brought civil engineering works more into the modern age.

Little is known of the navigators (navvies) who carried out the actual construction work. It is likely that most of the work was performed by men attracted in much the same way as the industries of the coalfield found their labour force. The promise of high wages and a relatively continuous employment drew in labour from agriculture. Although there is evidence that some Irish labour was used to build the Glamorganshire Canal it seems that the districts surrounding the coalfield, in particular the rural counties of Carmarthenshire, Breconshire and Cardiganshire, provided the main external source of labour.[42] It is likely that the contractors did secure bands of specialist workers, as were used on many of the English canals, but these normally made up only a small number of the total employed.[43]

The impact which the construction of the canals had upon the economic development of south Wales was crucial. Although Sir John Clapham, in highlighting the inadequate statistical record of the canals, argued that 'there is no way of measuring the economic gain to Great Britain from the canal system',[44] the fairly straighforward function of the south Wales canals makes this view somewhat misleading. All four major canals of south Wales were built to connect the northern parts of the coalfield with the coast, thus enabling the mineral resources of the upland districts to be effectively exploited. For the two eastern canals at least, the success of this is clearly shown by Harry Scrivenor's pioneering work, *History of the Iron Trade* (1854).[45] For much of the period, the *Mining Journal* also published, rather spasmodically, figures of iron carried down both canals, which do not vary significantly from Scrivenor's.[46] Although Scrivenor's series ends in 1840, the *Mining Journal* shows that in 1847, 240,977 tons of iron went down the Monmouthshire Canal, and 178,512 tons were transported by the Glamorganshire Canal and the Taff Vale railway combined. Indeed until the late 1850s only a small proportion of the total iron was transported by railways, so it is fair to assume that both canals continued to increase their iron traffic significantly.

It is true that the figures for the iron traffic do not distinguish between pig and bar iron. It is therefore not possible to derive a perfectly accurate measurement of the relative significance of the iron transported down the canals, compared to total production. However, all the bigger works, apart from Blaenavon, despatched the bulk of their output as bar iron, and the only significant flows of pig iron were periodic inter-works transfers within the area.[47] In the absence of substantial local customers it seems likely that the major part of the iron produced during the first half of the nineteenth century found its way to markets via the Glamorganshire and Monmouthshire Canals. The total iron output estimated for the region in 1804 was 505,000 tons; of which the major part, around 90 per cent, came from the northern rim of the coalfield. In that year, the two canals between them accounted for the trans-shipment of 312,000 tons, or almost 70 per cent of the district's output. Although of lesser significance, the shipment of iron down the Swansea Canal began to increase in importance as the Ystalyfera, Ynyscedwyn and Ystradgynlais ironworks expanded output during the 1830s.

An interesting feature of Scrivenor's figures is the extent to which the Monmouthshire ironworks were transporting and presumably producing as much, and after the late 1820s, increasingly more than their more illustrious Glamorganshire counterparts. By 1840 the Monmouthshire Canal was shipping almost 50,000 tons a year more than the Glamorganshire Canal. Contrary to popular belief the four Merthyr works did not completely dominate the iron-smelting industry of south Wales.

Such was the scale and pace of the iron industry's expansion that from a position of producing a mere 12,500 tons, less than 20 per cent of Britain's total pig iron output in 1788, south Wales was by 1830 Britain's major iron producing region, with 277,643 tons, 41 per cent of total output. From then on south Wales's comparative position declined as new iron producing regions emerged. None the less its total output continued to increase to 505,000 tons in 1840 and 840,000 tons in 1855,[48] an expansion largely facilitated by the canals.

The main contribution of the canals to the economic development of south Wales, was that of releasing the iron-smelting industry from the constraints of its location. However, their role in initiating a vibrant coal trade did not fall far behind. The two western canals were promoted largely with this in mind. As early as 1801 the Swansea Canal carried down 54,225 tons of coal for trans-shipment[49] and in 1810 the Neath Canal, which was more narrowly dependent on the coal trade than the others, transported 90,000 tons down to Neath.[50] Statistical evidence is fragmentary for both canals though it is reasonable to assume that the bulk, probably three-quarters of the coal that left Swansea in the first half of the nineteenth century, came down the Swansea Canal, and after 1824 when George Tennant completed his Neath and Swansea Junction Canal, down the Neath Canal as well. Judging from the growth of the revenue and dividends of both canals their coal exports continued to expand throughout the first half of the nineteenth century. In 1820, the Swansea Canal carried 150,000 tons. In 1840 Swansea exported nearly 600,000 tons of coal and culm. Of this latter total, approximately half was anthracite, mostly in the form of culm (small anthracite) for lime and malt burning.[51]

The Glamorganshire Canal had a limited coal trade until the 1830s largely because of the substantial advantage the exemption from coastwise duties gave to Newport and the Monmouthshire Canal until 1831. Before 1830, therefore, the Monmouthshire Canal dominated the coal trade of the eastern half of the coalfield. As early as 1809 Newport was exporting 148,000 tons of coal, a volume not equalled by Cardiff until the early 1830s. However, from then on the expansion of coal-mining in the valleys of Glamorganshire resulted in the substantial growth illustrated in the figures of coal traffic.[52] The Aberdare valley was the first district to experience the irrepressible growth of steam-coal mining which was to transform the eastern half of the coalfield during the second half of the nineteenth century; between 1840 and 1853 sixteen steam-coal pits were opened there, and during the 1840s the Aberdare Canal's tonnage more than trebled.[53] Indeed the rate of growth of the coal trade quickly led to the substantial problems of congestion on the canals, especially on the Glamorgan Canal, which occasioned the introduction of directly competing railways. However, such was the effectiveness of canals in meeting the straightforward demands made on them by the economy of south Wales, and so central had they become to the infrastructure of the coalfield, that apart from the Taff Vale Railway, completed in 1841, the competition with the railways did not even begin until the second half of the nineteenth century. Sometimes as in the Vale of Neath, the railway (Vale of Neath line 1851) served one side of the valley and the canal the other, but generally the comparative advantage of the railways was not strong enough to cause the early demise of the canals. Not until the later 1860s and the 1870s did the advantages of the railways occasion a movement of traffic away from the canals. Even then all four canals continued to be significant carriers until the last decades of the century and the canal companies of south Wales were able to maintain their tonnages and comparatively high dividends longer than most of their English counterparts.[54]

The transport of coal and iron dominated the traffic on the canals of south Wales. The only other specific traffic of any real significance was the increasing importation of iron ore particularly after 1830, and mainly from Cumberland, as the south Wales ironmasters became increasingly aware of the advantages of mixing the richer haematite ore with the local ironstone, especially in the manufacture of rails.[55] Some copper ore was carried by the Swansea Canal to the copper smelters furthest inland, but the rest of the traffic was made up of a miscellaneous range of goods required by an industrializing economy. Thus in addition to foodstuffs and domestic goods taken up from the ports, the canals carried large quantities of stone for road-making and for building, timber for pit-props, limestone and lime. However, the export of finished bar iron and coal so dominated the traffic of the canals that all other goods are usually entered on the few returns that remain, as 'sundry items'.[56]

Not only did canals connect the ironworks and collieries of the northern parts of the coalfield with the coast, but they also each formed the basis for an elaborate transport network. Tram-roads (horse-drawn wagons on rails) were built, both by the canals and by other interests, to connect the canals with various locations in their respective valleys. This was an integral part of the programme of canal building in south Wales and provided a vital link in the transport chain between raw material and market. The building of tram-roads was revolutionized in 1799 when Benjamin Outram, the foremost tram-road engineer, recommended to the Monmouthshire, and to the Brecon and Abergavenny Canals that they should convert their early tram-roads into plateways, with the weight being borne by the rail as opposed to the wagon, resulting in a substantial increase in efficiency and a significant saving in transport costs. The use of tram-roads rapidly expanded and from only a few miles in the late 1790s, south Wales could boast of 150 miles of tram-road in 1811 and 350 miles by 1830. The region led the way in the strategic use of tram-roads and as Hadfield puts it, 'the system grew, within ironworks, from works and limestone quarries and collieries to each other; from all of them to the canal lines'.[57]

Although all the canals made effective use of tram-roads, it was the Monmouthshire Canal that developed them most comprehensively, investing more than half as much again of the capital cost of the canal on the tram-road network. The Monmouthshire Canal was built with two relatively short branches, both of eleven miles, to Crumlin and Pontnewynydd just north of Pontypool, respectively, barely reaching half-way to the main ironworks and coal-mining districts. The connection was completed by a series of tram-roads which linked the producing areas with the heads of the canal, and as in the case of the Sirhowy and the Rhymney tram-roads, also ran all the way to Newport. The Monmouthshire Canal itself built nine separate tram-roads, with a total length of 41 miles, including the 9½ mile Beaufort tram-road from Crumlin to the Ebbw Vale and Beaufort ironworks. In addition over 90 miles of the tram-roads were built by various independent interests, including the Abersychan tram-road built in 1827, a distance of 4 miles, to link the Abersychan ironworks with the Blaenavon tram-road and the Canal. So well were the Monmouthshire, and the Brecon and Abergavenny Canals served by tram-roads, that many of the ironworks, such as Nantyglo and Blaenavon, had the choice of a tram-road link either south to the heads of the Monmouthshire Canal, or eastwards to join the Brecon and Abergavenny, on which toll charges were lower.

In addition the canals had a developmental effect upon economic activity in their respective valleys. During the course of the early nineteenth century a number of new enterprises set up along the canal banks. Thus in 1816 the Brown Lennox Company came from Millwall to Pontypridd, where it could ensure adequate supplies of iron from Merthyr for its chain manufacture.[58] Other concerns, especially in the western valley, built short canals to connect with the main arterial waterway. Thus in 1839 the Vale of Neath Brewery built a short navigable cut to link it up with George Tennant's Neath and Swansea Junction Canal.[59] The canals also had a significant developmental effect upon the towns at which they joined the sea. The four ports, Newport, Cardiff, Swansea and Neath, which during the nineteenth century became major urban centres, rapidly developed as the centres of manufacturing and commercial services for the canals, and the trade which they promoted.

The canals were, as Clapham so aptly put it, 'both evidence and cause of that industrial development on and about the south Wales coalfield which was so marked a feature of the national economic scene in the new century. Like so many small unimportant canals and navigations around the coasts, their object was merely to bring an upland district in touch with tide-water. But their upland district was not some agricultural or secondary manufacturing region. It was trenched by the coal and iron valleys of Monmouth and Glamorgan'.[60] What the canals did then was simply to bring the cost of transporting the heavy bulky products that ushered in the industrial revolution in south Wales down to a level sufficiently low to enable them to effectively compete with areas rather more conveniently located, but without the advantage of the strategic combination of coal, ironstone and limestone in close proximity, or without highly prized coal reserves that could be relatively easily mined.

Although many estimates of the impact of the canals upon the cost of transportation have been made both by contemporaries and by subsequent historians, the most exhaustive and authoritative was conducted by W.T. Jackman in his classic work, *The Development of Transportation in Modern England* (1916). Jackman, as a result of a comprehensive comparison of the freight rates of canals and competing land transport, found that the average reduction in the cost of goods carried by the canals was around 65 per cent and that the difference between individual routes varied only between 50 per cent and 75 per cent of the cost of land transport.[61] Jackman agrees with the *Cambridge Chronicle and Journal* of 1813 that 'there was no instance in the Kingdom of conveyance by canal being above a half of the price of land carriage'.[62] Perhaps the most pertinent observation of the impact of the canals in south Wales was made by the Report of the Royal Commission on Canals in 1911, which stated that the Glamorganshire Canal, enabled boats of up to 60 feet in length to carry 20 tons of iron, a load which previously would have occupied 12 wagons, 48 horses, 12 men and 12 boys.[63] Although this advantage was to some extent offset by the slow speed at which goods were conveyed, an average of 2 miles per hour, and though the large number of locks on the south Wales canals made even this a rather optimistic figure, the scale of the canals' physical capacities ensured that the savings in transport costs were fully enjoyed.

During the 1790s then, some 77 miles of canal were built for less than £½ million, and these with their associated tram-roads opened up the south Wales coalfield to the main thrust of the industrial revolution which was already beginning to transform Britain.

Appendix

Coal and Iron Transported down the Glamorganshire and Monmouthshire Canals

i) Coal carried down the Glamorganshire Canal		ii) Coal carried down the Monmouthshire Canal	
Year	*Tons*	*Year*	*Tons*
1829	83,729	1829	489,762
1830	106,170	1830	533,408
1831	117,134	1831	490,813
1832	165,351	1832	491,718
1833	184,261	1833	456,897
1834	183,953	1834	456,060
1835	176,374	1835	499,096
1836	192,241	1836	487,061
1837	226,671	1837	517,066
1838	189,081	1838	497,374
1839	211,214	1839	518,916
1840	248,484	1840	558,104
1841*	245,467	1841	619,806
1842	325,825	1842	611,504
1843	353,108	1843	589,927
1844	416,138	1844	648,561
1845	521,388	1845	677,614
1846	581,444	1846	647,836
1847	622,235	1847	588,539

*Commencement of Taff Vale Railway.
Source: Newport Public Library, Doc. M000625 Acc.

Source: as i).

iii) Iron carried down the Monmouthshire Canal

Year	Ironworks															Tons Total
	Abersychan	Beaufort	Blaenavon	Blaina	Bute[2]	Clydach	Coalbrook Vale	Ebbw Vale	Garndyrus	Nantyglo	Pentwyn	Rhymney[2]	Tredegar	Varteg	Others[1]	
1802	—	—	1,091	—	—	—	—	—	—	—	—	—	—	—	—	1,091
1803	—	1,612	2,079	—	—	447	—	1,655	—	—	—	—	—	81	—	5,874
1804	—	2,950	8,490	—	—	1,266	—	2,890	—	—	—	—	—	771	—	16,367
1805	—	4,605	7,262	—	—	1,455	—	1,012	—	—	—	—	956	1,094	—	16,384
1806	—	3,989	6,594	—	—	1,599	—	3,252	—	—	—	—	3,124	2,482	—	21,040
1807	—	3,947	6,042	—	—	1,196	—	2,209	—	—	—	—	4,138	2,745	—	20,277
1808	—	4,004	7,163	—	—	963	—	1,553	—	—	—	—	5,529	2,379	—	21,591
1809	—	3,566	9,848	—	—	1,136	—	786	—	—	—	—	9,105	2,053	—	26,494
1810	—	3,948	12,254	—	—	1,372	—	2,758	—	—	—	—	7,696	1,676	—	29,704
1811	—	3,910	12,377	—	—	872	—	2,633	—	77	—	—	6,643	583	—	27,095
1812	—	3,995	14,579	—	—	1,774	—	4,648	—	1,168	—	—	7,862	120	—	34,146
1813	—	3,204	13,562	—	—	2,174	—	5,939	—	1,855	—	—	7,597	141	—	34,472
1814	—	3,146	12,438	—	—	1,472	—	4,752	—	2,292	—	—	9,131	—	—	33,231
1815	—	3,767	14,002	—	—	2,999	—	4,953	—	4,684	—	—	9,225	—	—	39,630
1816	—	3,164	11,773	—	—	2,658	—	2,949	—	6,160	—	—	7,499	—	—	34,203
1817	—	2,104	11,080	—	—	3,162	—	3,127	2,247	7,242	—	—	10,350	127	—	39,439
1818	—	2,100	8,771	—	—	3,947	—	2,476	5,097	7,325	—	—	8,258	—	—	37,974
1819	—	2,124	6,776	—	—	3,788	—	1,907	4,427	7,934	—	—	7,140	225	—	34,321
1820	—	3,132	9,423	—	—	3,397	—	3,605	2,798	8,826	—	—	8,211	360	—	39,752
1821	—	2,962	8,973	—	—	3,876	1,880	6,041	2,838	10,460	—	—	9,923	3,757	—	50,710

																Total
1822	—	3,786	5,831	—	—	4,225	919	5,960	3,476	10,906	—	—	8,102	4,453	—	47,658
1823	—	4,269	10,745	—	—	3,651	1,582	8,613	4,370	12,723	—	—	9,903	5,031	—	60,887
1824	—	5,347	11,265	212	—	3,617	1,541	10,101	4,517	15,134	—	—	11,444	5,290	—	68,468
1825	—	7,091	9,042	1,588	—	3,748	3,596	10,325	4,218	16,536	83	—	11,012	4,512	—	71,751
1826	—	6,028	8,059	2,098	—	3,660	2,874	10,297	2,145	11,512	738	—	10,962	5,128	—	63,501
1827	113	5,914	8,255	2,991	—	4,107	3,016	14,403	2,446	18,059	4,140	—	13,837	7,427	—	84,708
1828	6,478	5,701	9,766	3,507	6,320	5,183	3,756	15,479	2,645	19,032	4,147	—	14,341	8,131	—	104,486
1829	7,760	6,896	10,124	4,863	9,909	6,967	1,902	16,959	2,242	17,433	4,698	—	13,349	9,232	—	112,334
1830	7,615	5,065	9,397	4,195	5,728	6,771	1,905	18,133	3,654	17,115	5,425	—	12,303	8,988	—	106,294
1831	8,022	5,150	9,706	2,921	7,548	6,231	2,189	18,778	4,133	17,866	4,850	—	13,340	11,519	2,710	114,963
1832	7,751	6,052	8,986	7,960	7,180	6,542	2,396	19,740	1,833	21,333	4,038	—	13,304	11,171	2,680	120,966
1833	7,295	7,512	8,285	4,880	5,611	7,252	2,429	19,226	3,600	21,007	4,406	—	12,323	10,627	4,064	118,517
1834	8,430	9,808	8,406	6,324	3,662	6,261	2,898	20,228	2,214	22,594	4,057	—	12,858	14,762	4,077	126,579
1835	9,724	12,976	9,023	9,233	4,198	7,618	3,211	25,392	4,286	24,957	6,527	—	13,909	14,831	5,253	151,138
1836	12,278	14,567	7,606	8,911	2,346	7,640	3,754	23,120	4,297	25,384	8,201	2,963	12,133	11,209	3,341	147,750
1837	10,261	11,145	7,150	6,675	—	7,081	3,325	22,475	4,159	23,981	6,895	6,797	12,641	10,422	6,441	139,448
1838	11,857	10,903	8,074	7,482	—	9,283	4,000	23,579	—	25,263	7,444	13,547	15,526	9,857	12,268	159,083
1839	12,481	10,505	5,718	1,140	—	9,606	5,204	25,342	—	24,945	12,533	14,881	14,861	12,820	14,715	164,751
1840	12,290	10,049	7,347	—[3]	—	10,038	7,824	24,199	—	26,662	17,783	18,581	15,288	12,669	18,070	180,800

Source: H. Scrivenor, *History of the Iron Trade* (London, 1854), pp 127 and 158.
[1] Includes Cwm Celyn, Golynos, Victoria and Pontypool.
[2] Bute amalgamated with the Union Ironworks in 1836 to form the Rhymney Iron Co.
[3] Included in Cwm Celyn.

iv) Iron carried down the Glamorganshire Canal

Year	Ironworks										Tons Total
	Aberdare	Blakemore	Brown & Co.	Bute	Cyfarthfa & Hirwaun	Dowlais	Gadlys	Penydarren	Plymouth	Taff Vale	
1817	—	—	—	—	14,191	9,936	—	8,275	7,095	—	39,497
1818	—	—	—	—	15,706	9,694	—	8,834	7,377	—	41,611
1819	—	—	—	—	16,646	10,796	—	7,549	7,633	—	42,624
1820	2,626	—	—	—	19,010	11,115	—	8,690	7,941	—	49,382
1821	1,863	—	—	—	18,070	12,571	—	10,018	9,943	—	52,465
1822	2,023	—	—	—	17,137	14,557	—	9,924	8,833	—	52,474
1823	2,659	—	—	—	19,452	14,015	—	10,240	10,920	—	57,286
1824	4,234	—	969	—	20,399	12,594	—	10,358	9,499	—	58,053
1825	6,354	—	1,178	—	23,063	15,851	—	10,611	11,269	—	68,326
1826	6,686	—	57	—	20,206	16,601	—	8,691	7,836	—	60,077
1827	8,472	2,101	1,059	—	29,312	20,726	—	10,369	12,907	—	84,946
1828	9,864	2,056	720	—	30,011	23,575	414	10,223	12,976	—	89,839
1829	8,644	2,001	767	166	24,768	23,352	559	10,085	13,534	—	83,876
1830	6,765	2,702	621	—	19,892	27,647	—	11,744	12,177	—	81,548
1831	6,903	2,947	626	36	15,465	22,075	—	11,819	10,498	—	70,369
1832	5,997	3,042	757	572	24,668	29,395	—	10,582	9,200	—	84,213
1833	6,964	3,519	890	434	37,380	35,072	214	12,150	12,093	3,461	112,177
1834	8,497	3,194	1,163	127	34,952	33,477	731	12,752	12,073	3,739	110,705
1835	9,261	4,020	1,854	124	35,090	39,145	1,828	12,834	12,631	3,068	119,855
1836	9,981	3,957	2,437	22	34,654	39,286	1,816	12,537	13,573	4,723	122,986
1837	9,830	3,594	2,756	—	33,580	38,914	1,756	12,834	15,353	6,171	124,788
1838	12,247	3,474	3,394	—	36,986	39,361	1,127	12,707	16,143	5,198	130,637
1839	11,307	3,304	4,037	—	37,009	40,495	1,081	15,540	15,762	4,246	132,781
1840	10,327	3,175	2,476	—	35,507	45,218	1,345	16,130	12,922	4,902	132,002

Source: H. Scrivenor, *History of the Iron Trade* (London, 1854), pp. 124 and 257.

The Supply of Raw Materials to the South Wales Iron Industry, 1800–60

MICHAEL ATKINSON

The purpose of this paper is to assess the role played by the supply of raw materials, especially of iron ore or ironstone, in the development of the south Wales iron industry between 1800 and 1860. This period has been chosen because it formed a transitionary phase between two more commonly recognized stages of development within south Wales. Before 1800, the industry was based solely on local supplies of coal, ironstone and limestone which of course was the main reason why the industry was attracted to the area in the second half of the eighteenth century. After 1860 local ironstone was no longer the main source of iron, being replaced by imported, mainly foreign, haematite ores. This change eventually resulted in the construction of new steelworks on the coast and the demise of smelting at the heads of the valleys, although the shift in location was delayed by many years in part due to the heavy investment required. Between 1800 and 1860, the industry progressed technologically to such an extent as to alter the basis of location in the traditional iron-making belt of the north-east rim of the coalfield. Through dramatic improvements in furnace fuel economy, by substantial increases in the cost of mining local ironstone, and the development of the embryonic science of metallurgy and the resulting ability and need to use ores of varying properties, the industry found itself facing a very different raw material supply situation than it had at the end of the eighteenth century.

The raw material element in the production cost of manufacturing iron consisted of the cost of extraction, of transport to the furnaces, and the royalty payment. Since royalty payments to land, or mineral, owners varied a great deal both over time and between the different works, they cannot be ignored in any comprehensive study of raw material supply, especially since it can be argued that differences in royalty arrangements can partly explain the varying fortunes of the iron companies. However, since this paper does not seek to analyse such variations within the district, royalty arrangements are not discussed. Therefore, the paper divides into three main sections: firstly, a summary of the importance of raw material supply in determining location; secondly, the effect of fuel economies on the relative importance of the main raw materials used and therefore their effect on location; and thirdly, a detailed study of the sources of iron ore and ironstone and the reasons behind changes in these sources. This latter section has been dealt with in some detail for two reasons — firstly, it is a subject which has received little attention in the past and, secondly, when attempting to explain the decline of iron-making along the north-east rim of the coalfield, there was clearly no problem as regards coal and limestone which continued to be locally obtained. It is to iron ore supply that one must look to explain the movement away from the valleys.

Throughout its history, the iron industry has always been a raw-material based industry, locating itself as close as possible to the sources of those minerals. The reason for this is that the process of iron-making involves a substantial reduction of bulk so that it was cheaper to transport the product to the market than to haul the raw materials over long distances to the furnaces. In 1800 about 8 tons of coal,[1] 3½ tons of ironstone and about ½ ton of limestone were required to make one ton of pig iron. It then took at least 1½ tons of pig to make a ton of bar iron.[2] The locational 'pull' of raw materials in this period was clearly demonstrated in south Wales where a substantial industry was built up based on the export of the final product to often far-distant markets.

The cost of assembling the basic ingredients in the blast-furnace — coal, iron ore or ironstone, and limestone — was by far the major element in the cost of producing iron. The mineral agent of the Marquis of Bute, Robert Beaumont, estimated in various reports written in 1830–1 that raw material cost accounted for between 80 and 85 per cent of the total cost of producing pig iron.[3] Again in 1839, William Needham, then manager of the Varteg ironworks, estimated that raw material costs, excluding royalty, formed 73 per cent of total pig iron production cost,[4] while William Menelaus of Dowlais commented in 1857 that 'the cost of minerals makes up such a large proportion of the cost of finished iron, that economy in this department is of the greatest importance'.[5] In 1892, Isaac Lowthian Bell estimated that raw materials cost formed 88 per cent of the total production cost of pig iron,[6] whilst in 1906 James Stephen Jeans estimated that they accounted in Cleveland for 84.3 per cent.[7]

Since the cost of assembling all the required materials for the blast-furnaces was so crucial to the iron industry, it determined where it could be profitably carried out. Hypothetically, the optimum location for the production of pig iron would move as changes within the industry altered the relative importance of each of the ingredient raw materials. In reality, the forces of geographic inertia, resulting from the high capital cost of reconstructing a smelting site in a new location, condemned the industry to remain for years on sites which had long become effectively obsolete.[8] This inertia does not however preclude discussion of the 'pull' of raw material sources since only by fully appreciating the importance of these sources can one assess the position of the industry over time.

Of the three basic raw material inputs, limestone is the least significant in this context. Again, Bell commented in 1885 that 'of limestone there is so small a weight used that its geographical position rarely, if ever, determines the location of the blast furnace'.[9] Limestone was quite widely available in all of the iron-producing regions of the country and the technology of extraction (i.e., open quarrying) was so universal that it was not possible to discern any major differences between regions or individual works that would influence their relative positions.

It was the juxtaposition of coal and ironstone within the south Wales coal measures that drew the industry to the valleys in the eighteenth century. Both occurred in horizontal or near-horizontal seams, mostly interstratified but sometimes, as in the case of blackband ironstones, actually intermixed. Initially both could be cheaply worked simply by digging at the surface outcrop of the seams. The geological structure of the coal measures was such that the upper seams of both coal and ironstone outcropped on the north-eastern rim of the coalfield and it was this phenomenon which attracted industry to the particular siting of the valley heads. Surface working was carried out by 'scouring' whereby the force of flowing water was used to wash coal or ironstone out of the ground, or by 'patchwork' in which the raw material was simply dug away at surface, i.e., shallow quarrying. The physical limitations of such modes of working are obvious and eventually the seams had to be followed at depth.

It was the need to extract the raw materials from increasingly less accessible formations which caused the rise in the cost of local raw materials in the nineteenth century. The first stage in extracting coal or ironstone underground, facilitated by the indentured terrain, was the driving of levels into the hillside, but, as the upper seams became worked out, it was found necessary to sink shafts to the lower seams with all the increased expense which was involved, such as mechanical pumping, greater ventilation requirements, and the need to raise or lower men, materials and minerals. The coal of the north-eastern parts of the coalfield was particularly suitable for iron-smelting and provided a strong, stable attraction for the industry. The only significant change in its contribution was that, because of technological advance, the ratio of the quantity of coal to iron ore decreased as the period progressed, though this did not begin to influence the determination of the industry's location until the latter part of the nineteenth century.[10]

The supply position of the other major ingredient in the iron-making process, iron-stone or ore, did however alter significantly, and experienced variations over the period. The onset of increasing extraction costs in south Wales coupled as it was with the deterioration of ironstone seams coincided with the exploitation of richer ores elsewhere or the cheaper working of ores of similar content. The iron industry either had to tolerate the increased cost of ironstone or import its supplies from elsewhere. Clearly the cost of transport, which previously had been unimportant because the raw materials were all close at hand, now became significant. As will be seen, ore could be imported from other parts of Britain and delivered to the works more cheaply than the local ironstone could be mined.

As long as both the coal and iron ore were drawn from the same close vicinity, there was no competition in 'pulling' the centre of smelting activities towards one mineral or the other, and it is argued that the location of the iron industry on the coalfields following the spread of coke-smelting obscured the importance of ore supply since the ore was found, in most coalfields, along with the coal.[11] Once the sources were geographically separate however, the amounts of each mineral used in the process became crucial since the industry would have wished to locate where assembly cost was minimized.

Between 1800 and 1860, the relative amounts of each raw material used altered dramatically. The amount of iron ore used to produce one ton of pig remained comparatively static. The only way that iron ore input could be reduced was to use ores of higher metallic content such as haematites, but with the calcination of lower grade ironstone increasing its metallic content when it entered the furnace to over 45 per cent, the difference between calcined local ironstone and imported haematites was not so great as to dramatically alter the relative importance of ore and coal. It was improvements in fuel economy that really altered the relationship by reducing the amount of coal required to produce a given amount of iron. The invention in 1828 by J.C. Neilson of the hot-blast, which has been termed 'the most important single innovation in the industry in the age of iron',[12] resulted in truly dramatic reductions in coal requirements. Whereas before the hot-blast some 8 tons of coal were needed for each ton of pig, by 1860 this had been reduced to 3 tons or less.[13] Initially, coal was used to heat the blast but the use of waste furnace gases, pioneered by J.P. Budd of Ystalyfera works and later by G. Parry of Ebbw Vale,[14] allowed further economies in the use of coal.

To the ironmaster, the significance of these improvements in furnace technology was that they substantially reduced his production costs. To the industry in general, the long-term effect was to completely alter the factors influencing location, for by 1860 almost as much ore as fuel was required in the furnaces, although further coal supplies were needed to refine pig and to power the steam engines. Eventually, ironmasters had to rethink their strategies and in south Wales it became increasingly evident that the works at the heads of the valleys were placed in a disadvantageous position.

However, it is doubtful whether the improvements in fuel economy would have had an effect on the location of the industry had it not been for the switch that occurred in the source of iron ore. Whilst it is well known that from the late 1860s the south Wales iron and steel industry imported increasing quantities of foreign, mainly Spanish, haematite, it is not generally appreciated that it imported large quantities of ore from other areas of the United Kingdom well before that time. The use of external supplies of ore has been mentioned by Birch, Roepke, Daunton, Isard and Watts,[15] but the point has never been pursued in any depth. Although Evan Jones stated that over a quarter of a million tons of foreign haematite was imported into Newport in 1847,[16] this was not the case for the exact figure he quoted was in fact iron exports from the port. Indeed, figures of imports of foreign ore show that the foreign trade was insignificant until the 1860s. However as will be shown, ores from other parts of Britain were being used in the early nineteenth century and by 1860, before the spread of the Bessemer process made haematite ores indispensable, they were being used in very substantial quantities. Such a major switch in ore sources must have had good causes and serious implications and warrants an attempt to trace its development and to analyse the reasons behind it.

It is known that as early as 1796 ore was shipped from Combe Martin in north Devon, to Llanelli[17] but whether this was a regular trade or not is unclear. The stock accounts of the Cyfarthfa works show that from at least 1812 small stocks of Lancashire ore were held at the works on a regular basis,[18] so the practice of using non-indigenous ores can be traced back at least to the end of the Napoleonic Wars, although there is as yet no clue as to the use to which it was being put nor to the extent of the trade. By 1819, a Furness iron ore trader was writing that 'we shall not ship more than 10,000 tons . . . most of our customers have said enough, except Guest, Crawshay and some of the Chester ones',[19] indicating that trade in ore had become quite substantial.

Figures of ore shipments from the Furness area show that between 1824 and 1839 an annual average of 12,075 tons of haematite were sent to south Wales.[20] In this period there appears to have been no increasing trend in tonnages shipped but from 1840 there certainly was, with the annual average tonnage sent between 1840 and 1844 amounting to 21,238 tons. Although stock accounts give no idea of the amount of ore actually used, the Cyfarthfa stock accounts indicate a similar increase.[21]

There is clear evidence that Furness was not the only area supplying ore to south Wales in this period. In 1825, Anthony Hill leased haematite mines at Crowgarth in West Cumberland to supply his Plymouth works at Merthyr,[22] and in 1829 he gained control of Box Bush mine in the Forest of Dean from a free miner.[23] In 1832 Josiah John Guest acquired the Westbury Brook mine and in 1834 William Crawshay obtained a three-fourths holding in the Buckshraft mine, both in the Forest of Dean.[24] In the south-west of England, the magnetite mines at Haytor in Devon were being worked for the Welsh market in the 1820s and 1830s,[25] whilst in 1840, Mushet reported that ore was being sent from Plymouth to south Wales.[26] The Dowlais Letter Books contain several references to ore suppliers in Cornwall in the 1840s,[27] whilst in 1844 John Taylor commented that large quantities of Cornish ore were being delivered to south Wales.[28] The earliest reference to activity in Somerset, later to be the scene of quite intense activity on the part of the south Wales ironmasters, was the working of iron ore mines near Dunster by Crawshay in 1836, supposedly with 'great vigour'.[29] Certainly ore from Minehead and Bristol appears in the Cyfarthfa stock accounts in 1847–9.[30]

The survival of a large body of business records for the Dowlais works allows a more detailed picture of the growth of haematite trade to be pieced together. As early as 1826–7, a total of 3,341 tons of ore were recorded as being shipped up to the works from their Cardiff wharf.[31] Since the accounts for this item covered 16 of the 24 months, the implication is that Dowlais was receiving about 2,600 tons of haematite annually. In 1833 some 4,780 tons of ore were sent to the works.[32] By 1838, the use of ores from other orefields in Britain had clearly increased substantially for in the year from December 1837 to November 1838, a total of just over 20,000 tons of 'imported' ore was used in the furnaces, with two-thirds coming from Cumberland and the rest from the Furness area, the Forest of Dean and the ports of Brixham in Devon, and Fowey in Cornwall.[33] From 1836, with only occasional exceptions, stocks of more than 10,000 tons of mainly Cumbrian and Cornish haematite were held at the works.[34] It is significant that by the late 1830s, haematite had become so important to furnace operations at Dowlais that, on requesting urgent shipments from Cardiff of 'red ore', (i.e. haematite), Thomas Evans wrote in 1836 that 'I have been obliged to stop the Blast on the Furnaces for want of supply today, and I am directed not to use more of our own Mine than if we had a regular supply of the Ore, therefore one day is of the greatest importance just now'.[35]

By the late 1840s, the quantity of haematite used had again increased substantially. Figures of ore used in the Dowlais furnaces, available for intermittent periods between

1845 and 1852, show that between 35,000 and 50,000 tons were being used annually,[36] a figure corroborated by details of orders placed for ore by Dowlais. Total ore contracts placed in 1847 amounted to 56,400 tons, mostly drawn from south-west England,[37] whilst orders for ore placed between January 1852 and February 1855 averaged 56,108 tons per year, mainly from Furness and West Cumberland.[38] Direct involvement in haematite mining, noted in the Forest of Dean, was otherwise apparently limited at this stage, the only other operation in which Dowlais became directly involved, without much success, being in Eskdale in Cumberland where ore prospecting was carried out in the late 1840s.[39]

By 1850 Dowlais works alone was using externally supplied haematite ore at the rate of some 50,000 tons per year. In this it was not alone but the evidence available for other works is not so abundant, although it does indicate that the use of haematite was becoming more widespread after the 1820s. In 1828, the Clydach works was reported as having already charged one furnace with local ironstone and Lancashire ore and to be commencing to similarly charge another.[40] In 1837, the Abersychan works was reported to be using haematite as part of the furnace charge,[42] whilst in 1839 the Rhymney works was being supplied with ore by Harrison, Ainslie and Co,[42] then the largest Furness haematite mining firm. Details of raw materials fed to the Crawshays' Hirwaun furnaces reveal that the amount of haematite used grew from 1,632 tons in 1839 to 5,904 in 1848.[43]

It appears that the mid 1830s saw an unforeseen expansion in the use of haematite, and the Directors of the Taff Vale Railway reported in 1836 that 'the iron ore imported into Cardiff is also an article . . . exceeding what was assumed for it in the calculations laid before Parliament'.[44] By 1846, the Taff Vale Railway was carrying more than 50,000 tons per year,[45] with the Glamorgan Canal transporting similar amounts.

A further indication of the size of the trade at this time can be found in the figures of iron ore output presented by Braithwaite Poole in 1849.[46] According to these, some 87,000 tons of ore were sent that year from Furness to south Wales, whilst a substantial proportion of the total of 100,000 mined in the Whitehaven area must also have found its way there. The Dowlais Company's and the Crawshays' mines in the Forest of Dean yielded 31,000 and 30,000 tons respectively although, with the Crawshays operating the Cinderford furnace in the Forest, not all of their ore would have gone to Cyfarthfa. The total of 118,000 tons mined in the south-west in 1849 would also have gone mainly to south Wales.[47]

By 1856, the Dowlais works had become dependent on British haematite ores for its iron output. In that year, according to the manager William Menelaus, the furnaces used 90,000 tons of haematite, accounting for more than half of the total pig iron make of the works,[48] whilst in the same year, the Ebbw Vale works used 84,000 tons of haematite.[49] In a report to Lord Leconfield in 1853, a major west Cumberland haematite royalty-owner, his mineral agent George Dixon described Cumberland haematite as 'an almost indispensable article of trade' to the south Wales works.[50] In evidence to the Select Committee on the Rating of Mines in 1856, Menelaus maintained that 'if we confined ourselves to Welsh ore . . . the works would be shut up',[51] and William Llewellin stated that although south Wales had long imported haematite, it was 'nothing like the extent to which we import it now'.[52]

In the 1850s, the south Wales works also began to use lower grade ore from Wiltshire and Northamptonshire, and even from the Isle of Wight. As early as 1853, the *Mining Journal* reported that 1,000 tons of Northampton ore were being sent weekly to south Wales,[53] whilst in the late 1850s, the Rhymney works was ordering ore from Pell in Northampton and the Ebbw Vale works was using 400 tons per week.[54] In the early 1860s, the Abersychan works was using ores from Cumbria, the Forest of Dean, the Brendon Hills, Northamptonshire, Elba, Spain and Cherbourg,[55] whilst Percy reported that ore dredged by fishermen off the Isle of Wight was being delivered to Cardiff and used at Ebbw Vale.[56] The late 1850s also saw the Dowlais and Plymouth concerns actively exploring Exmoor as a source of ore to reduce their dependence on Cumbrian suppliers,[57] although their efforts in Somerset came to nothing. From 1851, however, the Ebbw Vale Company did exploit large deposits of haematite and spathose ores in the Brendon Hills in Somerset, the spathose ores at a later date being used to produce 'speigeleisen' for use in Bessemer Converters.[58] Clearly therefore the south Wales works found external supplies of haematite essential for their operations far earlier than is commonly thought. The mere fact that major works like Dowlais, on the eve of the advent of cheap steel and before the influx of foreign ores, had become dependent on external ore supplies demands some explanation.

The two factors constantly present throughout the period in question were the steadily increasing cost and the decreasing quality of local ironstone. Whereas Welsh 'mine' had cost 5s. per ton in 1800, by 1830 it was costing between 8s. and 9s. per ton, and by the 1850s ironmasters were paying 14s. or more.[59] By contrast, the price of the richer haematite ores remained fairly stable. For example, during the period 1834–52 the cost of haematite delivered to Dowlais from Furness varied between 18s. and 21s. per ton,[60] about half of which was made up of the transport cost from the main shipping ports of Barrow and Whitehaven to the works. Ore stocks at Cyfarthfa in 1837–9 were costed at 20s. per ton.[61] In the same period, haematite ores of 50–55 per cent metal content were being sold at the ports of Barrow and Whitehaven to south Wales ironmasters for between 9s. and 12s. per ton.[62] The ores from the south-west and the Forest of Dean with an average metal content of 45 per cent and with much less distance to travel, sold at substantially lower prices. In 1844, Cornish ore was being delivered to Cardiff at 9s. per ton, whilst in 1852 Restormel ore cost 10/9d. per ton at Cardiff.[63] After transport to the works, these ores were costed at between 12s. and 15s. per ton, with Dean ore commanding the highest price.[64]

By the mid 1850s, a situation had been reached whereby the higher grade haematites had become cheaper both to purchase and to use than local ironstone. Before the Select Committee on the Rating of Mines, it was stated that 'the ironmasters can now buy iron mine in Somerset and the Forest of Dean, and in the North of England, a great deal cheaper than they can raise their own ironstone; that is a fact, I know'.[65] The cost-reducing effect on furnace operations was noted by Menelaus in 1857 when he commented that 'With regard to mine we cannot hope to see the cost reduced much, it is every year becoming more difficult to get, the men have comparatively low wages — by becoming colliers they can easily earn more money, this keeps up a continual drain of men from the mine works into the collieries, which will end in raising permanently the cost of mine. To meet this scarcity we are using as little mine as possible, the result will be seen in the account No. 2, where it is seen that by substituting red ore for Welsh mine, the cost has been reduced 1/4d. per ton of Pigs, while at the same time we have not lowered the quality'.[66] All the witnesses giving evidence for the south Wales area to the Select Committee on the Rating of Mines supported the view that it was simply cost-reduction that lay behind the import of haematite. For example, Dobson claimed that 'if the ironmasters could get it (local ironstone) now at a moderate expense, they would still rather use their own mine than mine coming from other districts', a view shared by other witnesses.[67]

However, the comparative cheapness of haematite ores in south Wales in the 1850s obscured a further, and perhaps more important, reason for their use both then and in the preceding decades when such a cost advantage was not so obvious. There were strong technological reasons for its use, both in the furnace and in the puddling process. The primary reason for the introduction of haematite into the furnaces was almost certainly the need to remedy inherent defects in the pig iron produced purely from Welsh mine. Writing in 1830, William Needham reported that 'There are some works in Wales where the iron has a tendency to be red short, and others where the opposite quality is most to be dreaded. A cold short iron is generally produced from a lean ore, that is, one containing only a small percentage of iron, and at several works in south Wales, it is found advantageous to mix the rich hepatic ores of Lancashire and Cumberland with the poorer iron stone of their own district. The mixture gives strength to the iron and prevents it from being cold short'.[68]

Since iron produced from haematite alone tends to be red-short, the art behind the use of haematite and ironstone mixes was in the selection of the correct quantities both of ores and of coke, and in this sense it would not be too fanciful to consider iron-making analogous to the baking of a cake. In 1850, E. Talbott of Tipton wrote that 'a judicious combination of ores in the first process will supply a suitable quality of pig iron, and, this obtained, red-short and cold-short may be all but annihilated'.[69] However, many ironmasters showed typical conservatism and unwillingness to experiment in perfecting the charge to the furnace, complaining of the poor quality of the iron brought about by their own inexperience with the mixtures. Thus in 1840, David Mushet commented that 'The manufacturer, therefore, finding his operation with these ores so subtle and precarious, frequently abandons their use, in the firm belief that their application, in quantity, is incompatible with the existence of good melting pig iron'.[70] The problem lay not only with the need to carefully select the mixture but also with the insufficient carburisation of the iron, and the remedy proposed by Mushet was the addition of extra fuel to ensure a sufficient level of carbon in the furnace to take up the excess oxygen produced by haematite ores. According to Mushet, it was the advent of the hot-blast that allowed much greater facility in achieving good results from the furnaces,[71] a fact that may explain the expansion of haematite imports in the late 1830s. Mushet in fact claimed that the use of hot-blast had 'removed all difficulties' as far as proper carburisation was concerned.

There is, however, further reason why the use of haematite should have expanded so much in the late 1830s and 1840s. South Wales, as is well known, specialized heavily in the rail trade and the defect of cold-shortness was much detested by customers. There was nevertheless contemporary disagreement over the effect on quality accompanying the use of haematite. For example, William Truran was quite damning in his comment that 'the general quality of *forge iron has been lowered in consequence* of the increased use of cinders and rich ores, there can be no question, but we may remark, that, for many purposes to which bar iron is now applied quality is a *secondary* consideration; and the use of cinders and rich ores in moderation is attended with numerous advantages to the manufacturer'.[72] On the other hand, John Percy maintained that iron made from a mixture of haematite, cinders and Welsh mine 'may be considered best Welsh common forge-pig'.[73] The principal advantage, as regards the rail trade, seems to have been that the use of haematite in the production of forge-pig allowed a degree of control over the final product not possible with the pure Welsh mine-pig. In the production of bar iron, 'piles' of bar were erected in the balling furnace in a manner suited to the needs of the final product, and jealously guarded by the manufacturer. The ability to produce iron of different qualities for different purposes, even if applied only to the requirements of rails, was of positive advantage. Mushet summed it up when he stated that 'Those works whose situation enables them to draw their supply from fields of ironstone, impressed with all the various characters of mixtures, possess many advantages which those more insulated are frequently deprived of. With equal ease ought the manufacturer to be able in these cases to fabricate with certainty a quality of iron capable of forming to advantage the most minute piece of casting, or the heaviest piece or ordnance; at pleasure he might form a quality fit for the forge, or of value in the pig iron market. In short, where such variety of ores exist, iron of every quality, comprising fusibility and strength, may at pleasure be manufactured, suited to the many and various wants of a foundry and forge'.[74] It is perhaps not coincidence that the works which most heavily used haematite such as Dowlais, Cyfarthfa, Ebbw Vale and Rhymney, were those which specialized most in rails. Indeed, according to J.T. Smith, it was for the purposes of the rail trade that haematite was sent to south Wales in this period.[75] How does all this then improve our understanding of the development of the south Wales iron industry?

Clearly, at an earlier date than is commonly realized and certainly by the late 1830s the Welsh iron industry could no longer rely on local sources of raw materials to meet all of its requirements. In this it was not alone for the Staffordshire and Scottish industries were also drawing supplies from Cumbria. However, if the Furness ore trade is typical, south Wales formed the chief market for haematite ores, taking about three-quarters of Furness ore exports between 1824 and 1845. South Wales appears to have been in a particularly precarious position as regards ore supplies, a point fully emphasized when Spanish ores flooded in, in the 1860s and 1870s, making south Wales from the outset the main user of such ores.[76]

It is not suggested that before 1860 the situation had become such as to warrant any major geographical shift in the Welsh iron industry. Local ironstone remained overall the main source of the metal iron throughout the period in question and, anyhow, the total coal tonnage needs of the works (including refining and power) were still greater than ore requirements. It is suggested, however, that it was clear to those concerned in the industry that major changes were afoot, that the seeds of the eventual destruction of the industry on the north-east rim were germinating, even during the heyday of the Welsh wrought-iron trade; that the specific needs of the trade in which the works specialized, i.e., rails, led to changes in raw material supplies which, when later reinforced by the demands of steel-making, destroyed the logic of location at the heads of the valleys. In essence, in the valleys at least, one can push back the starting date for the decline of the Welsh iron industry.

Coal-Mining in the Llanelli Area
— Years of Growth, 1800–64

M.V. SYMONS

By 1800 Llanelli's coal industry had been established for some three centuries, the area having emerged as one of Britain's early coalfields in the sixteenth century. This early rise can undoubtedly be attributed to the area's favourable geological structure and location which had brought seams of the free-burning bituminous coal required by sixteenth-century consumers to shallow, workable depths close to the sea-shore and the ships of the export trade. In the hands of local people with limited capital, the industry had failed to realize its true potential until the middle of the eighteenth century when an influx of developers from outside the area had first introduced modern mining techniques and metal-smelting works to the Llanelli coalfield. These early attempts at full industrial-ization had soon come to a halt, however, and it had taken a second influx of capitalists and entrepreneurs in the 1790s to establish the proper base for a widespread and permanent industrialization process.[1] This paper provides a brief summary of the subsequent growth of Llanelli's coal industry between 1800 and 1864.

The geographical area of this study, covering some 20 square miles (approximately 1/40th of the south Wales coalfield), is shown in Figure 1 on page 54. It was a sub-coalfield in its own right, developing separately from its neighbouring sub-coalfields (Loughor and Burry Port) and possessing a unique history capable of being unravelled only by detailed study of a localized area. The area extends from the Ordnance Survey National Grid line SN 04 in the north (delineating a barren inland zone between bituminous and anthracite surface coal where little exploitation has taken place), down to the shoreline of the Burry Estuary in the south. The Plas Isaf Fault, which represented a natural barrier to eastwards advancing coal-workings from within the area and to westwards advancing workings from the Loughor sub-coalfield, has been taken as the eastern boundary. Similarly, the Moreb Fault, which provided a natural discontinuity between workings of the Llanelli and Burry Port sub-coalfields, has been taken as the western boundary.

The coal mined at Llanelli was predominantly bituminous in nature, pure anthracite being absent.[2] Some seams, particularly those to the north-east of the area, yielded coals with properties intermediate between bituminous coal and anthracite, referred to as 'semi-anthracites' or, more commonly, as 'steam-coals'.[3] Llanelli was the pioneer of the Welsh steam-coal trade and the world-wide demand for its steam-coals played an important part in the area's development after 1830.[4]

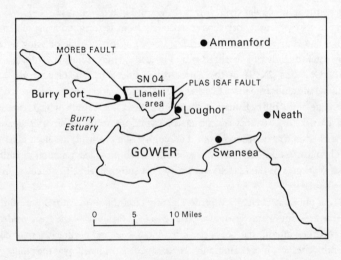

Figure 1
The Llanelli area

Coal-mining 1800–64

The period 1800 to 1864 may be conveniently divided into two approximate halves of distinctly different character in terms of the development of Llanelli's coal mining industry.

The first period — 1800 to 1829 — was an innovative time with the first real large-scale exploitation of the area's coal resources and the allied establishment of smelting-works and other industries. It was a period notable for the ruthless competition between the newly arrived industrialists and for the reckless speculations which bankrupted many of them. By 1829, only one of the late eighteenth/early nineteenth-century industrialists, R.J. Nevill, was still in business at Llanelli and significant changes were taking place in the ownership and development of the local coal industry.

The second period — 1830 to 1864 — was a time of consolidation and new development despite the adverse national economic climate of the 1830s and 1840s. Two companies — the Llanelly Copperworks Company and the Llangennech Coal Company — monopolized the local coal industry, although a new feature of this period was the emergence of numerous small concerns, sometimes consisting of only a few working miners in partnership, which operated alongside the larger enterprises employing hundreds. The combined output of the large and small concerns increased steadily after 1830 with a peak export, and presumably production, plateau reached in the late 1850s/early 1860s.[5] By this time, however, the seeds of decline of Llanelli's coal industry had already been sown with the result that growth ceased after 1864.

These two periods are now examined in greater detail.

1800–29

The first 30 years of the nineteenth century saw unparalleled industrial growth throughout most of Britain, and events at Llanelli mirrored this national trend. Llanelli's second phase of industrialization, initiated in the late 1790s, was continued and strengthened by the advent of a number of English industrialists who invested heavily into the exploitation of the area's coal resources, the establishment of metalworks, the formation of railway networks, and the construction of docks capable of accommodating large vessels. Some of the new industrialists also invested in land purchase. As a result of these developments, the population of the town approximately doubled between 1800 and 1829[6] with coal exports from the area increasing fivefold over the same period. As the new metalworks and increased population were consuming more coal locally, it can be safely assumed that the increase in coal production was greater than the fivefold increase in coal exports; unfortunately, accurate estimates of production cannot be achieved for this period because output records of the numerous collieries were either not kept or have not survived.

Estimated coal exports between 1800 and 1829 are shown in Figures 2 and 3. Figure 2 provides export quantities for the 230 years between 1650 and 1880 in order that the 1800 to 1829 period can be put into context and an appreciation gained of the unprecedented expansion of Llanelli's coal industry during the early nineteenth century. Figure 3 shows coal exports between 1800 and 1880 to a larger scale and also provides population figures up to 1881.[7]

Coal Exports ('000 tons)

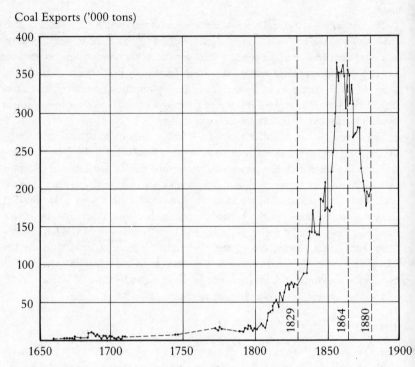

Figure 2
Coal exports from Llanelli 1650–1880

Chief amongst the new industrialists at Llanelli were: Alexander Raby, a London ironmaster, who arrived just before 1800 and committed his large personal fortune (possibly as much as £175,000) to the development of the area's coal resources and the establishment of ironworks; John Symmons of Paddington, a London coppermaster, who purchased almost 4,000 acres of land in the early 1800s in order to acquire a coalfield on which metalworks could be erected; General George Warde of Bradfield, Berkshire, who was assigned extensive coal leases in 1802 by the grandsons of Chauncey Townsend who had been one of the major figures in Llanelli's mid eighteenth-century industrial development; Charles Nevill of Birmingham, manager of a copperworks at Swansea, who came to Llanelli with his son Richard Janion Nevill, in 1804, to establish the Llanelly Copperworks Company[8] for John Guest (a Birmingham merchant and industrialist) and William Savill (a London copper merchant); the Pemberton family from the north of England who, in 1804, took over collieries previously worked by local coalmasters and

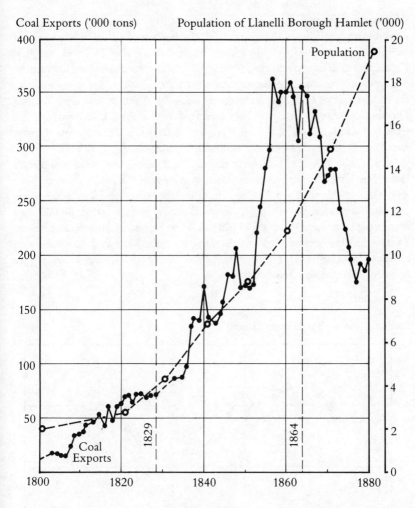

Coal Exports ('000 tons)   Population of Llanelli Borough Hamlet ('000)

Figure 3
Coal exports from Llanelli 1800–80; population of Llanelli 1801–81

also purchased lands; and the Earl of Warwick and John Vancouver who purchased John Symmons's lands and collieries in 1804.[9]

These people competed for the most advantageously situated and potentially profitable coalfields, and the rivalries and intrigues which ensued between them provide a fascinating insight into the motives, outlooks and methods of operation of south Wales's early nineteenth-century industrialists. It is a cautionary tale, however, as few of them prospered and many lost their entire fortunes in the Llanelli coalfield. Alexander Raby and General Warde, after many financial crises, ended up so deeply in debt to R. J. Nevill and the Llanelly Copperworks Company that they had to surrender all their industrial interests and live in reduced circumstances; the Pembertons, after an expensive but abortive colliery venture, withdrew from the area; the Earl of Warwick and John Vancouver had to surrender Symmons's lands and collieries back to him and neither they, nor Symmons, profited from the transaction. By 1829, only R. J. Nevill survived from the entire influx of early nineteenth-century industrialists and he, and the flourishing Llanelly Copperworks Company, held control of most of the coalfield with only the recently formed Llangennech Coal Company (founded in 1825 by four London merchants) presenting any form of rivalry to their monopoly.[10]

Even though most of them failed financially, Llanelli's early nineteenth-century industrialists all contributed to the development of the local coal industry between 1800 and 1829 and Figures 2 and 3 show that, apart from interruptions in certain years, exports, and undoubtedly production, increased steadily over the period. By 1829, coal exports were running at more than 71,000 tons, an average annual growth rate of almost 7 per cent having been achieved over the thirty-year period: it may be concluded with certainty that Llanelli had taken part in the rapid economic growth that was such a major feature of early nineteenth-century Britain.

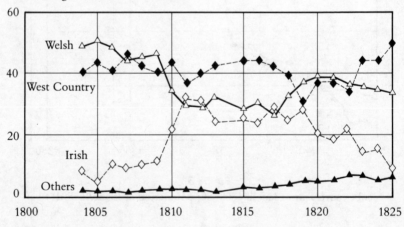

Figure 4
Distribution of coal sailings 1804–25

A valuable insight into the factors influencing the development of the local coal industry is provided by considering the distribution, in terms of export markets, of the ships sailing out of Llanelli laden with coal. This consideration can be made for the 22 years from 1804 to 1825.[11] Llanelli's coal was exported to three main markets — other Welsh ports (particularly Carmarthen and Cardigan); West Country ports (particularly St Ives, Barnstaple, Bideford and Plymouth); and Irish ports (particularly Waterford, Wexford, Cork, Kinsale and Wicklow). Ships also sailed with Llanelli's coal to other English ports, the Channel Islands, Copenhagen and, after the Napoleonic Wars, to French ports (particularly Brest), but these sailings constituted only a small percentage of the total coal export trade. Figure 4 shows the extent of Llanelli's coal trade with these markets, from 1804 to 1825, in terms of the percentage of the total coal vessel sailings taken by each market (these percentages will differ slightly from the percentage of the actual tonnages of coal exported to each market as the vessels engaged in the Irish and foreign trade were somewhat larger than those employed in the Welsh and West Country trade). It can be seen that the Welsh and West Country markets normally took most of Llanelli's coal export ships, except for the years between 1811 and 1819 when the Irish market took approximately one-quarter of the vessels and probably more than that in terms of tonnage. This period coincided with efforts on the part of some of Llanelli's coalmasters to attract the larger ships of the Irish trade which could, for the first time, be accommodated because of improved harbour facilities and a more organized pilotage and navigation of the difficult Burry Estuary. The West Country trade was maintained during all these years because of the profitable two-way trade of copper ore import and coal export; a trade which assumed particular importance after R. J. Nevill took control of Alexander Raby's and General Warde's collieries between 1816 and 1818. Nevill, acting for the Llanelly Copperworks Company, concentrated on the West Country copper ore import/coal export trade with a consequent increase in sailings to that market and a complementary decrease in sailings to the Irish ports.

A similar insight can be gained by considering the cargoes carried by the vessels sailing in to Llanelli between 1804 and 1829.[12] Ships entered Llanelli laden in one of three ways: in ballast; with copper ore; with other commodities (lead ore, iron ore, bricks, grain, timber etc.). Figure 5 on page 60 shows the distribution of vessels sailing in to Llanelli on this basis and, additionally, gives the percentage of vessels sailing out from Llanelli with coal. In 1804, over 90 per cent of vessels entered Llanelli in ballast and, as some 96 per cent left laden with coal, it may be concluded that the shipping trade depended almost entirely on coal at this time. The situation changed quickly over the following two years as copper ore imports to the Llanelly Copperworks commenced and as the commodities required by a rapidly expanding industrial area were brought in. As a consequence, less than half the vessels entered in ballast in 1806 although as many as 88 per cent still left with coal. As the area became more self-sufficient the situation reverted back and, by 1810–11, some 80 per cent of ships entered in ballast, the cargoes of the remaining 20 per cent being more or less equally divided between copper ore and general materials. At this time some 92 per cent of vessels left Llanelli laden with coal. There was little change in this pattern until 1816–18

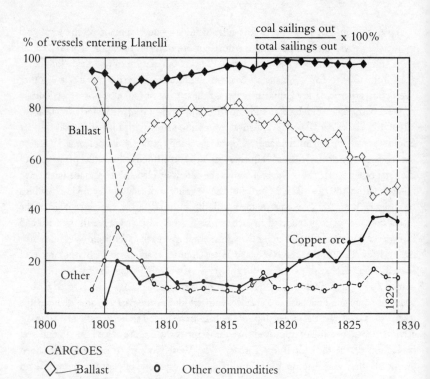

Figure 5
Distribution of import vessels 1804–29

when R. J. Nevill's control of most of the local coal industry led to an increase in the percentage of vessels entering with copper ore and a corresponding decrease in the percentage entering in ballast. The coal industry retained its strong hold on Llanelli's shipping trade throughout all these changes, however, with 98 per cent to 99 per cent of vessels leaving the port laden, or partly laden, with coal between 1819 and 1826.

1830–64

Llanelli's coal industry was virtually monopolized by two companies in 1830 — the Llanelly Copperworks Company and the Llangennech Coal Company. The Llanelly Copperworks Company, locally controlled by R. J. Nevill, held major leases of coal throughout the Llanelli area by virtue of its acquisition of Alexander Raby's and General Warde's interests; the Llangennech Coal Company held most of the well-known 'Llangennech' steam-coal in the north-east sector of the area. There were a number of smaller concerns in operation but only two were of significant size — the Pemberton Family's collieries, sub-leased to George Bruin of Pentonville in 1829[13] and the Pwll Colliery, opened by Martyn J. Roberts in 1825.[14]

The Llangennech Coal Company embarked upon major developments in the early 1830s with the opening of the 700 feet (213 metres) deep St David's Pit in 1832 (at that time the deepest pit in Wales)[15] and the construction under an Act of Parliament[16] of a connecting railway and large floating dock. The dock, capable of accommodating the largest class of collier ship of up to 1,000 tons, was named the New Dock on its opening in 1834 and was the first public floating dock in Wales.[17] The Company was also involved with its sister concern — the Llanelly Railway and Dock Company — in obtaining a further Act of Parliament in 1835[18] to allow an extension of its railway system into the Carmarthenshire hinterland in order that the anthracite and other mineral trade could use the New Dock as its shipping port. The Llanelly Copperworks Company also initiated considerable colliery developments in the 1830s. A report on the potential of its coalfields was obtained in 1836[19] and the recommendations were implemented from 1837 with the sinking of new pits and the redevelopment of existing collieries.[20] The Company soon became the largest single concern in the Llanelli area and, by 1841, employed just over one-third of the local colliery workforce (454 out of an estimated 1300).[21]

Llanelli's coal industry continued its steady expansion throughout the 1840s, 50s and early 60s despite the fact that the Llangennech Coal Company experienced acute financial difficulties as early as 1842[22] and offered to sell part, or all, of its collieries to the Llanelly Copperworks Company in 1844.[23] Although the Llangennech Coal Company survived this crisis, its scale of operations from the mid 1840s onwards was limited in relation to the hopes held a decade previously with the opening of the St David's Pit and the New Dock. The failure of the Llangennech Coal Company to realize its full potential was, however, compensated by the continuing success of the Llanelly Copperworks Company and the emergence of numerous smaller concerns which exploited previously unworked thin seams at shallow depths, removed pillars of coal left behind to support the roof in old workings in thicker seams working out any untouched areas in the process, and generally acted as gleaners of the coalfield. It is estimated that at least 39 different concerns, ranging in size from a few working miners in partnership to companies employing up to 100 men, operated in this manner in the Llanelli area between 1830 and 1864.[24]

Total output figures for the Llanelli area are available for only the final year of the period considered and, as for the years from 1800 to 1829, coal exports have to be taken as the indicator of the local coal industry's development. Figures 2 and 3 (on pages 56, 57) show that coal exports increased at an average annual rate of almost 5 per cent between 1830 and 1857 with 363,000 tons of coal exported in the latter year. Exports remained around this high level until 1864 but then rapidly decreased and had dropped to under 200,000 tons by 1880. Llanelli's bituminous and steam-coal industry had gone into irreversible decline and, in terms of export quantities, had passed its peak after 1864.

Explanations for this change from growth to decline in such a short time can be provided by considering both national and local factors. In the national context, Llanelli's coal industry initially reflected that of the United Kingdom with steady growth to meet the increasing demands of industry and population until 1857 when general commercial depression, attributed by contemporary observers to over-manufacturing in all branches of trade and industry,[25] led to a cessation of growth in the output of coal. This trade depression lasted into the late 1860s[26] and was followed by the strikes and lock-outs of the 1870s. These national factors adversely influenced Llanelli's coal industry[27] and certainly help explain the standstill in export growth between 1857 and 1864. They do not, however, explain why it was that Llanelli's coal industry fell into permanent decline after 1864 when the United Kingdom's coal industry, and that of south Wales in particular, continued to grow.[28] Convincing local explanations can be found to account for this decline. Firstly, Llanelli was an old coalfield and most of its accessible and profitable coal had been worked out. Secondly, Llanelli was no longer attracting the coal export trade vessels, partly because of failure to improve port facilities at a time when superior harbours were being constructed at Swansea, Cardiff and Newport, and partly because of the problems of navigation caused by shifting sandbanks within the Burry Estuary. Evidence of this failure to attract vessels was provided in 1859 when it was reported at a meeting of the Llanelly Harbour Commissioners that the Llangennech Coal Company had forfeited a Government contract for the supply of steam-coal because of the reluctance on the part of the ships' masters to enter the Estuary[29] and again, in 1862, when it was reported that Llanelli's coal export trade to the East Indies 'had been lost in consequence of defective dock accommodation'.[30] Additional factors contributing to the decline were: the growing recession in Britain's copper industry which adversely affected the Llanelly Copperworks Company which was the area's largest coal-mining concern;[31] the development of the steam-coal resources of other parts of the south Wales coalfield which took markets that had previously used Llanelli's coal;[32] and possibly, the loss of R. J. Nevill's entrepreneurial skills on his death in 1856.[33]

Full production and market disposal figures are available for the Llanelly Copperworks Company's collieries for the years from 1838 to 1880.[34] The Company was by far the largest of Llanelli's coal-mining concerns, accounting for at least 60 per cent of the area's total production in 1864,[35] and examination of its colliery accounts must reflect the pattern of growth and subsequent decline of Llanelli's coal-mining industry. It must be borne in mind, however, that the Company differed from other coal-mining concerns at Llanelli in that a significant percentage of its production was specifically for consumption at its own copper and allied works. Figure 6 shows the Company's coal production for the years 1838–39 to 1879–80 and also its disposal in terms of three markets — exported coal, coal supplied to the copper and allied works owned by the Company, and other locally consumed coal (tin and ironworks after 1845, steam-engines at the Company's collieries, the Company's colliers, and the local population). Figure 7 expresses the quantities taken by each of these markets as a percentage of the Company's coal production. It can be seen that production increased steadily to 1857, levelled off until 1862 and then increased to its peak of 291,145 tons in 1864. High levels of production were maintained until 1872–73 but fell rapidly thereafter. Coal exports also peaked in 1864 confirming the choice of that year as the transition point between growth and decline in Llanelli's coal industry. The export trade was the main market for the Company's coal for most of the 1830 to 1864 period with exports accounting for 57.2 per cent of production in 1858 and still running

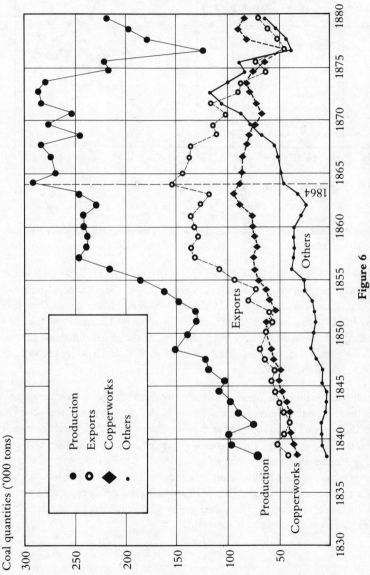

Figure 6

Coal production and market disposal figures for the Llanelly Copperworks
Company 1838–80

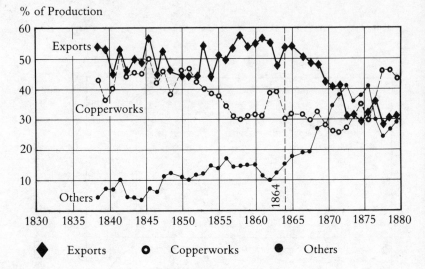

Figure 7
Market disposal of the Llanelly Copperworks Company's coal production
1838–80

at 53.3 per cent of production in 1864. It was not until the early 1870s, when the iron and tinplate industries had become well established at Llanelli and the population had increased to some four times that of 1830, that local consumption surpassed exports (Figures 6 and 7). The fortunes of the Llanelly Copperworks Company and Llanelli's coal-mining industry were strongly interrelated during the period considered and the explanations provided for the growth and decline of the area's coal industry also apply to the Company's mining interests.

Llanelli's coal industry had thus experienced significant changes during the first 65 years of the nineteenth century. A small industry in 1800 with an annual production of less than 20,000 tons,[36] it had expanded to meet local and export trade demand until a peak production of just under half a million tons (7 per cent of the south Wales coalfield, excluding Monmouthshire) had been reached in 1864.[37] During these years of growth coal-mining had not only been a flourishing industry in its own right but had also established the pattern for Llanelli's future by attracting the metalliferous industries of copper, iron, steel and tinplate which were to play such a major part in the area's late-nineteenth and twentieth-century economic life.

Banks and the Economic Development
of South Wales before 1914

R.O. ROBERTS

Over recent decades two issues have increasingly challenged economic historians concerned with banking. Firstly, there is the matter of the role of banks in economic growth. The main question here is whether banks (in establishment and operation) were market-determined institutions, responding passively to the demands for their services; or whether, and to what extent, they were initiators and propagators of expansion. A second challenge has been that of tackling these and other issues in a regional context. Here the centre of interest has moved from the often sketchy histories of individual banks to studies of banking activities throughout a region — recent investigations of the banks of Lancashire and the Birmingham area being prime examples.[1] It is hoped that studies of this latter kind may provide better understanding of country-wide banking operations, and illumine the inter-country comparisons (which also are now being re-assessed). For this type of investigation the southern half of Wales might appear to be an eminently suitable region, but it has to be noted that the available records leave very much to be desired.

A commercial bank, of course, performs a number of functions, of which the most important are receiving and protecting funds deposited with it, making advances and loans, and arranging transferences of money. By operating according to the fractional reserve principle, a bank's lending greatly exceeds the total of its reserves and deposits: it thus creates purchasing power. R.S. Sayers, in a classic study, emphasized that banks are 'not merely *purveyors* of money but also, in an important sense, *manufacturers* of money'; and he added that, through the way they distributed money, they governed 'the direction of the flow of production'.[2] (Interestingly, the agent of the 'Branch Bank' of the Bank of England at Swansea in 1835 stated that much tact was needed in persuading a banker to become 'a mere dealer in money and not a maker of money';[3] but this observation — reflecting the current restricted view of bank-money — related only to the issuing of banknotes, and did not encompass other forms of money based on credit.)

In the later Middle Ages and the early modern period in a number of countries — notably Italy, the Low Countries and England — various traders, scrivenors, lawyers and goldsmiths undertook one or two of the banking activities mentioned; and there evolved bills of exchange, promissory notes and cheques, and also the practice of extending credit in excess of the reserves held. Such limited-function intermediaries, however, were not bankers, nor were their later counterparts in rural Wales — i.e., the drovers who, engaged as they occasionally were in transferring money, borrowing or lending, have been credited quite erroneously with the establishment of banks. In fact, it is clear that a mature commercial bank performs not some but all of the financial functions noted above. Such banks first emerged in England in the seventeenth century, whereas establishments of this kind did not appear in Wales until the last third of the eighteenth century.

Three phases may be distinguished in the history of true banking in south Wales before 1914. The first, which saw the establishement of banking partnerships, extended from the beginnings in the 1770s until the financial crisis of 1825–6 — by which time the region's banks were becoming 'every man's affair' and were even providing metaphors for contemporary versifiers.[4] The second period lasted from 1825 until 1859, during which time the Bank of England Branch at Swansea had a considerable influence in the region; and the third from 1860 onwards when joint-stock banks grew both 'naturally' and by amalgamation. These divisions, of course, are far from rigid; some of the partnerships survived until the late nineteenth century, and one (the Black Ox Bank) until 1909; whereas a few joint-stock banks had operated since the 1830s. Because of such overlaps the following account does not deal in turn with each of the periods mentioned but rather, in succession, with the so-called 'private' banks, the Bank of England Branch (usually known as the 'Branch Bank') and the joint-stock banks. The private banks, in fact, were partnerships, and both they and the joint-stock banks in England outside London and in Wales have been referred to as 'country banks'.

The Private Banks

The private banks of south Wales were set up by people with various interests — landowners, yeomen, traders, industrialists and lawyers — for almost all of whom banking was a subsidiary occupation. Each of the up to six partners would invest a few hundred pounds: for example, the Union Bank of Haverfordwest was founded in 1802 with a capital of only £3,000 invested by five partners; a Chepstow bank in the same decade had a capital of £20,000 equally provided by five persons; while the four partners of Wilkins & Co., Brecon each subscribed £1,000 for its establishment in 1778.[5] The main bases of the banks' businesses, however, were the funds deposited with them.

In the case of Wilkins & Co. half the deposits were left at its Brecon and Merthyr branches in the 1830s for over six months at 3 per cent interest.[6] For the Wilkins Bank the ratio of deposits to the reserve (of gold and silver) was 2.0:0.1 (or 0.2), and the ratio of deposits to the note circulation was 2.0:1.0.[7] Such ratios were probably not untypical — though another rare item of evidence on such matters shows that deposits were £12,000 and notes in circulation £10,000 in the Knighton section of the Kington and Radnorshire Bank in 1836.[8] A number of the private banks had branches or were linked with other banks by a large measure of common ownership. And the unlimited liability of each partner for the debts of the establishment meant that all his material resources together with his reputation were pledged, whilst information or rumours about the assets of a deceased partner could have a marked effect on confidence in the bank.[9]

The private banks of the region, like those elsewhere, issued their own promissory notes payable on demand. And people were prepared to receive payment in the notes of various banks; thus, H.G. Allen, Landshipping, wrote around 1830 that he would 'take the notes of the Aberystwith, Carmarthen, Landovery and Wilkins of Brecon's Banks provided they continue to pay'.[10] On such matters, indeed on all the operations of the region's private banks, the testimony of John Parry Wilkins in June 1832 to the Parliamentary Committee on the Charter of the Bank of England provides the only substantial available account.

During the second quarter of the nineteenth century there was an argument between prominent bankers in south Wales about the desirability of continued issuing of the private banks' own paper. Wilkins put forward two main reasons for such a continuation by banks like the one bearing his family name — to which he had just returned after spending six years as agent of the Bank of England Branch in Swansea. He stated that in places other than the larger industrial centres deposits were insufficient to enable the banks, without their own note issues, to advance to traders on a remunerative scale. Secondly, he held that almost all the return from advances — say 5 per cent interest plus commission less stamps and expenses — would accrue to the private bank if it granted accommodation with its own notes, whereas if it did so with Bank of England notes its net income from the advances would have been reduced by the Bank of England's discount charge.[11] It may be added that Wilkins also observed that the private banks generally, and his own in particular, issued their notes according to the demand for them in relation to the reserves held without being directly affected by the foreign exchanges or the Bank of England's paper.[12] Wilkins's immediate successor as Branch Bank agent in 1835, on the other hand, suggested the counter-arguments that, by abandoning its own notes for those of the Bank of England, the private bank would save the cost of manufacturing notes and the stamp charges on them; would avoid the necessity of maintaining a large balance with a London bank; would save most of the commission payable to a London banker; would be relieved of the costs and risks of protecting its own circulation, enabling its assets to be more effectively deployed; and would gain from a reduction in 'the hazzard of making cash remittances'.[13] The notes of the private banks clearly met a need. At its peak in 1827 the circulation of Wilkins & Co. at Brecon and Merthyr was £124,000, and that of Waters, Jones & Co., Carmarthen was £100,000 in 1825 — whereas the peak issue by the Swansea Branch Bank in the early 1840s was no more than £107,000. Before 1826 'very few' Bank of England notes circulated in the Merthyr–Brecon area, and this was doubtless true of the whole of south Wales.[14]

The region's banks soon evolved clearing arrangements for the various notes coming into their possession: early provision for such clearing in the Merthyr area is mentioned; and Wilkins stated in 1832 that, at the clearings in the extensive district of his establishments, notes would be exchanged and the balances paid in London on demand or, in the case of notes from fairly distant banks, with bills of 21 days or longer usance. Cheques had appeared in the region by the beginning of the nineteenth century,[15] and by the late 1830s the banks also took each other's cheques — as when the Wilkins bank in

Llanelli took drafts on Biddulph Bros., Carmarthen (being payments for work on building the Llanelli–Llandeilo railway). Despite such co-operation, however, there was keen competition between private banks in issuing notes as in other respects: each banker sought, in Wilkins's words, 'to withdraw as much of his neighbour's paper as he can from circulation and put out his own'.[16]

The private banks issued their notes mainly by providing advances for farmers and for dealers in agricultural requisites and produce, by discounting bills representing industrial and urban transactions and by a moderate amount of longer-term lending. Some banks were notable for their advances on the promissory notes of drovers to enable the latter 'to go to the fairs' and otherwise to acquire animals for their trade: such were the banks of David Jones & Co. (the Black Ox) of Llandovery and Llandeilo, Waters, Jones & Co., Carmarthen and some of the branches of Wilkins & Co. The latter were more cautious than the others and would only lend up to £2,000 on the joint note of the drover and his surety (-ies), whereas Waters, Jones & Co. would lend up to £7,000 at a time to a 'very considerable' Carmarthenshire drover on the latter's 'own responsibility' without security, and David Jones & Co. seemingly would advance upwards of £10,000 'without any security . . . [other than] . . . his [the drover's] own responsibility'. Certainly around 1830, such advances without collateral were 'in part . . . the general custom of doing business . . . in that neighbourhood'.[17]

From 1829 until c.1832–3 there was much distress in the farming districts of south-west Wales, largely as a result of a sharp reduction in the liberal accommodation that had been provided by banks for the drovers: it was a reduction of about four-fifths in the case of Wilkins & Co. This severe contraction in turn had been substantially due to the compulsory and sudden withdrawal in 1829 of all banknotes of less than £5 in value. The period of distress was extended by the failure of the bank of Waters, Jones & Co. in February 1832, and for a time there was some reluctance to advance on promissory notes. The subsequent recovery of the cattle trade, however, led to further large-scale financing of drovers and farmers by the banks: in fact Wilkins & Co. were said to have reaped a profit of as much as £30,000 in their dealings with small farmers (and drovers?) by the early 1840s. The promissory notes on joint securities representing this trade were frequently renewed, and thereby yielded interest of 20–30 per cent annually, together with a commission charge in London — which shows that the paper was rediscounted.

Wilkins & Co. preferred to advance on promissory notes payable in London than to do so on those not thus negotiable — 'we charge a higher commission on the unconvertible paper' — but a 'good' note which was inconvertible elsewhere would be advanced upon to a drover known only at Wilkins's bank to be creditworthy. Paper not convertible with facility in the London market would become negotiable with Wilkins's endorsement, but the bank disliked sending endorsed bills to London or to the Branch Bank in Swansea for rediscounting. J.P. Wilkins added that banks in large cities would seldom advance on promissory notes, but it has been shown recently that the practice continued in the Birmingham area as 'late' as the early 1830s: the Bank of England branches would never advance on such notes; and Wilkins & Co. stopped doing so in 1841.[18]

Until the later decades of the nineteenth century the banks also provided short-term finance for industrialists and urban traders, and put banknotes into circulation, mainly by discounting bills of exchange. The total value of such paper arising from inland transactions was still increasing in England and Wales around the middle of the nineteenth century, and the instruments were of three kinds: small bills mainly drawn on, or by, retailers, of average value £22 and average usance three months; medium bills chiefly drawn by manufacturers and wholesalers upon retailers, of average value £127 and three and a half months average usance; and large bills drawn by importers on manufacturers and wholesalers and by the latter on exporters, their average value being over £1,000 and the average usance a little over four months.[19]

Bills of these three kinds — and with an extremely wide range of usance — were employed in south Wales. 'Good' six-month bills of the iron trade, and six-months bills on London drawn by copper-smelting firms (to pay for ores) were important; and medium and small bills with usance down to a few days were common — 'for such', stated the Bank of England agent in Swansea, 'is the system of doing busines in these districts'.[20] Many of the small bills were drawn by traders in coal and in 'drugs, wine, groceries and oats', and they were made payable at London houses such as Cocks, Biddulph & Co. and Child & Co. They remained important despite the greater incidence of stamp duties on them than on their larger counterparts. As in other parts of Britain, the adjective 'good' was used to describe a bill which it was considered could safely be taken for discounting: what was usually required by the banker was 'solidity of the parties' — i.e. of both the drawer and the drawee of the bill, and generally also the knowledge that it genuinely represented trading transactions and was not an 'accommodation' device drawn by one member upon another in a firm seeking finance. There were complaints, however, about the difficulty of obtaining 'sound information' about those presenting bills in Swansea, and the 'unmercantile character of the bills in circulation' in the town — which probably was not unrepresentative of much of south Wales in these respects.[21]

Bill discounting, of course, could lead to longer-term lending by the renewal of bills — just as the periods covered by rural promissory notes often were extended — and the trade bills would thus become virtually 'accommodation' or 'finance' paper. Such a practice was not uncommon in south Wales. Some of the indebtedness of Nevill & Co., Llanelli to the bank of Esdaile & Co., London — a debt amounting to £79,300 in December 1825 — was on bills whose repayment period had been much extended; and in 1830 Walter Coffin obtained finance from William Crawshay by bill renewal.[22] The Bank of England in the late 1820s and 1830s found it necessary to discourage the handling of renewed bills at their Swansea Branch Bank, and to observe that 'Messrs. Wilkins are hardly justified in paying the bills discounted under the Loan Account by the discount of others, as they thereby lengthen out its period'.[23]

Apart from rediscounting, however, there are numerous examples of outright lending by the private banks: indeed, such lending has been seen by P.L. Cottrell 'almost ... to have been the standard practice in South Wales' — with the implication (from the context of his statement) that this was not usual elsewhere.[24] Certainly, even the examples of such

Table 1
Some of the loans granted by private banks of the region

Date(s)	Bank	Amount (£s)	Recipient
1791	Fendal, Jelf & Co.		Partner in Aberpergwm Colliery[25]
1790s	Wilkins & Co.		Hirwaun Forge[26]
1790s	id.		Brecknock & Abergavenny and Glamorganshire Canals[26]
1804–14	id.	15,000 'at least' in 1814	Tappenden & Co., Abernant Iron Works[26]
1813	id.	54,000 outstanding	Hill & Co., Plymouth Iron Works[26]
1831	id.	do.	id.[26]
1813–37	id.	5,000–c.27,000	Frere & Co., Clydach Iron Works[26]
1840–90	id.		Owners of small vessels, regd. Llanelli[27]
1847	id.		Owner one sixty-fourth of steam tug[27]
1804, 1810	Waters, Jones & Co.	5,000 for 4 months initially	Daniel, Nevill & Guest, Copper Works, Llanelli[28]
1812	Buckle, Williams & Co.	3,000	Monmouthshire Canal[29]
1818	Gronow & Co.	1,500	Charles Tennant[30]
c.1820–23	Haynes, Day, Haynes & Lawrence and 'a Carmarthen Bank'	Short- and long-term loans	Alexander Raby, Colliery Proprietor, Llanelli[31]
1823	Wood & Co.	Debts c.35,000	and assets largely in fixed capital[32]
late 1820s	William & Rowland	3,000	Landore Iron Co.[33]
1830s–1841	Walters, Voss & Co.	overdrafts — c.7,000 in 1841	Sir John Morris, Millbrook Iron Co., Swansea Valley[34]

accommodation that have been noted are so many that it seems best to set them out in tabular form (Table 1).

Some so-called 'banks' were set up in the period 1815–35 mainly as the financial note-issuing arm of the industrial enterprises whence they sprang — major examples being Guest, Lewis & Co.; Taitt, Lewis & Co.; Homfray & Forman; and Crawshay, Hall & Bailey.[35] In each of these cases, however, the finances of the two or more industrial and financial concerns involved seemingly were so scrambled together that it appears unlikely that evidence will emerge of 'bank' lending to the parent.

Individual bankers became investors and lenders, and this clearly had implications for the private banks in which they were partners with unlimited liability. As examples there may be given the investments after 1815 by John Wood Jnr of Wood & Co., Cardiff, 'in real estate, canals and railways and exchequer bills'; [36] George Buckle of the Chepstow Bank's involvement as a partner in the embryonic Varteg Ironworks in 1802; the case of T. Hill and S. Hopkins — of Hill, Kinsey & Co., Abergavenny — who in 1815 were partners in the Blaenavon Ironworks; and the investment in 1810 by Lewis Osborne, also of Hill, Kinsey & Co., in the Llanvihangel Railway, to which Phillip Jones — of the bank of Jones, Davies & Co., Abergavenny and Pontypool — lent over £1,200 in 1822.[37] Again, John Biddulph, of Biddulph Bros. Carmarthen (and also Branch Bank agent in Swansea) was a partner in the Cwmamman Colliery in 1840 and in the Abercarn Tinplate Works of Biddulph & Spence from 1845. In addition, individual partners of Wilkins & Co. took shares in, and provided loans for, a considerable number of vessels in the period 1840–90, while John Parry de Winton (alias Wilkins) was a promoter and a director of the Brecon–Merthyr Railway in the late 1850s and early 1860s.[38] Despite such occasional references to involvement in railway development, however, and unlike the situation in England, [39] bank and banker lending for this purpose in south Wales appears to have been very small: indeed, in the railway speculations of the mid 1840s the bankers of Swansea appeared to have avoided 'advancing on shares or debentures'.[40]

The Swansea Branch Bank

The private banks were highly vulnerable because of the immobilization of their funds, their dependence on the personal assets and reputation of each of the six (or fewer) partners, their reliance in many cases on the economic fortunes of a fairly small district, and their links with banks elsewhere. Such vulnerability became particularly manifest in the financial crisis which spread across England and Wales in 1825–6. This reached south Wales through the closure of some of the London correspondent banks, and through the domino-effect spread of the calamity along the chain of Gibbins banks from Banbury and Birmingham to Swansea, Neath, Llandeilo and Hay, while there was inevitably a run on neighbouring banks.

People in Government circles concluded that the principal requirement was increased Bank of England control over the quantity and 'quality' of the banknotes in circulation. The Country Bankers' Act was thus passed in May 1826. This allowed joint-stock banks with note-issuing powers to be established outside the London region, and also made clear that provincial branches of the Bank of England could be set up. One such branch, the third to be founded, was opened in Swansea in October 1826. The following account of its establishment and operations is a very brief summary of what has been published elsewhere.[41]

The main object of the Branch Bank was to substitute its own notes for those of other banks in the region, and it came to do this mainly by paying them in discounting bills of exchange. Discount accounts subject to strict rules were granted by the Branch Bank to acceptable trading and banker customers: each bill had to have two securities independently of the discounter, and 'accommodation' or 'finance' bills were not allowed. Until the 1840s the Branch Bank undertook more discounting for banks than for traders — discount accounts for the banks, on favourable terms, being allowed only if they confined their issues to Bank of England notes.

From the middle 1830s onwards, probably under the influence of competition from new joint-stock banks, the Bank of England allowed its branches to provide some advances. The Swansea Branch Bank was permitted to advance 'a moderate proportion' of the value of bills sent by it to London correspondent banks on behalf of its banker customers, and in the late 1840s it was also allowed to advance for a month on six-month bills which were four or five months from maturity.

By around 1840 the Branch Bank agent at Swansea was able to write that country bank notes were 'out of vogue' and 'shut out' of 'this part of Wales', though they continued to fight a losing battle in the rural hinterland. This supersession was only partly due to the operations of the Branch Bank (whose note circulation at its maximum was less than that of Wilkins & Co. alone, at Brecon and Merthyr, immediately before 1829). Other reasons were the statutory withdrawal of all notes of below £5 by 1829, and the growing use of gold sovereigns, half-sovereigns and cheques as means of payment.

On the whole the Branch Bank's business became smaller from the mid 1830s onwards, though it still continued to perform useful functions. It was described in 1832 as 'a very great convenience . . . in the supply of precious metals and Bank notes' — a function which, among other things, enabled banks in the region to keep smaller reserves. And the 'hazzard of making cash remittances' was reduced for traders and bankers by enabling money and bills to be transmitted on their behalf by the Branch Bank to London and other centres. By its work of receiving most of the taxes in south Wales in the second quarter of the century, the establishment made its presence known in towns and townships throughout the region and, beyond its normal economic activities, it also performed a few services for social reasons. Thus, in 1831–32, exceptional secured loans of £30,000 and £20,000 were made by it respectively to the banks of Waters, Jones & Co. and Wilkins & Co. to enable them to relieve the distress of farming communities in their districts. It made a further notable contribution in 1842 by exchanging at a small discount the light sovereigns which were said to have derived from the Bristol area and which had caused discontent because they could only be spent at a heavy cost.

By the 1850s, however, it could be stated that 'the West of England and South Wales

District Bank and the Glamorganshire Banking Company . . . command the whole Trade of the Town and vicinity' of Swansea. The Branch Bank was closed in 1859 and its residual business was transferred to its Bristol counterpart.

Joint-Stock Banks

The Glamorganshire Banking Co. and the West of England and South Wales District Bank illustrate two ways in which joint-stock banks came to be established in the region from the mid 1830s onwards. The Glamorganshire was created by amalgamation of three private banks in Swansea and Neath — though a number of its shareholders lived in England. The West of England and South Wales District Bank, on the other hand, was set up by 'very opulent bankers' who lived — as did most of the shareholders — outside south Wales. These two institutions together with all the main joint-stock banks established branch networks, the latter being extended from around 1880 onwards through amalgamations involving both joint-stock and private banks whose activities previously had been concentrated on particular districts with their own distinct needs and types of business. Such mergers further enabled balancing to take place within the larger institutions between their high-lending and low-lending branches — by internalized adjustments which had been anticipated in the Gibbins group of the 1820s, and within the Liverpool-based North and South Wales Bank with its 'fusion of varied undertakings' from the 1830s onwards.[42] These developments involved the disappearance of the remaining private banks: Lloyds Bank absorbed Wilkins & Co. in 1890 and David Jones & Co. in 1909.

From their first appearance in the region the joint-stock banks, as they sought to expand their business, pursued a liberal discounting policy.[43] And the accounts of a few of the banks in Glamorgan in the 1870s and 1880s show that such discounting continued on an appreciable scale — though, then and later, the relative importance of the domestic bill appears to have been declining in Wales as in England. In the 1870s banks in south Wales and Gloucestershire had ratios of advances plus discounts to deposits which were around the English-Welsh average.[44] And, undoubtedly, in the second half of the nineteenth century, as earlier, the granting of such short-term accommodation led to longer-term lending.[45]

Table 2 on pages 74, 75 gives examples — mainly for Glamorgan and by no means exhaustive — of the long-term loans provided by joint-stock banks having branches in south Wales. It is clear that such banks continued, and perhaps extended, the lending practices of their private counterparts. In most decades the loans seem to have been neither numerous nor large, but it should be noted both that some were revolving commitments extending over more than a single decade, and that the list is incomplete.

The largest items listed are the West of England and South Wales District Bank's loans totalling about £750,000 in the period 1855–80, and the £357,000 borrowed before World War I by public companies in the coal, iron and steel industries. The latter amount was obtained by nine companies, out of the thirty whose files were inspected: four of the nine received loans of around £50,000 each and one had been lent £70,000, but the proportion of the total borrowing which came from banks without offices in south Wales has not been traced.[46]

Table 2
Examples of loans provided by joint-stock banks having branches in south Wales[49]

Date(s)	Bank	Amount (£s)	Recipient
From late 1830s	West of England		Geo. Insole & Son, coal-mining, Rhondda[50]
c.1840	id.		Hill & Co., Plymouth Ironworks
1850s	id.	c.10,000 overdraft	Monmouthshire Canal Co.[51]
1860s	id.	1,500	Thomas Rees, tinplate mnfr. Llangennech[52]
1870s	id.	35,000	Garth Iron & Tinplate Co., Rhiwderyn Works[52]
1855–80	id.	c.750,000	Coal, iron and tinplate firms. The book value of the investments in 1878 was £777,000. Of this £746,742 was tied in four south Wales firms, the largest being Booker & Co., Melingriffith, and the Aberdare & Plymouth Co. Ltd. Expected on realization to yield only £160,000[52]
1840s	Glamorgan Banking Co.		Benson, Logan & Co., Colliery, Penclawdd
1847	id.	1,500 overdraft	G. Byng Morris, Millbrook Iron Co., nr. Swansea[53]

Table 2 — continued

Date(s)	Bank	Amount (£s)	Recipient
c.1848–52	id.		Penrose & Evans, Eaglebush Colliery, nr. Neath
1850s–1860s	id.	50,000–60,000	Hallam & Madge, tinplate mnfrs., Morriston
1870s	id.		Kenway & Rees, corn merchants, Bristol and south Wales
c.1880	id.	8,000	Glamorgan Tinplate Co., Pontarddulais
early 1880s	id.		Biddulph, Wood & Co., tinplate mnfrs.
early 1880s	id.		Townsend, Wood & Co., tinplate mnfrs., Briton Ferry
c.1870–90	id.	Overdraft to 10,000	Vivian & Sons, copper smelters, Swansea[54]
1841	Mon. & Glam. Bkg. Co.	17,000	Oakwood & Argoed Iron and Coal Co., nr. Pyle
pre 1848	id.		Jevons & Wood, Venallt Coal and Iron Wks., nr. Neath
1880s–91	Metropolitan Bank, Swansea		Vivian & Sons, smelters, Swansea[54]
1908	id.	5,000	British Metal Extraction Co. Ltd.
1911–14	id.	5,000–10,000 (overdrafts)	Swansea Vale Spelter Co. Ltd., Llansamlet

A few of the banks undoubtedly granted loans beyond the limit of prudence. This was held to be so in the case of the Monmouthshire and Glamorganshire Banking Co., operating mainly in Monmouthshire; a correspondent in the *Mining Journal* in May 1845 complained of its 'over-active interest in industrial concerns and of its provision of accommodation almost unprecedented . . . to men of no property, and as little character, with the natural consequences'.[47] It was, however, the over-extended industrial financing by the West of England Bank which brought about the worst financial collapse — involving the closure of this institution in 1878 and the serious distress of shareholders (including charitable organizations) in the west of England, south Wales and London. The liabilities of its shareholders, after realizing certain assets, totalled about £300,000. In the early 1880s the Glamorganshire Banking Co. also went through a period of crisis due to heavy withdrawals (arising from trade depression and failures), bad debts (which totalled £168,000 in February 1884) and some accounting inaccuracies; but with the help of some powerful loyal customers it weathered the storm. Other banks in south Wales suffered losses but, overall, the region's banks managed to expand their operations, enlarge their reserves and declare substantial dividends in the period 1850–1914.[48]

Services obtained from banks outside south Wales

Various enterprises which entered south Wales during the eighteenth and nineteenth centuries continued to be customers of banks in England. (Such links, of course, were distinct from the services obtained indirectly by firms in south Wales from correspondent banks or from the head offices of joint-stock institutions.) The direct connection included, in the one direction, deposit and investment in London banks[55] and, in the other, the receipt of short-term finance and longer-term accommodation by some south Wales concerns — evidence for which can be briefly summarized.

Alexander Raby in 1802 arranged that all Monmouthshire Canal business should go through Edwards, Templar & Co., London,[56] and six years later the Hirwaun Iron Co. was receiving advances from and having bills discounted by Fry & Co., also of London. The financial transactions in Cornwall of both the Llanelly Copperworks Co. and Vivian & Sons, Swansea, were conducted by the Miners Bank, Truro (with which each firm shared a partner). Vivian & Sons, on an experimental basis, were able to have some of their workers paid by the Miners' Bank in 1804, and the same bank's disbursements on account of Vivian & Sons's purchases of ores were around £200,000 annually in the 1820s.[57] In 1804 the Llanelly Copperworks Company were allowed by Martin, Waters & Co., Carmarthen to draw on the latter's London correspondent bank, Barclays: in the 1820s the Miners' Bank was discounting bills for them; and, in the same decade and the next, they enjoyed the facilities and acceptance of Esdaile, Hammet & Co., Lombard Street.[58] Henry Burgess in his *Circular to Bankers* (1828) observed that some of the south Wales ironmasters had establishments in London where discount and other transactions could be arranged; the Crawshays in the early 1820s could obtain up to £10,000 in gold from a London bank 'against the next Pay'.[59] The second Marquess of Bute employed a number of banks in England and Scotland, but for his south Wales estates he mainly dealt with Messrs. Coutts and the London and Westminster Bank, the former being owed £15,000 on short-term in 1828 and the latter allowing an overdraft up to £20,000 in 1835.[60] Vivian & Sons were discounting bills on London in the 1840s, as also were Benson, Logan & Co., the Penclawdd colliery firm, and Joseph Price of the Neath Abbey Iron Co. — 'because he can have his bills done cheaper in London'.[61]

An account of some of the longer-term accommodation granted by banks outside south Wales is given in the accompanying Table 3. The provenance of the large loans to the nine public companies (noted on the last line of the table) has unfortunately not been traced.

Table 3
Examples of loans provided for firms in south Wales by banks outside the region

Date(s)	Bank	Amount (£s)	Recipient
1789	Bate & Robins, Stourbridge		Blaenavon Ironworks Co.[62]
1802	Edwards, Templar & Co. London		Monmouthshire Canal Co.[63]
1824	Miners' Bank, Truro	10,000	Llanelly Copper Works Co.[64]
1820s	id.	Overdrafts 32,000 in 1823	Vivian & Sons, copper smelters[65]
1820–3	Esdaile, Hammet & Co.	20,000–30,000	Llanelly Copper Works Co.[66]
1826	Bank of England	10,000	id.[67]
1827	Garfit & Claypon, Lincs.	98,000	John Christie, Brecon Forest Tramroad, etc.[68]
from 1830s	Wright & Co., Nottingham	7,000 (1841)	Oakwood & Argoed Iron & Coal Co., nr. Pyle[69]
do.	'a Newcastle bank'	11,000 (1841)	id.[69]
pre 1841	Walters, Bath	Over 1,500	Vale of Neath Brewery Co.[70]
1841	London Joint Stock Bank		Cambrian Iron & Spelter Co., Maesteg[71]

Table 3 — continued

Date(s)	Bank	Amount (£s)	Recipient
early 1840s	North Wilts Banking Co.		Maesteg Ironworks Co.[71]
1840s	Bank of England		Benson, Logan & Co., Colliery, Penclawdd[72]
do.	Burnett, Hoare & Co.		id.[72]
1847–52	Bank of England	270,000	Co. of Copper Miners, Cwmafon[73]
late 1840s	Royal British Bank		Maesteg Ironworks Co.[74]
early 1850s	id.		Cefn and Garth Collieries, nr. Pyle[74]
1855–9	Union Bank	30,000	Bute trustees (dock construction)[75]
do.	National Provincial Bank	30,000	do.[75]
pre 1878–90	Robarts & Co.	30,000 (overdraft limit)	Vivian & Sons, copper etc. smelters[76]
1887	Coutt's Bank	60,000	Bute Docks Co.[77]
1889	National Provincial Bank	60,000	do.[77]
1910	Various	357,000	nine public companies in coal, iron and steel[78]

Conclusions

Banks clearly have been involved in the processes of saving and investment, in facilitating trading transactions, and in the smooth running — the tribology — of economic systems. Reference has been made to the question of whether their emergence was merely a response to existing demands or whether they had a more creative role as stimulators of economic expansion (and hence of further financial demands). One comparative study of the banking history of a number of countries has led to the conclusions, (a) that the responses of banks to the various financial demands were by no means always automatic and efficient, and (b) that financial institutions occasionally did make an innovatory, 'supply-led', contribution to economic expansion.[79]

The traditional account of English and Welsh banks has described them as concentrating almost exclusively on the provision of short-term, largely self-liquidating, credits for their borrowing customers. A contrast has been drawn — especially for the period c.1880–1914 – between the restricted sphere of operations of British banks, thus viewed, and what has been seen as the wider role, and greater participation in long-term financing, of the banks in France, Germany and Belgium. Recently, however, this assessment has been questioned if not overthrown. It has been shown that there was much more long-term lending by British banks than had previously been supposed, while the contribution of 'Continental' banks to the provision of fixed capital for the mining and manufacturing sectors of their respective countries was exaggerated: thus, despite the industrial origins of a number of them, the German credit banks of the mid nineteenth century primarily are shown to have supplied long-term finance mainly to government and railway authorities, and — according to some — they may even have hindered economic growth in the German states.[80]

The demands for banking services that developed in south Wales in the late eighteenth and early nineteenth century were by no means simple — though they were probably less complicated than those of the more diversified economy of the Birmingham area at the same time.[81] On the coalfield there were rapidly expanding industrial enterprises requiring finance for their circulating and fixed capitals from various sources including the banks. The rural areas, on the other hand, were losing much of their isolation, developing links with other districts, and increasingly shifting from peasant self-sufficiency into a monetary economy — a change to which drovers and other intermediaries contributed both before and later alongside the early banks.[82] In relating to these demands, the history of the banks' operations, until say the mid nineteenth century, may be seen as the story of the tentative acts of a large number of separate concerns. These were frequently amateurish, pursuing their own interests, competing with each other but co-operating to a limited extent, being similarly linked to the London money market. The following statement about the activities of the banks of west Yorkshire before 1850 seems also to be applicable to those of south Wales in the same period: 'no laws and frequently little practical business acumen governed policies with respect to posting of collateral, holding of bank reserves against deposits, ratio of overdrafts to borrower's level of profits, or even the special privileges granted to stockholders and directors'.[83] Difficulty in obtaining satisfactory collateral security was clearly a feature which banks in south Wales shared with those of other regions.[84] During the second half of the nineteenth century, however, some of the hindrances were overcome and the region's banking system developed towards the more professionalized and satisfactory state which it reached before the First World War.

In south Wales, as in other parts of Britain, the major demand for bank finance was that for short-term credit; and, in the way in which they concentrated upon satisfying this demand, there seems little to distinguish its banks from those elsewhere — particularly from those in other areas which were net importers of capital. The magnitude of the provision of short-term bank accommodation is indicated by sparse items of information about note issues — the considerable size of which was closely related to the amount of paper that was discounted — and the profits made by such financing (as noted for the rural operations of Wilkins & Co. in the later 1830s). And the general importance of bank credit is illustrated by the plight of the Carmarthenshire and Breconshire farmers when its supply was so suddenly curtailed around 1830 or, again, by the fact that the overdraft of £32,000 allowed by the Miners' Bank to Vivian & Sons in 1823 was about a quarter of the latter's entire capital. The greater willingness of banks in rural areas than in the towns to lend upon limited, one-person, security is of interest, as also is the contrast (which had also developed in England by the 1830s)[85] between the types of paper presented for the short-period borrowing in rural and in urban districts. In the case of the urban areas, the fact that traders continued to seek accommodation from the Branch Bank between the 1820s and 1850s has suggested that other banks in the Swansea area did not differ much from it in their discounting policies.[86]

Short-term finance — which, for example, might be for purchasing raw materials — could release funds for fixed-capital formation and, as noted for south Wales and elsewhere, short-period advances were frequently renewable. Furthermore, the amount of outright longer-term lending to industrial firms in south Wales was quite substantial: the tables above lend support to Arthur John's statement that in this region 'long-term loans for fixed capital purposes by bankers were more common than is supposed'.[87] Noting the contrast between the late eighteenth and early nineteenth centuries' evidence in this respect for south Wales and also the Hull area, on the one hand, and Lancashire, on the other, Cottrell has suggested that 'only when capital requirements had a degree of lumpiness, as with deep mining and primary metalworking, or in the case of areas where the informal supply of capital was extremely limited, did banks become important providers of fixed capital'.[88] Cottrell also observes that the banks only rarely supplied long-term loans for the initial financing of new enterprises; and no evidence of accommodation for such purposes has been found for south Wales — whereas the records for west Yorkshire have provided an abundance.[89] Again, it has been concluded that the evidence for medium and long-term lending by English banks in the period after 1830 'is not as well developed yet as for the industrial revolution'. For south Wales, however, the balance is otherwise, and the admittedly partial evidence of the three tables above shows that such lending continued fairly strongly into the late nineteenth and early twentieth centuries — a period when the London-based English banks became more unwilling to lend long.[90] And while, from the beginning, some of the bank lending was misdirected one concludes that overall it was a useful source of long-term finance in supplementation of equities, other lending and plough-back from profits. The banks and many of the individual bankers appear to have been active participants in the economic development of their districts: in the words of Arthur John over thirty years ago — in opposition to what he regarded as an earlier accepted view — 'the early banking system . . . played a not unimportant part in the industrial development' of the region.[91]

Section B
*c.*1840–*c.*1914

Farming in South-East Wales c.1840–80

DAVID HOWELL

The industrial development of south-east Wales and elsewhere created a big new demand for agricultural produce. Generally, Welsh farmers did not grasp these marketing opportunities. The unfavourable physical terrain and wet climate meant, of course, that Welsh farmers were faced with real disadvantages. In particular, the large areas of wet uplands confined farming to a narrow range of activities and the wide tracts of unenclosed moorland obstructed improvements in livestock breeding. There were manifestly other obstacles to Welsh agricultural improvement in the nineteenth century. The physical conditions and remoteness from large markets (even after railways were built there were many remote areas of the Principality with unsatisfactory transport facilities) influenced the persistence of small farms. Population growth imposed a pressure on land resources which generated land hunger with its consequent tendency to stabilize or increase rents. Limited communication with more advanced parts of the United Kingdom, aggravated as this was by the barrier of language, curtailed the spread of ideas on improved farming. Because of all these factors, the general run of Welsh farmers possessed neither the capital resources to invest in improvements nor the mental attitudes and equipment to do so. Possibly unwillingness to adventure capital was of the greater importance partly because it was shared by the many small Welsh landowners, and partly because, had the desire to invest existed, credit might have been forthcoming from sources such as the country banks.[1]

Absence of compensation for unexhausted improvements outside Glamorgan before it was made compulsory by the Agricultural Holdings (England) Act of 1883 may have accounted for the reluctance on the part of large Welsh tenant farmers to invest.[2] Tenant right, however, was not a factor in curtailing small peasant-tenants[3] (the majority-type in Wales) from carrying out improvements, for the sums of money required from the incoming tenant to compensate the outgoing one would have been simply too burdensome for most Welsh tenants. The problem was not a peculiarly 'Welsh' one. Thus stated a Nottinghamshire witness before the Parliamentary Commission on Tenant Right in 1847: 'An extensive tenant right would require more capital and would consequently shut out men of small means'.[4] How then are we to explain the unwillingness on the part of the small Welsh tenant to invest? In so far as the tenant on small estates was concerned (and such estates covered most of the acreage of the

Principality), it can partly be explained out of his fear that rent increases would automatically follow any improvements undertaken on his part. But not all small tenants farmed under the unsatisfactory tenurial conditions which obtained on small estates. It was not the general practice on large estates for owners to confiscate the efforts of their tenants by automatically charging high rents. Yet on large and small estates alike the Welsh peasant mentality looked upon any rise in rents as a result of permanent improvements as a calamity, given their attitude of equating 'successful' farming with low expenditure. Rent was an important item in the structure of farm costs which had to be maintained at a stationary level. The possibility of rent increases implied that the farmer consciously refrained from showing any outward sign of prosperity. There was thus a total inhibition against all improvement. The uncommercial attitudes of the Welsh farmer, and his hoarding of money arising from his preoccupation with keeping his rent as low as possible, largely accounted for the underdeveloped farming in Wales in the 1870s.[5] The *Cambrian News* pertinently observed on 16 July 1880:

> Yearly tenancies, it is to be feared, do not account for all the reluctance on the part of Welsh farmers to rear fat stock; for agriculturalists who live on their own land, and many who hold long leases, or are tenants of landlords who neither evict nor increase rents, follow the practices of those who are less secure, and by no means their own masters.

The picture was not universally gloomy, however, for in the Vale of Glamorgan, in the southern areas of Monmouthshire and, to a lesser extent, in southern Gower intensive farming was practised in the middle decades of the nineteenth century. These three areas will be considered separately although discussion will be concentrated on the Vale of Glamorgan.

By the middle of the century, farming in Glamorgan was improving in response to the growing demand from the industrial towns and to the competition from imported foodstuffs. The impact of the industrial demand was reflected in the increased amount of barley being grown and the widespread cultivation of potatoes.[6] Albeit, poor transport facilities in the pre-railway era considerably reduced the impact of the industrial market and, in the case of corn, enabled outside supplies from certain areas to be sent to the 'works' nearly as, if not more, cheaply than supplies within Glamorgan. It was thus claimed by Evan David of Radyr Court Farm in the county that Irish corn and corn from the coast of south-west England could be conveyed to Merthyr in the 1830s more cheaply (or, in the case of Irish corn, perhaps nearly as cheaply) than half the Glamorgan farmers could convey theirs. Irish corn could be brought to south Wales cheaply, he explained, because of the great export of coal from Glamorgan to Ireland, the coal vessels returning in ballast had they no farm produce to bring over.[7] Such difficulties of transport facing Glamorgan farmers and the advantage this gave outside suppliers, together with the high price of producing Glamorgan corn compared with that of Irish farmers,[8] meant that in the mid 1840s some three-quarters of the flour consumed in Merthyr and its vicinity came from Ireland, Bristol and Devon.[9] The difficulties of inland transport between the Vale and the manufacturing population of the 'works' resulted in corn grown in the Vale being exported to Bristol, from which market it was often returned as flour or malt to Cardiff to be forwarded to Merthyr via the Glamorgan Canal or the Taff Vale Railway.[10] Poor inland transport facilities also led to corn grown in the Vale being shipped from Aberthaw to Neath and Swansea. Because of the uncertainty and delay involved in shipping, a small amount of corn from the Vale had to be sent overland to Cardiff and Neath involving long haulage.[11]

Improved marketing facilities came with the construction of the South Wales Railway which reached Swansea in 1850, but the want of direct rail communication between the Vale and the mining towns was still a constraining factor on agricultural progress down to the mid 1860s. This is clearly revealed by witnesses before a Select Committee of the House of Commons in 1862 concerning the Cowbridge Railway Bill.[12] John Carne of Dimlands Castle testified that the South Wales Railway had done much to improve Bridgend, but Cowbridge had fallen off because the line went so far to the north of it. Accordingly, Carne and other large landowners like his brother Nicholl Carne of St Donats, Mr Humphry of Penlyne and Rowland Fothergill were promoters of the desired line in 1862 'not upon the instigation of any Railway Company but from their desire to have it in their district'. The problems which the farmers about Cowbridge experienced in sending their produce to the mineral districts were emphasized. Even after allowance is made for a degree of exaggeration natural in evidence of this kind, it is clear that farmers in the southern Vale were severely hampered through absence of rail facilities.

John Carne elaborated upon the various ways in which farm produce found its way to the mineral centres of Merthyr and Aberdare from the Cowbridge district. Livestock were driven chiefly. The journey took a considerable time and it was not unknown for fatstock to have failed to make the journey and having to be butchered on the road. If not driven, livestock were taken by farmers in the Cowbridge district to Bridgend station and sent by rail to Neath and up the Vale of Neath Railway to Aberdare. Merthyr, Dowlais and Aberdare also furnished the chief market for the farmers in the vicinity of Cowbridge for hay (of which a very large quantity was grown south of the borough), straw and oats. This produce was either carted to Llandaff station and so up the Taff Vale Railway or else it went to Bridgend and down the broad gauge line to Neath and then up the Vale of Neath.

Another witness was Daniel Edwards, a surgeon of Cowbridge, who testified to markets being held every week in the town and to the fact that one of the market days once a month was set aside for a larger market than usual, termed as 'high market'. Some of the cattle sold at Cowbridge market were taken to Llantrisant station or Bridgend and sent westwards to Neath and up the Vale of Neath Railway to Merthyr. This involved a rail journey of 54 or 55 miles. The distance from Cowbridge to the same destination by the proposed railway, it was pointed out, would be about 24 miles. The fact that farmers in the Cowbridge district were anxious to procure rail facilities was shown in the subscription list which included many names of local farmers subscribing amounts varying from £2 to £50. Apart from these, three gentlemen subscribed £100 each and another three £50 apiece.

Jenkin Thomas, a farmer and cattle jobber living near Cowbridge also gave evidence. For a number of years he had purchased a large quantity of cattle and sheep from the Vale south of Cowbridge and had sold them in the Aberdare market and at the works in that district. His cattle were sent from Cowbridge to Aberdare by first driving them to Llantrisant from which station they were sent by the Neath railway route. Such a journey took from say 6pm one evening to 1pm the following day — a notable improvement, he pointed out, on the three days which it had formerly taken him to drive his cattle from Cowbridge to Aberdare. This recourse to rail transit contrasted with the practice of driving cattle over the twenty-four miles of road between Cowbridge and Aberdare followed by an Aberthaw cattle dealer, one Daniel Thomas. He explained that he did not send them by rail through Neath to Aberdare because they failed to get there in time owing to the fact that they were delayed so much along the route. Lack of good rail accommodation, he alleged, disallowed him to carry on as extensive a business as he would have liked. He claimed that he had deliberately held back from purchasing cattle and sheep at Cowbridge market because he knew they could not walk the twenty-four miles by road, a two-day journey which even cattle in good condition had often failed to make. Another farmer who gave evidence was Thomas Wilson, who lived in a village two miles south-west of Cowbridge. He was also a hay merchant, supplying hay and straw to the industrial centres. Most of his purchases were made in the Vale, and he sent from 600 to 1,000 tons of hay and about 100 tons of straw a year to the 'works' at Merthyr and Dowlais. He sent his hay and straw by road to Bridgend, Llantrisant or the smaller station of Peterstone on the same line, from which stations it went via Neath to Merthyr. This witness once again pointed to the reduction in mileage which would be achieved if the proposed line was constructed. He claimed, however, that he did not care so much about the matter of mileage. What bothered him was the loss of time and loss of trade under the present system.

Another witness from the other side of the trade who advocated railway facilities directly linking Cowbridge and Merthyr was John Nixon, a coal-proprietor at Mountain Ash. There were upwards of 200 horses at his works and they consumed nearly 400 tons of hay a year. He obtained a large quantity of hay and straw from the Vale. This fodder was sent from Cowbridge in wagons to Cardiff whence it went up the canal or Taff Vale Railway to his works. Nixon observed that if the projected line was made, the expense of the carriage would be considerably reduced and that, furthermore, farmers about Cowbridge would be enabled to get coal more cheaply in order to burn the local Aberthaw limestone. Similar evidence from the demand side of the trade was given in March 1861 before the Select Committee on the Llantrisant and Taff Vale Junction.[13] George Thomas Clark testified that the Dowlais works employed altogether directly and indirectly about 600 horses and he claimed that the proposed line would open up hay for horses from the Vale. He stated that the Dowlais works purchased about 1,800 tons of hay a year and added: 'Of course we are anxious to get it as cheap as we can and if the agriculturalists about Cowbridge sell it cheaper than we get it from Ireland or Somersetshire we should be happy to buy it'.

The Cowbridge Railway Bill became an Act on 29 July 1862. In February 1865 a line linking Llantrisant and Cowbridge was opened enabling a train to run from Pontypridd to Cowbridge. Significantly, the first day saw Cowbridge celebrating a general holiday.[14]

Unfortunately no work seems as yet to have been done on the amounts of the different products supplied from various rural areas of south-east Wales to the different marketing centres. Quantitative evidence is hard to come by and what I have obtained from Railway Returns from 1865 onwards does not take us very far. In 1865 livestock numbers carried on the Taff Vale Railway (which included also the 'Aberdare', 'Llantrisant and Taff Vale Junction', and 'Cowbridge' lines) comprised 744 cattle, 9,741 sheep and 196 pigs. Numbers carried on the same railway (excluding the 'Cowbridge' line) in 1867 comprised 786 cattle, 13,637 sheep and 228 pigs. From 1868 down to 1873 and perhaps beyond, all we are provided with are the gross receipts from carriage of livestock on the Taff Vale complex. Even if we assume that livestock flows were towards the industrial towns in the hills, which in itself carries risks, no precise knowledge is gained of quantities of livestock bought in one market — whether that market was in south-east Wales or elsewhere — and sold in another. Besides, no information is provided as to the quantities of hay, straw and oats carried by rail.[15]

The lack of quantitative precision is unfortunate. None the less the evidence indicates that it was only with the development of adequate rail communications that farmers in the Vale could take full advantage of the big demand for produce from the industrial centres in the north of the county. Commenting on the farming of south Wales in 1872, Thomas Bowstead wrote: 'Doubtless, Welsh farming has within the last few years made amazing progress, and this improvement may be in a great measure attributed to the rapid extension and marked prosperity of the mining and manufacturing industries'.[16] A high-wage earning population demanded 'good and abundant' food. Beef and mutton, he observed, commanded as high a price in towns like Newport, Cardiff, Swansea, Neath, Aberdare and Merthyr as in the largest English towns, while dairy produce was in big demand. 'In fact, everything the farmer has to sell realises a highly remunerative price; and the resources of the land, if they are not already made the most of, must soon be called into the fullest action'. Thus clover hay sold briskly at £4.10s. to £5.5s. a ton and wheat straw sold at from £3.10s. to £4 a ton. Many enterprising farmers, particularly those having few buildings, took advantage of these prices and sold off a large proportion of their straw and some hay.

Once the marketing conditions were favourable farmers in the Vale could invest with confidence by virtue of the protection afforded them by the Custom of Glamorgan over tenant right. Writing in 1885 of the agriculture of Glamorgan W. Little of Aberaman commented that 'doubtless to it nearly everything good in the farming of this division of the county (the Vale) owes it position'.[17] The tenant right incorporated in the Custom of Glamorgan was in use in central and east Glamorgan, between the river Avon in the west and the river Rhymney in the east.[18] It was observed earlier that this was the only district in Wales which could boast a well-developed tenant right compensating the farmer for unexhausted improvements which he had carried out on his holding. Arguably, it was also superior to many of the local Customs which were operative in various English counties. Thus Daniel Owen of Ash Hall, a farm three miles from Cowbridge, claimed in a pamphlet which he wrote sometime in the 1880s that generally English Customs were infused with the spirit of inequality and injustice. The Bedfordshire Custom, for example, did not compensate the tenant for either manure or drainage. Likewise, the Customs of Berkshire, Hampshire, Leicestershire, Lancashire, Cheshire, Middlesex, Oxford, Somerset, Staffordshire, Surrey, Wiltshire, Worcestershire, the North Riding and north Wales were deemed inadequate.[19]

The Glamorgan Custom was unwritten until about 1840, having been, according to John Howells of St Athan in 1882, 'handed down for generations from father to son, constantly advancing and adapting itself to the necessities and growth of the agriculture of the district'. John Davies has suggested that the development of the Custom may have owed something to the practice of giving compensation which prevailed on the Bute estate in the early decades of the nineteenth century. Another modern writer asserts that tenant right emerged because of the low level of prices of the 1830s: 'Intensive agriculture, if a viable means of maintaining a profit margin by increased production and sales of produce during an era of low returns, necessitated a vehicle for the guarantee of capital investment in an economic milieu so prone to price fluctuations and the vagaries of nature'.[20] According to John Howells, the main landlords and tenant farmers of the counties of Glamorgan and Monmouth, meeting on a number of occasions at Cardiff around the year 1840, 'formulated it into a system'. He went on to claim that such a procedure checked the natural development of the Custom by assuming that it was full-grown. If this contention was indeed true then the situation here contrasted with what happened in England, where between 1843 and 1875 Customs in some districts had 'moved with the times'. In those areas, new, more capital-intensive and market-orientated farming practices witnessed Customs being extended to provide the necessary confidence and support to tenants to continue practising improved husbandry.[21]

Whether developing or not there is no doubt that in the 1880s the Custom was well-developed. The tenant right bill on well-managed farms amounted to sums between 20s. and 60s. an acre, according to the state of cultivation and cleanliness of the holding.[22] After a careful study of the Custom, Jones writes that: 'The custom was limited to those sectors of the county east of the river Afan and dedicated to arable husbandry, especially the cultivation of wheat. Towards the western borders of the Vale of Glamorgan only the barest elements were visible and the scope, in addition to the scale, of compensation gradually contracted. For example, lime, the traditional manure of Welsh agriculture, was the basis of compensation in the western Vale'.[23] The Custom did not allow for the construction, enlargement or repair of buildings; for haulage towards such purposes; for laying down to permanent pasture; and a tenant could not remove any machinery he might have erected on his holding.[24] Despite these constraints, it was popular with tenants. Indeed, they preferred the 'old custom' to the Agricultural Holdings (England)

Act of 1883 which, as we have seen earlier, for the first time made compensation for unexhausted improvements compulsory.[25] On 27 May 1884 Daniel Owen read a paper before the Cowbridge Farmers' Club in which he argued that the Glamorgan Custom was in a number of respects superior to the Act. Such contemporaries even rated the Custom as superior to the celebrated Lincolnshire one.[26] An example of the kind of allowance which could be paid to the tenant of a substantial, well-run farm in the Vale was that made to Rees Thomas of Rock Farm and West Aberthaw Farm, adjacent holdings south of Cowbridge extending over 475 acres, in 1882. The judges awarded him £1,125.[27]

Progressive farming in the Vale was also encouraged by the fact that much of the land was in the hands of great landlords.[28] These included in 1873 such magnates as the Marquess of Bute, the Lord Windsor, the Earl of Dunraven and Christopher Rice Mansel Talbot of Margam.[29] The correspondent from Wales to *The Times* in 1889 was J.E. Vincent, an ardent defender of Welsh landowners during the debate over the Welsh Land Question. He claimed that while the great landlords of Glamorgan were business-like in the royalties they charged their mining tenants, they were wholly generous in their relationship with their agricultural tenants.[30] The Earl of Dunraven, owner of an estate of nearly 24,000 acres in Glamorgan, laid out 27½ per cent of his gross rental on average every year between 1872 and 1893 on improvements. Lord Windsor likewise treated his farm tenants generously.[31] John Davies has remarked of the Bute estate: 'Apart from the low percentages of the late-1820s and the 1830s, when the agency lacked a dedicated agriculturalist and when expenditure on the dock was at its height, the proportion of the gross rents spent on repairs and improvements by the Bute estate in the nineteenth century was remarkably high'. The state of farm buildings on the estate in the 1840s, even those in the Vale, was deplorable and so Davies convincingly argues that: 'The Bute estate had both the need for a higher investment and, by the late-nineteenth century, the means to finance it'. Meanwhile farm rents between the late 1840s and the end of the century were static. Under the third Marquess (1847–1900) 'income from non-agricultural sources rendered unnecessary the management of the agricultural estate on strictly commercial lines and thus there were no rent increases during the agriculturally prosperous 1850s and 1860s'.[32] In so far as the other great estates of Glamorgan were concerned it seems that landlords charged their rents on a supply and demand basis (indeed, Daniel Owen in 1881 claimed that rents in Glamorgan were higher than in England) but then proceeded to 'treat their tenants with the utmost liberality'.[33]

The many large farms of the Vale were conducive to improvements in farming. W. Little stated in 1885 that there were a few holdings from 500 to 800 acres but that the average size in the better parts of the Vale was about 200 acres. Writing of the Vale about the same time, J. Darby observed that farms of between 200 and 300 acres predominated, although there were a few bigger and some smaller.[34]

Another stimulus to intensive farming in the Vale from the 1840s down to the early 1880s was the various forms of encouragement given farmers towards carrying out improvements in their husbandry. Local farmers' clubs played a part. Thus the

Cowbridge Farmers' Club drew its membership from among local men of 'capital and position'.[35] J. Darby noted in 1885 that this club was one of the best of the local farmers' clubs, its monthly discussions which took place at the Bear Hotel, Cowbridge, serving to advance 'the spirit of emulation' in farming along improved lines.[36] Similarly, the remarkable increase in the membership of the Glamorganshire Agricultural Society from a long-static level of about 100 members to some 350 in 1877 reflected the growth of interest in the technical advances of the period[37] and stimulated the adoption of improved methods. It is also likely that covenants enjoining improved farming, such as those introduced on the Bute estate from the 1830s, were beneficial towards raising the poor standard of husbandry which persisted in the county down to the 1840s. The Vale of Glamorgan was one of the few areas in Wales suited to the practice of the Norfolk system,[38] and the covenants imposing a four-course system were widely practised in the Vale in the second half of the century[39] and probably promoted agricultural improvement. The thinking of the second Marquess of Bute ran along these lines in writing to his agent in 1845: 'As a general rule where tenants are less acquainted with what they ought to do, more stringent covenants are required than in an improved country, and the tenants should be bound to do certain things in return for outlays by the landlord'.[40] On the other hand, it was claimed that certain of the provisions in agreements were oppressive, as, for example, the one restricting the tenant from selling any hay or straw.[41] (The fact that large quantities of hay and straw were sold off Vale farms suggests that this covenant was either blatantly ignored by farmers or that landlords easily waived it upon request). Linked with these progressive covenants were leases for specified terms of years or annual agreements. These were introduced in the Vale proper (as distinct from the Border Vale in the west and the highland regions of the county) in the early nineteenth century, because the long leases for lives would have prevented landlords from enjoining on their tenants progressive husbandry techniques.[42] Finally, the second Marquess of Bute, albeit with limited success, encouraged his tenants to increase productivity by introducing premiums from the 1820s and making available for the use of his tenants in the 1840s a threshing machine, a steam-engine and a sub-soil plough. The practice on the estate of making available certain equipment and services was increased later in the century.[43]

We must now look briefly at the features of intensive farming in the Vale. Most farmers practised mixed husbandry, but as late as the 1880s when the switch to grass was underway in response to agricultural depression two-thirds of the land was arable.[44] Improved cropping rotations were introduced on the large holdings in the first half of the century. C.S. Read, writing of the agriculture of south Wales in 1849 observed: 'The Vale of Glamorgan is, perhaps, the finest district and as well farmed as any in South Wales'. The more progressive farmers were now taking two corn crops at the most in succession.[45] By mid century more systematic rotations were characterizing the farming of the Vale, nitrogenous legumes, mangolds and turnips featuring as common elements.[46] Details of the cropping rotations on the best-managed farms of the Vale can be seen in the Report of the Farm-Prize Competition in South Wales and Monmouthshire sponsored by the Royal Agricultural Society of England in 1872. West Aberthaw, farmed by Michael

Spencer, was highly commended. The system of cropping was the four-course one, namely roots, barley or wheat, seeds and wheat; and this same four-course system was followed on the highly commended Rock Farm tenanted by Rees Thomas. In 1885 W. Little observed that the four-course rotation had been 'long practised' in the Vale, though at the time he was writing there were objections to the system on the grounds that the land not only got clover-sick but to some degree also root-sick.[47]

Progressive farmers in the Vale were using artificial manures such as guano, dissolved bones, nitrate of soda and mineral superphosphates.[48] By purchasing these along with artificial feedstuffs onto their holdings tenant farmers were important agents, along with their landlords who provided purpose-built outbuildings and drainage, in bringing about 'the second agricultural revolution'.[49] As early as the 1840s artificial manures, many of them shipped to south Wales, were allegedly 'extensive' in use.[50] Figures are available for a later period showing the large quantities of artificial manures which were shipped into Swansea and, to a far smaller extent Cardiff, from overseas. Over the five years 1874–78 Swansea's imports of artificial manures were as follows:[51]

1874	175 tons worth £1,546
1875	3,501 tons worth £8,531
1876	5,663 tons worth £13,470
1877	6,145 tons worth £15,305
1878	6,436 tons worth £15,446

Increased application of manures necessitated improved drainage, for they would lose their value if the land remained wet.[52] Drainage was expensive, but the situation was improved from the year 1846 onwards when it was to some extent financed on favourable terms from Government and public companies' loans to landowners.[53] If we look at all the Welsh counties for the amounts borrowed by landowners for drainage purposes under the whole range of Public and Private Acts between 1846 and 1892 then we find Glamorgan with £12,730.18s. 4d. (representing the drainage of about only 3,000 acres) falling in the lower half of the table.[54] Of this total, amounts borrowed by individual landowners are not available in every case. Even so, it is clear that Glamorgan's owners did not borrow to any great extent and from the evidence available it does not seem that the large owners in the Vale availed themselves of the opportunity to borrow.[55] It has been plausibly argued: 'The landed magnates with large amounts of capital drawn from commerce and industry had no need of Acts of Parliament'.[56] Between 1847 and 1863 nearly £7,000 was spent on the Bute estate on drainage, besides the cost of running the tile factory which had been established near the docks in 1845, again suggesting that, 'the Bute authorities had no need to seek government assistance to finance their improvements'. The amount expended on drainage by the Bute family by no means, however, represented the total spent on drainage on the Bute estate since the Bute tenants, receiving tiles at cost price from the estate factory, preferred to carry out their own drainage.[57]

Modern machinery was used for planting and harvesting. Grain crops were sown with a Suffolk drill and clovers and grass with a broadcast drill.[58] In so far as harvesting was concerned, the horse-drawn mowing machine and self-delivery reaping machine both came into popular use on large farms in the Vale from their introduction in the 1860s.[59] It was claimed that more threshing machines were being used in the Vale at the close of the 1840s than were usually to be seen in England.[60] By 1872 progressive farmers in the Vale were using portable threshing machines. Steam-ploughing, however, was not in use in 1872, Thomas Bowstead remarking that: 'the formation of steam cultivation companies, such as are now springing up in the great arable districts throughout England, would doubtless prove a profitable speculation'.[61] By the mid 1880s a steam plough was in use on the 700-acre Boverton farm in the Vale, a facility which allowed the tenant to dispense with four pairs of horses.[62]

Livestock management on the substantial holdings likewise contrasted with the general backwardness of the small family-farms. Rather than raising a number of ill-bred store animals, farmers with capital often fattened their livestock for the butcher. In 1849 the Glamorgan breed of cattle was the most popular on Vale farms, many of which were stall-fed on hay and turnips when four years old. During the winter months the yearlings were fed in sheds, some farmers turning them out in the daytime to feed off turnips and taking them in at night; two-year-olds were similarly treated except that they were lodged in an open straw-yard. Hereford cattle were more plentiful in the vicinity of Cardiff, it being noted that 'the general farming is of a very superior description in that locality'.[63] From that time Herefords grew in popularity throughout the Vale. The fattening beasts were fed off linseed or cotton-cake, cut roots and loose hay, and on the best farms they were stall-fed for the butcher.[64]

It was observed in 1872 that the sheep which were kept on lowland farms of south Wales and Monmouthshire (presumably including the Vale) were mainly Cotswolds and Oxford Downs, with a few flocks of Leicesters and Shropshires. They were managed along the most improved lines. The leading breeders visited the Gloucester September fair to purchase the best rams. The lambs were dropped early in March and under the best management they were soon taught to eat cake before going on to turnips and, by the end of the year, cut swedes. As time progressed they were fed with more varied feeding stuffs as peas, linseed or cotton-cake, Indian corn and crushed oats. This had the double advantage of bringing the animals on quickly and of keeping up the manurial value of the land. The wether tegs were sent to market at 13 or 14 months. The management of the ewes during the winter was as good as that for the lamb stock. Plenty of hay was fed to them and also a moderate supply of roots.[65]

Before closing this discussion on farming in the Vale a few observations about its general character need to be made. In the first place, it must be emphasized that not all farming in the Vale was progressive. W. Little observed in 1885: 'Many of the farms are as well managed as those of the best-farmed English counties, but others again are conspicuous only for their slovenly management'.[66] Secondly, at the close of the 1840s farming technology was most advanced in the eastern Vale. Further west that excellence gradually fell away.[67] Finally, it is important to consider whether the farming practised on the sizeable farms in the Vale constituted what has been termed 'high farming'. In Caird's sense of the term, 'high farming', to quote J.D. Chambers and G.E. Mingay, meant 'a high outlay of capital to achieve a high output per acre — by means of artificials and stocking with good quality breeds of cattle, drilling of the best seeds and the use of machinery to harvest and thresh the crops, together with his requirements of thorough drainage, removal of "unnecessary obstructions to economical tillage", "convenient farm-roads", and "well-arranged buildings".'[68] If we use the term in this sense then it is fair to claim that high farming was practised in the Vale, although we must note the considered view of J. Darby in 1885 that Vale farming was 'in no case extraordinarily high, but very generally of a nature to compare with that of most well-cultivated regions of Wales or the West of England'.[69] However, 'high farming' in a more technical sense of the term was, as E.L. Jones has pointed out, 'an extension of mixed farming', the latter epitomized by the Norfolk system, 'with its close-knit cycle of fodder and grain crops, its arable flock, and its yard-fed bullocks'. To this system high farming brought the generous feeding of purchased oilcake to the livestock in order to produce both meat and dung; the latter, along with purchased artificial manures, was in turn richly applied to the arable lands to stimulate high yields of cereal crops and of fodder crops for the livestock. 'The greater the scale of feeding farm-grown and bought-in fodder and the heavier the application of farm-produced and purchased fertilizer, the more the saleable produce and the more manure for the next round of cropping, that is, the higher the farming'. While in the 1840s the richer feeding of livestock for the sake of better dung in order to boost cereal crops lay at the heart of the system of high farming or 'high feeding', by the 1860s there had come about an adjustment within the system of mixed farming in response to the increase in prices of livestock products compared with the stagnant level of wheat prices. The new relationship between cereals and livestock enterprises shifted in favour of livestock, the manure from the stall-feeding now being devoted not so much to the wheat crop as formerly but to the roots as further feed for the livestock.[70] A.W. Jones plausibly concludes that the system of farming followed in the most advanced areas of Glamorgan agriculture in the middle of the nineteenth century was not high farming in this latter sense of the term. Rather it was the Norfolk system which predominated. He argues that the concentration upon hay and corn for the mining districts 'was more conducive to alternate husbandry than high feeding for corn and cattle production'. Artificial manures were not used for the implementation of high farming but rather to prevent soil exhaustion. He continues: 'It was an expensive method to reap immediate high profits and meet market demands. Roots were still the mainstay of fattened cattle under this system and enabled the farmers to export vast quantities of hay'. In forwarding this view Jones relies in part upon the observation of Read in 1849 that the land in the Vale was injured by the great amounts of hay and straw sent to the mining centres, 'the loss of which in almost every instance, is inadequately supplied by manure not made on the farm'.[71] Later, in 1872, Thomas Bowstead pointed to the lack of sufficient farm buildings as an inducement to farmers in south Wales to sell straw and hay and also indicated how the manure problem was solved. 'Many good managers, especially those scantily supplied with buildings, avail themselves of these prices, and sell off a large proportion of their straw and some hay; and, by bringing back all they can produce of town-made muck, and supplementing it with the best artificial fertilizers, they can easily maintain unimpaired the manurial condition of their farms'.[72]

Some doubt remains as to how soon agricultural depression, which set in in the Vale from 1878 or 1879 in so far as corn crops were concerned,[73] began to diminish the degree of intensive farming practised there. Daniel Owen observed in his paper to the Cowbridge Farmers' Club in 1881 that in the severest period of depression there were no farms vacant in the area despite the fact that rents were higher in Glamorgan than in England and the rainfall greater than throughout the average of England. He concluded: 'Our prosperity is due, in my opinion, to an equitable tenant right'.[74] Although W. Doyle was to remark in 1882 that the Glamorgan Custom of tenant right obviously could could not afford complete protection, albeit the local press and public speakers were contending in 1883 that Glamorgan farmers, if not wholly exempt, were not as hard pressed as their English neighbours. However, the position by 1885 had altered: 'There are at present more farms in the market and more land in the owners' own hands than has been the case for forty years. The high farming for which this division (the Vale) has long been noted is not now being maintained'.[75]

In Monmouthshire, in the neighbourhoods of Abergavenny, Monmouth, Usk, Newport and Chepstow, farming was similarly progressive, reputably, indeed, superior to that practised in the Vale. The same consumer demand from the teeming new centres of population was felt. Farms were frequently from 300 to 400 acres in size, and large, square fields were encountered between Chepstow and Newport. Finally, of great importance in stimulating improvement was the Tredegar agricultural show, which was founded in 1818 by the Morgan family of Tredegar and continually supported by them thereafter. W. Fothergill claimed in 1870 that 'it stands almost without a rival as the best local show in England'.[76] In 1851 Sir Charles Morgan, as the sponsor of the show, gave 16 silver cups, and cups were also donated by other land-owning families.[77]

It is not surprising, therefore, that a Monmouthshire farm was awarded second prize in the competition of 1872. This was the Slough Farm, held by Mr Valentine Parsons. It was about 292 acres in size and was located 4½ miles outside Chepstow. Three other Monmouthshire farms were in fact included within the short-list of the twelve best kept holdings. (The other eight comprised seven from Glamorgan and one from Pembrokeshire).[78] We have seen that drainage was an important element of intensive farming in Britain at mid century and, in Monmouthshire, a considerable amount was carried out by the aid of government grants and by private enterprise.[79] Monmouthshire thus saw an outlay of £21,230 (this was higher than any sum borrowed by any county in Wales) charged for drainage under the Public Money Drainage Acts between 1847 and 1872 and an outlay of £8,562.8s.2d. sanctioned as a charge on estates in Wales for drainage under the several Improvement Companies Acts, the Improvement of Land Act, 1864, and the Limited Owners' Residences Act between 1855 and 1892.[80] Individual landowners prominent in borrowing were John Herbert of Llanarth Court (£5,000 between 1852 and 1856), Sir Charles Morgan of Tredegar Park (£4,117 between 1855 and 1857), Robert Bateman of Llantrisant (£1,623 between 1862 and 1865) and Sir Benjamin Hall of Llanover (£1,452 in 1852–53).[81] The course of cropping followed was generally swedes, barley, clover and wheat or, to a lesser extent, winter oats. Cattle were all fed under cover in stalls, usually on roots and meal, with meadow hay and straw. By 1870 folding of sheep on roots, with corn and cake was widely practised. Cotswolds were the main breed stocked on the farms in the south of the county.[82] A number of farmers, including Parsons of the Slough Farm, sold large quantities of wheat straw.[83] If so, as already suggested, they would not have been practising high feeding in so far as cattle management was concerned. None the less, it is clear that intensive, progressive farming was a feature of the agriculture of lower Monmouthshire in the four decades or so after 1840.

A brief mention must also be made of the improvements made in the farming of southern Gower. By the 1840s the opportunities presented by the Swansea market meant that the parishes of Port Eynon and Oxwich were mainly given over to grain and crop production for that market.[84] Potatoes were grown on a big scale in Gower to feed the Swansea population. The system of farming, however, was only beginning to undergo improvement. Thus in 1849 corn crops were taken in succession until the soil was exhausted. Nevertheless, the cultivation of turnips and mangolds was 'extending rapidly'.[85] The example of alternate husbandry was first set by C.R.M. Talbot, Esq., on his home farm at Penrice Castle in 1844 and the practice was publicized in a pamphlet written by him in 1850 and circulated in the Swansea area.[86] According to W. Little, the system was gradually adopted by tenant farmers, 'and by slow but sure degrees the whole aspect of Gower became changed for the better'.[87] By 1885 either the four- or five-course system of cropping was being practised on large farms in Gower.[88] Indeed, such was the transformation in Gower farming that W. Little claimed in the 1880s that 'No portion of the county has made greater strides in improvement during the present century than this'. By then roads had become greatly improved, good crops of roots, grain and grass were being grown, and cattle had in the recent past been greatly improved, principally by using Shorthorn bulls. Likewise sheep had been improved by crossing the mountain breed with Shropshire Down and other rams. Improved breeding of stock had been fostered and encouraged by the chief landlords of the district (as C.R.M. Talbot and Sir Hussey Vivian of Park Hill) introducing pure-bred animals. All this meant that rather than store stock being raised and sold off to other parts of the country as was the case in the 1830s and 1840s, livestock was chiefly fattened off on roots for the butcher.[89] In the immediate vicinity of Swansea the land was kept under grass or market gardens and maintained in a high state of fertility, small farmers keeping two or three cows to provide Swansea with milk.[90] For all its improvement, however, it would be erroneous to place the farming in southern Gower on the same advanced footing as that which prevailed in the Vale of Glamorgan and southern Monmouthshire. Significantly none of the twelve best managed farms in south Wales and Monmouthshire described by Bowstead in 1872 was located in Gower.

The industrial market of south Wales gave rise to intensive farming in the Vale, southern Monmouthshire and southern Gower. Other areas of south Wales also responded to the marketing opportunities, even if the general level of farming of those areas remained low. Moreover, in the Castlemartin area of south Pembrokeshire, the Towy valley and the region running westwards from Carmarthen to St Clear's and Laugharne some improvement took place in the standard of farming practised. I have indicated elsewhere how in the pre-railway period produce from south-west Wales like corn and butter reached the industrial valleys to the east via the roundabout route of Bristol where it was re-shipped to Cardiff and Newport and sent on to the industrial districts by canal or the Taff Vale Railway. Before the railway, butter, pigs and poultry were also sent to Merthyr from south-west Wales by carts. Fat pigs, too, from the region were sometimes driven to the industrial towns in the years before the railway. In addition butter was sent to the industrial towns from Brecknockshire and corn from Radnorshire in the pre-railway era. But transport costs curtailed the opportunites for supplying the needs of the new industrial market. Thus to have supplied oats from Brecknockshire would have been too costly, involving conveyance over high land between the Usk valley and Merthyr.[91] Although rearing of storestock persisted in most areas of south Wales after the railway network had been constructed, cheap transport did, however, lead to an increase in livestock fattening in certain fertile areas to serve the industrial market of the south-eastern valleys. Farmers of the Castlemartin area increasingly fattened their cattle for the butchers, although, as was the case with many farms within the Vale of Glamorgan which fattened stock, the large feeding farms of south Pembrokeshire lacked the requisite housing facilities for stall-feeding. Carmarthen and St Clear's were prominent marts for the sale of fat cattle produced in the Towy valley and in the belt extending westwards from Carmarthen to St Clear's and Laugharne. Even before the railway, *The Welshman* for 7 June 1850 reporting on the June fair (probably that of Carmarthen) observed: 'The notice of intention to change the day of the fair not having received sufficient previous publicity, many dealers and butchers attended from Merthyr, Swansea, Llanelly and Cardiganshire and were exceedingly wrathful on learning of the change'. Butter was sent by rail from south-west Wales to the 'hills' of Glamorgan and Monmouthshire, and the farmers of that region clung on to producing the heavily-salted tub butter partly because of their conservatism but partly also because the Glamorgan colliers continued their preference for that brand. The hill districts of Glamorgan supplied Caerphilly cheese to the Glamorgan colliers with whom it remained popular because it did not crumble easily. With the exception of farms in close proximity to the 'works' and the principal towns like Cardiff and Swansea, liquid milk was not supplied off the farms in south Wales having good access to the industrial areas. Welsh farmers went in for butter- and cheese-making, and the industrial market of the Glamorgan hill district and Cardiff was provided with milk down to the end of the century chiefly from Somerset and Monmouthshire.[92]

A number of points need to be made in conclusion. Those hill districts of Glamorgan resting on the coal measures did not entirely fail to respond to the new demand for farm produce. In the 1880s the Cyfarthfa home farm of W.T. Crawshay, Esq., some 350 acres in extent, was run on highly improved lines, and not only this home farm but the 300-acre

Vaynor Farm which he also had in occupation were greatly improved by drainage, heavy manuring and high feeding of stock. About a mile from the upper part of the Cyfarthfa home farm was a tract of land belonging to the Dowlais Ironworks Company and stock was taken in to graze at a certain sum per week. Cowkeepers stocked their dairy cows there to supply the Dowlais inhabitants with milk.[93] Little was the first observer to mention the 'colliery farms', groups of small mountain farms tenanted by the colliery companies for the purpose of feeding pit-ponies, sheep and cattle.[94] As we have seen, the small tenants of the hill farms made cheese for sale to the colliers. The coalfield area, however, could produce only a small fraction of the food required for the mining population which drew the major part of its requirements from outside the mining area. Some of this came from certain favoured agricultural districts within south Wales which came to specialize in producing foodstuffs for the new industrial markets and the ports on their doorsteps. However, part (in the mid 1840s three-quarters of Merthyr's flour) was brought from outside the region for two main reasons: firstly, the fact that the agricultural sector could not meet the demands of the urban and industrial market[95] and, secondly, the adjoining farming districts could not compete with the sea-borne produce because of the higher cost of transporting by land (especially by cart) compared with the cheapness with which produce could be brought to the ports and thence taken by canal or the Taff Vale Railway to the mining towns.[96] The extension of the railway network enabled the farming districts of south Wales to supply a larger proportion of the needs of the urban and industrial markets.

Capital Formation by Railways in South Wales, 1836–1914

TOM TAYLOR

The main purpose of this essay is to make available two new series of historical statistics, gross and net fixed capital formation by railways[1] in south Wales, 1836–1914 as a modest addition to existing national series of railway capital formation.[2] It is not intended to give a historical account of railway development as such. Much of this ground has already been covered by many writers, none of whom has, however, paid much attention to economic matters.[3] The published series tend to emphasize railway capital formation as a component of total capital formation and are national in scope, although it must be said that Kenwood has also made important contributions at the regional level.[4]

The title of this essay requires some discussion. Firstly, the term 'south Wales' is not unambiguous. Thus the geographical limits of the area studied are set by the counties of Gwent, South, Mid, and West Glamorgan, and the southern part of Dyfed.[5] These embrace the coal measures which were such an important factor in the development of the area. There is a certain arbitrariness in the geographical limitation of railway activity and in one or two important instances, parts of lines outside the counties named are included in the survey.[6]

Secondly, the meaning of the term 'railway' should be made clear. The criteria adopted here are those proposed by Lee. 'Broadly the modern railway may be regarded as a combination of four main features, namely: (a) specialized track; (b) accommodation of public traffic; (c) conveyance of passengers; and (d) mechanical traction'. To these we welcome Robbins's addition of '(e) some measure of public control'.[7] This list presents a mixture of technical, economic and political factors but together they remove ambiguity since any enterprise simultaneously fulfilling all these five conditions is commonly understood to be a railway, a definition generally implied by those operating in the field of railway capital formation. 'What is a railway?' may seem a commonplace and even trivial question,[8] but in this case the importance of a precise and explicit definition is obvious. The compilation of a statistical series requires a firm and clear basis and it is in the nature of railways that this particularly should be so. As Robbins[9] points out, 'all five features have to be present together before there is a railway; when one or more of them is absent, then there is a tramway, or a light railway, or a private means of transport, or something else'. Also, the simultaneous character of these features must be stressed as they keep cropping up singly or in part throughout history — specialized track for the accommodation of wheeled vehicles, for example, being encountered in Babylonia, Greece and the Roman Empire. Hence the need for a precise definition. It follows from this that the definition clearly excludes tram-roads of which there had been a significant development in south Wales prior to railways.

Not so easily resolved is the question of what are conventionally called ancillaries. In the history of railways in Britain, these strictly speaking non-railway activities have been wide-ranging and numerous, particularly after 1870. Some companies became hotel proprietors and dock and steamship owners in a big way,[10] and at least one south Wales company dabbled in paddle-steamers with disastrous consequences.[11] By the twentieth century, railways were operating motor road vehicles, both for passengers and goods. The State was slow to recognize the importance of ancillaries and it was not until 1911 that provision was made for the first time for their operations to be recorded separately from railway working.[12] These activities were not unimportant commercially and were economically justifiable as examples of vertical integration. Further, they indicated, in some instances at least, an attitude of mind that railways were in the transport business rather than the railway business, which if nothing else was good marketing. In spite of all this, ancillaries were, nevertheless, still subsidiary in importance. By definition they could be excluded without further consideration (or at least treated separately) if it were not for the especial significance for railways in south Wales of one particular ancillary, namely docks and harbours.

The purpose of many railways in this area was so obviously to connect industry with port facilities that the relationship between dock and railway is particularly close. Dock companies developed into railways;[13] railways acquired or leased or sought access to docks;[14] the railway and the dock were at the outset conceived of as a single integrated system.[15] This is reflected to some extent in the titles of south Wales railway companies,[16] the words dock, harbour or port occurring in at least ten instances, and after 1922 when almost the whole railway network of south Wales came under the single ownership of the Great Western Railway, that company could claim the ownership and operation of the largest dock system in the world.[17]

A considerable part of railway capital was thus tied up in harbours and docks and to exclude these from our study would be misleading. Such an exclusion would reduce, for example, the Cardiff Railway to an enterprise of minor significance in terms of capital employed; in the case of the Barry Railway it would be an act of arbitrary and unmeaningful dismemberment. Thus it is reasonable to include harbours and docks within our concept of railway, although preparing separate estimates for these works as far as sources make possible. Such an inclusion eases a difficulty. It is not always clear from the evidence available how much of an expenditure on way and works is in respect of docks on the one hand and 'railway proper' on the other. Within any dock area there is provision of facilities essential to and characteristic of railway operation — track, signalling, buildings, even stations, and most significant, sidings. Other ancillaries were less important, and in any case do not constitute the problems posed by harbours and docks. They are excluded by definition and omitting them has presented no problem as they are generally identifiable.

The third point to consider is the period under review. This is taken as 1836 to 1914 and has been decided on several considerations. The starting-point is more or less precisely determined by the definition of a railway. The first enterprises fulfilling all the necessary conditions were incorporated about that time and construction of any significance was begun in the late 1830s. Indeed, much can be said for taking 1836 as the starting-point, the year of incorporation of the Taff Vale Railway. Prior to that date there is no evidence of capital investment by railways as such. The end of the period could be taken as 31 December 1922, after which date amalgamation was required, if it had not already proceeded, under the terms of the Railways Act, 1921. In fact the year 1922 in south Wales was one of smooth and steady amalgamation in accordance with the Act,[18] adding little but complication to our enquiry. The Great War and its immediate aftermath were untypical and can be reasonably excluded as a period of overall state control and direction. In fact, there is a more particular reason for excluding this period. Government control, as exercised under Section 16 of the Regulation of the Forces Act, 1871, played havoc with commercial decision. In particular, charges for services rendered between companies were discontinued, as was also the settlement of 'through' traffic receipts. In effect, what each company collected it held as its own receipts, a procedure which clearly did not accurately reflect its commercial activity. Recognizing this, the Board of Trade authorized the accounts for the year 1914 onwards to be published in modified and abridged form and this was done until the end of 1921.[19] Realistic data is not easily available for this period. Thus, 31 December 1913 is selected as the end of the period, giving a span of almost 80 years.

No single, simple index can be regarded in itself as a completely adequate measure of railway performance and development. Several obvious magnitudes come to mind — paid-up capital, receipts, traffic, employment, route or track mileage, working stock and perhaps profits and dividends. All these offer insights and may be regarded as necessary complements in a comprehensive measure of railway performance. The present study follows common practice in attaching major importance to an index of capital. The term is used in the economic sense of fixed capital formation, of which estimates of gross and net figures have been prepared. The distinction between gross and net is widely known, as are the reasons for normally employing the gross concept in series of capital formation, but it so happens that the data on which the present series has been based makes estimates of net capital formation a relatively simple matter.

Capital formation as an index is considered firstly because of its economic significance. Moreover, as the stock of physical assets employed is equally accepted as one significant index of the size of a concern, a series of fixed capital formation rates highly as an instrument for analysing the growth of railways and their impact on the economy. Secondly, fixed capital formation is a particularly appropriate index in the case of railways because of their nature as economic enterprises. They come under the category of public utility which embraces enterprises supplying not only a variety of transport services, but such things as water, gas, electricity and other forms of energy. These enterprises have at least one characteristic in common, important in this connection, and that is that the greatest part of the capital sums raised is transformed into fixed assets which are employed to earn revenue and are not for the purpose of resale. Many of these fixed assets in the case of railways, as in other kinds of public utility, are of long durability, some of which are technically described as 'permanent'.[20] Thus a series of fixed capital formation can reasonably be regarded as a fairly representative indicator of railway development. Thirdly, such a series can be constructed without encountering insurmountable difficulties. Adequate data is available, even if it requires some interpretation, considerable reformulation and a certain amount of estimation. Fourthly, a series of fixed capital formation is particularly important simply because other series of fixed capital formation covering the period, or the greater part of it, already exist. In particular there are the series of fixed capital formation by railways in the United Kingdom or parts of it; as well as series of total capital formation for the whole economy. Thus direct comparisons can be made with these series.

The basic problem involved in the construction of a series of fixed capital formation by railways is the transformation of the available data into economic terms. The main primary source of the data is the surviving published Reports and Accounts of the companies concerned.[21] Useful supplementary sources are Herapath's *Railway Journal, The Railway Times, The Railway News,* Bradshaw's *Railway Manual* and *Shareholder's Guide,* also Slaughter's and Tucks and the Board of Trade Returns.[22]

Ideally, the Reports and Accounts of all companies in south Wales having separate existence in the period would be used. Unfortunately, not all of these exist. The series is based in the first instance on the records of the 42 companies which are available (see, Appendix 2 on page 114), but is supplemented from other sources. Altogether, there were at least 109 identifiable corporate bodies in existence within the period, but a number of these consisted of no more than a short section of track, or a junction, or disappeared after a short period as a result of amalgamation, or were Joint Managing Committees whose financial records were kept by the parent companies, which is very much in line with the British experience as a whole.[23] It is chiefly in respect of these companies that records are not available, and if no allowance is made for them, this is not likely to have a significant effect on the results. The 42 companies undoubtedly account for the greatest part of the south Wales railway network, all the most important companies being included. On this basis, an unsupplemented series can be regarded as adequately representative of the whole.

To appreciate fully how the series on capital formation was derived from accounting records, it is necessary to outline the basic principles underlying railway accounting and to make some reference to railway accounting practice, particularly in the earlier part of the period.[24] Railways were statutory companies and the form and practice of their accounting were derived from Acts of Parliament. Throughout the period the sources of their authority were Standing Orders and the Special Acts[25] which each company had to obtain to gain corporate existence. The accounting provisions in these were minimal and not uniform, leading to a great diversity of practice. When additional powers were required further Special Acts had to be obtained. The three General Acts[26] passed in 1844 and 1845 went little beyond requiring that the directors should cause full and true accounts to be kept and did nothing to secure uniformity.

This absence of uniformity was constantly criticized and the need to secure it amply recognized, but nothing serious was done about the problem until the establishment of the Royal Commission on Railways, 1865–7. The ensuing Report, referring to the three general Acts of 1844 and 1845, criticized them for not securing a uniform system of accounts, thus leaving companies free to adopt whatever form they chose. The result was 'that no adequate means are afforded by which to compare the financial affairs of two companies or even to compare the accounts of the same railway from time to time.'[27] However, in spite of the diversity of accounting practice and malpractice, the custom had grown among railways of adopting a particular system of accounting — the double-account system. The Royal Commission recommended uniformity and the Regulation of Railways Act 1868 which followed the Report required all railways to submit their accounts half-yearly according to the forms prescribed in the first schedule to the Act. The system adopted in these forms was the double-account system and this appears to be its first statutory recognition.[28]

Although Pollins has referred to the Act of 1868 as 'a turning point in the history of railway accounting after a long period of uncertainty', it is clear that as far as railway accounting practice is concerned, it did not, in fact, secure its objective of uniformity.[29] Certainly, companies were required to submit accounts half-yearly, constructed on the double-account system, in accordance with the prescribed forms. Unfortunately, this is where uniformity ended. Although the forms were there, there were neither laid-down arrangements for prescribing which items should be included under the various headings, nor the machinery for exercising compliance. Thus, as far as railway accounting is concerned, all the 1868 Act secured was uniformity in structure but diversity of content. Worse, the extension of the railways' operations into ancillaries after 1868 was marked and the Act made no statutory provision for this.

The problem of diversity of accounting practice which had bedevilled railways since their outset was not finally tackled until the passing in 1911 of the Railway Companies (Accounts and Returns) Act, which had followed the Report of the Railway Companies' Association Committee in 1905 and that of the Departmental Committee of the Board of Trade in 1909.[30] The first year for which accounts were published in the new form was 1913, the last year of our period and as, for our purposes, no difficulty was encountered in maintaining continuity with the form of the 1868 Act, nothing further will be said about what the 1911 Act prescribed.

All the above might understandably lead one to the conclusion that nineteenth-century railway accounts are almost useless for anything apart from a study of accounting pathology. The difficulties may be summarized as primitive accounting, errors, malpractice and lack of uniformity. The last is characteristic of railway accounting throughout the period until 1913, the first three a feature of the first half of the period, particularly the earlier years.

In the matter of capital formation, however, these problems are not quite so serious as may first appear — fortunately since the accounts are an indispensable source. As far as primitive accounting and errors are concerned, the accounts have to be used whatever, as they are the only records available, with little or no means of supplementing them or amending them. In the case of malpractice, the most significant activity seems to have been that of charging to capital that which should properly have been an expense against revenue. In terms of physical assets, this means that estimates of gross capital formation are unaffected, although the net figure is increased by the extent of the malpractice and the replacement figure correspondingly reduced. To correct for these irregularities is extremely difficult and their extent cannot be judged apart from suggesting that they are not too important when the results are compared with estimates of gross and net figures arrived at by any other methods. Finally and fortunately there is no real problem as far as diversity of practice is concerned. Physical assets are generally itemized, and where they are not, they can often be unscrambled. Taking all the above into consideration, railway accounts are not only almost the sole source over a long period for estimates of capital formation on a regional basis, they can be regarded as acceptably accurate for this purpose notwithstanding their reputation.

The double-account system which was customarily employed by railways before 1868 and statutorily required afterwards until nationalization is, by accounting practice, comparatively modern and was generally used by public utilities. It was regarded as appropriate to enterprises where the bulk of the capital was transformed into long-life, revenue-earning physical assets which wear out over a long period of time in the performance of their services. Its essential difference from conventional business accounting is most clearly seen in the treatment of two of the principal accounts and of the balance sheet — respectively, receipts and expenditure on capital account, revenue account, and general balance sheet.

The capital account shows on the receipts or credit side the total of money subscribed, under the categories of stocks and shares, loans, debenture stock, and premiums on stocks and shares sold. Since we are concerned with physical assets, we must concentrate on the expenditure side or debit side of the capital account which shows how the financial capital was spent on promoting and obtaining authorization, on the acquisition of land, on constructing, and on equipping the railway, under the broad headings of lines open for traffic, lines in course of construction, and working stock. Further detail is shown in two other statements — details of capital expenditure for half year ending, and return of working stock (for the half year). The former statement is particularly valuable in that it shows capital expenditure further broken down into land and compensation, construction of way and stations, and law and parliamentary charges. Thus, the expenditure side of the capital account and the two statements are the first source for data on capital formation.

The balance on the capital account, and it is normally a credit balance, is transferred to the general balance sheet which summarizes the short-term liabilities and assets. Thus in the double-account system, the items found in the conventional balance sheet are presented in two accounts, the capital account and the balance sheet; as Pollins neatly puts it, 'one dealing with fixed capital and the other with circulating capital'.[31] The balance sheet of the double-account system, is therefore of no use to us.

It is otherwise with the expenditure side of the revenue account. On the face of it, the items here are what we would expect to be charged against revenue, but the first three items — maintenance of way, works and stations, locomotive power, and carriage and wagon repairs require further examination. Details of these are contained respectively in three abstracts (A, B and C). In addition to the conventional charges for repairs and maintenance, these contain charges for complete renewals and repairs and partial renewals. This is an essential feature of the double-account system.

Leaving aside for a moment the issue as to whether or not repairs and maintenance are a component of capital formation, any estimate of capital formation must be based not only on the relevant items in the capital account but also on the entries for complete and arguably partial renewals shown in the revenue account. This follows from the layout and the functions of the three accounts discussed above.

The principle underlying the practice of the double-account system in this regard is that the capital account records the capital subscribed to establish and equip the concern and shows how most of it is transformed into the long-life revenue-earning assets required. The duty of the company in this connection is to maintain these assets at their full revenue-earning capacity and this is a proper charge against revenue, not only in respect of repairs and maintenance, but also for renewals, both partial and complete. Assets shown in the capital account are added to only when expansion or improvement take place, or are subtracted from when assets are displaced and are not replaced. In no way are they written down as they would be in a normal balance sheet. This is because the original authors of the double-account system considered that separate provisions for depreciation were not necessary and that occasional rather than regular (half-yearly) renewal out of revenue would suffice. This judgement was statutorily recognized in a negative way in the 1868 Act form of accounts which made no provision for depreciation funds (but did not forbid them). That the 1911 Act form of accounts required such provision in the general balance sheet for specifically named renewal funds indicated a change of policy, the thinking behind which is worth examining.

If the principles of the double-account system are adhered to, then the assets in the capital account, which are recorded as a total to the end of the previous accounting period and as amounts for the current accounting period, represent the value of net fixed capital formation. Also, the assets in the revenue account (complete and partial renewals), are a measure of the capital wastage replaced and thus represent depreciation. Gross fixed capital formation is a matter of addition of the assets in the two accounts, and is likely to be less inaccurate an estimate than those for its components which depend crucially on proper charging to capital and revenue. Current practice, certainly earlier in the period, would enhance net capital formation and correspondingly reduce replacement. Another factor affecting the accuracy of these estimates is 'betterment', which at its simplest is the difference between the estimated replacement cost of a displaced asset and the cost of the new asset. Basically, it is a reflection of technological change, and the problem was recognized by railways from their inception. Strictly speaking, betterment is properly chargeable to capital; in practice its treatment was diverse and customarily often charged to revenue. Here again, practice does not affect gross capital formation but may mis-state the net figure and depreciation.

If betterment was early recognized and a matter of discussion, depreciation was early recognized and a matter of controversy.[32] The issues involved do not directly affect the procedures we have adopted, but a knowledge of these issues does lend support to our treatment. Clearly, whether or not assets wear out in use was not at stake. The argument was about how to provide the funds required to make good that wear and tear. Central to the issue was whether to establish separate depreciation accounts, thus making renewal a regular charge or simply to meet the payments when the occasion required. The latter position is implied in the double-account system and the most forceful argument for it in practice has been supplied by Price Williams. 'There is no need, any more than there is in the analogous case of the railway, for the provision of sinking funds either for the recouping of the capital invested in those undertakings (waterworks), or for the renewal of the operating works and plant which have become worn out'.[33] Price Williams's case is based not only on his knowledge of public utilities in general and waterworks in particular, but on very detailed data on locomotive stock of the London and North Western Railway over a thirty-year period and on the data for a number of railways over a shorter period. Notwithstanding this the case is confounded by the fact that many railways did keep depreciation accounts, although the practice was far from uniform or universal.

The issue is essentially financial rather than economic and we do not believe that its resolution materially affects our procedures. Occasional charging of renewals results in an uneven annual charge to revenue and a time-lag between revenue earned and the charge. When the undertaking is approaching or at maximum development, the charge for renewals is fairly regular from year to year and cannot give rise to real complaint, unlike the company in the course of development where the time-lag assumes much greater importance. The purpose of depreciation accounts is to reserve funds from current revenue at regular (half-yearly) intervals, for renewals made in the future. Thus the controversy is about the balancing of charges to revenue over time and does not affect our problem. The double-account system records when the renewals are made and, if partial renewals are included, probably gives a better indication of the course of wear and tear than any estimates based on depreciation accounts which for the most part are operated on principles more akin to the amortization of a debt. The 1911 Act's requirement to provide renewal funds was recognition of a change in practice which had become widespread and was considered desirable, and the use of the term 'renewal' rather than the customary 'depreciation' was a reflection of the growing influence of rising costs in shifting the emphasis from original to replacement costs.

Fixed capital formation is not an entirely unambiguous concept and in making the estimates there are two acceptable procedures open to us. The first is to add to the expenditure on assets in the capital account, the expenditure in the revenue account in respect of new (replacement) assets. This gives us a measure of the expenditure incurred in creating assets, whether net additions to the stock or replacement. It is a minimum concept of gross fixed capital formation since it confines itself to the cost of creating assets both as additions and replacement, and excludes repairs and maintenance. Is this an entirely satisfactory concept of gross fixed capital formation? It is essentially the procedure used in the United Kingdom national accounts and in those of many other countries. It is also the basis on which Mitchell worked.[34] The justification for its adoption in the United Kingdom is that it 'has the advantage of conforming more closely to accounting definitions of capital expenditure; but that it has the admitted disadvantage that the difficulties of distinguishing in practice between ordinary maintenance and improvement, render the definition of capital expenditure somewhat imprecise'.[35]

This clearly indicates that the other procedure is equally worthy of consideration, namely that gross fixed capital formation is not merely the cost of acquiring new assets, both as net additions and complete renewals, but also the cost of maintaining the existing assets at a proper level of revenue-earning capacity. Thus on this basis, gross fixed capital formation would be the total expenditure on assets in the capital account, plus the total amount for repairs and maintenance charged to the revenue account, whether in respect of complete renewals or merely for the renewal of parts, or repairs. This is a maximum concept which in our view is more correct. Conceptually there is no difference between the total replacement of a worn-out asset and the replacement of a worn-out part. Both actions have precisely the same objective, that of maintaining an asset in full working order and therefore able to provide its revenue-earning service. This implies the not exceptional proposition that capital formation is a continuous process throughout the life of an asset and is not confined to the cost of initial acquisition.

That this is in line with the physical behaviour of assets, particularly long-lasting ones, can be seen from Price Williams.[36] The thirty-year life of a locomotive is basically determined by the durability of the main frames, the longest-lasting major part of the structure. Most of the other parts of the machine, major and minor, require to be replaced at least once and in some cases several times over, if the life of the machine is to be sustained. A similar pattern is indicated by the studies of builders' mechanical plant by the Building Research Station.[37]

We shall therefore include the full amount of expenditure on repairs and maintenance in our calculation of gross fixed capital formation as we consider this more realistic and conceptually more correct. There are precedents and justification for this. Until 1951 current maintenance on buildings and works was included in gross fixed capital formation in all UK national income publications and it is still the practice in the Scandinavian countries. Further a full allowance for repairs and maintenance is included both by Cairncross and Kenwood in their series.[38] There is also a practical advantage — an area of uncertain estimation becomes one of more accurate calculation. Until the 1911 Act, railway companies were not obliged to distinguish in their published accounts, between complete renewals on the one hand, and repairs and partial renewals on the other. In practice, few of them did before 1913 and even where they did, they did not always consistently do so. Thus expenditure on complete renewals prior to 1913 has to be estimated, and Mitchell who does so, clearly recognizes that the margin of error may be quite wide. This difficulty resolves itself by including all repairs and maintenance as a part of gross fixed capital formation.

It is clear from the foregoing that if a series of net fixed capital formation is required, expenditure on the capital account will give us this, provided the principles of the double-account system have been properly adhered to, in particular if a proper allocation in respect of betterment has been made and if repairs and renewals have been sufficient to maintain capital intact. These are big ifs and it is clear that railway accounting practice has fallen from the ideal in this respect. Nevertheless, it is our view that the capital account provides an estimate of net fixed capital formation as accurate as by any other method. On the basis of the general principles outlined above, the series is built up by abstracting from the accounts of the 42 companies, figures, in accordance with the following fairly broad categories — way and works, working stock, docks, land. The total expenditure half-yearly on these items as recorded in the capital account is a measure of net fixed capital formation; the revenue account, recording complete renewals and repairs and partial renewals, measures the maintenance of capital intact; the sum of the two is gross fixed capital formation.

Further disaggregation of the categories may for certain purposes be considered useful. It may, for example, be important to identify expenditure on permanent way as distinct from other works which embrace a considerable range of assets. Likewise between locomotive power and the several kinds of rolling stock. Unfortunately the wealth of detail made obligatory by the 1911 Act is generally absent before 1913, and a breakdown further than has been given would present serious difficulties.

There seems to be some uncertainty about land as an element of gross fixed capital formation. It is excluded by Cairncross and Kenwood, but included by Mitchell. Certainly, it disappears in the aggregate national accounts since purchases cancel out sales — it is in effect a transfer — although factor incomes stemming from its transfer remain as a positive element. Land does not, however, disappear within a sector of the economy and is thus included, not only because it is an essential prerequisite of way and works, but also because it represents a not inconsiderable investment of capital.[39] It has been calculated as far as possible net of parliamentary costs.

For the most part the compilation of the series in terms of the above categories presents no real difficulty, the categories in almost every case being immediately identifiable in the accounts. In the several instances when they are not, it has been possible to make reasonable estimates based on supplementary sources, as is also the case where certain of the accounts have not survived.

The estimates of some important items encountered difficulties. The figures for docks is one case. While the capital accounts in general clearly specify this asset, the revenue accounts before 1913 in the main do not. In fact, only a partial and incomplete record of dock repairs and maintenance can be identified. Inspection of relevant accounts since 1912 indicates that the amount spent annually on repairs and maintenance is approximately 2 per cent of the aggregate sum in the capital account in respect of docks.[40] Thus the expenditure on dock repairs and maintenance in each year prior to 1913 is estimated to be 2 per cent of the total capital sum expended on docks up to that year. The margin of error is not considered to be unduly wide, taken over a period of time, although this may be otherwise in a given year.

A greater difficulty, with the possibility of much more serious effects on the accuracy of the calculation of capital formation, is encountered in the accounts of the two largest companies in south Wales — the South Wales Railway and the Great Western Railway with which latter company the former was amalgamated in 1863. The fundamental difficulty arises from the fact that the Great Western was basically an English company and prior to 1863 its system was entirely outside south Wales. On its acquisition of the South Wales Railway and the West Midland Railway, it became the largest company with operations in south Wales and retained this position throughout our period by further development and amalgamation. Naturally the accounts are for the whole system and do not give a direct record in themselves of the company's south Wales interest. It was this difficulty which Howells encountered and did not proceed with further.[41]

A not dissimilar difficulty exists in the accounts of the South Wales Railway, which from its inception had a close connection with the Great Western Railway. The Act of Incorporation of the South Wales Railway contains a leasing agreement with the Great Western Railway whereby the latter company provided most of the working stock and operated the former against a payment.[42] The South Wales Railway accounts thus provide directly no adequate record in respect of working stock. Both capital expenditure and repairs and maintenance in respect of these assets have to be estimated.

The leasing agreement obliges the Great Western Railway to provide the following: locomotives, rolling stock except for minerals and similar articles conveyed in large quantities or at special rates, engine drivers and stokers, all other staff necessary to the efficient working of the stock, and all stores and materials incidental to the locomotive department. The expenses of all the above have to be met by the payment to the Great Western Railway, including an allowance for the cost of repairs and maintenance not only of the working stock but also a proportion for workshops. There is also a charge for the interest on the capital so tied up, plus depreciation, where this is not adequately covered by repairs and maintenance. Thus the South Wales Railway accounts record the capital expenditure and repairs and maintenance only of the mineral wagons excepted by the terms of the agreement. To these figures must be added estimates in respect of the Great Western provision of stock based on the annual payments to that company.

The estimates for repairs and maintenance are calculated as follows. It is known that in September 1859 there were 64 locomotives operating the South Wales Railway, and that the average annual expenses for repairs and maintenance per Great Western locomotive was £251.8. Thus the total cost of repairs and renewals for locomotives can be estimated for that year as £251.8 × 64 = £16.1 thousand. The Great Western revenue accounts for the thirteen-and-a-half-year period 31 December 1850 to 31 December 1862, the period stock was supplied, show that the totals spent on repairs and maintenance of locomotives and of carriages and wagons for the whole system were £1,060.0 thousand and £806.1 · thousand respectively.[43] Thus repairs and maintenance to carriages and wagons amounted to 73 per cent of locomotive repairs. Applying this percentage to £16.1 thousand, the estimated amount of locomotive repairs and maintenance on the South Wales Railway in 1859, gives a figure of £11.8 thousand for repairs and maintenance to carriages and wagons in that year. The total paid in 1859 to the Great Western Railway for the services rendered is shown in the South Wales Railway accounts as £109.1 thousand. Thus repairs and maintenance to locomotives and to carriages and wagons are 15 per cent and 10 per cent respectively of that total. Assuming that these percentages remain constant throughout the period in question, expenditure on repairs and maintenance is 15 per cent and 10 per cent of the annual payment to the Great Western Railway.

The amount of capital expenditure on working stock has now been estimated. The first supply of this in 1850 is known to be valued at £76.0 thousand.[44] By 1853, the first year in which a regular payment is recorded, the cumulative value of the stock supplied is assumed to have risen to £100.0 thousand, bearing in mind the further developments of the line. In that year the calculated expenditure on repairs and maintenance is £15.4 thousand. If it is assumed that the proportion between the two remains stable, which is not unreasonable, it is possible to calculate the cumulative totals and therefore the annual totals of capital expenditure for subsequent years on the basis of the figures for repairs and maintenance in those years.

Thus estimates of the capital expenditure and repairs and maintenance of working stock provided by the Great Western Railway are produced, to which are added the known figures for the stock purchased by the South Wales Railway. It is agreed that the above is a somewhat elaborate procedure based on few known facts and a number of assumptions, but it is considered that the results which cover a relatively short period of time are satisfactory.

The greatest difficulty is encountered with the Great Western Railway, which after the middle of 1863 became the greatest single railway enterprise in south Wales. The effect of the amalgamation of the South Wales Railway was that separate accounts of that company ceased to be published, as was the case with subsequent amalgamations with other companies in south Wales. The problem therefore is to obtain from the records of the whole Great Western system a measure of the capital formation of that part located in south Wales.

Fortunately the capital account offers some assistance. The abstract of the capital account itemizes, in considerable detail, expenditure on way and works and land, both in terms of type of asset and geographical location. In some cases expenditure in south Wales can be unambiguously identified. In other cases it cannot, several items located both within and outside south Wales being grouped together under one total expenditure. An abstract of the accounts was prepared, distinguishing between south Wales and common expenditures. The question of the allocation of the common expenditure proper to south Wales has been settled by applying to the annual total, the annual proportion of Great Western route mileage in south Wales to the total route mileage of the whole system.[45] Two major items of construction are given specialized treatment. These are the Worcester, Hereford and Aberdare extension, and the Severn Tunnel Railway. In each case, 50 per cent of the total expenditure is allocated to south Wales. In this way an estimate has been made of the capital expenditure on way and works and land by the Great Western Railway in south Wales since 1863. The capital expenditure on working stock and repairs, and maintenance expenditure on way and works and working stock have been derived by again applying to the relevant annual totals, the annual proportion of Great Western route-mileage in south Wales to the total route-mileage of the whole system. The above procedures are necessarily unsatisfactory, which is particularly unfortunate since the Great Western Railway may well have been responsible for anything between 25 and 50 per cent of the capital expenditure by railways in south Wales in any year. They do, however, provide a plausible estimate not previously available and are based on the only information at present available. It is recognized that route-mileage is not the most refined of indicators, although it is certainly more relevant to way and works than working stock. However, unless further research can reveal how much of the total stock was located in south Wales or provide some other indirect method of calculation, route-mileage must be used in this case also.

The purpose of this paper has been to make available two series on capital formation, one gross, one net, by railways in south Wales. No attempt has been made to place these within the wider context of the south Wales economy. They do, however, constitute the first net figures for railway capital formation over a long period, the first published series for south Wales and the second regional series. Because of the regional character of the series, much more detail has been given of the construction of the indexes and of the accounting records on which they are mainly based. The work has suggested further lines of investigation which are being currently undertaken: a comparison with other published series, and an extension of the scope of the enquiry to include not only private traders' investment in railway wagons but also in private or industrial railways. For south Wales, these last two were particularly significant.

Appendix I
Fixed Capital Formation by Railways in South Wales, 1836–1913

£'000

Year	Way and Works		Working Stock		Docks		Land	Fixed Capital Formation	
	C.E.	R. and M.	C.E.	R. and M.	C.E.	R. and M.		Net	Gross
1836	1.9	—	—	—	—	—	—	1.9	1.9
1837	14.3	—	—	—	—	—	1.0	15.3	15.3
1838	50.6	—	—	—	—	—	39.6	90.2	90.2
1839	128.4	—	9.9	—	—	—	17.8	146.2	146.2
1840	109.9	—	15.0	—	—	—	4.8	124.6	124.6
1841	92.4	0.6	2.7	0.6	—	—	—	107.4	108.6
1842	22.4	2.5	1.9	2.0	—	—	0.9	26.0	30.5
1843	12.0	2.9	3.8	1.7	—	—	0.6	14.5	19.1
1844	1.4	3.2	13.5	2.5	—	—	0.5	5.7	11.4
1845	57.1	3.3	28.6	2.9	—	—	6.6	77.2	83.4
1846	208.2	2.6	38.7	3.6	—	—	76.6	313.4	319.6
1847	495.2	3.3	22.4	3.4	—	—	127.7	661.6	668.3
1848	607.2	5.3	32.9	5.6	0.9	—	70.7	701.2	712.1
1849	611.8	6.7	95.0	7.0	0.9	—	109.2	754.8	768.5
1850	473.7	7.8	20.4	8.1	0.2	—	30.7	599.6	615.5
1851	330.4	13.4	53.9	10.6	—	—	53.7	404.5	428.5
1852	384.4	22.1		8.3	0.3	—	66.8	505.4	535.8

Year									
1853	370.4	38.6	102.5	31.2	—	—	45.7	518.6	588.4
1854	429.7	52.5	144.4	41.3	—	—	27.5	601.6	695.4
1855	257.3	64.5	68.4	45.9	—	—	24.0	349.7	460.1
1856	256.9	74.8	52.1	54.8	—	—	45.2	354.2	483.8
1857	387.4	96.2	90.1	67.8	27.7	0.6	102.1	607.3	771.9
1858	244.3	85.0	48.9	87.5	70.6	2.0	24.5	388.3	562.8
1859	412.0	91.8	51.3	84.9	52.8	3.0	56.2	572.3	752.0
1860	381.2	94.1	40.1	91.2	46.3	4.0	35.0	502.6	691.9
1861	511.0	103.9	29.3	85.2	37.0	4.8	28.2	605.5	799.4
1862	431.9	62.1	39.0	66.8	55.7	5.8	28.0	554.6	689.3
1863	720.3	94.7	29.2	97.1	60.6	7.0	201.1	1011.2	1210.0
1864	1368.9	128.0	49.1	134.4	89.4	8.8	26.6	1534.0	1805.2
1865	1288.3	123.8	120.2	129.9	76.5	10.4	23.2	1508.2	1772.3
1866	869.2	142.6	137.9	138.1	114.4	12.6	43.9	1165.4	1458.7
1867	531.5	144.1	92.6	125.4	61.6	13.8	27.9	713.6	996.9
1868	525.2	144.3	59.3	146.1	93.2	15.8	57.9	735.6	1041.8
1869	192.3	169.3	61.6	161.7	65.0	17.0	34.0	352.9	700.9
1870	273.8	173.3	60.4	161.2	47.7	18.0	21.7	403.6	756.1
1871	236.1	172.9	82.3	157.9	45.8	19.0	62.5	426.7	776.5
1872	242.2	189.2	119.1	169.4	44.7	19.8	16.0	422.0	800.4
1873	290.8	217.8	125.1	189.7	44.0	20.8	23.2	483.1	911.4
1874	306.4	242.9	132.9	195.8	42.8	21.6	31.6	513.7	974.0
1875	370.2	295.9	95.2	194.2	105.9	23.8	34.6	605.9	1119.8
1876	439.5	274.0	33.6	187.3	53.0	24.8	47.1	573.2	1059.3
1877	401.8	329.0	26.3	195.4	—	24.8	45.4	473.5	1022.7
1878	233.1	300.5	28.3	188.4	—	24.8	17.7	279.1	792.8
1879	166.0	280.2	14.0	189.8	0.2	24.8	41.1	221.3	716.1

Appendix I — continued

Year	Way and Works		Working Stock		Docks		Land	Fixed Capital Formation	
	C.E.	R. and M.	C.E.	R. and M.	C.E.	R. and M.		Net	Gross
1880	258.8	262.5	31.6	220.4	—	24.8	21.4	311.8	819.5
1881	224.8	275.9	45.1	231.8	10.8	25.0	12.4	293.1	825.8
1882	289.4	298.6	19.1	241.6	68.3	26.4	27.6	404.4	971.0
1883	452.7	299.7	49.9	253.3	66.4	27.8	21.3	590.3	1171.1
1884	727.9	287.6	101.2	257.8	44.3	28.6	43.5	916.9	1490.9
1885	500.9	269.2	96.2	246.0	26.3	29.2	40.9	664.3	1208.7
1886	581.5	255.7	26.4	243.5	1.6	29.2	45.5	655.0	1183.4
1887	713.8	266.6	8.8	252.0	38.5	30.0	74.0	835.1	1383.7
1888	816.6	275.3	63.2	259.5	18.2	30.4	25.2	923.2	1488.4
1889	534.4	285.4	152.0	259.2	42.3	31.2	31.3	760.0	1335.8
1890	378.6	298.1	178.8	259.4	66.4	32.6	60.7	684.5	1274.6
1891	257.7	305.4	157.1	281.8	136.8	35.2	37.1	588.7	1211.1
1892	222.9	309.2	76.1	285.7	129.9	38.0	41.9	470.8	1103.7
1893	174.3	314,5	42.8	292.3	126.3	40.6	34.1	377.5	1024.9
1894	240.9	334.6	74.8	300.3	114.3	42.8	94.8	524.8	1202.5
1895	374.7	334.0	127.8	303.4	183.3	46.4	143.5	829.3	1513.1
1896	688.0	345.6	131.6	328.3	415.1	54.8	116.1	1350.8	2079.5
1897	534.3	389.4	200.6	338.6	709.7	69.0	126.4	1571.0	2368.0
1898	600.5	404.2	144.9	288.6	393.1	76.8	131.9	1270.4	2040.0
1899	747.6	453.6	151.7	401.6	409.0	85.0	106.6	1414.9	2355.1

Year									
1900	484.3	476.1	279.6	424.5	411.0	93.2	92.8	1267.7	2261.5
1901	455.5	592.3	82.5	459.2	370.6	100.6	95.9	1004.5	2156.6
1902	278.5	490.4	106.9	473.3	329.8	107.2	82.7	797.9	1868.8
1903	290.1	485.8	70.7	481.9	242.9	112.0	47.0	650.7	1730.4
1904	308.6	493.8	96.3	499.2	288.4	117.8	60.5	753.8	1864.6
1905	228.8	482.1	154.4	501.9	336.5	124.6	87.7	807.4	1916.0
1906	319.5	533.3	106.1	572.4	359.3	131.8	42.5	827.4	2064.9
1907	306.1	559.0	141.6	611.4	515.6	142.2	79.3	1042.6	2355.2
1908	324.8	569.9	109.8	645.8	424.1	150.6	122.5	981.2	2347.5
1909	487.7	565.8	20.9	629.5	267.6	156.0	47.9	824.1	2175.4
1910	413.1	565.2	14.0	619.3	214.5	160.4	42.3	683.9	2028.8
1911	322.0	570.5	5.1	618.5	152.2	163.4	27.2	506.5	1858.9
1912	275.0	567.5	134.4	617.5	170.8	166.8	33.4	613.6	1965.4
1913	336.5	634.6	184.8	617.3	291.1	172.6	86.6	899.0	2323.5

Appendix 2
Railway Companies in South Wales 1830–1914

  1. Aberavon Harbour Company
  2. Aberdare Railway Company
  3. Aberdare Valley Railway Company
*4. Alexandra (Newport and South Wales) Docks and Railway Company
*5. Barry Railway Company
*6. Brecon and Merthyr Tydfil Junction Railway Company
  7. Bridgend Railway Company
  8. Bristol and South Wales Union Railway Company
  9. Briton Ferry Dock and Railway Company
 10. Brynmawr and Blaenavon Railway Company
 11. Brynmawr and Western Valleys Railway Company
*12. Burry Port and Gwendraeth Valley Railway Company
 13. Burry Port and North Western Junction Railway Company
 14. Cardiff Docks and Railways Company
*15. Cardiff and Ogmore Valley Railway Company
*16. Cardiff, Penarth and Barry Junction Railway Company
*17. Cardiff Railway Company
*18. Carmarthen and Cardigan Railway Company
 19. Carmarthenshire Railway Company
 20. Central Wales and Carmarthen Junction Railway Company
*21. Coleford Monmouth Usk and Pontypool Railway Company
*22. Cowbridge and Aberthaw Railway Company
*23. Cowbridge Railway Company
*24. Dare Valley Railway Company
*25. Duffryn Llynvi and Porthcawl Railway Company
 26. Dulas Valley Mineral Railway Company
*27. East Usk Railway Company
*28. Ely and Clydach Valleys Railway Company
 29. Ely Tidal Harbour and Railway Company
*30. Ely Valley Railway Company
 31. Ely Valley Extension Railway Company
 32. Fishguard Bay Railway and Pier Company
 33. Fishguard and Rosslare Railways and Harbour Company
 34. Great Western and Port Talbot Railways and Dock Companies
*35. Great Western Railway Company
 36. Great Western and Rhondda and Swansea Bay Railway Companies
 37. Great Western and Rhymney Railway Companies
 38. Grosmont Railway Company
*39. Gwendraeth Valleys Railway Company

40. Hereford Hay and Brecon Railway Company
41. Kidwelly and Burry Port Railway Company
42. Llanelly and Mynydd Mawr Railway Company
*43. Llanelly Railway and Dock Company
44. Llangammarch and Neath and Brecon Junction Railway Company
*45. Llantrisant and Taff Vale Junction Railway Company
46. Llynvi and Ogmore and Great Western Railway Joint Committee
*47. Llynvi and Ogmore Railway Company
*48. Llynvi Valley Railway Company
49. London and North Western and Brecon and Merthyr Joint Committee
50. London and North Western Railway Company
51. London and North Western and Rhymney Railways Joint Committee
52. Maenclochog Railway Company
53. Manchester and Milford and Pembroke and Tenby Joint Committee
54. Manchester and Milford Railway Company
55. Merthyr Tredegar and Abergavenny Railway Company
56. Midland Railway Company
57. Milford Haven Dock and Railway Company
58. Milford Haven Railway and Estate Company
59. Milford Railway Company
60. Monmouth and Hereford Railway
61. Monmouth Railway Company
*62. Monmouthshire Railway and Canal Company
63. Monmouthshire Railway and Canal and Great Western Railway Companies Consultative Committee
64. Mumbles Pier and Railway Company
65. Narberth Road and Maenclochog Railway Company
*66. Neath and Brecon Railway Company
67. Neath Pontardawe and Bryn-aman Railway Company
68. Newport Abergavenny and Hereford Railway Company
69. Newport and Pontypool Railway Company
70. Newport and Sirhowy Railway Company
71. Newport Street Joint Committee
72. North Pembrokeshire and Fishguard Railway Company
*73. Ogmore Valley Railway Company
74. Oystermouth Railway Company
*75. Pembroke and Tenby Railway Company
*76. Penarth Extension Railway Company
*77. Penarth Harbour Dock and Railway Company
78. Penarth Harbour Dock and Railway and Taff Vale Railway Joint Committee
79. Penarth Sully and Barry Railway Company
*80. Pontypool, Caerleon and Newport Railway Company

Appendix 2 — continued

*81. Pontypridd Caerphilly and Newport Railway Company
 82. Port Talbot Company
*83. Port Talbot Railway and Docks Company
*84. Rhondda and Swansea Bay Railway Company
*85. Rhondda Valley and Hirwain Junction Railway Company
*86. Rhymney Railway Company
 87. Rosebush and Fishguard Railway Company
 88. Ross and Monmouth Railway Company
 89. Rumney Railway Company
 90. Severn Tunnel Railway Company
*91. Sirhowy Railway Company
*92. South Wales Mineral Railway Company
*93. South Wales Railway Company
 94. Swansea and Carmarthen Junction Railway Company
 95. Swansea and Mumbles Railway Company
 96. Swansea and Neath Railway Company
 97. Swansea Vale and Neath and Brecon Junction Railway
 98. Swansea Vale Railway Company
 99. Swansea Valley Railway Company
*100. Taff Vale Railway Company
*101. Treferig Valley Railway Company
 102. Usk and Towy Railway Company
 103. Usk Valley Railway Company
*104. Vale of Glamorgan Railway Company
*105. Vale of Neath Railway Company
 106. West Midland Railway
*107. Whitland and Cardigan Railway Company
 108. Whitland and Taff Vale Railway
 109. Wye Valley Railway Company

*Companies whose accounts have survived.

Fixed Capital Formation in the Ports of the South Wales Coalfield, 1850–1913

A.G. KENWOOD

During the second half of the nineteenth century dock and harbour construction in south Wales was dominated by the shipping needs of a rapidly expanding coal export trade. Before 1850, the construction of canals and tram-roads had supported a steady expansion of the coastwise trade in coal, and with the coming of the railways in the 1840s there was also a rapid acceleration in the region's coal export trade. It was largely this growth in coal shipments from south Wales that had brought into being the port facilities which were to develop so rapidly after 1850.[1] This subsequent rapid expansion of regional port facilities was based on two interdependent developments: the spread of a railway network throughout the south Wales coalfield and the phenomenal growth of the steam-coal trade which eventually made south Wales the greatest coal-exporting region in the world.

Railway companies were largely responsible for the development of dock facilities in south Wales after 1880. Other major contributors included the trustees of the Marquis of Bute, and, after 1886, the Bute Docks Company, both of which bodies were responsible for considerably expanding the dock facilities at Cardiff originally begun in 1839 by the second Marquis of Bute. Still later, in 1897, the docks became the property of the Cardiff Railway Company. In Newport too, early dock construction was the work of private dock companies, and not until the 1880s did these works and their future expansion become the responsibility of a dock and railway company. Among the major south Wales ports, only in Swansea did the provision of dock facilities remain throughout our period the sole responsibility of an undertaking other than a railway company. Here a public harbour trust was formed in 1854 to take over control of the dock and harbour from the town council.[2] By the middle of the nineteenth century harbour commissions with powers to improve and maintain local harbour facilities as well as to provide dock facilities where needed but not already provided by private dock or railway companies, were in existence in Llanelli, Neath and Newport.

II

The construction of additional dock and harbour facilities in south Wales after 1850 involved considerable capital expenditures of an income-generating kind, namely expenditures which created employment not only within the construction undertakings themselves, but also in the large number of industries concerned with supplying the dock and harbour authorities with materials and equipment.[3] Moreover, once the new facilities were created, their operation and upkeep involved a substantial increase in the workforce, for despite some increase in the use of mechanical power, dock operations remained a relatively labour-intensive activity.[4] The estimates of fixed capital formation in the table in the Appendix refer to the total of expenditures on the 'real' capital which goes to make up the physical plant of docks and harbours, that is, works, quays, storage facilities, and machinery. These estimates are in *current* prices. Annual estimates of expenditure on repairs and renewals by the various dock and harbour authorities are also included in the table, and these estimates are combined with the capital expenditure figures to make up annual estimates of gross fixed capital formation in the south Wales ports during the second half of the nineteenth century.

The annual estimates of gross capital formation for the south Wales ports have been plotted in Figure 1. The series exhibits four substantial waves of investment in dock and harbour construction averaging sixteen years from trough to trough and around seventeen years duration from peak to peak.[5] The first wave of investment rose from a low point in the mid 1840s to a peak in 1859 before declining sharply to a new low in 1861. The second long fluctuation covered the period 1861 to 1878, with the peak in investment activity coming in 1874. The third investment fluctuation had troughs in 1877 and 1892 and a peak in 1888; and the fourth, troughs in 1892 and 1911 and a peak in 1907. One other feature of investment activity in dock and harbour construction in south Wales after 1850 needs to be noted, and that is the strong upward trend imparted to the series by the region's rapidly expanding demand for shipping facilities. This is reflected in the relatively short-lived downswing in investment activity associated with each of the four long fluctuations described above. Thus over the four fluctuations in gross fixed capital formation in docks and harbours the upswing from trough to peak averaged thirteen years whereas the downswings from peak to trough average only four years.

During the first two investment fluctuations dock construction continued to be concentrated mainly in Cardiff and its environs, and in Newport.[6] In Cardiff, the Bute East dock was opened in stages between 1855 and 1859, and the Roath basin, which was started in 1868, was opened to traffic in July 1874.[7] Four years later a timber pond which extended over six acres was built between the Bute East and West docks to cater for the rapidly growing imports of timber. At Penarth, the Ely tidal harbour was opened in 1859, and a dock in June 1865. Parliamentary powers to extend the Town dock at Newport to 12 acres were obtained in 1854 and these works were completed and opened early in 1858. In Swansea, a harbour trust was incorporated in 1854 to take over control of the local shipping facilities from the town council, including the North dock of 16½ acres which was opened in the same year. From the outset, the Harbour Trust had to face the possible threat of competition from a private company that had been set up in the early 1850s to construct another dock in Swansea, the South dock. The company soon ran into financial difficulties however, and its works were taken over by the Harbour Trust in 1857 and completed and opened to traffic in 1859.

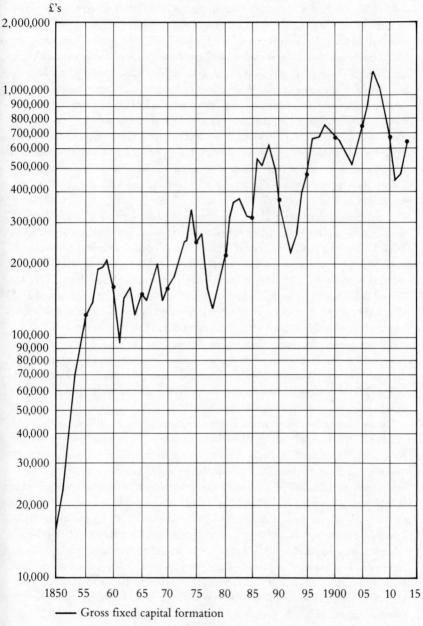

Figure 1
Gross fixed capital formation in docks and
harbours: south Wales, 1850–1913

Dock construction was also under way in the late 1850s in Briton Ferry, where a dock of about 14 acres was opened in 1861. In the 1860s interest in the harbour at Porthcawl was revived with the construction of the Llynvi Valley and Ogmore railways which linked the collieries of those two valleys with the port. A dock of 7 acres was built at the northern end of the existing tidal basin at a cost of £250,000 and opened for traffic on 22 July 1867.[8] Elsewhere in south Wales the port improvements were less striking. In Neath, the harbour commissioners were given powers in 1874 to divert the river by constructing a navigable cut, and then to convert the river into a floating dock by the building of a lock entrance and basin. These works however, with the exception of the navigable cut, were never completed. At Port Talbot, where a dock had been opened in 1837, the only works of any significance to be undertaken before the formation of the Port Talbot Railway and Dock Company in 1894 involved the lengthening of the lock entrance in 1874.

In the 1880s dock construction became common in the major ports of south Wales. In the Cardiff district the Penarth dock extension was opened in 1884 and the Roath dock in 1887. These efforts proved insufficient to meet the needs of the expanding local coal trade however, and a number of colliery owners, driven to desperation by the inadequate shipping facilities at Cardiff, undertook to build a new dock at nearby Barry. This was opened in 1889. Further west, the East, or Prince of Wales dock, with an area of 27½ acres had been opened in Swansea in 1881. It was built largely in connection with the export of tinplate, although the newly-built Rhondda and Swansea Bay coal railway also had its terminus at the dock. Competition between the two rival dock companies in Newport was finally removed with their amalgamation in 1882 under the name of the Alexandra (Newport and South Wales) Docks and Railway Company. This merger was followed by the construction of a dock extension of 20 acres and a new entrance lock, both of which were opened to traffic on the 6 June 1893.

During the fourth long boom in port investment activities in south Wales covering the years 1892 to 1911, the Prince of Wales dock in Swansea was extended in 1898, and the King's dock opened in 1909. In Cardiff, where the Cardiff Railway Company had taken over the docks from the Bute Dock Company, the new Queen Alexandra dock, 52 acres in area, was opened in 1907. An increase in the district's dock facilities had occurred earlier in 1898 with the opening of the Barry No. 2 dock with an area of 34 acres, and fitted out on the north side for the coal export trade and on the south side for the import trade. Powers to extend the docks at Newport were obtained in 1904 and 1906. The south dock extension was completed in 1907, and the remaining 28 acres of new dock area plus an entrance lock was opened in 1914. In Llanelli the harbour commissioners, under threat from the expansion of dock facilities occurring elsewhere along the south Wales coast, were finally moved to action in 1896 when an Act was obtained to construct the Commissioners', or North, dock which was opened to traffic in 1903. At Port Talbot, the Port Talbot Dock and Railway Company set about extending the water area of the dock and a new lock was constructed and brought into use in 1898.

III

The growing volume of investment in the port facilities of south Wales was largely a consequence of the region's rapidly expanding coal export trade, but technological changes in shipbuilding, including the changeover from sail to steam, and the continuing increase in the size and number of steamships, meant that dock entrances had to be enlarged and the size of the docks themselves increased or new, larger docks built. The need to speed up the turn-round of vessels — a process which depended on the length of quays available, the power and number of mechanical appliances in use, and the facilities for removing cargoes once they were landed — made improvements in these aspects of port organization imperative. Of particular importance in this respect was the use of hydraulic power to work dock plant and machinery. This method of working the intermittent operations characteristic of docks, such as the opening and closing of dock and sluice gates, turning swing-bridges and capstans, and working cranes and lifts, proved to be far more economical than steam. By 1885 it had been adopted at most of the important English and Welsh ports.[9]

Table 1
Gross capital formation, the value of exports and total trade, and coal exports: south Wales ports, 1851–1915. Overlapping decade averages

Overlapping Decades	Gross Capital Formation 000s		Value of Exports m.		Value of Total Trade m.		Foreign Exports of Coal m. tons	
	Volume	Change in Col. (1)	Volume	Change in Col. (3)	Volume	Change in Col. (5)	Volume	Change in Col. (7)
1851–60	126.7	—	—	—	—	—	1.1	—
1856–65	159.3	32.6	3.4[a]	—	—	—	1.9	0.8
1861–70	151.1	– 8.2	4.3	0.9	—	—	2.6	0.7
1866–75	206.4	55.3	6.2	1.9	—	—	3.4	0.8
1871–80	219.2	12.8	6.2	0.0	10.8[b]	—	4.7	1.3
1876–85	263.0	43.8	6.6	0.4	11.4	0.6	7.3	2.6
1881–90	426.8	163.8	9.6	3.0	14.6	3.2	10.1	2.8
1886–95	423.0	– 3.8	11.9	2.3	17.3	2.7	12.4	2.3
1891–1900	512.9	89.9	13.6	1.7	20.2	2.9	14.9	2.5
1896–1905	660.4	147.5	17.3	3.7	26.1	5.9	18.0	3.1
1901–10	785.9	125.5	22.9	5.6	34.2	8.1	22.4	4.4
1906–15[a]	788.1	2.2	27.4	4.5	40.4	6.2	24.9	2.5

[a] Eight year average   [b] Nine year average

Source: Gross capital formation: Table, in Appendix. (see page 126)
  Current value of exports: *Annual Statement of Trade.*
  Current value of total trade: *Annual Statement of Trade.*
  Coal Exports: 1851–73: *Returns in sessional papers annually.* 1874–1913: F.A. Gibson, *A Compilation of Statistics of the Coal Mining Industry of the United Kingdom, the various coalfields thereof, and the Principal Foreign Countries of the World* (Cardiff, 1922), table, p. 82.

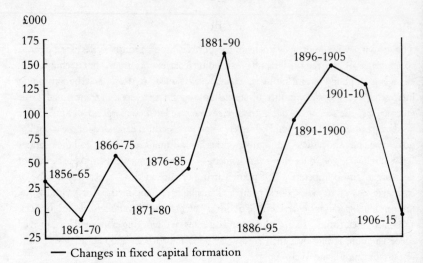

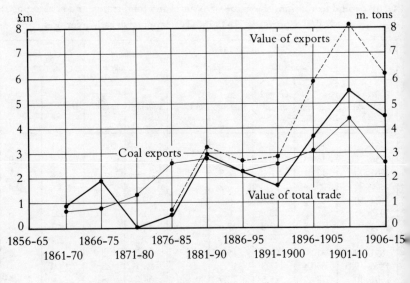

Figure 2
Changes in fixed capital formation, value of exports and total trade, and coal exports: south Wales ports, 1851–1915. Overlapping decade averages.

Table 1 and Figure 2 illustrate the close relationship between changes in the volume of overseas trade passing through the south Wales ports and changes in the level of capital expenditures in those ports' facilities. The changes are described by decade averages, overlapping by five years. The decade is employed in order to eliminate short-term movements associated with business cycles or other transient disturbances.[10] From an examination of the series plotted in Figure 2 it is obvious that the long swings in the growth of overseas trade synchronize well with the changes in the level of fixed capital formation in docks and harbours. Thus as the growth in the volume of south Wales's overseas trade accelerates or retards, so does the increase in the volume of the region's fixed capital formation in docks and harbours.

IV

Taken together the estimates of fixed capital formation in the docks and railways [11] of south Wales, and the housing index for the south Wales coalfield constructed by Hamish Richards and J. Parry Lewis [12], cover a substantial part of the total fixed capital formation undertaken in south Wales during the second half of the nineteenth century. According to Feinstein's estimates of gross fixed capital formation, for example, these three types of construction activity accounted for around 46 per cent of total gross fixed capital formation in the British Isles in the period 1861–65; 38 per cent in 1881–85; and 29 per cent during the years 1901–5.[13] In Figure 3 (page 124) therefore we have plotted these three sets of data, using the net capital expenditure estimates for docks and railways because the housing index refers to new housebuilding only.[14]

Over the period 1860 to 1913 each of the three series exhibits three long fluctuations in investment activity, with capital formation in railways and docks tending to precede that in residential building. This relationship is particularly marked in the long swing covering the period of the 1860s and 1870s. Railway investment reached very high levels around the mid 1860s when dock investment and residential building activity were increasing in extent but at relatively low levels. Their peaks in activity during this period were registered around the mid 1870s when there was some slight upsurge of investment in railways though at levels substantially below those reached in the railway boom of the mid-sixties. The period after 1880 and up to the eve of the First World War has been described by Brinley Thomas and others as one in which the south Wales economy became geared almost entirely to the export trade sector of the British economy.[15] In this period, too, an examination of the plotted data in Figure 3 suggests that investment in transport facilities tended to lead the upswings and downswings in residential construction.[16] The relevant major turning-points in the three series are shown in Table 2.

The mechanism relating these three forms of constructional activity is not difficult to envisage. Thus a sustained rise in the export demand for coal would lead eventually to an increased need for additional railway and port facilities, once any excess capacity had been utilized. The resulting burst of constructional activity, added to the expansion of coal output needed to supply the export markets, would create, in turn, an increased demand for labour which would initially be met locally through a reduction in unemployment,

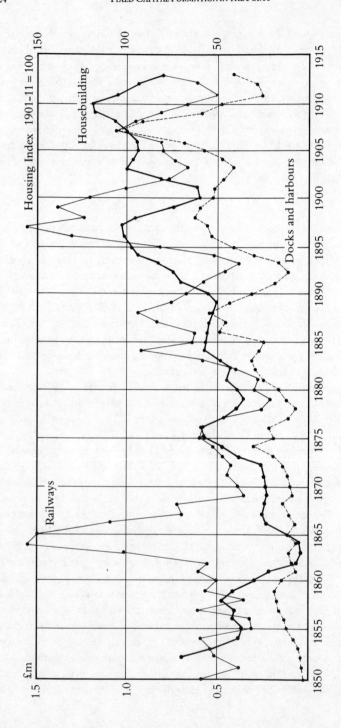

Figure 3
Net fixed capital formation in railways, docks and harbours,
and house-building: south Wales, 1850–1913

Table 2
Major turning points in long fluctuations in construction activity in south Wales, 1850–1913

Sector	Trough	Peak	Trough	Peak	Trough	Peak	Trough
Railways	1858	1864	1879	1888	1893	1899	1911
Docks and Harbours	1861	1874	1878	1888	1892	1907	1911
Housebuilding	1863	1876	1879	1897	1900	1909–10	—

Source: Figure 3

and perhaps through an increase in hours worked. However, if the assumed expansion of export demand continued to generate higher levels of investment activity in docks and railways, then at some stage the labour force in the export economy would be enhanced by migration in response to the new employment opportunities in the region.[17] This migration of labour, moreover, has a special significance for the regional growth process, since it has a much greater impact than the other sources of labour input (the locally unemployed, increased hours, etc.) on household growth in the area. Newly-established households generate demands, not only for housing, but also for general urban services and for the furnishing of new houses. Thus the increase in households typically associated with migration inflow leads to further growth, not only in consumer spending but also in private and public investment, and it is this induced rise in the growth of aggregate demand which tends to sustain and prolong the expansion. Of course, many other factors, not merely the level of investment activity in transport facilities, played a part in determining the demand for housing in the south Wales coalfield, not least the level of incomes of labour, which, in turn, was closely related to the movement in the price of coal.[18] Nevertheless, the rising levels of investment activity in railways and docks obviously played a leading role in generating the growing real incomes necessary to support an expansion of housebuilding activity in the region.

The data in Figure 3 tends to give substance to Brinley Thomas's thesis that after 1880 the Welsh economy became geared largely to the British export sector. But a great deal more research needs to be done before that thesis can be adequately analysed and tested. There is obviously a need for investment series relating to the major industries of south Wales, particularly coal-mining, and there are other forms of capital spending by local authorities, public utility undertakings, shipping companies and so on, which would help considerably in determining the precise pattern of investment activity in south Wales after 1850. Neither should the rest of the Welsh economy be ignored, and the construction of estimates of capital formation in housebuilding for the rest of Wales, and for agriculture throughout Wales would provide the basis for a more thorough-going analysis of the part played by the Welsh economy in the economic growth of Britain during the second half of the nineteenth century.

Appendix

Gross and Net Fixed Capital Formation in Docks and Harbours of South Wales 1850–1913

Year	Net F.C.F.	Reps & Maint.	Gross F.C.F.	Year	Net F.C.F	Reps & Maint.	Gross F.C.F
1850	12.8	3.4	16.2	1882	305.6	55.4	361.0
1851	18.9	3.8	22.7	1883	313.7	57.5	371.2
1852	39.2	3.7	42.9	1884	265.0	56.5	321.5
1853	66.9	5.1	72.0	1885	251.9	58.4	310.3
1854	87.8	5.5	93.3	1886	499.0	58.4	557.4
1855	119.0	6.4	125.4	1887	456.8	62.7	519.5
1856	131.5	8.2	139.7	1888	569.9	63.9	633.8
1857	183.4	10.2	193.6	1889	430.0	67.8	497.8
1858	185.7	10.8	196.5	1890	311.1	69.8	380.9
1859	197.7	11.6	209.3	1891	205.2	73.9	279.1
1860	152.8	14.3	167.1	1892	144.0	78.1	222.1
1861	81.6	15.2	96.8	1893	180.8	85.3	266.1
1862	130.5	17.0	147.5	1894	310.4	84.4	394.8
1863	142.5	19.8	162.3	1895	388.5	90.1	478.6
1864	101.5	23.1	124.6	1896	558.1	102.8	660.9
1865	130.4	25.5	155.9	1897	571.6	99.0	670.6
1866	113.8	29.2	143.0	1898	666.3	95.5	756.8
1867	141.3	30.7	172.0	1899	621.9	103.9	725.8
1868	171.6	34.5	206.1	1900	557.8	116.8	674.6
1869	105.3	36.6	141.9	1901	522.5	122.5	645.0
1870	121.8	39.5	161.3	1902	452.3	130.8	583.1
1871	136.9	42.3	179.2	1903	375.9	140.2	516.1
1872	173.5	44.5	218.0	1904	470.3	146.5	616.8
1873	207.3	43.8	251.1	1905	601.7	152.7	754.4
1874	295.0	46.8	341.8	1906	717.2	155.8	873.0
1875	202.2	47.2	249.4	1907	1063.6	168.9	1232.5
1876	224.0	49.5	273.5	1908	928.0	175.3	1103.3
1877	107.8	50.8	158.6	1909	666.1	180.6	846.7
1878	81.6	49.8	131.4	1910	496.7	191.8	688.5
1879	117.6	51.3	168.9	1911	246.8	196.8	443.6
1880	167.0	52.8	219.8	1912	278.5	196.3	474.8
1881	259.2	55.3	314.5	1913	437.9	204.7	642.6

Sources: The capital formation estimates in the above table are based on financial data
taken from the following sources:-
    (i) Railway company half-annual reports and accounts for the:
        Alexandra (Newport and South Wales) Docks and Railway Company
        Barry Railway Company.
        Briton Ferry Dock and Railway Company
        Burry Port and Gwendraeth Valley Railway Company
        Cardiff Dock and Railway Company
        Duffryn, Llynvi and Porthcawl Railway Company
        Fishguard and Rosslare Railways and Harbours Company
        Llanelly Railway and Dock Company
        Llynvi and Ogmore Railway Company
        Llynvi Valley Railway Company
        Ogmore Valley Railway Company
        Penarth Harbour Dock and Railway Company
        Port Talbot Railway and Dock Company
        Rhondda and Swansea Bay Railway Company
        Taff Vale Railway Company
        Vale of Neath Railway Company
    (ii) Dock Companies: Reports and Accounts for the:
        Alexandra (Newport) Dock Company
        Bute Docks
        Milford Dock Company
        Newport Dock Company
        Swansea Harbour Trust
    (iii) Other Sources:
        (a) Government returns relating to expenditures on docks and harbours:
           A/P, 1876, Vol. LXV; A/P, 1883, Vol. LXII; A/P, 1903, Vol. LXII:
           Local Taxation Returns, Annual, 1881–1914.
        (b) *A History of the Alexandra (Newport) Dock Company from AD1864 to
           AD1877* (1882). This history bears no author's name and was prepared
           for private and confidential circulation.

Investment in Public Health Provision in the Mining Valleys of South Wales, 1860–1914

HAMISH RICHARDS

Introduction

In December 1982 I was looking for a space to park my car in Twynrhodyn, Merthyr Tydfil. Bright Place had no space: neither had Dyke Terrace where I managed to do an eight-point turn to try elsewhere. Eventually I found a spot in Cobden Crescent. It was only when I parked that I realized the significance of the names of the streets that I was driving in. The name Bright Place was not related to the south-facing aspect of the late nineteenth-century houses. Similarly, the name Dyke Terrace had nothing to do with the twenty-foot wall which ran down one side of the street. Of course, if in true Geneva style, they had been called John Bright Place, Richard Cobden Crescent and Dr Thomas J. Dyke Terrace, I would have realized that the early Merthyr Labour councillors had been honouring nineteenth-century social reformers in naming the streets built at the turn of the century. Cobden and Bright, yes. But Dyke, who was Dyke? Perhaps of the three, Dyke was the most relevant to be honoured at that place and time. Dr Dyke probably did more for the social development of Merthyr Tydfil in particular and the south Wales industrial valleys in general than any other person in the nineteenth century. He was a medical officer of health with a bee in his bonnet. In fact, two bees: a pure water supply and an efficient sewerage system. His *Annual Reports* submitted to the Merthyr local authority are models which any self-respecting medical officer of health in any developing part of the world should attempt to emulate. He was concerned not with the eradication of disease but with the prevention of disease. While his report itemizes deaths in the preceding year he uses these data to extol the need for better water and improved sanitation facilities. In these pleas he was ably supported by Mr Samuel Harpar, the surveyor to the Local Board of Health.

In 1852 the average age at death in Merthyr was 17½ years; 527 children out of every 1,000 born died under the age of one in that year, and the overall death rate was 36 per 1,000. In that year, the surveyor submitted a proposal to the Board on 20 September in the form of an estimate for sewers and drainage:

Sewerage	£23,725/ 2/-
Drainage	£9,331/17/-
Total	£33,056/19/-

In the presentation he stated that if charged to the General District Rate and spread over a period of thirty years (it) would require a rate beginning at 6*d*. in the £ and ending with 2*d*. in the £ to liquidate the amount with 5 per cent interest. Consideration was adjourned.

However it was not adjourned for long. Dr Dyke wrote in 1866: 'With the establishment of this Board in 1850 a brighter day dawned: since then gradually but safely various means for the promotion of health have begun: the widespread good which has resulted may be seen in better health, less sickness, longer life . . . What the sanitary results have been may be seen in the following comparisons of facts as they were in 1851/52 and in 1866:

The death rate has diminished from 36 to 25 per 1,000: infant mortality from 527 to 434 per 1,000 live births: the number of persons attaining the age of 70 has increased from 55 to 89 per 1,000 deaths and the average age at death was extended from 17½ to 24½ years.

The Board may congratulate themselves on the success of their endeavours to improve the health and prolong the life of every one of the fifty-four thousand human beings who reside in Merthyr Tydfil'.

Coverage

Although, according to the title, this paper sets out to consider investment in public health provision in the mining valleys of south Wales, both 'public health provision' and 'mining valleys of south Wales' have been defined in a relatively narrow sense: the latter due to the non-availability of data for certain areas and the former to a perhaps misplaced delicacy in wanting to exclude the word 'sewerage' from the title. Public health provision in its broadest sense could include hospital provision and maintenance as well as waterworks provision. But it is only provision for sewerage and draining that will be considered in this paper.

The original intention had been to look at investment in sewerage schemes throughout the south Wales coalfield from Blaenavon in the east to the Gwendraeth valley in the west, but time constraint plus the non-availability of data limited the actual study to certain valleys converging on Cardiff. In fact the data collected relate to the Taff–Cynon–Rhondda valleys including both Cardiff and Barry but excluding Penarth. Data are also available for the Rhymney valley but these have not been examined. Indeed, it is evident from the little material that has been examined that historical documentation exists to enable a thorough study to be undertaken by an enthusiastic postgraduate student. It is simply the intention of this paper to expose the potential.

Sources

The data exists in Council Minutes, Minutes of Local Boards of Health, Medical Officer of Health Reports, and Surveyors' Reports. These original documents may be found in council archives, in the County Records office, in public libraries and in Welsh Water

Authority offices. With the establishment of the Welsh Water Authority in the 1970s many local undertakings disappeared and so did their records. In some cases the records were destroyed but mostly they survived in unlikely and often inaccessible locations. Ironically, it is quite likely that nineteenth-century data will survive in the old council minutes, but the prospects for twentieth-century material in the form of specific reports of the smaller bodies such as the Rhymney Valley Board are not so favourable. These documents are currently stored in unsuitable places and will inevitably deteriorate, probably in a relatively short time. Hence for anyone interested in twentieth-century developments, time is short; for those interested in earlier periods, the records are mostly safe and accessible.

The hypothesis

Very little investment took place in sewerage systems in south Wales between 1914 and 1960. In fact the amount of investment during the first six decades of the century was exceedingly limited. While it is true that there was relatively little house building in south Wales during the inter-war period the hypothesis which stimulated this study was that the capacity of the south Wales sewerage system must inevitably be strained by the sixties due to the post-war building boom and the expansion of light industry in the valleys; particularly at Treforest Industrial Estate and the smaller light industry development in and around the Rhondda. Implicit in this hypothesis was the assumption that the sewerage system, developed in the second half of the nineteenth century, was designed for the then prevailing needs and would even have been 'pushing the limits' as a result of the building activity in south Wales between the turn of the century and the outbreak of the war in 1914 during which period approximately 70,000 houses were built in the coalfield and consequently would have been connected up to the existing system. On the basis of this assumption the system was ready to 'blow-up' or 'break-down' at any moment.

The reality

The system in the second half of the twentieth century is not about to 'blow-up' or 'break-down', but does in fact have a considerable amount of excess capacity. This, however, does not reflect the foresight of the early civic leaders of the mining communities which may seem to be the natural assumption to make. Instead, it is related to the rather devious calculations of the consulting engineer engaged by the Ystradyfodwg and Pontypridd Main Sewerage Board.

Mr Chatterton, a London based consulting engineer, submitted his report and proposals to the Ystradyfodwg and Pontypridd Board in May 1886. The scheme proposed by Mr Chatterton involved a capital outlay of £159,000. Mr Chatterton had developed his proposals on the assumption that the total population of the area would increase to 300,000 by the end of the century. On considering the Report the Board felt that the population estimate was far too high and consequently that the proposed scheme and with it the capital outlay, not to mention Mr Chatterton's percentage fee, were all too large.

(In this respect the Board was correct. The highest-ever population of the area was reached in 1921 when the census figure was 214,780). The Board requested the engineer to recalculate his proposals on a more realistic population figure of 150,000 (anticipating, of course, a reduction of about 50 per cent in the size and hence the cost of the scheme). Mr Chatterton was not happy to do this but he eventually agreed and went off to 'do his sums' again. This time, however, he discovered that his original estimates had made insufficient allowance for the run-off surface water especially in the northern parts of the area which had an exceedingly high annual rainfall. He also discovered that he needed to increase the flow per head of population. His revised figure in consequence was not approximately half his original figure — in fact, it was not substantially reduced. Neither was his commission, and the area had a sewerage system to last a century. Perhaps occasionally and in hindsight there is something to be said for less than honest London-based consulting engineers. At an early stage of this research it thus became clear that its central hypothesis was untenable. But not everything was flushed down Chatterton's high-capacity sewers. There is still much to learn from the development of the south Wales sewerage system. We have already briefly considered the enthusiasm and foresight of Dr Dyke. Other aspects that will be considered are the arguments used to justify investments in sewerage schemes; the sources of funding; and the inter-area politics. These aspects, which will be considered in turn, are clearly revealed in the existing records of the Merthyr Tydfil, Aberdare and Mountain Ash, Ystradyfodwg and Pontypridd, Cardiff and Barry authorities.

Arguments to justify investment in sewerage schemes

In 1850, Mr T.W. Rammell presented the report of his 'preliminary inquiry into the sewerage, drainage and supply of water and the sanitary conditions of the inhabitants of Merthyr Tydfil' to the General Board of Health in London. This enquiry was conducted following a petition on the part of more than a tenth of the rated inhabitants praying for such an enquiry. The enquiry which lasted from 16 to 24 May 1850 revealed that there were no sewers in the town. Filth, if it was removed, was washed into the Taff. There was no adequate water supply. Something had to be done, especially as the population of about 45,000 was growing, with about 10,000–11,000 finding their way into the town each year 'the length of their sojourn depending upon the opportunity of obtaining employment'. This record of the incidence of temporary seasonal migration is interesting especially in the light of an earlier statement of Mr Rammell concerning the length of his enquiry which exceeded his original expectations due to the need to translate his questions into Welsh and the answers into English.

Rammell made three main recommendations: he urged the establishment of a Local Board of Health; the provision of 20 gallons of water per day for each inhabitant (50,000) which would cost £23,000; and the provision for an adequate refuse-drainage system costing £17,000. The total cost of his proposals came to £40,000 but his proposals were not universally welcomed. John Williams, a miner of Caepant-y-Wyll, stated that he objected to paying 1½d. a week for water when it cost him nothing to fetch it from the river. 'My reason is that people have not enough to buy food and have nothing to spare for water. I don't know if I would rather pay 1½d. a week for the doctor than for water; half a pint of beer costs 1¼d. I should not be inclined to give half a pint of beer for a supply of water for the week'. That was in May. By September, John Williams and another 1,480 inhabitants of Merthyr had been swept off with cholera and diarrhoea. Nearly three per cent of the population died in just four months. This gives adequate emphasis to the conclusions and recommendations of Mr Rammell who attaches street-by-street statistics of this death rate as a postscript to his report. It places the beer or water alternative of John Williams in its true perpsective.

The Local Board of Health was established in 1850. Dr Dyke — a leading figure in the Rammell enquiry — became its medical officer of health and from then on began his campaign for better water and better sewerage schemes in Merthyr Tydfil. By 1866, as we saw earlier, death rates had fallen and life expectancy had increased by substantial proportions as compared with the situation when the Local Board of Health was established. And the reasons were not far to find. Of the 9,880 houses in the area in 1866, as many as 9,148 or 92 per cent were connected with a pure water supply and 5,485 or 60 per cent had conveniences connected to the 10 miles of mains sewers that wended their way through the town and to the sewerage farm located just outside the Local Board Area south of Troedyrhiw.

As the years passed Dr Dyke continued to report with unabated enthusiasm on the success experienced in his area. In 1882 he wrote:

It is most satisfactory to find that Enteric Fever and Diarrhoea have caused so few deaths (EF.3:D.5) (Dr Paine reported for Cardiff EF.15:D.110) . . . The conclusion I have come to is that in the formation of a well constructed system of sewerage, you have done away with the exciting cause of the former malady and by the abundant supply of pure water, you have almost wholly banished the latter disease from your list of causes of death.

Moreover, the benefits were extended as the administrative area expanded and the coal industry developed in the new areas. In the same report Dr Dyke recorded that:

The houses built in Merthyr Vale were of a roomy substantial character, the place is well sewered and drained and supplied with the pure water of Merthyr.

In 1883 the Annual Report of the Medical Officer of Health contains the following paragraph:

The new colliery villages of Merthyr Vale and Treharris grow with vigour. The annual additions of new streets and of well built stone houses supplied with every hygienic necessity to render life healthy to the occupants, these and the high rate of wages earned by the men, conduce to produce a high standard of health. Needless to say, the phrase 'every hygienic necessity' covers both piped drinking water and adequate toilet facilities.

Dr Dyke built on the Rammell report. The three recommendations of Rammell were the establishment of the Local Board of Health and provision for a water supply and a sewerage system. It was likely that once a Local Board was established they would then be more or less bound to expedite the implementation of the other two recommendations of Rammell. Given the interest and drive of Dr Dyke, who in turn was no doubt further fired by the disastrous cholera outbreak of 1850, sanitary progress in Merthyr Tydfil was converted from a likelihood to a probability.

It was not so easy in other places. In Cardiff, for example, the medical officer of health had to argue his case most strongly before the members of his Local Board. As a by-product, however, the report of the medical officer of health on the sanitary condition of Cardiff in 1866 contains a most interesting calculation in justification of investment in sanitary reform. It is pointed out that between 1853 and 1856, the sum of £26,624. 15s. 7d. was spent on a sewerage scheme in the Newtown district of the Board. In the following two years the scheme was extended and the total cost reached £37,000. It was argued that by 1856 with the completion of the drainage works an improvement in the sanitary condition had become evident. Until 1856 the mean annual mortality rate was 30.12 per 1,000 but between 1856 and 1866 it was reduced to 22.20 per 1,000 showing an annual saving of eight lives in every thousand of the inhabitants. With an average population of 36,000 this was a saving of 288 lives a year or over the ten years a total saving of 2,880. The total cost of saving these 2,880 lives is shown as follows:

	£
Main Drainage Works	37,000
House Drainage Works	20,000
Street and Court Improvements	10,000
Sundry Works, say	3,000
	£70,000

(The street and court improvements were an important investment in this context since they eliminated stagnant pools and filth).

In order to show that independently of the important saving of 2,880 lives, the £70,000 had been wisely expended from a monetary point of view, the following calculations were carried out; the whole exercise being labelled *Sanitary Economy* and being based on the cost of sanitary works lasting for 25 years.

1st	Assuming that 288 lives per annum are saved by sanitary measures, taking half as males 144 and $\frac{4}{10}$ as productive, i.e. 58, the gain to these at £300 per life will be £300 × 58 =	£17,400
2nd	Take the productive females at half the value =	£8,700

3rd	Taking the loss by incapacity to work in 9,000 families at £4 which in a town made healthful is saved (9,000 × £4)	£36,000

A total annual saving of	£62,100
Which at 25 years purchase would produce	£1,552,500
Deducting outlay for sanitary works	£70,000

This leaves a net gain to the community of	£1,482,500

This figure compares with one of £14,378,113 for Liverpool: a community roughly ten times the size of Cardiff in 1866. The Liverpool balance-sheet was presented by the Assistant Town Clerk of Liverpool to the Social Science Association Meeting in 1858. The Cardiff medical officer of health report states that the estimate of a productive human life to the community is based on an elaborate inquiry conducted by a Dr Farr into the money value of a man AND IS DECIDEDLY MODERATE (at £300 *per life*).

This is a most interesting concept, and a fascinating balance sheet. As the Cardiff Local Board invested over half a million pounds on sewerage programmes in the following half century, the Board and its successors may have been influenced by this sophisticated statistical cost benefit analysis which also contained the rider that no provision was made in the calculation for 'the mental as well as bodily suffering prevented through the reduction in deaths which, though of the greatest moment, are incapable of reduction to a money standard'.

While the Merthyr Tydfil Local Board seemed to be highly motivated under the guidance of Dr Dyke, and the Cardiff authorities were being presented with original if complex arguments from their interested officers, the Pontypridd and Ystradyfodwg Boards were subject to external pressures. Although the Rammell report which sparked off activity in Merthyr Tydfil could be described as an act of the central Government, it must also be remembered that the Central Board of Health was reacting to a petition drawn up by a tenth (albeit a disputed tenth) of the population of the town. Hence the initial impetus at Merthyr Tydfil in 1850 was local in character. But this was far from being the case in Pontypridd. In May 1880, a Mr Lomax had prepared a report on the situation in which he pointed out that 'at present the whole of your district is drained by surface drains into the rivers Taff and Rhondda which receive the excretia from many of your closets'.

In December 1881, a special meeting of the Pontypridd Urban Sanitary Board met to consider the Lomax report. That was nineteen months after the report was presented and a full twelve months after an earlier ratepayers meeting. It was resolved to do *nothing* until the experience of the Ystradyfodwg Local Board was clear. Nothing happened. It was a clear case of shadow-boxing. The two Boards did not want to work together. Yet the geography if nothing else dictated that they should. In consequence the Local Government Board exerted pressure for the development of a Joint Sewerage Scheme but even as late as May 1885 when the Local Government Board presented a Draft Provisional Order, following a Public Enquiry held in March 1885, setting up a United Sewerage

District, the Pontypridd authority was against the proposal. Eventually the Ystradyfodwg and Pontypridd Main Sewerage District Provisional Order received the Royal Assent on 22 July 1885 and the provisions came into effect on 29 September 1885. It was only on 1 October 1885 that the Pontypridd authority selected its four members to the Board. This is some indication of the opposition that existed in Pontypridd.

Sources of funding

The basic problem of funding sewerage schemes was that although dedicated exponents of such programmes could expand on the social benefits to be derived, especially in the long run, the direct returns to such investment in financial terms was nil. Money had to be borrowed and provision made for the repayment of debt plus interest charges, but there were other problems too.

First, capital investment in a sewerage scheme was merely the beginning. Clearly, maintenance and repairs were current costs that also had to be anticipated. For example, in 1912 the Merthyr Borough Council spent £1,675 on the maintenance of sewers and drains. This sum was more or less the annual average for the period from 1891 to 1913. To some extent the situation in the mining valleys must have been more acute than in other areas because of the prevalance of faulting and subsidence. For example, the Ystradyfodwg and Pontypridd Joint Board had to spend £20,896 in 1914 to provide a new section to the main sewer in Trealaw in order to overcome a 24ft subsidence which necessitated a diversion of 1,135 yards.

The second problem in the south Wales valleys in the last quarter of the nineteenth century was the expansion of the area itself and consequently the need to borrow more and more in order to invest in an expansion of the system. In some cases the sum involved was small: the Merthyr Authority had to find £2,850 in 1905 to finance the Graigbethlwyd scheme and the Public Works Loan Board (PWLB) readily provided the resources. At the other extreme, the Cardiff Corporation Act of 1901 gave the Authority borrowing powers to raise £181,000 in order to construct the western district sewer. Between 1901 and 31 March 1913 the total capital cost of the western district sewer reached £339,723. 14s. 11d.

In many instances the authorities raised the required capital from the PWLB, though this was not the only source of capital. In the case of the Mountain Ash Board, the clerk was instructed in June 1890 to borrow up to £2,500 on a 30-year loan in order to connect Ynysybwl to the main sewer. The specific instructions were 'to get the loan at the best possible terms'.

It is interesting to note that often the consultant sanitary engineers gave advice. For example the famous or infamous Mr Chatterton in his report of 1886 to the Ystradyfodwg and Pontypridd Joint Board stated that:

> The total cost of the proposed sewer would be £159,000. If the sum is borrowed for a period of 50 years at 4 percent it would require an annual payment of £7,401 to pay interest and repay the capital, which is equivalent to a rate of 5.54 pence in the pound of the rateable value of the Joint Sewerage Board in 1885.

The good Mr Chatterton went on to outline an alternative proposal to his main scheme which was a trunk sewer to the sea. The alternative was for a sewerage farm at Upper Boat. In this case the initial capital cost would only be £123,000 (and would incidentally, include the purchase of 356 acres of land from Jesus College, Oxford). The total annual repayment on this amount would be £5,967 giving a saving of £1,434 when compared with the Trunk Sewer proposal. But with the sewerage farm scheme an annual cost of £1,250 for pressing sludge would be necessary. Hence the annual saving would be reduced to £184. Chatterton further pointed out that there would inevitably have to be greater investment in the processing plant at Upper Boat as population increased, hence the capital cost of the Upper Boat scheme would not be limited to the initial £123,000 investment. Finally, he emphasized the point that with a trunk sewer to the sea, other villages could be joined up to the main and *charged* for the service. Chatterton urged the more costly initial scheme perhaps partly because his percentage would be then based on the larger sum. Whatever the motive, Chatterton's foresight was correct. All the communities between Pontypridd and Gabalfa (Cardiff) were connected to the Ystradyfodwg and Pontypridd system at various dates prior to the First World War.

For the period from 1895 to 1909 the Cardiff City records provide three sets of financial data pertinent to sewerage activities. These were: new capital investment, maintenance and repair costs, and loan charges. During the period in question the new capital investment was confined to the western district sewer where expenditure amounted to £148,283 between 1901 and December 1908. The relationship between maintenance and repair costs on the one hand and loan charges on the other are as follows:

Cardiff Borough Council: sewerage charges 1895–1909

Year	Maintenance and Repairs	Loan Charges
1895	£2,220	£8,500
1896	2,400	8,500
1897	2,440	9,400
1898	2,500	9,500
1899	3,280	8,999
1900	3,175	9,013
1901	2,566	9,032
1902	2,795	9,086
1903	2,349	9,966
1904	2,605	11,447
1905	2,517	11,461
1906	2,373	11,210
1907	2,455	11,446
1908	2,427	10,660
1909	3,035	10,991

The interesting feature in this table is the more or less constant nature of both series over time. The loan charges, of course, increase after 1904 due to the borrowing for the western district scheme. It will be recalled that the Merthyr Tydfil data also show a relative stability in the cost of maintenance and repairs over the same period.

One final aspect of funding which may be considered is the source of the loans. The clerk to the Mountain Ash authority could not have been the only official in south Wales instructed to obtain 'the loan at the best possible terms'. More often than not the best terms available for work of this nature could be obtained from the Public Works Loan Commissioners but often other sources also had to be tapped. In August 1890 the Barry authorities obtained a loan at 3½ per cent from Messrs. C. Dagnall & Co. This was of a sum of £4,000 which supplemented the £23,000 loan approved by the PWLB only two months earlier.

In 1901 the Merthyr Tydfil Urban District Council borrowed £32,140 17s. 9d. for sewerage works. This total was derived as follows:

	£	%
Public Works Loan Commissioners	22,139-10- 6	69
Lords of the Admiralty	8,318- 7-10	26
U.K. Assurance Company	1,181-13- 2	4
Prudential Assurance Company	323- 6- 3	1
Liverpool Friendly Society	178- 0- 0	—
Total	£32,140-17- 9	

The following year a sum of £24,000 was raised for similar works. Again, the PWLB was the main source (64 per cent of the total) with the remainder coming from the Lords of the Admiralty, the Prudential and the Liverpool Friendly Society. The Cardiff Corporation, on the other hand, issued £100,000 worth of consols at £89,304 in order to fund the initial stages of the western district sewer begun in 1901. These data from Merthyr and Cardiff are fascinating. Were they exceptions or did most authorities borrow from a variety of sources?

It would be interesting to look at similar records for other Boards to substantiate the hypothesis that residual sums had to be sought to supplement the limited resources available from the PWLB. It is, however, necessary to qualify the use of the word 'limited' in this context as the commissioners appear to have been providing the bulk of the capital in Merthyr, Barry, Aberdare and Ystradyfodwg and Pontypridd. In all probability this PWLB role was repeated elsewhere throughout not only south Wales but the United Kingdom as a whole. But nevertheless the Commissioners, despite their significant input, could not completely satisfy the active demand and consequently Boards had to borrow limited amounts from other sources.

Sources of conflict (inter-district politics)

Mention has already been made of the difficult birth of the Ystradyfodwg and Pontypridd Joint Sewerage Board. Almost half a decade passed as the one authority watched and waited for the other to make a false step. The geographical features were such that Joint Boards were a logical outcome especially as large economies of scale could be anticipated. The problems, however, were inevitable given the fragmentation of the Local Boards of Health. In fact, it was only the Merthyr Tydfil Board of Health that covered a geographical entity that had some meaning at the turn of the century. In the Cynon valley, Aberdare and Mountain Ash vied with each other in the same way that Ystradyfodwg and Pontypridd did in the Rhondda valley.

The sewerage schemes being developed were based on the slope of the valleys and to contain schemes within 'geo-political' boundaries did not make economic sense. Chatterton's argument for a trunk sewer to the sea rather than a sewerage farm at Upper Boat made monetary sense and it became a better proposition if more communities were to participate in it. The rivalries in the valleys may be seen as little more than community or personality issues although one can share the sensitivities of the four Pontypridd representatives wending their way up the valley to the initial meeting of the Joint Board held at Ystrad on 30 October 1885.

There was, however, the potential for a more substantial issue, namely an environmental one and that involved the Cardiff Corporation vis-à-vis the valley authorities. Initially the Taff had been an 'open-sewer' but in the years following Dr Dyke's initiatives the situation had improved. The Cardiff authorities were, however, opposed to the Ystradyfodwg and Pontypridd proposal to have the trunk sewer discharge into the channel at Rhymney. According to the Cardiff Borough Engineer, the Ystradyfodwg and Pontypridd scheme was superior to that existing in Cardiff at the time, and although it was anticipated that the scheme would have an outflow of 2 million gallons of sewerage per day, the Borough Engineer regarded this, to use his own phrase as 'only a drop in a bucket'. The medical officer of health, however, was not so amenable. He was against the proposal on the basis that the tides and currents in the channel would result in the valley sewerage becoming an environmental hazard to the citizens of Cardiff. He succeeded in persuading the Corporation to set up a Special Committee. This Committee advised the Cardiff Council to oppose the plan despite the fact that the Cardiff sewerage system was of a much lower technical standard than the plans submitted by the Ystradyfodwg and Pontypridd Joint Board. On the advice of the medical officer of health and contrary to that of the engineer, the Council opposed the proposal and it was only in the latter half of 1888 that they relented and agreed not to block the valley proposal any longer. As a result of the successful introduction of the valley system the Cardiff Council then began planning to renovate their existing system which eventually resulted in the development of the Cardiff western sewer in the opening decades of the twentieth century. Ironically, however, the Cardiff western sewer became the subject of another inter-council conflict.

In 1904 the Barry Urban District Council expressed the desire to link Barry and Barry Dock with the Cardiff western sewer. This request was made despite the fact that the Barry Sewerage Board had in 1892 developed an effective sewerage system sufficient to provide for 60,000 people. The Cardiff Council was not prepared to accede to this request. It would, however, appear that this negative attitude was based on political rather than technical or economic factors. However, the political forces won the day and the Cardiff western sewer remained an exclusive Cardiff possession.

Conclusion

The Rammell Report was a significant milestone in the social and economic development not only of Merthyr Tydfil but of the entire south Wales coalfield. The recommendation to set up a Local Board of Health at Merthyr Tydfil had ramifications throughout the coalfield, not because a Local Board of Health was established but because of the evangelical zeal of the appointee to the post of medical officer of health with respect to pure water and proper sewerage. Dr Dyke could well become the patron saint of public health practitioners — he was an effective proponent of the practice of preventative medicine almost a century before that concept became established. As a result of what Dyke did in Merthyr Tydfil, the spread of interest in improved health facilities and the importance of proper sewerage systems encompassed the other valley authorities and an effective system was established. That development has a lot to teach public health and social welfare students of the twentieth century.

Because of both spatial and time constraints this paper has not achieved its intention of charting out a precise record of the way and extent to which a 'quiet' revolution was achieved in south Wales between 1850 and 1914. What it has, however, done is to indicate that a wealth of material exists to be tapped; that there are interesting phenomena waiting to be recorded; and that it is a subject that has a vital relevance in other societies at the present time.

Labour and Technology in South Wales, 1870–1914

M.J. DAUNTON

The history of work is in its infancy. Although the Society for the Study of Welsh Labour History (Llafur) is flourishing, it has largely concentrated upon collective bargaining, strikes, ideology and leadership to produce an account which emphasizes the union meeting rather than the daily experience of work. Similarly, economic historians attempting to explain technological change have concentrated upon changes in the relative costs of capital and labour, and have neglected the social relations in the workplace which could become important constraints upon purely economic assessments of best practice technology. The aim of this paper is to place work at the centre of attention, in a way which will bring together the concern of labour historians for the experience of the working class and of economic historians for the rationality of entrepreneurial behaviour.

Richard Price has recently complained that labour history is marked by 'near-obsessive concern to trail over the old ground about the emergence of the Labour Party, the continual attention to organisational history and the perpetual interest in the leadership personnel of the Labour movement'. The dynamics of change are seen as residing within the movement itself: the process is internal and linear and unambiguous. Price indicates in his study of building workers that the conventional approach is flawed. Unions were accepted by the employers because recognition allowed the use of the leadership to impose discipline and order upon the rank and file. The control of work on the shop-floor becomes of crucial significance: the desire of employers to impose stricter discipline met the desire of the workers to maintain their autonomy. The union leadership achieved recognition and collective bargaining over pay and hours in return for surrendering traditional work practice. The 'rise of labour' was an ambiguous process which was determined by forces outside the boundaries of the labour movement.[1] The 'frontier of control' in the workplace has recently become a topic of concern for labour historians, ranging from David Montgomery on the American experience to Royden Harrison on the 'independent collier'.[2] But the primary concern is still the nature of the labour movement. Price chastises labour historians who fail to consider the experience of work largely on the ground that 'the forces, pressures, and changes in the workplace conditioned, shaped and altered the institutional structures upon which labour came to wield its influence and power'.[3]

Economic historians, for their part, have been concerned with the analysis of the divergences between the technology of Britain and its major competitors in the late nineteenth and early twentieth centuries. The view that British entrepreneurs were conservative, clinging to an outmoded technology, has given way to the orthodoxy that they were making rational decisions, selecting a technology which was appropriate to the relative cost of the factors of production at their disposal.[4] This reinterpretation by the 'new economic historians' is based upon the application of a rather simple and crude version of neo-classical economic theory to the past which makes a number of assumptions about the nature of the labour market and technology. These assumptions are as follows. There was a single unified labour market within which all employers and workers operated. This free and open market allocated labour according to marginal costs and distributed income according to marginal productivities. Workers migrated to and from jobs according to marginal differences in wages. Skill had an objective technical basis, and higher wages reflected payment for knowledge and the job-learning time. Technology was selected and developed according to rational decisions based upon the changing relative cost of labour and capital. In more sophisticated versions natural resources are added, so that in America abundant and cheap raw materials and energy could be substituted for both labour and capital. The relative cost of skilled and unskilled labour may also be stressed, so that capital-intensive technology in Germany and America was a response to shortages of skilled labour in particular rather than labour in general. These assumptions form the basis of the recent reinterpretation of British economic history between 1870 and 1914.[5] But perhaps they are not so axiomatic as is usually believed.

An alternative set of propositions could be put forward. Rather than a single labour market allocating workers according to marginal costs, there could be a split between an internal and external, a primary and a secondary, market. The internal labour market allocated workers within the firm, offering employment stability and a defined hierarchy of advancement. The wages paid might not reflect marginal costs and productivity, but might rather be established by the desire to control workers within the firm through a bureaucratic social system. This internal or primary market connected with the external or secondary market at defined entry points, and the interesting historical question is who acted as gatekeeper, imposing what entry requirements. This pattern applied above all to employment by the State and large service occupations — the Post Office and the railway companies are important examples before 1914 — but might also be found in industry. However, many occupations in the nineteenth century still relied predominantly upon the external labour market, which resulted in a lack of job stability and little prospect of systematic advancement. The exact limits of the two methods of allocation need to be established by empirical research. The rationality of businessmen may indeed operate in directions different from those specified by 'new' economic historians relying on neo-classical theory. Whilst technical change might create homogenized jobs, employers might manipulate the internal labour market to create strictly demarcated job ladders. Wage differentials might therefore represent not the rationality of marginal productivity, but rather the rationality of segmentation of the labour market in order to control the workforce.

It might be the case, therefore, that objective technical factors did not determine the social structure of work. Technology alone did not create the labour system, but only defined the realm of possibilities. The higher wage paid to skilled men might not reflect a genuine basis in scarce knowledge or learning time, but might rather be socially constructed through the artificial delimitation of certain work as skilled. This might simply be anachronistic survival, or might be created in a more positive sense, either by the collective organization of the workforce, or by the employers as a technique of control over subordinate grades. The social construction of skill was not necessarily opposed by the employers as a restrictive practice, for they might in certain circumstances collude in the process. The task of the historian of labour and technology is to distinguish between 'genuine' skill with an objective technical basis, and skill which was socially constructed by the workforce or the employers acting in co-operation or in opposition. The relationship between technology and the labour market was not deterministic, for there were two independent systems which mutually interacted. The labour system created at one stage of technological development might create resistances to future technical change, despite the realignment of relative factor costs. Alternatively, the labour system might be modified in the absence of technical change. This would appear to be the case in the building trades considered by Richard Price, and in the slate quarries of north Wales. The relationship between technology and the labour market must be carefully specified for each major occupation.

These comments amount to a denial of the approach of neo-classical economics that labour is simply purchased as a commodity with a relative factor cost. Social relations at work cannot be reduced to exchange relations, for in purchasing labour the employer must also erect structures of control. This might result in behaviour which was 'irrational' in terms of neo-classical economics, but perfectly rational in terms of assuring that work was undertaken by the labour which had been purchased.[6] It might indeed be the case that economic historians should reject neo-classical theory and accept instead a form of institutional theory.

The most illuminating example of an occupation which has been approached from both standpoints is the Lancashire cotton-spinning industry.[7] The present aim is merely to substitute some case-studies taken from south Wales. It does not pretend to provide the results of any new research; neither does it claim to supply a rounded picture of labour and technology in the area. The intention is a modest one, of suggesting some lines of enquiry which have not been considered by historians of the Welsh economy. Work is not a theme which may be relegated to the periphery of the historian's concern. It must become an integral part of any analysis of the Welsh economy since the industrial revolution.

I

The coal-trimmers employed in stowing coal in the holds of ships at Cardiff provide a clear example of the social construction of skill, and the creation of wage differentials which were unrelated to variations in marginal productivity.[8] Shipowners had originally required trimmers to stow coal so that it would not shift and endanger the vessel. In sailing ships with narrow hatches and irregularly shaped holds, this was a vital job. But by the 1880s changes in the design of ships had made trimming a job which was less vital for safety. Technical change had undermined the objective or genuine basis of skill. The development of steamers with large hatches and uncluttered holds removed many of the problems of trimming. In particular, the development of 'self-trimmers', especially trunk and turret steamers, threatened the trimmers, the very name being a denial of their strategic importance. The result was that 'a steamer is oftener trimmed by the winches than by shovel'. By moving the shoot of the tipping machinery in the hold, coal could be directed more or less as required without the intervention of the trimmers. It could be claimed that the coal-trimmer had become an unnecessary luxury, and the tariff charged 'a swindle of the first magnitude'. One trimmer admitted that the only training required was a day or two's practice, yet this occupation retained its position as the élite of the Cardiff waterfront. It did so through the social construction of skill in the absence of any objective technical basis.

The internal structure of the trimming workforce was based upon a division between a smaller body of 'gangmen' who were paid on a piece-rate for every ton of coal loaded, and a larger group of 'hobblers' who were paid on a time or 'turn' rate. There was a form of internal subcontract which had no objective technical basis but which must rather be understood as the product of the politics of the workplace. The gangmen were organized in groups of eight to twelve men, and they would share equally in the payment for loading a ship. It was not necessary to handle every ton of coal loaded, and the bulk of the work was concentrated in the final stages when the gangmen would themselves employ additional hands from the ranks of the casual hobblers. It was clearly in the interest of the hobblers to demand payment of the full tariff rate and they were, potentially, a threat to the position of the gangmen whose 'skill' lacked both a clear technical basis and a scarcity value. The ability of the gangmen to retain their privileged position in fact rested upon a careful balancing of two sets of social relationships.

The first involved the coal-shippers and shipowners. Whilst the shipowners *paid* for the trimming, the trimmers were *controlled* by the coal-shippers. The coal-shippers paid the trimmers in the first instance, but then claimed from the shipowners the amount paid to the trimmers plus an allowance for superintending the work. Trimming did have some benefits for the coal-shippers who stressed the care needed to prevent the creation of worthless small coal. This enabled the Cardiff Coal Trimmers' Union to exploit the division between shipowners paying for a service which they did not want, and the coal-shippers who had some reason for continuing a service about which they did not have to be cost-conscious. Strong feeling was created between the shipowners and coal-shippers. The shipowners complained that they were paying for the trimming but had no control over the men and no say in fixing the tariff, which tended to be too high because it was determined by coal-shippers who did not personally pay. The great danger for the trimmers was that the coal-shippers might at some stage agree with the shipowners and consent to a drastic reduction in the tariff. The union was in fact remarkably successful in winning the support of the coal-shippers against the shipowners. When the tariff was revised in 1907, the shipowners had gathered information to convince the shippers of 'the superfluous character of the work with which the men fill their time and the small amount of real work done, especially on self-trimmers'. This the shipowners significantly failed to do, and the shippers refused to agree to determine a tariff which could be presented to the trimmers as a *fait accompli*. Rather, the coal-shippers felt that the shipowners were being unreasonable, and instead the union and shippers settled a tariff between themselves which was imposed upon the shipowners as a *fait accompli*. The success of the trimmers rested less upon the technical basis of their skill than upon their ability to exploit the division between their employers.

The second set of social relationships was within the workforce. The gangmen trimmers were hired by foremen in the employ of the coal-shippers. In theory the foremen were paid out of the allowance received by the shippers for superintending the work, but in practice they 'stood in' with the gang, taking a share of the earnings. The gangmen might resent this, but the foremen did perform the vital function of controlling entry to the grade. However, reliance upon the foremen threatened to alienate the hobblers. 'The exclusiveness of the trimming gangs was notorious on the waterfront . . . the cult of coal trimmer is somewhat in the nature of a close borough'. The task of the gangmen had to be to propitiate the foremen whilst not alienating the hobblers. The result was a subtle shift of emphasis depending upon the immediate threat, a process at which the gangmen were remarkably successful despite a number of strained periods.

The continued privileged position of the gangmen trimmers on the waterfront was no simple matter to be taken for granted. It arose not from any firm technical basis, but from the ability to prevent shippers and shipowners from forming a common policy, whilst keeping foremen and hobblers more or less in line. The politics of the workplace were vital for an understanding of the distribution of income within the trimming workforce.

II

Social processes were of importance even where skill had an objective technical basis, for the expertise could be learned in a number of ways. N.B. Dearle in 1914 suggested three methods by which skill was attained in London. The first was by regular service, in which an employer gave the lad an opportunity to learn the trade and did not simply pay him for the current value of his work. The second method was learning by migration, either between firms or between occupations within firms. Thus, a lad might enter a firm without the prospect of continuity of employment and without a definite right to an opportunity to learn. He was simply a wage-earner who was paid for the current value of his work, and took his chance of acquiring the trade. A full knowledge of the trade was gained by moving from firm to firm as a migratory improver. Migration might also occur within a firm where work was graded according to the skill required. Lads would move from machine to machine and grade to grade in a process of promotion within the internal labour market of the firm. Service was regular, but there was no specific period set aside for training, and the boys were paid for the current value of their work at each stage. The third technique of acquiring skill was 'following up'. This applied to boys who worked as 'mates' or assistants to a skilled man or squad of men for several years. This was not a period devoted to learning the trade, for the lad undertook various tasks for the skilled man on the squad which did not necessarily involve the techniques he would require as an adult. He was serving and helping, but not himself undertaking the work of the skilled man.[9]

The method by which skill was acquired might vary between the same trades in different parts of the country: a given technology did not necessarily impose a given method of acquiring skill.[10] The coal-mining industry provides a clear illustration of this assertion. In the north-east of England, adolescents would enter the pit as 'drivers', employed in driving the horses on the main roads underground. They would move on to 'putting' at some time between the ages of 16 and 18, which involved pushing full tubs from the face to the main roadways, and returning empty tubs. The next stage was to become a 'putter and hewer' for about three months, when the adolescent mainly worked as a putter but undertook hewing as required. The 'putter and hewer' then became a 'hewer and putter' for a period ranging from three months to a year, during which time he would be mainly employed in hewing but worked as a putter when required. Finally, in his early 20s the young miner in the north-east would become a full hewer. This most closely fits Dearle's second classification, of migration from grade to grade within the firm, whereas miners in south Wales were trained by the third method of 'following-up'. In south Wales, boys did not go down the pit as drivers, working their way up in an established way from driving to putting to hewing. Rather, boys would go down the pit as either trainee hewers or hauliers. The hewer would be assisted by a helper, usually under the age of 21 and often a son or relative, whom he would pay by the day. Haulage was not, as in the north-east of England, a specifically adolescent occupation. In south Wales in 1906, only 3.4 per cent of the haulage workers were boys under the age of 16, in contrast to 30.4 per cent in Durham. But whereas in Durham no boys under the age of 16 worked at the face, the proportion of face-workers in south Wales under the age of 16 was 14.5 per cent. Although the technology of extraction was the same, the labour system differed between the two areas, and not only in the manner in which the young were taught the skills of life underground.[11]

Dearle developed his classification in order to explain the methods by which skill was acquired in the trades of London. In south Wales, however, there was one important group of industries which was unrepresented in London: process trades such as the manufacture of iron, steel, copper and tinplate. It might be suggested that machine-tending trades required manual skill on machines which performed a discrete operation: an engineer would learn to use a lathe, a cotton-spinner to operate a pair of mules. Process work was different.

Process work involved material which flows rather than is moved in discrete stages; it therefore usually necessitates limited manual skill, as the material itself is often not handled at all by the operator; what is needed are what have been called 'control skills', that is the ability to identify, and react correctly to, malfunctionings in the process; before instrumentation . . . the duties of operators also frequently included the actual formulation of the material, and the monitoring of the subsequent stages of the process as the material became modified by chemical or mechanical action.

It must be emphasized that, in the absence of instrumentation, it was the knowledge of the process-operator which controlled the changes in the materials: the accumulated experience of the workforce was essential to determining the point at which to tap the furnace or the moment at which bars could be rolled.[12] These process trades, which were so important in south Wales, were usually organized on the basis of squads of men who would handle the whole of the process. A boy would be attached to a squad, and progress from grade to grade as he acquired a 'feel' for the material which was handled. Skill was learned by 'following-up', although there might also be migration between branches of the process. The internal labour market was crucial, for it was usually only possible to gain access at one entry point as a boy, and then to progress from grade to grade within the squad, according to strict rules of seniority. In the case of the iron and steel industry, the progression on open-hearth furnaces 'was from chargewheeler, which was basically a labouring job, up through third and second to first melter; samplepassers, the equivalent of foremen, were recruited from first melters'.[13] It is worth considering one process industry — the tinplate trade — in some detail.

III

A tinplate works was divided into two sections: the mill in which steel plates were produced; and the tinhouse in which the plates were coated with a layer of tin.[14] These were two distinct processes, involving a different set of skills and separate teams of workers. In the mill, steel bars were heated in a furnace, passed through the rollers, reheated and rolled again, doubled upon themselves and squeezed flat. The doubled sheets were then heated, rolled, folded and squeezed twice more so that they eventually had eight layers. These tasks were undertaken by a squad of four men: the furnaceman heated the steel to the required temperature; the rollerman, who was in overall charge, passed the steel through the rollers; the 'catcher' or 'behinder' received the steel and returned it over the top of the rolls to the rollerman; and the 'doubler' folded and squeezed the sheets. The rolled and folded steel was then cut to the size required for the finished plates by a shearer who was assisted by a boy. The laminated sheets were opened by a team of women and girls, who used a knife or cleaver to tear them apart. Whilst the rolls were operated continuously by three eight-hour shifts, the shearers and openers worked one eight-hour shift. The next stage was to clean the sheets in acid and to heat them in a furnace for ten hours: this was black-pickling and black-annealing. The plates were then cold rolled to give them a good surface, after which their pliability was restored by 'white-annealing' or heating for about seven hours. The final stage was to clean the sheets in a weaker solution of acid, which was known as 'white-pickling'. A plant with six sets of rolls would

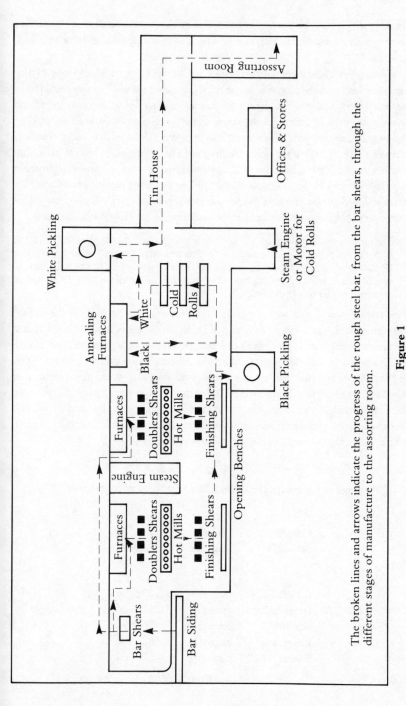

Figure 1
Rolling mill, Tinplate works

The broken lines and arrows indicate the progress of the rough steel bar, from the bar shears, through the different stages of manufacture to the assorting room.

employ two picklers, two wheelers and ten or twelve women to control the pickling process, and eleven men to handle the annealing. The cold rolling was undertaken by boys and girls.

The career progression for boys in the mills was to start work on the cold rolls. In their late teens they would be promoted to the hot rolls, and would work up from behinder or catcher, to furnacemen, doubler, rollerman and shearer, as vacancies occurred and according to strict seniority. An alternative career progression was to enter the pickling and annealing department, where the ultimate aim was to become an annealer. The boys received relatively high wages from the first, and the proportion of boys to male adult workers was small enough to provide a 'substantial guarantee' of permanent employment as a skilled man. J.H. Jones was confident that 'the prevailing method of recruiting the ranks of skilled workers is quite effective and eminently satisfactory'. The Secretary of the Employers' Association pointed out at the beginning of the First World War that

> The custom of the trade, which is most rigorously looked after by the men's Unions, is that every person is promoted according to seniority. Any boy of 14 starting in a tinplate works knows for an absolute certainty that, provided his health is all right, he will before he is 20 be earning from 35s. to £2; and that before he is 25 he will be earning from £3 to £4 per week.

The average wages paid to each grade in 1906 (see Table 1) indicate the income differentials which arose from this system of grades. In some process industries, a system of subcontracting survived by which one worker was paid on a piece-rate, and he then paid the men below him. This remained a major issue in the steel industry in south Wales, and the Webbs reported that 'the great bulk of the men here would like the system of subcontracting to be abolished altogether and all the men to be paid through the office'. In the tinplate trade, by contrast, 'there is absolutely no subcontracting' and all workers were paid direct from the office. Group payment and internal subcontracting had given way to individual payments in the mid nineteenth century.

Table 1
Average net earnings (full-time), last pay week of September 1906

Boys			
Cold rollers	time rate	13s.	1d.
Behinders	piece rate	22s.	0d.
Men			
Behinders	piece rate	26s.	9d.
Furnacemen	piece rate	47s.	3d.
Doubler	piece rate	50s.	9d.
Rollerman	piece rate	62s.	10d.
Shearer	piece rate	61s.	3d.

Source: J.H. Jones, *The Tinplate Industry* (1914), p.266.

The technology in the rolling branch of the tinplate trade underwent little change between 1870 and 1914. J.H. Jones pointed out in 1914 that 'the rate of output is not determined by the speed of the machinery; the men control the machines, the machines do not control the men'. This gave the workforce an element of discretion: they had the practical knowledge of the process; they could control the pace of work. The outcome was the 'stinting' of work by the men, so that 'the daily output per mill had for many years been limited by custom to an amount far below producing capacity'. The customary limit was gradually raised from 20 boxes of plates a shift in 1850, to 25 in the 1850s, 30 in an eight-hour shift or 36 in a twelve-hour shift by 1870, and 36 per eight-hour shift by 1890. The Webbs explained that 'the output is "stinted" to 36 boxes per man per shift and this amount is practically produced daily by each man or he would be discharged. If a man makes more one day he must make less the next or subject himself to a fine by the Union'. The aim was to prevent the market from being overstocked which would result in prices, and wages, being reduced. The result of this 'stinting' of output below the capacity of the mills was, argued Jones, to create technological inertia, for 'no inducement existed to improve the machinery; additional expenditure in this direction brought no advantage'. But in 1902 limitation was abandoned. It might seem paradoxical, at first sight, that this followed the establishment of the Conciliation Board in 1899 which gave recognition to the unions, incorporating them into a formal institutional structure of collective bargaining. In fact, the coincidence is not surprising. The stinting of output rested largely upon customary expectations informally imposed within the workplace, designed to influence wage levels in the absence of a formal machinery of collective bargaining; the unions, in the absence of official recognition before 1899, could only hope to utilize the customary control over output. When the Conciliation Board was established the initial aim was to preserve control over output, at the expense of raising the stint to 40 boxes per shift. But the employers pressed for the abolition of controls, and in 1902 the unions agreed to abandon any practices which restricted output. The men were 'to follow the machinery . . . We instruct our members to utilise the full period of time of their turn and the machinery in use'. The success of the union was ambiguous. Part of the task of the leadership was now to impose work discipline upon the members. The 'frontier of control' had been pushed forward by the employers, and in return for the abandonment of autonomy and controls on output the union had gained recognition and, in effect, a closed shop. Frequent local strikes to impose quotas and rates gave way to a more orderly pattern of labour relations. The average weekly production of a mill rose from 500 to 750 boxes, which Jones felt would remove technical inertia. 'Since increased efficiency is reflected in the output, and consequently in cost, a sum spent upon improvements may be repaid in increased profits within a short space of time'. It is perhaps not surprising that employers started to compel defaulters to pay their union subscriptions, and became strong supporters of the benefits of collective bargaining.

The position in the tinhouse differed in important respects, for here there were significant changes in the technology. The tinning of the steel plates was undertaken up to the 1860s using a range of six cast-iron pots, and a team of four men and three girls. The tinman dipped the plates into grease and then tin; they were placed in the first part of the washpot from which they were removed by the washman who wiped off the surplus tin; he then dipped them in the second part of the washpot which contained the purest tin; any excess tin was next melted off in a pot of hot grease; the third workman or 'riser' subsequently placed the plates in a pot of melted tallow; and, finally, the fourth workman or 'lister' removed the bead of tin which had formed on the lower edge of the plate by dipping it in the list pot and striking it with a stick. The plates were subsequently cleaned and polished by girls. In the tinhouse hand labour was gradually replaced by machinery, and the level of skill reduced. In the 1860s a set of rolls dispensed with the list pot and lister; about 1890 the washman was replaced; and shortly afterwards the riser was discharged. In 1892 a cleaning machine displaced two girls. The result was that a team had been reduced from four men and three girls, to a tinman, a riser and a duster. The plates were guided through the various metal and grease mixtures by sets of rollers, so that it was merely necessary for the riser to feed in the plates, and the tinman to remove them. This changed the pattern of promotion in the tinhouse. The hierarchy had run from lister to riser to washman to tinman. The relationship between juvenile and adult grades was upset by the truncation of the promotion hierarchy. The danger was that boy labour in the tinhouse could become a blind-alley occupation: surplus adolescents for whom no permanent positions were available could be sacked at the age of 20 and a new cohort taken on from school. However, this did not occur, largely because of the desire of the adult grades to prevent an overstocking of the labour market which might undermine their position. The issue was settled by the dispute over the 'twopenny touch' in the mid 1880s. It had been the practice for the washman to receive 3d. per box for the lister. Initially, 2d. went to the boy, ½d. to the washman, and ½d. to the employer for spoiled sheets; after six months the boy received 2d. and the washman 1d.; and at the end of a year the boy received the full 3d. and was eligible for promotion. But in 1885–6, the employers retained 1d., allowing nothing to the washman, and paying the boys 2d. per box. This was opposed by the adults, who insisted that the whole 3d. should go to the boys, and that

Table 2
Average net earnings (full-time), last pay week of September 1906

Boys		
Risers	piece rate	17s. 1d.
Men		
Tinmen	piece rate	43s. 6d.
Assorters	piece rate	50s. 5d.

Source: J.H. Jones, *The Tinplate Industry* (1914), p.266.

new workers should be engaged only when absolutely necessary. The system of systematic promotion was maintained up to the First World War, with the prospect of advancing from riser to tinman and, in some cases, to assorter who sorted the plates and acted as superintendent.

Table 3
Variable costs in the manufacture of tinplate, 1905

	per cent
Steel	48.6
Tin	21.2
Wages	21.1
Coal	4.2
Boxes, acid, grease	4.8

Source: W.E. Minchinton, *The British Tinplate Industry. A History* (1957), p.84.

The employers had little desire or need to overturn the labour system in either the rolling mills or the tinhouse. The major variable cost was not labour but raw materials. In the mills, an attempt to drive labour would not greatly influence the cost of rolled plates, and provided there were sufficient skilled men forthcoming there was no great incentive to adopt more capital-intensive techniques. It would only be necessary to deepen rather than widen the capital base if shortages of skilled men created a bottle-neck. This did not arise, and the production of plates was a clear example of the influence of the labour market upon technology. The change of 1902 led, J.H. Jones notwithstanding, merely to a more effective use of existing machinery and not to the initiation of technical change. In the tinhouse, technical change could reduce the cost of raw materials by saving on the use of tin, which fell from eight or nine pounds a box in 1857 to just over two pounds in 1888. There was also, of course, some saving in labour costs but any attempt to disrupt the system of orderly promotion would be difficult in view of the highly competitive and fragmented nature of the industry. In the absence of concerted action, an attempt by one employer to overturn the labour system would simply result in a loss of output to the benefit of competitors. The workers had indeed been able to defeat the 'twopenny touch' by calling out the men from one works and maintaining them by subscriptions from those who remained in employment at other works. The potential danger that juvenile labour in the tinhouse might become a blind-alley occupation was avoided up to 1914.

IV

It would be possible to apply the concepts which have been proposed in this paper to a variety of other occupations in south Wales. The railways which carried coal from the mines had an internal labour market within which skill was learned by 'following-on' from engine cleaner to fireman to driver in a rigid hierarchy.[15] On the other hand, the ships which carried the coal away from the docks relied upon the external labour market, with little prospect of promotion, few controls over entry, and endemic instability.[16] But the intention is not to provide a comprehensive coverage of the south Wales economy: it is rather to suggest some avenues of enquiry which have been neglected; and to stimulate debate on the interrelationships between the labour market, social structure and technical change. It should be asked of any occupation whether skill was the genuine product of technical factors, or the social construction of workers and employers; how skill was acquired; whether there was an orderly progression in the internal labour market or allocation by the external labour market. Technology might create skill, but the existence of abundant skilled workers might also shape technology by removing the need to substitute capital for hand labour. The labour system created by one method of production might become an independent factor, creating a dead weight against future changes in productive processes, and constraining the entrepreneur's choice of what constituted best-practice technology. The distribution of income in society was the outcome of social processes at the workplace; the social structure of Llanelli or Ferndale was influenced by the relationships between grades in the tinplate works or down the pit.

The analysis presented here does have major shortcomings. The emphasis has been upon the individual factory or dock or mine, and it is clearly necessary to increase the scale to cover the regional labour market in aggregate. The analysis is also static, neglecting the differences in patterns of recruitment and promotion between expanding, stable and declining trades as the regional distribution of employment changed. There are certainly ample opportunities for further research on the nature of work, technology and the labour market in south Wales, and this paper has attempted to suggest some possible lines of approach, rather than to provide any definite conclusions. Two morals should have emerged. First, economists should take care neither to treat labour as an inert, homogenous factor of production, nor to view technical change as a residual in economic development. Secondly, labour historians should take care neither to treat unions as an unambiguous triumph of class aspiration, nor to relegate the workplace to the periphery of their analysis.

Growth in the Coal Industry: the Cases of Powell Duffryn and the Ocean Coal Company, 1864–1913

TREVOR BOYNS

Between 1864 and 1913 the south Wales coalfield experienced a rapid growth of output from about 11 million tons to 56.8 million tons and this growth was accompanied by a massive rise in the number of persons employed, from about 47,000 to slightly over 233,000. By 1913 it had become the largest single coalfield, producing an output slightly greater than that of the great north-east coalfield of Northumberland and Durham. This rapid growth and development led to an increase in both the number and size of collieries in operation, and also to a greater concentration of output within the hands of large companies, particularly in the steam-coal section of the coalfield.[1] The growth of output and its concentration in larger collieries and larger companies, however, did not proceed at a uniform rate, being largely tied in with the ebb and flow of the trade cycle. Whilst colliery sinkings and the flotation of new firms might occur even in depressions, it is noticeable that there were marked bursts of activity during the major booms of 1871–4, 1890–1 and 1900–1. Not all of the new collieries and firms which came into being during such booms would survive for long, particularly since coal prices and therefore profits had often fallen dramatically by the time new collieries came into production. Thus the growth and development of the south Wales coalfield in the fifty years to 1913 is marked by the short lives of a large number of small collieries and small firms, whose overall contribution to that growth was negligible.

Overall the period from 1864 to 1913 did see an increase in the number of collieries from 418 to 621 (it had reached a peak of 688 in 1910). The vast majority of these collieries, however, were small and, in 1913, 292 of the 621 collieries employed less than 100 persons. Not only were the collieries themselves small, but so too were the 'firms' which owned them. Table 1 shows, for both 1860 and 1913, the number of collieries owned by each undertaking[2] in the south Wales coalfield. As can be seen, in both years the typical colliery undertaking controlled only one or two collieries, but there had been an increase in the number of undertakings controlling five or more collieries during the period. Unlike the situation in some of the older coalfields, e.g., Lancashire, Staffordshire and Scotland, these large undertakings tended to control large collieries. The number of collieries controlled is thus not necessarily the best indicator of an undertaking's size, a better measure being the output controlled by a concern. Using the annual summaries of the Monmouthshire & South Wales Coal Owners' Association it is possible to gain an

Table 1
Number of collieries owned by each undertaking, 1860 & 1913

Year	No. of collieries owned														Total No. of Firms	Collieries in Coalfield
	1	2	3	4	5	6	7	8	9	10	11	13	14	19		
1860	183	32	12	6	4	2	1	1	—	—	—	—	—	1	262	373
1913	291	55	13	6	8	6	1	1	2	1	1	1	1	—	387	621

Source: R. Hunt, *Mineral Statistics of the United Kingdom for 1860* (HMSO), and *List of Mines for 1913* (HMSO).

insight into the most important firms in terms of output, though it must be pointed out that in the pre-1890 period a number of the large companies were not members of the Association.

Table 2 shows the output levels of the major producers at various points throughout the 1863–1913 period. When the first coalowners' association was founded in 1864 it did not represent the major iron companies whose coal production at that time was for their own consumption rather than for sale purposes. After 1873, however, the association included both coal and iron companies and it is therefore possible to gauge the relative sizes of such enterprises. The largest sale-coal producer in 1873 was Powell Duffryn with an assured output of 1 million tons, which was slightly less than the 1.02 million tons of the Ebbw Vale Steel, Iron and Coal Co. Ltd. These two companies, together with two other iron firms, were producing substantially more than the three next largest coal undertakings each of which produced about ½ million tons. By 1913, however, there had been something of a change. One company, Powell Duffryn, now produced an output level much greater than that of the other leading coal producers. Of the eight largest colliery companies in 1913, those in third to eighth place had output levels little different from one another, but only half that of Powell Duffryn. Compared with 1873 it is also noticeable that the iron and steel companies were less in evidence amongst the largest coal producers in 1913, only GKN and Ebbw Vale Co. appearing in the list. Another notable change during the period was the rapid rise to prominence of the Ocean Company, which in 1894 produced an output over one million tons greater than Powell Duffryn or any other company. By 1913, however, this company's output had fallen slightly whilst Powell Duffryn's had expanded to 4 million tons.

The figures presented in Table 2 thus indicate that firms grew at different rates throughout the period, and therefore the eight largest firms in any one year need not be the same as those in a later year. The table does not, however, fully illustrate the growth of large companies in the south Wales coalfield since companies which retained a separate legal identity, but which were part of a combine or holding company, are recorded separately. In general this causes little problem since amalgamations and mergers of this

Table 2
Largest coal-producing companies, 1863–1913

1863	Output (tons)
T. Powell & Sons	489,558
Nixon, Taylor & Cory	251,113
D. Davis	228,034
United Merthyr Steam Colls. Co.	116,894
Lletty Shenkin Coal Co.	113,731
Gadlys Iron Co.	101,375

	Assured Tonnage		
	1873	1894	1913
Powell Duffryn	1,000,000	1,529,392	4,178,000
Ocean	500,000	2,594,617	2,402,959
Ebbw Vale	1,020,000	1,097,018	2,013,615
GKN Ltd. (Dowlais)	800,000	1,256,053	2,006,500
Nixon's Navigation	—	1,344,581	1,945,181
Cory Bros.	—	—	1,855,000
D. Davis & Sons	535,000	1,524,052	1,836,250
Lewis Merthyr	—	—	1,799,217
Tredegar Iron Co.	564,608	954,908	—
Blaenavon Iron Co.	915,613	—	—
United National Colls.	—	840,223	—
Glamorgan Coal Co.	500,000	—	—

Source: W.G. Dalziel, *Records of the Several Coal Owners' Associations of Monmouthshire & South Wales, 1864 to 1895,* and National Library of Wales, South Wales Coalowner's Association records, Annual Summary for 1914–15.

type had not become widespread in the south Wales coalfield before 1913; however a notable exception is the Cambrian Combine formed by D.A. Thomas (later Viscount Rhondda). The combine, which was initially formed in 1895 to acquire the Cambrian Navigation colliery, by 1914 controlled directly four companies with a combined output of 3½ million tons, and had links with concerns producing a further 3½–4 million tons.[3] This is, of course, to be contrasted with Powell Duffryn's output of 4 million tons, or 7 per cent of the coalfield's output, in 1913. The Cambrian Combine was then a major concern in the south Wales coal industry on the eve of the war and cannot be ignored in any study of the growth of the coalfield. The achievement of success through amalgamations, however, was unusual during this period when most companies expanded as a result of internal growth, i.e., the sinking and development of new collieries. Internal growth was the most important factor in the development of the Ocean Coal Co., David Davis & Sons and Powell Duffryn, though these last two companies did on occasions buy up collieries which lay contiguous to their existing pits. Because expansion through internal growth was far more prevalent than growth by amalgamation, this paper will concentrate upon two of the major coal companies which expanded chiefly in this manner, namely Powell Duffryn and the Ocean Company. Let us begin then with an account of the development of Powell Duffryn.

I

The Powell Duffryn Steam Coal Co. Ltd.
(a) Output growth, 1864–1913

Powell Duffryn was registered as a limited liability company on 28 July 1864 to purchase the steam-coal collieries belonging to Walter and Henry Powell for the sum of £365,000.[4] The company was registered with a nominal share capital of £500,000 divided into 100 shares each of £5,000 which were divided between nine persons, one of whom, George Elliot, had been instrumental in the purchase of the collieries and in the setting up of the company. The collieries bought by the company numbered seven, six of these being situated in the Aberdare valley — Lower Duffryn, Middle Duffryn, Old Duffryn, Upper Duffryn, Abergwawr and Cwmdare — and one, New Tredegar, in the Rhymney valley. In 1865, the first full year under the company's control, these collieries produced 624,806 statute tons of large coal,[5] the bulk of the production coming from Lower Duffryn (200,200 tons) and Middle Duffryn (137,344 tons). As Table 3 shows, the company's output of large coal expanded to over 1 million tons in 1870, but once the boom of 1871–4 had come to an end, production fell back somewhat in the depressed times of the late 1870s and 1880s. Thus, in 1890 output of large coal at just under 1.1 million tons was only slightly above that in 1870. This, as will be seen below, was a period of many troubles for the company, and it is only after 1895 that the company starts to expand output once again. By 1913 output of large coal had risen to 2.8 million tons, and total coal output to 3.9 million tons.

Thus the expansion of output occurred in two different phases, separated by a long period of stagnation. The initial expansion phase occurred in the late 1860s and early 1870s, and appears to have had two causes. The first was the acquisition of further collieries in the late 1860s, and the second, the boom in the coal trade of 1871–4. Powell Duffryn acquired the High Duffryn (or Ynyscynon) and Treaman collieries in 1865 for £8,750, the Aberaman Estate (including the Aberaman Colliery) for £125,000 in 1865,

Table 3
Growth of output, Powell Duffryn, 1865–1913

Year	Coal Output (statute tons)		Employment
	Large	Total	
1865	624,806	668,262	—
1870	1,032,449	—	3,643[a]
1875*	532,812	—	—
1880	875,487	—	—
1885	1,190,239	1,367,687	—
1890	1,083,336	1,311,701	—
1895	1,208,908	1,478,858	5,681
1900	1,551,575	1,937,906	6,432
1905	2,007,709	2,737,042	10,118
1910	2,404,128	3,218,951	13,495
1913	2,817,821	3,873,780	14,779

Note: [a] Excludes New Tredegar.
     * Strike year.

Source: Large coal — GRO D/D NCB 23, P.D. Cost Books, 1865–1913.
     Total coal — GRO D/D NCB 23, P.D. Output Books, 1885–1913.
     Employment — List of Mines (HMSO) 1895–1913.

and the Cwmneol and Fforchaman collieries in 1866 for £81,000.[6] These latter acquisitions, particularly those of the Fforchaman and Aberaman collieries, added greatly to the company's productive capacity and explain how it was that the company was able to expand output during the 1871–4 period and thereby to take full advantage of the boom conditions within the coal trade at this time. Output in 1871 was affected by the coalfield strike, but in 1872 the company produced almost 1.2 million tons of large coal, and in 1873 output again topped the one million ton mark. When the boom broke in 1874, however, the company's output dropped, and did not exceed a million tons again until 1883.

The late 1870s marked a period of retrenchment for Powell Duffryn, with a number of its collieries being closed, some of them never to produce again. Thus in 1875 the company closed the Abergwawr, High Duffryn and Cwmdare pits, with only Cwmdare being re-opened, and then only from 1880–91. The continuing poor state of trade in the middle 1880s led to the company also closing down the Middle Duffryn colliery in 1885, and in the following year the No. 1 pit at New Tredegar and the upper pit at Lower Duffryn — none of these ever re-opened for production. Thus it was that the Powell Duffryn Company was forced to close a large number of the collieries which had been purchased in the early years of its life, mostly due to the high cost of production at these pits. Despite the closures, the number of collieries in production, which had been eleven in 1870, had only been reduced to nine in 1890. The closures of the 1870s and early 1880s had been partially offset by new sinkings, e.g. West Elliot (1885) and No. 2 pit, New Tredegar (1885). Also the Treaman colliery, which had been acquired in 1865, after having remained idle for seventeen years, finally entered production in 1882. With the growth of the new collieries, the company's output of just under 1.1 million tons of large coal in 1890 was spread fairly evenly amongst the collieries, with five collieries producing between 160,000 and 190,000 tons.[7] It was the growth of these new larger collieries and further similar developments later which were to account for the rapid growth of output at Powell Duffryn after the mid 1890s.

Thus the second phase of expansion from about 1895 to 1913 was different from the earlier phase, being associated with the sinking of new collieries rather than with the acquisition of existing collieries. Perhaps of equal importance though, was that these new sinkings took place in the Rhymney valley and led to a shift in the centre of gravity of the company's production from the Aberdare valley to the Rhymney valley.[8] The coming into production on a regular basis of East Elliot (1896), Bargoed Steam pits (1902) and the Bargoed House pits (1904) helped to add materially to the company's output levels in the early years of the twentieth century. The expansion of output at these new collieries, the acquisition of Lletty Shenkin in 1900, and the continued expansion at older collieries, e.g., Aberaman and New Tredegar No. 2 pit, enabled the company to produce just short of 4 million tons of coal in 1913.

Despite the company's initial spurt of output growth, the first twenty years of its existence were not marked by any real growth. It was only after the mid 1890s that the company began to expand. The next section considers the problems faced by the company in those early years and how it overcame them.

(b) Profits, capital expenditure and growth

Perhaps the best way of indicating the changing fortunes of the Powell Duffryn company over the period to 1913 is to consider the dividends paid out by the company. Between 1864 and 1888 the company paid no dividends on its ordinary shares with the exception of 1877 when a 9.77 per cent dividend was paid in the form of bonus shares 'in respect of profits made in previous years but expended on Capital Account'.[9] In stark contrast, however, between 1889 and 1913 the company paid a dividend on its ordinary shares in every year with the sole exception of 1898, due to the five-month coalfield strike of that year (see Table 4).[10] In the first 25 years or so of its existence then it is clear that Powell Duffryn was either not making profits, or that the profits which were being made were being ploughed back into the concern or used to pay off debts which had been incurred. Table 4 shows, amongst other things, the level of gross profits for the company for 1866–9 and 1871–3. The impact of the boom of 1871–3 is seen very clearly with the massive increase in gross profit levels experienced in 1872 and 1873. Similar large increases in profit levels during periods of boom in the coal trade are shown in 1890–1, 1900–1, 1907–8 and 1913. Further, there is evidence of a much higher general level of profits after 1899 than before this year. These years of regular profit were in contrast to the early years of struggle during the 1870s and 1880s.

Table 4
Profits, capital expenditure and dividends,
Powell Duffryn Steam Coal Co. Ltd., 1866–1913

Year	Profits (£)		Capital	Dividend (%)[a]
	Gross	Net	Expenditure (£)	
1866	17,417	—	—	—
1867	30,519	—	—	—
1868	33,512	—	—	—
1869	17,781	—	—	—
1870	—	—	—	—
1871	17,994	—	—	—
1872	211,080	—	—	—
1873	284,728	—	—	—
1874–87	No information on profits or capital expenditure. The Company paid no dividends at all between 1874 and 1887, with the exception of a 9.77% bonus share issue made in 1887.			
1888	20,676	—	—	0
1889	95,481	—	—	3*
1890	152,066	—	—	12.5*
1891	127,411	—	—	7.5*
1892	56,146	—	—	1.5*
1893	33,034	—	—	1.5*
1894	92,611	—	—	5*
1895	56,139	—	—	1.5*
1896	65,856	—	—	1.5*
1897	75,258	—	—	2.5*
1898	40,741	—	—	0
1899	163,928	—	28,350	7
1900	367,570	—	63,195	7*
1901	269,624	—	54,440	7*
1902	211,858	—	68,555	7*
1903	191,598	—	62,418	7*
1904	257,417	76,155	76,349	7*
1905	174,006	81,965	158,254	7*
1906	227,958	140,169	102,991	7*

Table 4 — continued

Year	Profits (£)		Capital Expenditure (£)	Dividend (%)[a]
	Gross	Net		
1907	453,756	346,358	152,327	20*
1908	406,319	322,718	113,646	20
1909	258,981	198,293	106,714	15
1910	328,388	253,349	90,796	20
1911	266,929	224,769	125,907	20
1912	—	248,473	106,712	20
1913	—	364,421	115,659	20 & 50% in bonus shares

Note: [a] Free of tax except where marked *.

Source: Gross Profit — R. Walters 'The Economic and Business History of the South Wales Steam Coal Industry, 1840–1914', (Ph.D. Oxon., 1975 — D16989/76), p. 291
Net Profit — E.M. Hann, *A Brief History of the Powell Duffryn Steam Coal Company, 1864–1921,* (No information), p. 34.
Dividend and Capital Expenditure — *Sankey Commission* (1912), Vol. III, (Cmd. 361), App. No. 71, Tables 1 & 2, pp. 205–6.

Even before the coal boom of 1871–4, Powell Duffryn was having its problems. The coal trade in the late 1860s was not good, and despite the sound capital structure of the firm, Powell Duffryn came close to dissolution in the deep depression of 1868–9.[11] It would seem that in its very early years the company over-stretched itself, particularly in acquiring a number of collieries between 1865 and 1867. In total, the company committed itself to expending £579,750 on colliery acquisitions in these years, though in the end the price paid for the Powell collieries was reduced, as was that for the Aberaman Estate and the Cwmneol and Fforchaman collieries.[12] In order to finance the last two acquisitions the company had to issue £100,000 worth of 12½ per cent preference shares in July 1866. Since the preference shares had been issued to the original shareholders in proportion to their holdings of ordinary shares, over these first few years the subscribers to the company were forced to dig deeply into their pockets.[13] The revival in trade in the early 1870s provided the company with a certain amount of breathing space as far as its financial affairs were concerned. With the ending of the 1871–4 boom, however, the company was once again beset by financial problems.

In 1875 the state of the coal trade was so bad that the company was forced to mortgage the Aberaman Estate to the Mortgage Trustees of the Rock Life Assurance Co. in order to secure a loan of £70,000.[14] Two years later the company increased its registered capital to

£755,000 by the issue of £30,000 of 10 per cent preference shares and 100 shares of £1,250 each, considered £550 paid. It was stated in the Special Resolution allowing this increase that the remaining £700 on each share, when called, was to be used to pay off the 1875 mortgage and interest. The state of the coal trade in the late 1870s however, remained bad, and the company appears to have made losses throughout this period.[15] In December 1878 the company's fortunes were not helped by an explosion at the New Tredegar colliery which killed 23 men. In the following year the company made a loss of £43,000 and was having great problems in just surviving. E. M. Hann, manager of the company's collieries could describe the company's position thus:[16]

> The Capital had . . . been increased, owing to the losses incurred, besides which there were in existence Lloyds Bonds £20,000, a temporary loan from the Rock Life Insurance £60,000, and an excess of debits over credits of about £80,000 to tradesmen, etc., a considerable overdraft at the bank; and it was generally considered both inside and outside the concern that the position was well nigh hopeless. For some time after this — in fact, up to about 1884, I think — it was a frequent occurrence for extreme difficulty to be experienced in raising sufficient funds for the workmen's wages on pay day.

As if this was not enough, the collieries themselves were in desperate need of renovation:[17]

> . . . in 1879 and 1880 the plant at the pits was worn out and obsolete; the ventilation, generally speaking, and with slight exceptions, in a positively dangerous condition.

The successful emergence of Powell Duffryn from these troubled times would appear to be almost phoenix-like.

As already noted, the growth of output from the mid 1890s was the bearing of fruit from the sinking of new collieries, some of which were begun in the 1880s. Despite the troubles of the 1870s and 1880s, it would seem that the company was still able to focus some attention on the future. Not that the company's first sinkings were totally successful, and it is possibly this which caused the company's problems to continue into the late 1880s. During these troubled times the Managing Director of Powell Duffryn had been Sir George Elliot, and when he finally retired in 1888 a committee was appointed to investigate and report on the affairs of the company. The upshot of this report was the setting up of a three-man management committee, consisting initially of Joseph Shaw, Graeme Ogilvie and Henry Bolden. This step seems to mark a turning-point in the company's fortunes and as Tables 3 and 4 clearly show, the company began on an upward path from the 1890s. However, it appears that the company nearly did not survive the troubles of the 1870s and 1880s. In his evidence to the *Sankey Commission* in 1919 Joseph Shaw, then Chairman of Powell Duffryn, stated (q.23,772) that when he was appointed to the Board of Directors in 1888 he felt that the company was an absolutely bankrupt concern and advised the directors to wind the company up.

One possible explanation for the continued survival of the Powell Duffryn Company throughout the 1870s and 1880s would appear to have been the very low costs of production at the Fforchaman and Aberaman collieries. Of the former colliery, Hann has written: [18]

> . . . nothing so much assisted the Company throughout the bad years of 1875 to 1882, as the very cheap working of Fforchaman Colliery; and since those years too, it has been a great factor in providing the funds for sinking the Elliot Pits and making other extensions and improvements.

Other collieries in the Aberdare valley also, at least ultimately, helped to provide funds for sinking new pits. In the years of bad trade at the end of the 1870s, Aberaman was barely managing to eke out an existence by working remnants of the upper coal seams. In 1881, however, it became necessary to sink the colliery to the lower seams, as became the case at all the company's Aberdare collieries in time. Though excellent sections of both the Yard and Seven Feet seams were proved at Aberaman, it was a number of years before a market for them was secured. A major help in securing a market was the low cost of production at Aberaman, and Hann could state that 'it is from the working of these seams at the Aberaman Colliery that to a great extent provided the capital to sink new pits'.[19] The sinking of the Lower Duffryn winding pit to the lower seams helped put that colliery on a profitable footing in the 1890s despite the fact that in the 1880s the colliery had become a 'synonym for everything that was bad'.[20]

It would appear then that the factor enabling the company to sink new collieries after 1880 was the low cost of production at certain of the Aberdare collieries. How much of the total cost of sinking the Elliot pits of £209,772[21] was actually contributed by the Fforchaman colliery is uncertain, but it seems clear that, without this colliery, the company would have been forced to raise far more capital in the form of loans, than the substantial amounts which were actually borrowed. The boom of 1890–1, whilst not being of anything like the proportions of that of 1871–4, nevertheless provided the company with welcome relief. Profits in excess of £100,000 in both 1890 and 1891 helped the company in financing its developments, which included the erection of 50 coke ovens and a Humboldt washery at the Elliot pits, the sinking of the Coed-y-Moeth Pit, and the deepening of the Middle Duffryn winding shaft to enable the centralization of pumping operations there for the company's Aberdare collieries. The last operation alone cost £30,000 during the early 1890s,[22] and because of this and the company's commitment to sinking deep pits in the Rhymney valley, the company tried to procure a loan from the Rock Insurance Company. The report of T. Forster-Brown and Arthur Sopwith, however, was unsatisfactory and the loan was not procured, the company's collieries etc. being valued at only £265,000.[23] It was from about this time, however, that the company's fortunes changed substantially for the better.

It has been suggested that the cause of this change in fortune was due to the setting up of the Management Committee in 1888. In addition, the boom of 1890–1 and the coming to fruition of the sinking operations at the Elliot pits helped the company substantially in the early 1890s. With the reversal in fortunes the company embarked on a massive campaign of expansion. In addition to the developments already noted, the company began sinking the Bargoed pits in 1896–7, and the Cwmneol colliery was deepened and re-modelled between 1893 and 1898. Forster-Brown, in a new report accompanying the issue of £50,000 worth of 5 per cent debentures in 1897, stated that between 1893 and November 1896 the company had expended £70,000 on improvements and developments and that this had increased the profitability of the company.[24] Further sinkings followed in the early years of the twentieth century, and the amount expended on sinking new pits, coke ovens, washeries, etc., between 1899 and 1913 is presented in column 3 of Table 4. As well as sinking major new collieries such as Penallta (1905) and Britannia (1910), it would seem that in the early twentieth century the company was in the forefront of technological progress, at least within the south Wales coalfield. Powell Duffryn was amongst the first to experiment with coal-cutters, the use of electricity and the setting up of a by-product plant. Further, in 1910 the company erected an experimental plant at Fforchaman to dilute coal dust with stone dust in order to try and find a method of preventing major colliery explosions.

Thus a company which had been on the verge of bankruptcy in 1888 had, by 1913, become the major producer as well as being a potent force for technological change. The story of the Ocean Coal Company which is examined in the next section shows the opposite pattern, i.e., an initial period of exceptional growth, followed by stagnation.

II

The Ocean Coal Company
(a) Output growth, 1867–1913.[25]

The Ocean Coal Company began its life in 1864 when David Davies of Llandinam and his five partners secured leases of 2,000 acres of mineral tract in the Rhondda valley from Crawshay Bailey and others. Two pits, Park and Maindy, were sunk on this property, reaching the steam-coal seams in 1866. With the success of these operations at Cwmparc and Ton the partnership, David Davies & Co., leased further land contiguous to the original taking giving them an unbroken mineral property of 8,000 acres. In the period to 1886 further collieries, Dare, Eastern, Western and Garw, were sunk on this property. Whilst these developments were under way at the extended Rhondda taking, Davies, Scott and Company was formed in 1884 to develop a property in the Ynysybwl valley where the Lady Windsor colliery was sunk during 1885 and 1886. In 1887 the two private partnerships of David Davies and Co. and Davies, Scott and Company were combined into a public limited company called the Ocean Coal Company Ltd. Between its formation and the First World War the new company and its successor, Ocean Coal & Wilsons Ltd., did not develop any new collieries, though in 1893 the company added to its capacity by purchasing the Deep Navigation colliery. This colliery lay contiguous to the Lady Windsor colliery, and thus from 1893 the Ocean Company operated two large and self-contained sections of the coalfield, viz. the extended Rhondda taking, and the

Lady Windsor/Deep Navigation taking further east. The original Rhondda taking was once again extended in 1912 by the acquisition of the Avon Pits from the Great Western Railway Co. However, being unprofitable, these pits had been stopped for some time and even after the Ocean Company acquired them they remained idle for some years before being redeveloped.

Thus in the period between 1864 and 1893 seven collieries were sunk and a further colliery was purchased. Not surprisingly the output of the company grew spectacularly during this period, as shown in Table 5. By 1870 the company already had a yearly output of 300,000 tons of large steam-coal, and even when the boom of 1871–4 ended, production of large coal continued to grow rapidly reaching 494,000 tons in 1876 and 997,000 tons in 1883 (total production in this year being 1¼ million tons). With the completion of sinking operations at Garw and Lady Windsor in the late 1880s, total coal production had reached 1.85 million tons in 1892. The acquisition of Deep Navigation in

Table 5
Output of the Ocean collieries, 1866–1913

| Year | Output (tons) | | Employment |
	Large	Total	
1866	8,891[a]	—	—
1867	79,553	—	—
1870	303,334	341,271	1,516[b]
1874	441,586	—	—
1878	705,603	—	—
1880	914,110	1,152,951	3,179[c]
1883	997,420	1,246,069	—
1889	—	1,673,900	4,871
1893	—	2,144,222	7,336
1894[c]	—	2,516,321	7,917
1899	—	2,589,025	7,167
1904	1,911,262	2,560,902	7,966
1909	1,822,996	2,506,173	8,532
1913	1,709,078	2,397,985	8,339

Notes: [a] Figure taken from R. Hunt, *Mineral Statistics* (1867).

[b] Figures taken from I. Thomas, *Top Sawyer* (1938), p. 157.

[c] First full year of production at Deep Navigation colliery.

Source: Output — 1866–1883 — NLW, A. Stanley Davies MSS.
              1889–1913 — GRO, D/D NCB 28/89.

Employment — *List of Mines*, (HMSO), 1889–1913.

1893 added a further half a million tons to output, and production exceeded 2½ million tons for the first time in 1894. Making due allowance for the strikes of 1889 and 1912, the company's level of output fluctuated between c.2.3 and c.2.6 million tons per annum throughout the 1894–1913 period.

The rapid rise of output during the 1870s and 1880s established the Ocean Company as the largest coal producer in south Wales at this time, and in 1894 it was producing over one million tons more than any other producer. The failure to sink any new collieries after 1894 contrasted with the happenings at Powell Duffryn, and eventually Powell Duffryn ousted the Ocean Company as major producer once again. Thus in the period between 1894 and 1913, when coalfield output grew by 70 per cent and that of Powell Duffryn by a massive 160 per cent, the output of the Ocean Company actually fell by 4.7 per cent. In the next section the growth and development of the Ocean enterprise will be examined in an attempt to explain how the company was able to grow at an extraordinary rate in the 1870s and 1880s, but then failed to expand thereafter.

(b) Profits, capital and growth

Since the stagnation of the Ocean Company after 1894 was in such stark contrast to the period of continuous growth which preceded it, it would seem appropriate to analyse the factors influencing this early growth before attempting to explain the stagnation thereafter.

As already noted, the Ocean Company began life in 1864 as David Davies & Co., i.e., David Davies and his five partners.[26] In 1867 the company was converted to an unlimited liability private joint-stock company, with an authorized capital of £240,000, seemingly so that new partners could be brought in and the original shares divided up. This probably reflected the need for new sources of capital, since the sinking of Park and Maindy had taken longer than expected. Indeed the sinkings nearly failed since in March 1866 it was decided to abandon work on the two pits. However, on 9 March 1866, before this was implemented, 'one of the finest seams of coal in the world was struck in the Maendy pit at a depth of 220 yards. It was the upper steam coal seam, and a little later the lower seam was met at a depth of 240 yards'.[27]

The Ocean collieries, as they became known, were thus nearly stillborn. Once coal began to be produced from the second half of 1866, however, the partners never looked back. By the end of 1871, after the expenditure of £123,952, David Davies & Co. had three collieries — Park, Maindy and Dare — in production and together valued at £210,000.[28] The early growth of the company was greatly helped by the booming fortunes of the coal trade between 1871 and 1874. Between 1867, the first year in which the company recorded a profit (see Table 6), and 1875 gross profits amounted to £493,823, 83 per cent of which accrued in the boom years 1872–4. These high profits enabled the company both to pay high dividends and to plough funds back into the concern and open new collieries. Of the £493,823, 41.3 per cent was distributed and of the remaining £289,650 the major portion, £182,000, was used for the payment of calls on

Table 6
Gross and divided profits, David Davies & Co., 1866–91

| | Profit | | Divided as a |
Year	Gross	Divided	% of Gross
1866	—	—	—
1867	7,222	0	0
1868	7,273	0	0
1869	7,406	4,080	55.1
1870	11,998	0	0
1871	16,334	0	0
1872	73,438	31,900	43.4
1873	184,411	94,040	51.0
1874	151,878	74,153	48.8
1875	33,328	0	0
1876	35,480	0	0
1877	29,426	19,200	65.2
1878	31,644	16,800	53.1
1879	31,427	28,800	91.6
1880	39,178	30,600	78.1
1881	44,409	33,774	76.1
1882	76,214	52,400	68.3
1883	71,992	62,400	86.7
1884	53,761	61,805	115.0
1885	28,339	47,484	167.6
1886	12,511	0	0
1887[a]	16,458	0	0
1888[a] [b]	16,173	—	?
	12,367	17,000	137.5
1889	—	—	—
1890	255,056	184,000	72.1
1891	218,408	188,000	86.1

Notes: — indicates that the figure is unknown.
[a] First half of year only.
[b] Second half of year only.

Source: National Library of Wales, A. Stanley Davies, MSS. Bundles 31 and 39, and
Llandinam MS 101.

new shares created to enable new collieries to be sunk — indeed the sinkings of the Eastern and Western collieries were financed by calls which were deducted from revenue before the division of profit was made.

During the 1880s the company continued to expand by sinking two new collieries. The Garw colliery, which was sunk between 1883 and 1886, was financed by the original company, but a new company, Davies, Scott & Co., was formed in 1884 to finance the sinking of the Lady Windsor colliery. The reason for establishing a new partnership to carry out this latter venture is unclear, although Davies's biographer suggests that it might have been due either to the desire to enable the London merchant David Cooper Scott to be involved or simply because the site of the Lady Windsor colliery was on a new taking which was separate from the extended Rhondda taking. Whatever the reason, Davies, Scott & Co. only had a short life, for in 1887 it was merged with David Davies & Co. to form the new public limited liability company called the Ocean Coal Co. Ltd., formed with a nominal capital of £800,000, of which David Davies and his son, Edward, held almost one half of the 8,000 shares.

Little is known about the levels of profit earned after 1891. During the two years of the 1890–1 boom the company amassed gross profits of £473,462. Such large profits may possibly explain why the company went ahead and purchased the Deep Navigation colliery in 1893, though plans for doing so had been originally put forward in 1890. In 1908 the Ocean Coal Co. Ltd. merged with Wilsons, Sons & Co. Ltd., a well-known firm of coal-shippers and foreign depot owners. Links between the two companies, however, had been in existence prior to this with three members of the Ocean Company's board, Messrs. Webb, Yarrow and Jenkins, also being directors of Wilsons. The new holding company, Ocean Coal and Wilsons Ltd., was registered in March 1908, to hold all of the share capital in the two firms. The success of the company was indicated by the fact that in the years 1910–12 the company paid a dividend on its ordinary shares of 14 per cent, which was raised to 16 per cent in 1913 and 1914. In 1914, moreover, a 50 per cent bonus issue of ordinary shares was made in April. Despite stagnating levels of output in the early twentieth century, the company still seems to have been able to make handsome profits.

III

Powell Duffryn and Ocean — an explanation of contrasting patterns of development

The successful growth and development of colliery companies depend upon three main factors: general market conditions, the geological conditions prevailing at the company's collieries, and the quality of the management. As far as the general market conditions are concerned, though these differed over the period — being on the whole more favourable in the early twentieth century than during the late 1870s and 1880s —, since both the Ocean and Powell Duffryn companies were producing essentially the same product, i.e., large steam-coal, it would be difficult to argue that differences in the market conditions faced by the two concerns could explain the different patterns of development. However, although the companies were producing the same product, they did so under differing circumstances. The original Rhondda taking of the Ocean Company was a highly favourable one; it was large, contained steam-coal of excellent quality, and the geological conditions were good. Thus once the coal had been reached there would be little difficulty in finding a market for it, and given that the seams were virtually free of any water problems, the cost of mining was low with pumping costs negligible. In contrast Powell Duffryn suffered major problems with water, both in its Aberdare pits and later in the Rhymney valley when it began to exploit that area more fully. On balance then, the more rapid growth of the Ocean Company in the 1870s must be, at least partially, attributed to especially favourable geological factors.

The influence of favourable geological factors tends to wane as the coal seams are depleted. However, the Ocean Company did not perhaps suffer seriously from this trend in this period; on the eve of the First World War the company could still boast its possession of 'the largest unworked area of the Four Feet Seam of Coal in South Wales'.[29] On the other hand, the less favourable geological conditions of Powell Duffryn should not be over-stressed. Despite the problems of water, two of the Aberdare collieries, Aberaman and Fforchaman, were the company's lowest cost producers for much of the period. Further, less favourable geological conditions could, within limits, be offset by exceptional managerial talent. In the case of the Aberdare collieries, for example, Powell Duffryn introduced a centralized pumping scheme at Middle Duffryn in the early 1890s to solve the water problem. How, then, did the two companies compare in terms of managerial and entrepreneurial qualities?

Whilst favourable geological conditions obviously helped the Ocean Company in the formative years, much of the company's success at this time was also due to the entrepreneurial drive of one man, David Davies. It was his skill and vision which saw the potential of the virgin coal resources of the Rhondda valley and carried through their development, despite initial setbacks. Whilst Davies remained in control, the company grew and prospered. Davies, however, died in 1890 and it would appear to be no accident that the company was rather less dynamic after this time. With Davies gone, there was nobody of the same quality within the company to continue developing its coal resources. After buying the Deep Navigation colliery, the Ocean Company appears to have been content to enjoy the fruits of its earlier endeavours, the shareholders preferring present dividends to future ones. Control of the company between 1890 and 1913 remained little changed, except that occasioned by death, and in 1913 many of the senior company personnel had been with the company for upwards of thirty years. William Jenkins, the general manager, for example, had been in this position since 1871, and had been a member of the board since 1886. Whilst Jenkins was well respected by the workmen and was proud of his record of never having experienced a major accident in any of the mines under his control, it is possible that his essentially conservative nature may have reflected that of many other board members, and thus help to explain why the Ocean Company did not continue to expand its collieries and output after the mid 1890s.

The 1890s also saw a vital change in the fortunes of the Powell Duffryn Company, though in this case the change was a marked improvement. Superficially, at least, managerial changes appear to be connected with this change of fortune. In 1888 George Elliot, who had guided Powell Duffryn's fortunes until that time, finally retired and control of development and planning was placed in the hands of a three-man management committee. This board continued the expansion plans which Elliot had begun and it was as a result of the development of the company's Rhymney valley property that the company was able to expand in the early twentieth century. Thus while it would be possible to argue that David Davies was a superior entrepreneur than George Elliot, and thus Ocean developed more quickly in the 1870s and 1880s, it seems clear that the growth of Powell Duffryn from the 1890s, in contrast to the stagnation of Ocean, was due to the former company's greater ability in overcoming the loss of its dominating entrepreneur.

Conclusion

Ebbs and flows in the coal trade obviously affect the fortunes of colliery companies. This is no less true of Powell Duffryn and the Ocean Company than of many others. However, the distinguishing feature of the performance of these two companies between 1864 and 1913 is in their long-term, rather than their short-run, development. Thus whilst the output of the Ocean Company expanded rapidly between 1866 and the mid 1890s and then stagnated, Powell Duffryn experienced an initial stagnation to the mid 1890s followed by exceptional growth thereafter. A company's success, however, cannot be judged simply by whether or not its output grew, and using the level of profits as a guide to success it would appear that the Ocean Company did not fail in the 1895–1913 period. In 1891, at the height of the coal boom, the Ocean Company earned gross profits of £255,055 compared to Powell Duffryn's £152,066, thereby completely reversing the performance of the two companies in 1873 when Powell Duffryn had gross profits £100,000 greater than those of the Ocean Company (i.e., £284,728 compared with £184,411). By the end of the period under consideration Ocean was still earning higher profits than Powell Duffryn. During the eight years ending 1917, Powell Duffryn earned gross profits of £3.1 million (see Table 4) whilst during the same period the Ocean Company paid out over £3.5 million in cash dividends, despite a lower level of output.[30]

Despite the profits success of the Ocean Company on the eve of the First World War, there is an uneasy feeling that the company was not performing as well as it might have done. The Ocean Company's early and successful growth, and the later successful developments at Powell Duffryn were, as we have already seen, largely associated with periods of new colliery sinkings. Continued development of new collieries thus seems to have been an important factor in continued output and profits growth. Failure to develop any new collieries by the Ocean Company in the late 1890s and early years of the twentieth century, possibly because of failings amongst its management, led to output stagnation and, possibly, lost profit. Whether profit was lost or not is, of course, unknown, but if Powell Duffryn's performance after 1895 is used as a yardstick then it would appear that the Ocean Company under-performed in this period, particularly in the light of its highly-successful past history, and in this respect perhaps the company's proud boast that all its principal officials, including managers and under-managers, were Welshmen,[31] was somewhat misplaced!

Trade and Shipping in South Wales —
The Radcliffe Company, 1882–1921

ROBIN CRAIG

Although the industrialization of south Wales required the deployment of a great quantity of merchant shipping, neither of the two principal ports of registry, Swansea and Cardiff, manifest much evidence, in the classical period of development, of there being a substantial body of local men who were prepared to invest heavily in ships. Of the two ports Swansea took the lead with Cardiff lagging well behind. Despite an increasing volume of trade in coal, iron ore, copper ore and manufactured iron and tinplate, most of this traffic was carried in vessels owned outside the Principality with West Country shipowners taking the lion's share.

It was not until the 1860s and 1870s, with the very rapid growth in the export of steam coal, that Cardiff-based shipowners began to purchase steamships on a considerable and increasing scale. With the advent of the economical, bulk-carrying steamship — the characteristic tramp steamer — Cardiff shipowners began to play a much more dominant role, with outward coal cargoes combining effectively with homeward freights of iron ore and pitwood. Next, the coal cargoes outwards were complemented by freights of grain from the Black Sea as that trade expanded rapidly in the 1870s, this being one major factor in the collapse of the high farming era in Britain: it was this conjunction of coal and grain which was to nourish the fortune of more than one Cardiff shipowner.

The advent of large-scale steamship owning at the Welsh ports required the emergence of a number of new and dynamic entrepreneurs, but this remains a neglected aspect of Welsh economic and social history, as has recently been pointed out by Sir John Habakkuk in his review in *Morgannwg* (1981, pp. 134–5) of Volume V of the *Glamorgan County History*. This weakness in Welsh historiography is in marked contrast to the attention lavished upon other aspects of Welsh history. A glance at the *Dictionary of Welsh Biography* is sufficient to confirm this neglect: religious and educational leaders are given great, and no doubt justifiable, prominence, as are leaders of organized labour and politicians. But entrepreneurs are accorded scant attention, despite their undoubted contribution to Welsh industrial and commercial growth. Readers of textbooks on Welsh history, such as the recent well-received study by Dr K.O. Morgan,[1] might be forgiven for concluding that industry in Wales was all Indians and no chiefs. In the field of shipping the apparent bias against entrepreneurs is particularly marked, since Welshmen played a crucial role in the international predominance of this peculiarly successful British industry. Readers of the *Dictionary of Biography* will look in vain for any reference to Owen Philipps (Lord Kylsant), and there is but a brief paragraph for that other remarkable Welsh shipping magnate, Alfred Jones, the Carmarthen boy who made good. Perhaps the failure to accord full recognition to figures such as these is to be explained away by the fact that men such as Kylsant and Jones made their fortunes outside Wales: moreover, many who *did* accumulate great fortunes in Wales, not least a number of shipowners, may perhaps be categorized among those of whom Leland Jenks wrote when he described British foreign investors as constituting '. . . . a rentier governing class, whose economic interests lay outside the community in which they lived and exerted influence.'[2] This paper, however, examines a Welsh-born shipowning family which was as manifestly successful as it was indubitably Welsh.

Thanks to the initiative and enterprise of Dr Geraint Jenkins of the Welsh Industrial and Maritime Museum, many records of Evan Thomas, Radcliffe and Company, a major Cardiff shipowning firm, have been recovered. They probably constitute the most representative collection of business papers that has survived from the years in which Cardiff shipowning was rapidly expanding. It has been possible to supplement these papers with others rescued by Mr Peter Frank of the University of Essex. This small but interesting additional material comprises circulars and accounts sent by Radcliffe's to a shareholder in Whitby, and these papers help us to fill some gaps in the Radcliffe collection, which is sadly incomplete, especially in respect of the first ten or fifteen years of the business.

Dr Jenkins, in his book *Evan Thomas Radcliffe: a Cardiff Shipowning Company* (Cardiff, 1982) has published a most useful short study in which he explores several aspects of the Radcliffe enterprise. The present paper is intended to do no more than supplement Dr Jenkins's account and it is based upon a preliminary (and therefore provisional) analysis of some of the predominantly financial records. It is hoped that this present study will be in some ways indicative of the manner in which a Welsh steamship company organized its business: but at the outset, it has to be made clear that much remains to be done on this and other shipowning firms. It is especially to be hoped that it may be possible in the future to study some of the less successful, or unsuccessful, enterprises in order that a rounded and complete portrait may be presented of a complex and dynamic industry in which the prosperity of a few had its mirror image in the failure of the many.

The three Radcliffe brothers, named Henry, Daniel and Charles, were the sons of Rees Radcliffe of Merthyr Tydfil, and all of them were to seek their fortunes in Cardiff's rapidly expanding shipping industry in the 1880s. There is a felicitous symmetry in the fact that Merthyr, described by Gwyn Williams as '. . . mother of iron and steel in south Wales' and the town that produced Wales's 'first working class martyr and its first working class press'[3] should have also been the birthplace of Cardiff's first millionaire.

The eldest son, Henry (1851–1921), was one of a number of subsequently prominent Cardiff entrepreneurs who served in a subordinate capacity in the offices of Messrs J.H. Anning, the Cardiff shipowner. Anning had come to Cardiff from the West Country and at first owned sailing ships, but he embarked capital in steamships from 1877. He was thus one of that generation of incomers which included such men as Morel, Hacquoil, Marychurch, Stallybrass, Strong, Wilson, Capper and Guèrét, who pioneered steamship owning in the port and gave training to a second generation of shipowners. The Anning business was clearly a fructifying influence: apart from Henry Radcliffe, W.J. Tatem (later Lord Glanely) received his commercial training there, and William Reardon Smith was master of an Anning ship before becoming the master of Tatem's own first steamer, *Lady Lewis*, and in turn a leader of the shipping industry in south Wales.[4]

From Aberporth in Cardiganshire came Evan Thomas, son of Hezekiah Thomas, a small-scale shipowner with sailing ships in the coasting trade. Evan became an experienced master-mariner in steamships, moving to Porthcawl as that port expanded largely under the influence of the Brogden family.[5] It is commonplace that the two paths to shipping success in the nineteenth century were via the profession of seafaring or via the counting-house. In June 1881, this characterstic conjunction of skills was manifest when Evan Thomas promoted his first steamship company, taking as his partner in the enterprise the young Henry Radcliffe, then aged 24, and poised to show the experience gained from his years with J.H. Anning.

The second Radcliffe boy, Daniel, was born in 1860, three years after Henry. He began his shipping career in a humble capacity as customs clerk in Messrs. Turnbull's at the age of sixteen. The firm of Turnbull's had achieved distinction in both shipbuilding and shipowning in Whitby, and the firm was one of a number of northern companies that opened offices in Cardiff in the 1870s attracted to that port by the immense growth in the coal trade which was bread and butter to every British tramp-shipowning company. In 1884, Daniel was described as an accountant when he witnessed a document signed by the Turnbull directors.[6] Altogether he served fourteen years with the firm, gaining during that time a thorough grounding in all aspects of ship management from one of Cardiff's foremost and most respected shipping enterprises. Daniel appears to have joined his older brother at about the same time as Evan Thomas's premature and untimely death in 1891, and thereafter devoted all his energies to the enterprise Evan Thomas and Henry Radcliffe had placed on such firm foundations. The departure of Daniel from Turnbull's appears to have been on good terms, and Daniel may have been influential in the decision to order a steamship from Turnbull's Whitehall (Whitby) shipbuilding yard. The *Peterston*, a 2,768-ton steamer, was delivered in 1892 and was a successful ship, earning good dividends and destined to serve the brothers until her sale in 1913 when she was replaced by larger and more up-to-date tonnage.

The third Radcliffe son, Charles, was born in 1862, but he only had a brief association with his elder brothers. In about 1890 or 1891 Daniel Radcliffe brought him into association in respect of the management of the Glamorgan Steamship Co. Ltd., floated with a capital of £30,000 to take over the second-hand steamer *Lady Armstrong*, which had been built much earlier, in 1883. This vessel had a very brief life under Radcliffe management, being lost by collision with a Dutch steamer off Folkestone in April 1891. The latter vessel was found wholly to blame for the collision after a somewhat protracted legal dispute, and thereafter Charles seems to have severed his links with his older brothers. It may perhaps be significant that Charles was brought into association with his brothers in the year when the senior member of the Radcliffe enterprise, Captain Evan Thomas unexpectedly died at the early age of 49: moreover, the years 1890–91 were somewhat exceptional in the history of the firm, as Radcliffe's purchased some second-hand vessels, none of which was to prove a happy investment. Perhaps Charles had brought to his brothers some much needed capital that served to replace that withdrawn on the death of Captain Thomas. Perhaps there were brotherly disagreements: at all events, Charles thereafter pursued an independent career in ship management, except in respect of the Glamorgan Steamship Co. Ltd. participating with others in a number of shipping ventures. However, Charles proved less successful than his older brothers in weathering the financial gales which were to batter Cardiff after the collapse of the post-1919 shipping boom, and his last steamers were to be disposed of in the great shake-out of Cardiff steamshipping in the mid 1920s: coincidentally, perhaps, two of his five vessels were to be purchased by Turnbull Scott Shipping Company, in which Daniel Radcliffe had served his training, and his three remaining ships were to be acquired by Court Line.

Two principal methods were adopted in raising capital for shipping ventures in the nineteenth century. One method was to divide shares in the enterprise into the 64th shares allowed for under the legislation regulating the official registration of merchant ships. The second, and later, method was to float joint-stock, limited liability, companies under which the investable funds were raised by purchasing equity in registered joint-stock enterprises. Such joint-stock companies were established after the Repeal of the Bubble Act in 1825, and their number was multiplied with the advent of the limited liability legislation subsequently enacted. At first, shipping companies were promoted mainly in the expectation of establishing fleets of vessels, and share denominations tended to be large. As a consequence, the sources of capital tended to be confined to those with considerable wealth, often closely associated with the shipping industry. The advent of limited liability, and the consequent possibility of dividing shares into smaller denominations permitted the attraction of capital from a wider and more heterogeneous public which was less likely to have commercial or professional interests in the shipping industry as such.[7] There was much more 'blind capital seeking its five per cent'. From the 1870s there was a new development in shipping with shipowners establishing a series of single ship companies, generally several under common management, with each vessel constituting a separate joint-stock limited liability enterprise.[8] The great distinction between such ventures and ownership under the older 64th system was that the latter method of raising capital involved sharing the risk of what was often a speculative commercial venture which involved ownership of the vessel as tenants in common: liability was absolute and participants were liable for the debts of the enterprise as well as sharing in due proportion any profits that might accrue. Of necessity, such associations of owners of 64th shares tended to have as their basis a common identity of interest and association in which trust and responsibility were reposed in a ship's husband or managing owner who was accepted by all and who merited the confidence of the participants.[9] Under limited liability joint-stock companies, which issued shares of smaller denomination, the relationships could be much more impersonal. Moreover, the single ship company reduced any possible liability which might arise from maritime claims for such eventualities as collision, where a relatively cheap ship might inflict prohibitively costly damage on an expensive one: here the concept of limited liability came into its own in a very direct context.

The Radcliffe enterprise began as an association of a limited number of individuals under the 64th system, promoted by Evan Thomas himself in a circular reproduced in Dr Geraint Jenkins's recent brief history of the firm. The 64th shareholders who were invited to subscribe to shares in the first steamer *Gwenllian Thomas* contributed on the basis of over £277 per 64th share, this representing the due proportion of the cost of the steamer in June 1881, then under the course of construction in Palmer's shipbuilding yard at Jarrow. Evan Thomas and Henry Radcliffe proposed to manage the ship, taking as their remuneration 2½ per cent on the gross earnings of the vessel, all brokerages, discounts and demurrages being credited to the ship, and therefore to the shareholders.[10] The shares were very widely distributed, numbering fifty-eight individuals, and Evan Thomas and Henry Radcliffe only subscribed one share themselves, jointly. At first *Gwenllian Thomas* was registered in the port of Swansea, which was the port of registry for most Porthcawl shipping. The vessel was subsequently re-registered at Cardiff when in common with the second and later vessels acquired, joint-stock company ownership was substituted for the 64th system. Beginning with *Iolo Morgannwg* Steamship Co. Ltd., registered in November 1882, all the later companies established by Evan Thomas Radcliffe and Company were single ship companies capitalized at very near the cost of the individual vessels when purchased. A list of these companies is shown in Table 1 on page 172.

When we turn to consider the sources from which capital was obtained for the acquisition of tonnage, we find that there was a distinct and significant shift in the source of funds over the years. Clearly, when Evan Thomas and Henry Radcliffe first launched into ship management, the decision to own their first vessel under the 64th principal necessitated their obtaining financial support from a limited circle of business acquaintances and friends: moreover, as we have indicated, the individual subscriptions were of necessity large — each shareholder had to venture about £280 for a single share. With the decision to register all subsequent vessels under joint-stock, limited liability single ship companies, the catchment area from which capital could be drawn was both extended and rendered more impersonal. Each of the thirty-four companies inaugurated between 1882 and 1908 issued shares of £100 or less, and the share capital in each company corresponded to the cost of the vessel owned by each company. The first Radcliffe single ship companies required a capital of between £22,000 and £27,600, with £35,100 being needed for the larger than average vessel *Walter Thomas* in 1884. By the late 1890s the nominal capital of the single ship companies was as much as £44,000, representing the economies of scale achieved by that time with the utilization of much larger steamships in the Radcliffe fleet. The declining cost of new tonnage in the depressed years after 1902 required companies of somewhat less capital — around £40,000 would secure suitable new tonnage in the middle of this decade.

Table 1
The Radcliffe joint-stock shipping companies

Name of Company	Date Registered	Capital (£s)
Iolo Morgannwg	17 Nov. 1882	22,800
Anne Thomas	14 Jly. 1883	25,600
Kate Thomas	1 Aug. 1883	27,600
Wynnstay	1 Aug. 1883	27,600
Walter Thomas	5 Oct. 1883	35,100
Bala	27 Feb. 1884	28,600
Gwenllian Thomas	28 Jly. 1884	18,100
W.I. Radcliffe	5 Feb. 1886	25,800
Clarissa Radcliffe	10 Apl. 1888	28,300
Sarah Radcliffe	10 Oct. 1888	26,100
Mary Thomas	30 Nov. 1888	26,600
Jane Radcliffe	23 May 1889	26,000
Douglas Hill	26 Oct. 1889	30,000
Llanberis	7 Dec. 1889	34,400
Glamorgan	23 Jan. 1890	30,000
Manchester	15 Mar. 1890	30,000
Anthony Radcliffe	17 Apl. 1893	26,800
Ethel Radcliffe	2 Mar. 1894	25,600
Dunraven	31 Mar. 1896	31,400
Windsor	2 Nov. 1896	33,000
Llandudno	20 Nov. 1896	33,000
Wimborne	21 Jan. 1898	35,000
Paddington	14 Feb. 1898	40,000
Euston	16 Apl. 1898	31,000
Swindon	6 Jly. 1898	39,500
Llanover	24 Dec. 1898	44,000
Llangorse	13 Jan. 1899	44,000
Llangollen	20 Nov. 1899	40,000
Llanishen	26 Nov. 1899	40,000
Llandrindod	28 Nov. 1899	40,000
Clarissa Radcliffe	14 Apl. 1904	38,500
Patagonia	15 Nov. 1905	43,800
Picton	15 Nov. 1905	40,000
Colonies	4 Apl. 1908	

Source: P.P., *Accounts and Papers,* Annual Lists of New Joint-Stock, Limited Liability Companies.

It has only been possible to make provisional analysis of the sources of capital for Radcliffe companies thus far, but we have attempted a brief summary of our findings in respect of the first venture, *Gwenllian Thomas,* initially owned in 64th shares; the Anne Thomas Steamship Co. Ltd., of 1890–1; and the Picton Steamship Co. Ltd., registered in November 1905. The subscribers to *Gwenllian Thomas* were predominantly resident in south Wales: 40 per cent of the shares were subscribed by individuals living in Cardiff, the percentage for south Wales as a whole aggregating 55 per cent of the total capital. Next came north Wales with 19 per cent of the equity, and the rest came from south-west England, including two shares subscribed by the Holman firm in London, an enterprise with widespread connections in Welsh steamshipping which also engaged in shipown- ing, ship-broking and marine insurance. John Price, manager of Palmer's shipyard held 2/64th shares as did ship-brokers in Malta and Palermo. Ship-brokers and agents in Mediterranean ports were frequently subscribers to Welsh shipping ventures, hoping, no doubt, to secure the agency of such vessels on their frequent visits to ports in the area with outward freights of coal.

With the advent of limited liability shareholding in £100 units or less, the number and variety of shareholders increased markedly. There were 209 initially registered shareholders in *Anne Thomas* in the 1890–1 share register of whom 61 per cent were resident in south Wales and a notable 36 per cent of the total number of shares issued were held by individuals resident in central and north Wales. Southern England was also a fruitful source of financial support, with smaller contributions originating from London and the North of England. With the *Picton* of 1905–6, the picture manifests profound change: only 29 per cent of the shares were held in south Wales, whereas the North of England, with 28 per cent, was only marginally less significant. North Walians played a subordinate role. The geographical spread now embraced England, Wales, Scotland and Ireland, with shares also held in Straits Settlements, Sicily, Russia and South Africa.

Not all of these subscribers to Radcliffe steamship companies vouchsafe their trade, profession or calling in the share registers, but some generalizations may perhaps be in order. The shareholders may be generally identified as middle class, and most of them had no obvious connexions with the shipping industry. Six women had held shares in *Gwenllian Thomas,* as did two men of the cloth, a doctor of medicine, and a north Wales bank manager. In the case of *Anne Thomas,* the cloth was exceptionally well represented: thirteen ministers were numbered among the subscribers, predominantly Calvinistic Methodists. No fewer than eleven north Wales quarrymen were also participants, and a few were employed on the railways, including an engine-driver, and two railway guards. There were some other working-class subscribers, including two colliers, a tinplate workman, and a tripe-dresser. There was also a sprinkling of schoolmasters, farmers, fitters, and proprietors of small hotels or public houses. Thus it may be suggested that Radcliffe's were tapping a widening sphere for funds, with passive, middle or even working-class investors predominating, remote both from Cardiff and from professional engagement in the shipping industry.[11]

The methods by which Radcliffe and other newly-promoted shipping companies publicized their prospectuses is worthy of particular attention since they provoked a good deal of critical comment in the local and national press — not least among journals that circulated widely in the shipping community. Both the shipping papers *Fairplay* and *Syren and Shipping,* as well as less widely distributed and somewhat fugitive news sheets such as *The Lighthouse,* were fiercely critical of the new single ship companies and the extent to which they painted an over-optimistic and extravagant picture of the likely returns available to those who might venture their savings in tramp steamer companies. The main burden of the complaints was that the promoters were too eager to issue tendentious and misleading circulars which were excessively sanguine of the possible rewards which would accrue to subscribers. The critics maintained that the companies were unduly speculative; that they contributed in no small measure to the periodical cyclical fluctuations that afflicted the freight market; and that they encouraged over-building in booms. The managers of such ventures were criticized, too, for taking their management fees from the gross earnings of the vessels that they purchased, which meant that the rewards of management were excessive and relatively risk-free compared with the risks borne by ordinary shareholders. While the freight market was buoyant, a good manager could indeed advertise splendid returns on the capital outlay — as much as 40 per cent being sometimes obtainable. But over-speculative shipbuilding, for which shipbuilders themselves were far from blameless, tended to increase what was in any case a highly volatile market, and the high dividends of one year were all too often followed by years in which little or no distribution was made to the trusting shareholders who had been induced into acquiring equity when trade was good. Moreover, it was argued by the critics that only rarely was depreciation provided for in the printed prospectuses circulated, so that an unrealistic return was calculated on an asset which, while it could fluctuate wildly, generally rapidly diminished over time. The need for a conservative depreciation policy was rendered the more necessary by the rapid pace of technological change which characterized steamshipping from the 1870s: older vessels could quickly become obsolescent or require expensive repair or refitting and, without some kind of sinking fund set aside from current earnings, the long-term future of the enterprise could be highly questionable. The need to depreciate fully the capital asset, which resided entirely in the ship, was of profound importance in enlightened ship management, but even the most prestigious of the major liner companies (e.g., Cunard, and Royal Mail Steam Packet Co.) were extremely vulnerable on this score. At all times shipping companies had to steer a precarious course between paying scant attention to depreciation in the short-term interests of the shareholders, and the salting away of large sums of earnings from shareholders under the heading of renewal funds which diminished the dividends currently available for distribution.

The main criticism that can be directed at the critics themselves was that they only rarely had the capacity to distinguish successfully the well-run from the badly-run company. Complaints that the promotion of single-ship companies destabilized the market were often sour grapes bestowed upon new enterprises regarded by established firms as interlopers. The shipping press showed little discrimination in this matter.

Radcliffe's became a target of much ill-merited and fractious abuse as were other well-run companies such as Reardon Smith, W. & C.T. Jones and the Field Line, whereas all too often the real rogues, of whom John Ruthen of Cardiff was perhaps the prime representative, escaped discriminating censure. On the shipowner's part, it has to be remembered that they were competing with each other for a finite supply of funds available for investment: there was intense rivalry between Radcliffe's and Tatem's, for example, who were each anxious to display their own operations in the best possible light in order to secure the favour of the investing public.

One of the less seemly incidents which played some part in giving Radcliffe's the reputation which prejudiced their standing in the shipping press related to the Reverend J. Cynddylan Jones, Welsh secretary of the British & Foreign Bible Society, a prominent Calvinistic Methodist Minister, and author of several books of Biblical exegesis. It is quite clear that the Reverend Gentleman promoted the sale of shares in Radcliffe steamers if not actually from the pulpit, then at least from a distance not very remote therefrom. For these services he received a pecuniary reward: between 1883 and 1888 he received £1,318 from Radcliffe's for commission on shares in their single ship companies on the basis of 2 per cent (or £2) per £100 share sold. From the evidence of the Radcliffe accounts Cynddylan Jones received commission on the shares sold in seven out of eight companies launched: moreover, he was apparently given half shares in some of the ships, notably *Iolo Morgannwg*, and *Anne Thomas*, and a whole share in *Kate Thomas*. He also received loans from Radcliffe's amounting to £445 between August 1884 and June 1887. It seems likely that payments of this kind were not unique: Dr Geraint Jenkins believes that at least one north Wales bank manager performed similar services for the Radcliffe enterprise and it also seems possible that a Bridgend bank manager acted in like fashion. The use of such intermediaries did not escape notice in the shipping press. The editor of *The Lighthouse* commented on the Reverend Jones in the issue of 18 December 1886, referring to him as a 'leading and highly respected minister in the Calvinistic Methodist connection', who had done much to advocate investment in Radcliffe-managed shipping. The editor continued:

> This recommendation, besides being in many cases attached to the prospectus, was also inserted in a Welsh newspaper circulating in north Wales, where the Calvinistic Methodists are very strong. As a large proportion of the shareholders of the *Anne Thomas Steamship Co. Ltd.* appear to reside in north Wales, the reverend gentleman's 'testimonial' apparently carried weight with it. We don't know of course that he had any particular motive in going out of his way to recommend shipowning, so presume that in doing so he only desired to do what he could to promote the welfare of his flock: but in any circumstances, he deserved to be appointed 'Chaplain to the fleet — that is presuming the fleet required a chaplain.

These remarks arose in the context of criticism of Radcliffe's published voyage accounts in respect of *Iolo Morgannwg* and *Anne Thomas* in 1886 which purported to cast a favourable light on the management of the two companies. The accounts were criticized by *The Lighthouse* on the familiar grounds that there were no allowances in them for depreciation, repairs or renewals, but, more fundamentally, the accounts, although independently audited, manifested errors which the journal was quick to sieze upon. Similar criticisms were voiced from time to time by at least two other journals, and *Fairplay* and *Syren & Shipping* remained critical of Radcliffe accounts until the mid 1900s when other scandals in Cardiff shipowning circles diverted their attention to more legitimate targets. The 1886 criticisms were factually admitted by Radcliffe's however, and the firm had to issue amended accounts in which their acknowledged errors were corrected.

This blunder precipitated further adverse publicity when a minority of Radcliffe shareholders, who had been induced to invest in their vessels by the Reverend Jones, publicly came together under his leadership to express dissatisfaction with the dividends being declared in a period of manifest shipping depression.[12] It was the Reverend Jones who circularized shareholders and expressed criticism of Radcliffe management: criticisms which did not go unnoticed in the press. He seemed intent upon damaging Radcliffe's probity, but he does not appear to have made explicit the extent to which Radcliffe's had given him commission on shares that he had exercised his influence to dispose of, nor does he appear to have acknowledged the loans and gifts he had received. The main burden of Jones's complaints was that Radcliffe was making large profits at the expense of his shareholders, and that he, Jones, ought to have participated more fully in the wealth that the firm was allegedly accumulating. Jones also criticized Henry Radcliffe for supposedly failing to compensate adequately the surviving members of Captain Evan Thomas's family after his untimely death. In fact, Radcliffe's did make provision for Captain Thomas's widow and children, although some payments may indeed have been agreed as the consequence of Jones's animadversions. It is worth pointing out in this context that Captain Evan Thomas does not appear to have made any great financial contribution to the foundation of the business, and it seems probable that both he and Henry Radcliffe started their business on a shoe-string. The level of compensation was, therefore, a matter of fine judgement. The Reverend Jones also argued in correspondence with Henry Radcliffe that his own popularity and reputation had suffered as a result of the poor dividend distribution during the depression years, and that his preferment had been prejudiced by his known connexion with the Radcliffe enterprise. It is to be noted, however, that he could nevertheless still seek from Radcliffe a loan on behalf of his son, and at the same time bemoaned the fact that Radcliffe was now planning to fund the building of new vessels by canvassing for shares in English towns. Jones wrote: 'True, you have English shareholders coming in: but they would not have patronized you had not the Welsh floated you'.

From the evidence of the share registers so far analysed, the reverend gentleman's criticism can be seen to be only partly justified. Admittedly, the preponderance of support that Evan Thomas and Henry Radcliffe had at first received was largely derived from Welsh sources, but they, in common with most of the other Cardiff shipowners, soon exhausted the potentialities of that catchment area, and found new and richer sources of capital in the North of England, with investment from the textile districts becoming much more important than the contribution from Wales. Indeed, English cotton-spinning masters located as far away as Russia played some part in furnishing capital for Radcliffe steamers. If the 1884-built steamship *Bala* made explicit Radcliffe's reliance upon north Wales capital, the christening of the steamship *Manchester* in 1890 was tacit acknowledgement that Radcliffe's support by that time lay outside the Principality.[13]

As for the criticism that Radcliffe accounting took no cognisance of depreciation, this was a superficial view that took no account of an important feature of Radcliffe policy. From the inception of the first Radcliffe Company until Henry Radcliffe's death in 1921, the firm only liquidated one of their companies. This was the Clarissa Radcliffe Steamship Co. Ltd., which went into voluntary liquidation in 1899. It seems likely that this solitary liquidation was the consequence of the distressing loss of life occasioned when that vessel foundered on her homeward passage. What the partners did as vessels were disposed of was to transfer or assign other vessels in their fleet to the existing companies at written-down values. Similarly, several newly-built vessels were transferred to pre-existing single ship companies either in whole or in part. For example, when the steamship *Wynnstay* was sold, half the value of the newly-built vessel *W.I. Radcliffe* (the second Radcliffe vessel of that name) was transferred to the older company in 1904. Similarly, the original company, the Gwenllian Thomas Steam Ship Co. Ltd., owned in succession the *Gwenllian Thomas* of 1882, the *Gwent,* purchased second-hand in 1909 as the *Evangeline,* the *Boverton,* a newly-built vessel of 1910 and, later the *Llandilo* of 1928, when *Boverton* was renamed *Llangorse* and transferred to another Radcliffe Company.

These transfers and injections of new capital assets into existing single ship companies make any analysis of this business enterprise extremely complicated and the present writer has not so far succeeded in completely mastering the financial implications of these arrangements in evaluating the overall profitability of each of the Radcliffe steamships. But two points need to be made: it might be suggested that Radcliffe's, by securing their management fees on gross earnings, and by having initially at least little of their own capital committed to the vessels they managed, secured profits at the expense of their shareholders and took relatively few risks themselves. On the other hand, it has to be remembered that Radcliffe's profits fluctuated considerably, in common with all shipowners active in the tramp shipping sector, but their managerial skills were quite exceptional and they secured better than average returns for their shareholders in the long run. Had Radcliffe's not been able to establish such a reputation they would have found it much more difficult to raise new capital than in fact was the case. The policy of transferring new tonnage to existing companies when the original vessels had outworn their usefulness or had been lost, ensured that shareholders had valuable and up-to-date assets to back their investments. Moreover, it is clear that although Radcliffe's did not initially invest heavily in their own vessels, they did, as time progressed, become the preponderant holders of share capital in their own companies, by being willing to purchase shares if and when they came on the market. The composition of Henry Radcliffe's estate on his death in 1921 gives abundant and conclusive testimony to this point.

The policy of Evan Thomas, Radcliffe and Company with respect to the acquisition of tonnage, and the disposal of old vessels seems to have been remarkably judicious, and this factor played a major part in the firm's success. Their fleet purchases and disposals are summarized in Table 2. Their first vessels were uncharacteristically ordered when freights were high, and this was reflected in the correspondingly high price of their initial purchases. As freight rates declined and ship prices declined in sympathy, Radcliffe's bravely continued to expand their fleet, thus having at their disposal vessels of the newest and most economical design to withstand the incidence of depression, while leaving the firm well-placed to take full advantage of the improvement in rates when the market recovered. When the highly-volatile market moved against them, they were ready to cancel contracts with shipbuilders even though penalty payments might be incurred. Twice, Radcliffe's cancelled contracts entered into with the West Hartlepool shipbuilders William Gray, the first occasion in 1884–5 and again in 1890 when a penalty of £1,250 was incurred.

Table 2
The Radcliffe Fleet, 1882–1913

Name	Acquired	Built	Gross Tons	Disposal
Gwenllian Thomas	1882	1882	1,082	Sold Dec. 1905
Iolo Morgannwg	1882	1882	1,292	Sold Dec. 1905
Anne Thomas	1883	1883	1,419	Sold 1905
Kate Thomas	1883	1883	1,558	Lost Oct. 1895
Wynnstay	1884	1884	1,542	Sold Jne. 1902
Walter Thomas	1884	1884	2,358	Lost Jly. 1901
Bala	1884	1884	2,014	Sold Nov. 1903
W.I. Radcliffe	1886	1886	2,077	Sold Mar. 1903
Clarissa Radcliffe	1889	1889	2,460	Lost Jan. 1898
Sarah Radcliffe	1889	1889	2,169	Sold May 1914
Mary Thomas	1889	1889	2,159	Sold May 1908
Jane Radcliffe	1890	1890	1,839	Sold Aug. 1911
Douglas Hill	1890	1890	2,172	Sold Aug. 1909
Llanberis	1890	1890	2,272	Sold Feb 1912
Rothesay	1890	1880	2,110	Lost Oct. 1890
Renfrew	1890	1880	2,124	Sold 1893
Manchester	1890	1890	2,072	Sold Feb. 1912
Glamorgan	1891	1883	2,066	Lost Apl. 1891
Peterson	1892	1892	2,768	Sold Jly. 1913
Anthony Radcliffe	1893	1893	2,866	Lost enemy action Oct. 1918
Ethel Radcliffe	1894	1894	2,874	Sold Feb. 1915
Dunraven	1896	1896	3,333	Lost enemy action Nov. 1916

Table 2 — continued

Name	Acquired	Built	Gross Tons	Disposal
Windsor	1897	1897	4,074	Lost enemy action Nov. 1917
Llandudno	1897	1897	4,064	Sold 1927
Paddington	1898	1898	3,903	Lost enemy action Oct. 1916
Euston	1898	1898	2,728	Sold 1926
Wimborne	1898	1898	3,466	Lost Nov. 1910
Swindon	1899	1899	3,847	Lost enemy action Jly. 1917
Llanover	1899	1899	3,840	Lost enemy action Feb. 1917
Llangorse	1900	1900	3,841	Lost enemy action Sep. 1916
Llandrindod	1900	1900	3,841	Lost enemy action May 1917
Llangollen	1900	1900	3,842	Sold 1926
Llanishen	1901	1901	3,837	Lost enemy action Aug. 1917
Hanley	1902	1902	3,331	Sold 1912
W.I. Radcliffe	1904	1904	4,749	Lost enemy action May 1918
Clarissa Radcliffe	1904	1904	4,703	Sold 1926
Patagonia	1906	1906	5,084	Lost enemy action Jly. 1917
Picton	1906	1906	5,083	Sold 1927
Washington	1907	1907	5,080	Lost enemy action May 1917
Aden	1908	1905	2,426	Sold 1915
Gwent	1909	1901	3,344	Sold 1912
Euston	1910	1910	2,841	Lost enemy action Oct. 1917
Llandudno	1910	1910	4,187	Lost enemy action 1917
Boverton	1910	1910	2,958	Sold 1930
Wimborne	1911	1911	6,079	Sold 1936
Windsor	1912	1912	6,055	Lost enemy action Oct. 1915
Patagonia	1913	1913	6,011	Lost enemy action Oct. 1918
Clarissa Radcliffe	1913	1913	6,042	Sold Apl. 1935

Sources: Company records, Welsh Industrial & Maritime Museum, Cardiff; Peter Frank
Collection; and J. Geraint Jenkins, *Evan Thomas Radcliffe: a Cardiff Shipowning
Company* (Cardiff, 1982).

Radcliffe generally pursued a policy of purchasing tonnage when there was a buyer's
market. This was true both in respect of new and secondhand tonnage, although ventures
into the second-hand market were not always happy. In 1890, the market depression
appears to have encouraged the firm to purchase two second-hand, 1880-built cargo

vessels, both products of Palmer's shipyard where Radcliffe's first six vessels had been constructed. This decision to acquire older vessels proved unsatisfactory: *Rothesay* was lost within a year of purchase when she was proceeding on a somewhat unusual voyage for a Radcliffe vessel, bound from Cardiff to Batavia. The second vessel, *Renfrew*, was soon sold to another Cardiff shipowner, J.H. Wilson, at a loss.

Despite these faulty judgements, the firm took advantage of every opportunity to deploy progressively larger vessels in their trades, thus securing considerable economies of scale. Their first ship carried little more than 1,600 tons of cargo, whereas by 1890, 3,000 tonners were being ordered. By 1900, the dead weight of their new vessels had increased to 6,400 tons, and between 1911 and 1913 they purchased four vessels of 9,500 tons dead weight, which kept Radcliffe's in the forefront of Cardiff shipowners. This policy of acquiring new and ever more economical vessels meant lower operating costs and freedom for several years of the expense of heavy repairs, renewals, dry docking and Lloyd's survey fees.

In the decade before the Great War, Henry, now joined in partnership by his younger brother Daniel, still purchased the occasional second-hand vessel when such tonnage could be secured at favourable prices. For example, *Hanley* was acquired in 1904 from Messrs. Woodruff, Shillitoe & Company of Cardiff at a bargain price consequent upon a precipitate decline in freight rates. This virtually new steamship of 5,550 tons dead weight had cost Woodruff's £45,000 in 1902, and Radcliffe was able to purchase her for as little as £32,000. Again, in 1908 and 1909, in a depressed market, Radcliffe's purchased the second-hand *Craigmore*, built in 1905 for £23,375, and in the following year acquired *Evangeline*, built in 1901, for £17,350. The former vessel stayed in the fleet until she was sold in 1915: as *Aden* she was registered in the name of the last Radcliffe company to be formed, the Colonies Steam Ship Co. Ltd., registered in 1908. *Evangeline* was sold at the height of the 1912 shipping boom for £22,589 which was over £5,200 more than the firm had paid for her three years earlier.

The firm had ordered new vessels in anticipation of the boom in 1899–1900, and were to enjoy successful years between 1909 and 1911, having secured new vessels at bargain prices before a rising market had influenced building costs. As a consequence, the firm possessed, on the eve of the Great War, a modern fleet that was to be cruelly tested in the ensuing conflict: no fewer than sixteen of Radcliffe's peacetime built fleet were to be lost by enemy action in the course of the war.

Radcliffe's emerged from the war with a severely depleted fleet: the immediate post-war boom in Cardiff shipowning saw them conspicuously standing aloof from the pervasive euphoria which was to cause such distress and bankruptcy for the many who had been lured into speculative frenzy. They purchased just one vessel, *Ethel Radcliffe,* at a grossly inflated price that the brothers must have regretted in the depression that was to ensue. In the longer run, however, this vessel probably proved a profitable investment until she was lost by enemy action in 1941. The temptation to embark capital in new tonnage in the immediate aftermath of the Great War must have been nearly irresistible. Two factors may have compelled caution: firstly, the burden of Excess Profit Duty and

Income Tax on shipping was especially severe in its effects on profits. Secondly, Henry Radcliffe died in 1921, and this probably adversely affected the business. The settling of Henry's estate must have been a preoccupation for his younger brother, and it was not until 1924 that the purchase of new tonnage was resumed. By this time, of course, the price of new ships had fallen dramatically, and Daniel could reap the benefit of restraint.

If the firm can be judged as markedly successful in the timing of its investments, it is also clear that technologically the firm made the most of the opportunities that presented themselves for embodying new technology in their vessels. The record of the firm with respect to casualties and loss of life was second to none, and this reflects great credit on the partners and their marine superintendents,[14] no less than upon their officers and crews, who found the brothers hard taskmasters. As Dr Geraint Jenkins has most interestingly shown, their masters were most often recruited in Cardiganshire that great nursery of seamen noted for its nautical skill, prudence and sobriety. Life on board a Radcliffe vessel was tough for the crew and apprentices alike:[15] tramp shipowners rarely prospered by being over-indulgent to their seagoing personnel, although long-serving officers were accorded by the Radcliffe brothers great respect and deference which was more than earned in the responsibilities that they shouldered. Only one Radcliffe steamer incurred loss of life in peacetime and this disaster clearly affected Henry and Daniel. *Clarissa Radcliffe* was homeward bound from Nicholaieff to Rotterdam in 1898 with a full cargo of grain. In force 11 gales, off Vigo, when hove-to, her hatches were smashed by heavy seas and the Second Officer and two seamen were actually swept off her deck and drowned. Later, her cargo shifted and her holds were waterlogged and she went down with the loss of nineteen of her crew. One or two other Radcliffe vessels were wrecked, but without fatalities and unattended by the suspicious circumstances that were the case with certain other Cardiff ships in the years before the Great War.

Although Radcliffe's ordered more or less standard bulk-carrying steamers, they chose their shipbuilders with discrimination, securing good bargains and quick deliveries from firms which built to the highest standards of naval architecture, under the supervision of Radcliffe's own marine superintendents. Radcliffe rarely experimented with the entirely novel (although they were early to adopt steel construction) and preferred the well-tested design. They quickly realized the economic advantage to be gained by adopting vessels of larger carrying capacity, and shallow draught, and their steamship *Walter Thomas,* constructed within a couple of years of the firm's inception, was, in her day, the largest vessel in the Black Sea grain trade. The firm was quick to adopt the more economical triple expansion marine engine with its pronounced economy in fuel consumption, which enhanced carrying capacity and economized in the size of the crew. They also ordered Ropner-designed trunk deck steamers which again conferred added carrying capacity, greater longitudinal strength and large hatchways with clear, unobstructed holds that speeded the process of loading and discharge of cargoes. Moreover, Daniel, who served on the Employer's side in the Cardiff Coal Trimmers' Committee was among the first to have his vessels categorized as 'easy trimmers', thus reducing the trimming charges which were so often a bone of contention in the south Wales ports.[16]

Radcliffe's were among the first steamship-owners to cut down the rigging of their steamers, doing away with the cumbersome yards and spars for the carrying of sails. Their marine surveyor, Thomas Hesketh, giving evidence to the House of Commons Manning of Merchant Ships Committee in 1890–1, made particular reference to this factor as important in reducing top hamper in their ships, thus diminishing the propensity to roll in heavy seas — an important factor in vessels accustomed to carrying large cargoes of Black Sea grain.[17]

A particular feature of their new-built ships was the equipping of more or less standardized tonnage with a range of extra fittings which added materially to the cost of construction, but which gave the ships increased economy and efficiency in performance. Indeed, most of the vessels built in the 1890s and 1900s had about £5,000 to £8,000 additional expenditure above their basic cost on minor but cumulatively significant variations on the basic specification, notably the installation of marine engines of a particular reliability combined with extra power so that a better performance could be achieved. All the firm's vessels were built to, or in excess of, Lloyd's Register's highest classification, and nothing was spared to ensure that the vessels were seaworthy and efficient units equipped especially for the grain trade which was to be the principal homeward cargo.

In summary, then, Radcliffe's record as shipowners, judged by the criteria of design, maintenance, and casualty experience was praiseworthy: there is nothing to identify the firm with the unsavoury scandals that plagued Cardiff shipowning in the 1900s and which forced Radcliffe, in common with other local shipowners, to eschew Cardiff registry and adopt London in its place in order to avoid the opprobrium attached to some less scrupulous shipowners in the Welsh port.

From the private ledgers we are able to glean some data as to the income generated by the firm and distributed between its principals. The partners' profit and loss accounts are summarized on an annual basis in the ledgers for 1886, in half-yearly periods between 1887 and 1894, and quarterly thereafter. Despite a few accounting errors, mainly trivial, and some occasional inconsistency in accounting practice, it is possible to distil these data in a summary form (Table 3 on pages 188 and 189).

So far as the income of the principals is concerned, Evan Thomas and Henry Radcliffe shared the profits equally between 1886 and Captain Thomas's death in 1891, except in respect of the income derived from their first steamer, where the division was 35/64ths to Thomas and 29/64ths to Radcliffe. After Captain Thomas's death, Henry Radcliffe paid sums out of profits to the widow by the way of goodwill: between June 1892 and December 1893 £200 was paid. A further £3,000 was paid in instalments to Thomas's children over the period June 1894 and June 1895. Whether the intercession of the Reverend Cynddylan Jones had anything to do with these payments is not known, but the profit figures in these years need to be considered in the light of such payments. Again, the heirs of Captain Thomas received further payments in 1896 and 1897 amounting in all to £1,500, and another £1,000 went the same way between 1898 and 1899. The year 1886 had seen the writing off of £2,327, mainly bad debts, which helps to explain the minimal profitability of the enterprise in that year — a difficult one for industry generally despite what Professor Saul would have us believe.[18] The unwisdom of purchasing second-hand tonnage in the uncertain years 1890–1 is revealed in the fact that *Renfrew* was sold at a net loss of £2,503 in 1893.

From 1901 Daniel Radcliffe was admitted to a share in the profits, they being divided 8/10ths to Henry, 2/10ths to Daniel. In 1904, Wyndham Ivor Radcliffe, Henry's only son, began to benefit, the proportions being adjusted to 69/100ths, with Daniel getting 30/100ths, and Wyndham 5/100ths. These proportions remained undisturbed until Henry's death in 1921.

One other feature of Table 3 is worth mentioning: in 1902, Henry must have grown tired of paying out heavy insurance premiums, and consequently inaugurated a new venture, a mutual insurance association. Insurance brokerage and commission income thus becomes a new feature of the accounts. The incidence of the wartime Excess Profits Duty and Income Tax is very striking: in all, the firm paid some £280,000 in these taxes between 1916 and 1924. Prior to the world conflict, Radcliffe's had borne the relatively trivial amounts of income tax levied, so that shareholders always received their dividends tax free. Given the incidence of tax on the wartime scale it is not altogether surprising that a handful of Britain's largest tramp shipowners decided to abandon business and sell their fleets during the Great War;[19] their number included Edward Nicholl of Cardiff, one-time marine surveyor to Radcliffe's, whose rise to eminence was even more striking than Henry Radcliffe's, and the redoubtable Walter Runciman. However, the latter reconstituted his shipping enterprise after the War — a decision that his family must have sometimes regretted in the 1930s.

The Radcliffe fortunes depended critically on coal voyages outwards and homeward freights of grain from the Black Sea. They toyed intermittently with indulgence in a transatlantic liner trade,[20] but this never achieved sufficient continuity to be regarded as a permanent feature of their activities. It is not possible here to analyse in detail the surviving voyage accounts of Radcliffe vessels, not least because the evidence is so discontinuous and fragmentary until after the Great War. However, the coincidence between profit and freight rates prevailing in the Black Sea grain trade is too close not to be remarked upon (see Table 4 on page 190).

When Henry Radcliffe died in 1921 he left a fortune in real estate and investments amounting to little short of £1.4 million. During his lifetime he had acquired freehold property that had cost him something over £250,000, mainly estates in Glamorganshire. He held some leasehold property in Cardiff dockland that realized £35,000 when it was disposed of. Around £96,000 was held in 5 per cent War Loan, and other investments were divided between outside shipping companies (a trifling £1,700), Dry Dock Companies (£40,000), Colliery Companies (£27,000), Railways Companies (£17,000) and other miscellaneous companies (£15,000). Of course, we do not know what he paid for this portfolio, but it seems likely that he must have come a cropper with his investments in the Cambrian Railway Company.

Radcliffe's main assets were his investments in his own shipping companies,

Table 3

Evan Thomas, Radcliffe & Co: annual profit of the partners, 1885–1922(£s)

Year	To:			By:							
	(a)	(b)	(c)	(d)	(e)	(f)	(g)	(h)	(i)	(j)	(k)
1886	500	3,098	—	31	1,974		793	—	862	—	3,629
1887	594	788	—	3,038	2,935		747	153	583	—	4,420
1888	493	251	—	3,796	3,161		610	67	702	—	4,540
1889	575	175	—	6,000	3,554	954	714	117	1,411	—	6,750
1890	859	2,535	—	8,241	4,854	3,607	553	148	2,474	—	11,636
1891	1,266	3,352	—	12,548	6,273	6,655	530	300	3,408	—	17,166
1892	1,582	1,018	—	6,817	4,588	3,318	724	348	438	—	9,416
1893	1,882	3,100	—	4,267	4,452	3,496	287	335	679	—	9,249
1894	1,787	2,549	—	5,433	4,525	3,588	528	370	758	—	9,769
1895	1,918	2,124	—	7,839	4,556	3,984	951	300	2,090	—	11,883
1896	1,300	208	—	7,714	4,016	3,649	913	134	509	—	9,222
1897	1,397	1,965	—	10,356	5,921	6,035	912	102	748	—	13,719
1898	1,692	1,079	—	11,930	6,614	6,819	756	220	788	—	15,200
1899	1,958	1,342	—	17,817	8,536	9,573	1,452	473	1,072	—	21,106
1900	2,242	559	—	22,648	10,645	12,092	1,699	536	378	—	25,350
1901	2,551	915	—	20,735	9,904	12,026	1,370	450	452	—	24,202
1902	2,622	2,095	—	17,291	8,562	10,951	1,405	389	296	405	22,008
1903	2,579	1,347	—	17,666	8,139	10,275	1,024	251	210	1,692	21,591
1904	2,749	1,028	—	15,144	7,412	9,851	959	252	305	141	18,921
1905	2,859	1,795	—	19,637	9,153	11,647	1,178	335	708	1,271	24,292
1906	3,093	1,516	—	20,928	8,765	12,159	1,586	319	521	1,146	24,496

Year	(a)	(b)	(c)	(d)	(e)	(f)	(g)	(h)	(i)	(j)	(k)
1908	3,156	1,641	—	14,808	7,042	8,844	1,476	419	599	1,227	19,606
1909	3,287	798	—	19,693	8,307	10,491	1,582	256	2,059	1,089	23,779
1910	3,428	797	—	24,466	11,073	13,166	2,001	375	694	1,379	28,691
1911	3,899	552	—	27,340	12,009	14,816	2,060	416	795	1,698	31,793
1912	4,114	1,295	—	40,513	17,432	21,772	3,595	634	809	1,680	45,920
1913	4,351	1,460	—	39,615	17,914	20,321	4,080	523	917	1,672	45,427
1914	4,505	929	—	21,437	9,632	10,452	2,883	1,011	900	1,992	26,871
1915	4,310	2,016	—	90,042	44,793	40,647	5,713	2,445	937	1,835	96,371
1916	4,845	3,676	23,003	120,931	67,154	65,845	6,801	7,031	1,500	4,127	152,458
1917	6,770	3,798	24,829	61,035	50,937	31,588	4,495	1,777	2,663	5,884	96,804
1918	5,575	3,464	54,506	9,596	41,689	21,771	1,530	106	1,131	6,914	73,141
1919	6,977	1,524	73,006	942	41,325	30,605	3,713	1,427	1,091	4,288	82,449
1920	7,708	2,582	61,476	46,138	65,245	40,134	3,787	1,586	1,467	5,685	117,904
1921	7,096	1,951	32,245	20,832	31,486	20,711	1,797	776	1,867	5,487	62,124
1922	6,713	1,545	15,185	5,146	8,963	11,927	2,666	1,549	1,195	2,289	28,589

Note: These figures have been derived from the private ledgers. Minor discrepancies are due to rounding.

Column (a) To: Salaries
 (b) Office and other expenses
 (c) Excess Profit Duty and Income Tax
 (d) Profit divided by Partners
 (e) By: Management
 (f) Brokerage: own vessels
 (g) Brokerage: other vessels
 (h) Commission on bunkers
 (i) Other items
 (j) Taff Insurance, brokerage and commission
 (k) Total of annual account.

Table 4
Highest and lowest yearly freight rates, homewards from Black Sea,
1884–1914 (shillings and pence)

Year	Highest	Lowest
1884	4/9	2/3
1885	4/9	2/6
1886	4/-	2/1½
1887	5/-	2/10½
1888	6/9	3/3
1889	5/-	2/9
1890	4/9	2/9
1891	21/-	11/-
1892	19/-	8/-
1893	19/1½	10/6
1894	16/9	10/9
1895	16/-	10/-
1896	25/-	8/3
1897	14/3	9/-
1898	17/6	9/6
1899	14/6	8/1½
1900	22/-	10/3
1901	17/-	8/3
1902	15/3	7/9
1903	13/6	8/6
1904	12/-	8/-
1905	15/-	9/6
1906	13/6	8/-
1907	12/9	8/3
1908	8/6	6/1½
1909	10/4½	7/-
1910	15/6	7/9
1911	14/6	7/6
1912	24/-	10/-
1913	15/-	8/3
1914	14/-	6/4½

Source: E.A.V. Angier (Compiler), *Fifty Years' Freights* (London, 1920)
Basis Danube, per quarter of wheat 1884–90; per unit, New Charter, 1891–1914.

amounting in all to something over £½ million. It is clear that the humble clerk from Merthyr, who had with great success cajoled a wide spectrum of investors to put their trust in his managing skills, had, over the course of his business career, used a considerable part of the profits he had derived from successful ship management to repurchase shares in his single ship companies, so that, at his death, he was by far the biggest shareholder in his own companies.[21]

'Man proposes, God disposes' is a tag that is too often ignored in business history. Close attention to accounts and other financial data, which may be readily transformed into long time series, may sometimes induce tunnel vision in the historian rendering him indifferent to the purely human exigencies. In the case of the Radcliffe enterprise, its manifest success was an object lesson to aspiring entrepreneurs. But it is worth reflecting upon the extent to which the firm owed its initial success to the random conjunction of a mature west Wales shipmaster and a young shipping clerk: the skill with which these two weathered the depression of the 1880s has to be seen in the context of a highly complex and uniquely competitive industry in which ease of entry was only equalled by the high incidence of failure. These two men possessed, in their different ways, strength of purpose and single-minded devotion to their interests of an exceptional nature. The unexpected death of Captain Thomas was a major blow. Then the younger brother joined the firm to help guide the enterprise through the unsettled years 1890–1, to enjoy the rewards of prosperity at the end of the nineteenth century, and to witness, as a result of their skills, only a relatively small reduction in profits in the years of depression in the 1900s. Once that storm was successfully weathered, the market recovery that immediately preceded the outbreak of the Great War permitted the Radcliffe brothers to enter the conflict with a modern and well-equipped fleet. The wartime years saw unprecedented profits, but quite unacceptable losses to their fleet, with no fewer that sixteen of their fine vessels lost by enemy action. Excess Profits Duty must have imposed a severe strain on the partners' resources between 1917 and 1921, and it was in the latter year that the senior partner in the enterprise died. Perhaps these two factors served to restrain the firm in the heady atmosphere that prevailed in Cardiff in the immediate aftermath of war. It is idle to speculate about what might have been, but the death of Thomas in 1891 and the death of Henry Radcliffe in 1921 seem to have been turning-points in the fortune of an enterprise which was one of the few shipowning firms from Cardiff's great days of prosperity that still owned tonnage in the early 1980s.

The Climacteric of the 1890s

JOHN WILLIAMS

A generation ago Phelps Brown and Handfield-Jones launched the idea that the 1890s were a turning-point for the British economy. It was an inspired touch to entitle their essay 'The Climacteric of the 1890s'.[1] Attention was arrested by the resonances of this term as commonly applied to the human condition to indicate a time of 'fundamental bodily change'. Applied to the economy, however, the intention of the authors was to draw attention to what they saw as a critical period. The assertion is that after a long period of confident and persistent, though not necessarily steady, economic growth the British economy was perceptibly checked in the period around the turn of the century, and that this marked a definite break in trend and not just a cyclical downturn. There was a deceleration in the progress of productivity improvement and this arose from tardiness in applying technical changes. The argument thus reinforced vague criticisms about falling enterprise, and intensified concern on this issue soon led to the assertion that by the late nineteenth century 'the British entrepreneur had lost much of the drive and dynamism possessed by his predecessors of the classical industrial revolution'.[2]

Claims as dramatic and sweeping as an 1890s climacteric and entrepreneurial failure have naturally not stood unchallenged. There have been disputes about dates. From the outset Coppock[3] accepted the concept of the climacteric but wanted it pushed back to the 1870s. The debate became enmeshed, as was probably unavoidable, with the longer-standing issue of whether the years from c.1873–96 constituted a 'Great Depression'.

A much stronger response was provoked when the hypothesis of entrepreneurial failure was directly challenged. Perhaps this was partly because one source of the challenge was by the proponents of the new economic history. Making a more explicit use of economic theory they — and especially McCloskey and Sandberg[4] — seemed to demonstrate that British entrepreneurs at the time behaved in an economically rational manner. The extent to which these entrepreneurs applied new methods and shifted to different products was, given the relative factor prices, consistent with a hypothesis of maximizing returns. The elegant demonstrations of the cliometricians have not, however, resolved the issue of entrepreneurial capability. Partly this is because doubts remain about the quality of the data being used and, more fundamentally, about the appropriateness of the neo-classical theory for the problem to which it has been addressed. More recently, it has been strongly questioned from within the neo-classical tradition whether a satisfactory short-run rate of return does indicate a 'correct' allocation of resources[5] — though this point has not yet been explicitly applied to the argument about late Victorian and Edwardian entrepreneurs.

Beyond these more or less technical considerations, however, the debate has not been resolved because the participants are nursing quite different concepts of 'the entrepreneur'. There are at least two radically different views of the function of the entrepreneur which are embodied in the literature. The one, which may be described as Marshallian, sees the entrepreneur as the provider of a fourth factor of production, organization, to ensure the most efficient use of the other three — land, labour and capital. The main function of this entrepreneur is to make marginal adjustments to the factor combinations in a way that ensures the maximization of the short-run rate of return. His time-horizons are short. The other view, which may be described as Schumpeterian, sees the entrepreneur as innovator. The main functions of this entrepreneur are to introduce new methods, supply new products and create new demand. His time-horizons are long. With such divergent and confusing views being held about the basic nature of the problem a consensus on its resolution was never likely. The entrepreneur of the new economic historians, whose marginal adjustments were by definition successful because they earned a satisfactory rate of return, bore little relationship to the entrepreneur who had failed to produce the new chemical dyes and electrical equipment. The entrepreneur which McCloskey thought he had redeemed was quite simply not the same person who earlier had been damned.

A rather different defence of British entrepreneurs was provided by writers like Charles Wilson.[6] This was to accept many of the strictures but to argue that they only applied to parts of the economy and especially to the older heavy industries like iron and steel. The border between entrepreneurial failure and success ran along a structural divide. 'The division can be made — though very roughly and with exceptions — into old industries and new industries, basic industries and light industries, industries largely based on home markets and others on export markets.'[7]

It is hoped that even so abrupt a summary will have suggested something of the complexity of the issues involved. They form an essential background. Fortunately, however, most of the complications in the extensive literature are concerned with the attempts at explanation, and especially the attempt to attribute a break in the rate of growth of the British economy to a decline in business enterprise. There is a much greater level of agreement that there *was* a fall in the rate of growth. Aldcroft and Richardson, drawing on calculations made by Matthews, Feinstein, Maddison, Lomax and others, demonstrated that for a whole range of economic indicators the performance of the British economy from c.1900 to 1913 fell below previous levels.[8] This was epitomized by the bare figures for the rate of growth of gross domestic product: in the forty-odd years from 1856 to 1899 this had averaged 2 per cent; from 1899–1913 it fell to 1.1 per cent (a difference between doubling the output of the economy in 35 years and taking nearly 70 years to do so).

It thus seems to be reasonably established that there was a decline in the rate of growth somewhere in the 1890s. In accepting this, however, it is not necessary to give the phenomenon the full significance bestowed upon it by Phelps Brown and Handfield-Jones. Their climacteric implied a fundamental long-run change. But the average growth rate for much of the inter-war period (1924–37) was back up to 2.3 per cent and that level — or more — was sustained for another quarter century beyond 1945. In this perspective the decline of 1899–1913 looks less decisive, not so much a permanent downward shift as a hiccup. Fortunately, again, the complications over significance need not for the moment detain us. What is reasonably clear and certain is that the British economy underwent a deceleration in growth in the decade or so before the First World War. Our question is: did Wales share this experience?

Paring the issue down in this way thus relieves us of some of the complications of the more general debate. At the same time, however, its very starkness forces some confrontation with the blunt questions: was there a Welsh economy and, if so, do we know whether it grew faster or slower at this particular period? The questions have been linked because they are, necessarily, linked.

The issue of what constitutes 'an economy' is fraught with definitional niceties. But the essence of the problem can be indicated at a high level of generality. 'An economy' needs some physical geographical basis and it needs to be given some reasonable economic coherence. This can be achieved through political action (the area concerned being the basis for economic and social decision-making by political units or agencies); or through the fact that the area is bound by natural economic links; or because the people (or influential sectors of them) think of the area as a single economic unit.

At the beginning of the twentieth century the concept of a Welsh economy fails most of these tests. It was true that Wales constituted a reasonably well-defined geographical area. But the area was not lent much economic coherence through political action. Despite the recent (1881) passage of an Act of economic significance which related exclusively to Wales (prohibiting the general Sunday sale of alcohol) — and despite the busy huffing and puffing that surrounded the Cymru Fydd movement in the 1890s,[9] Wales was almost never a unit for decision-making in economic policy. Nor did economic activity within the geographical area impose its own natural coherence. There were strong geographical barriers to limit the links between north and south Wales. These, reinforced by traditional ties, meant that north Wales commerce looked naturally to Liverpool and south Wales to Bristol (and, as transport improved, London). People's economic thoughts ran along much the same lines. This was not surprising for managers and capitalists: but even for many who subscribed to the unity of Wales in cultural and social matters, it was natural to turn to England and (perhaps even more decisive in its long-run effects) to English for economic affairs.

These doubts about the reality of a Welsh economy are reinforced by the paucity of statistical data relating to Wales. Figures *do* exist. But they do so mostly as a by-product of information being collected on Great Britain, the United Kingdom or — that most irritating of fictions — 'England and Wales'. Wales, then, occasionally appears as a convenient regional unit but more often has to be reconstructed by adding together the figures for individual counties (and remembering to retrieve Monmouthshire from touch) or for north Wales and south Wales (since even in county tables the Welsh counties are often not separately listed — and Monmouthshire still has to be retrieved). All this simply underlines the obvious fact that Wales was not seen as a meaningful economic unit.

In other respects such considerations are, for the issue presently under discussion, largely academic. This is because the claim that a British climacteric had been discovered rested largely on figures relating to economic growth and to international trade. And on these issues, even if the concept of a Welsh economy had had substantial content for other purposes, there would still have been no separate statistics for Wales. Indeed, for economic growth there were, at the time, no figures for the British economy either. Changes in economic growth require the annual measurement of the national income, which has only been systematically provided since the Second World War. But for the UK as a whole national income accounts have been reconstructed retrospectively to carry the series back at least to the mid nineteenth century.[10] The same has not been done, and probably cannot be done, for Wales precisely because the necessary statistical bricks for such an edifice are still only available for very recent times — and even then their quality is suspect.

The second main statistical foundation for the climacteric thesis was information on international trade and commerce. But this too does not and, in any realistic sense, cannot exist for Wales. Foreign trade statistics necessarily coincide with sovereign political units. It is possible to extract information on the value of goods exported from, and imported through, each Welsh port. But aggregating these would not provide answers sufficient for our purpose: it is at least probable that for Wales viewed as a separate entity the largest volume of foreign trade (and finance) was conducted with England. And for that activity no reasonably reliable indicators exist.

It is clear, therefore, that any discussion of the possibility of a Welsh climacteric will have to rely on more indirect approaches. In the main these involve placing reliance on three main aspects. First, in the absence of any single measure — like an index of industrial output or of national income — which purports to capture the behaviour of the whole of industry or the entire economy, attention is concentrated on the particular experience of a small range of industries. In the case of Wales, and especially industrial south Wales, the exceptional dominance of a single industry in terms of male employment makes such an approach less hazardous and haphazard than would otherwise be the case. Second, it is also possible, in the case of the coal industry, to take up one of the main issues of the general debate: the extent to which the climacteric was associated with a decline in efficiency indicated by falling productivity trends. And finally some attempt will be made to indicate how contemporaries viewed the performance and prospects of the economy. It is realized that such a survey will be even more selective and even more subjective than the other indicators, but it is none the less relevant to enquire whether a change substantial enough to be labelled 'climactic' strongly impinged itself upon the public consciousness of the time.

The figures that are available on the rate of growth of output for some of the major

Table 1

Decadal percentage[1] changes. Economic indicators. Wales 1855–1914

	OUTPUT							EXPORTS		Value of Coal Output[2]	Value of Tinplate Exports
	Coal			Pig Iron	Tinplate	Slate	Lead	Coal	Tinplate		
	N. Wales	S. Wales	N & S Wales								
1855–64 to 1865–74	56.3	45.9	47.3	–1.8	N.A.	N.A.	9.0	N.A.	N.A.	103.8	103.1
1865–74 to 1875–94	5.5	42.7	37.4	–11.0	N.A.	N.A.	–20.1	104.4	110.5	10.5	45.1
1875–84 to 1885–94	12.6	42.1	38.9	–3.4	84.2	N.A.	–50.5	79.6	84.8	53.8	39.3
1885–94 to 1895–1904	10.6	32.0	30.1	1.3	–1.6	+5.6	9.5	45.9	–23.3	54.3	–31.5
1895–1904 to 1905–14	5.0	33.5	31.3	8.6	32.9	–23.6[3]	–8.9	43.6	49.2	63.1	

[1] i.e. shows increase in the total output for the indicated decade as a percentage of the preceding decade.
[2] Output × f.o.b. price of large coal.
[3] Includes estimate for 1914.

Welsh industries (Table 1) seem to be broadly consistent with identifying a decline in the rate of growth from somewhere about 1890. The rate of growth of coal output falls quite sharply and this is reflected (and magnified) in the figures for coal exports. Tinplate shows a similar downward trend although the exceptionally sharp fall in the 1890s, when there was a drop in the absolute level of output as well as its rate of growth, was caused by the specific collapse of the industry's major market in the United States as a result of the McKinley tariff of 1890. Slate, too, conforms to the pattern although this cannot be satisfactorily indicated on a decadal basis since the output series for slate only begins at 1882. The annual figures, however, show a pronounced peak in the late 1890s which is then followed by an absolute and accelerating decline.

The evidence of the coal industry is in many respects crucial. It is crucial because of the extent to which it came to dominate the Welsh economy from the mid nineteenth century. In the absence of national income figures this dominance is best illustrated from the occupational distribution of the Welsh population. In 1911 almost one-third (32 per cent) of all men in Wales were engaged in Mining and Quarrying and nearly 90 per cent of these were in coal-mining. Since most Welsh counties had no coal this was an extraordinary proportion for a single industry out of the twenty-three occupational groupings used by the census. It implies, of course, an even greater preponderance within the mining counties: Glamorgan and Monmouth, easily the two most populous Welsh counties, each had 40 per cent of the occupied male population in coal-mining: in Denbigh over one-quarter (25.6 per cent) of the corresponding population was similarly occupied.

It is significant therefore that the coal industry does, indeed, seem to provide supporting evidence of a break in trend towards the end of the nineteenth century. Two major items can be cited. The most thorough recent statistical investigation of the coal industry[11] has established a definite break in the annual growth rate for coal output in south Wales. For the period from 1874 to 1914 the rate of growth is 4.21 per cent per annum until 1890, and 2.88 per cent per annum after that date. Moreover the significance of this is reinforced because it can be demonstrated that, contrary to the previously received opinion,[12] for the United Kingdon coal industry the average annual growth rate remained steady throughout this period (at just under 2 per cent per annum). The second aspect relates to productivity trends. For the United Kingdom, Taylor[13] argues that productivity (in the sense of output per man year) was declining from the 1880s. For south Wales, Rhodri Walters[14] paints a more complicated pattern. There is still a substantial fall from about 300 tons per man year in the late eighties (1888) to less than 250 tons in the years just before the First World War. The fall is, however, neither steady nor persistent. Indeed, nearly all the decline takes place at the beginning and the end: either from 1888 to 1890 or after 1906.

There is thus a respectable body of statistical evidence supportive of a contention that Wales experienced a break in its economic development around 1890. Moreover, the evidence from the major industry of coal-mining indicates not merely that there was a sharp deceleration in the rate of growth but that this was accompanied by declining productivity. This seems to be consistent with another aspect of the general hypothesis of the climacteric: namely, that it was associated with a decline in enterprise and innovation. This, too, is apparently given extra weight by the fact that the degree of modernization in south Wales before 1914 was lower than in most other coalfields. In 1913 only just over one per cent of output in south Wales was mechanically cut. Nevertheless, the evidence is suggestive rather than conclusive. Closer examination of its statistical basis raises doubts about drawing firm conclusions, and these doubts are reinforced when more qualitative material is brought into consideration.

To start with the productivity propositions. Here the shape of the path taken by the decline in productivity is important. As already noted, the decline in output per man year effectively took place either between 1888 and 1890, or after 1906. In between there were fluctuations (very sharp in 1898 and 1899 because of the long strike and the recovery in output which followed and was intensified by the Boer War boom), but they were not fluctuations around a discernible downward trend: the level of output per man year in 1906 was the same as that for 1890. The significance of this pattern is that it makes it (on *a priori* grounds) less plausible to seek the explanations of declining productivity in such factors as diminishing returns, less intensity of effort by workers and falling enterprise by owners and managers, factors which would produce their effects persistently over long periods. The two quick bursts of declining productivity suggest that rather more weight might be given to *ad hoc* factors.

The exhaustive investigations of Dr Boyns largely confirm these deduced expectations. His concern was with the United Kingdom as a whole but, fortunately, his most detailed work was on south Wales. The findings here draw upon three layers of evidence: for the coalfield as a whole; for some 64 individual collieries; and, in still more detail, for the operations of two of the major companies, Powell Duffryn and Ocean. These various approaches allowed cognisance to be taken and tests to be made of such variables as days worked, the ages of collieries and colliery size. From all this what emerged was that the most important influences on output per man year were the number of days worked and wage rates. Disregarding the many complications and qualifications the most pertinent conclusions for the immediate purpose were the two negative findings: for the period between 1890 and 1913 (see Figure 1) the industry did not suffer from decreasing returns to labour nor from generally diminishing returns (i.e. the influence of diminishing returns was being offset by other factors such as technical change). The actual falls in productivity can, however, be substantially explained by *ad hoc* factors. At the end of the period the effect of the Eight Hours Act was followed by the Cambrian strike of 1910–11 and the national strike (the first of a very small number) of 1912. There are also specific explanations, though of a less decisive nature, at the beginning of the period. The Coal Mines Regulation Act of 1887, which reduced the number of hours worked by boys, was followed by Mabon's Day, which was introduced in 1888 and reduced the number of days worked by declaring the first Monday in each month a miner's holiday.

There is, in any event, a simpler interpretation of the overall experience from about 1870, one which would indicate that the stress placed on the fall of productivity in the 1890s is misplaced. This could be summed up by saying that the reason for the 1890s was

Tons per man year

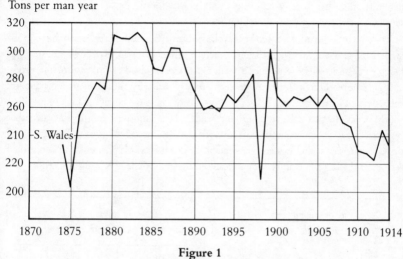

Figure 1
Annual labour productivity of coal-mining, 1874 - 1914

the 1880s. That is to say, the experience which stands out as exceptional is the very high level of labour productivity from 1880 to 1888. It was an experience which perhaps reflected the opening of a large number of new and well-equipped pits under the stimulus of the extraordinarily high level of prices and profits of the early seventies. On this reading the experiences of the 1890s simply meant that after the effects of this big lump of capital investment had been digested there was a reversion to a more 'normal' productivity level. It would be pressing too hard to spirit the entire problem away in this fashion, but the contemplation of such possibilities does contribute to keeping the productivity issue in perspective.

A further by-product is to lower the presumption that there was a substantial failure of innovation and enterprise. The most usual indicator of this is the slow progress made in mechanical cutting and conveying in south Wales before 1914. This was never a very reliable guide, even when it was assumed that there was a long and continuous decline in productivity to be explained. The conditions in south Wales were never particularly suitable to such machinery, given — and it is an important qualification — that the labour cost of cutting remained relatively low and was fairly directly related to the selling price of coal. The geological conditions in south Wales militated against the use of machinery in two broad ways. The unsettled nature of the seams, with 'working' (movement) of both roof and floor, made difficult the smooth, continuous working of the machines. But these conditions also reduced the contribution which could be made by machines since the pressure from the roof often eased the actual problem of cutting the coal: many Welsh miners ended their shift by under-cutting the seam in the sure knowledge that when they returned next morning much of the overhanging coal would have been brought down. The most general criticisms of technical backwardness were thus always misdirected. The demonstration that there were, in any event, no significant signs of diminishing returns suggests that they were also superfluous.

The conclusion would seem to be that the failure of diminishing returns to show up as a significant factor must mean that its inherent influence in an extractive industry was being successfully offset. And such a result must have involved a fair degree of innovation and enterprise. Diminishing returns can be held back by more efficient production methods and by the opening up of new coal areas. There is evidence of each in pre-1914 south Wales. In particular underground haulage was improved and, in this and other respects, there was a significant shift towards the use of electrical power. The continued drive towards new sinkings and the tendency to shift towards previously underworked sectors of the coalfield can be economically illustrated by the following figures:

No. of collieries sunk in Rhondda valleys		Dates of sinking of S.W. collieries still in existence in October 1922	
		All	Anthracite
1855–84	60	96	12
1885–1914	7	175	38

It can also be illustrated by a brief extract from the *South Wales Daily News* of 1 July 1891 — just at a time when the decline in activity was supposed to be taking place. At a meeting of Cardiff Chamber of Commerce it was reported that *at the present time*: 'the new Clydach pit was being developed (and it is rumoured that another was to be sunk); Naval Colliery Co. is going to sink a new pit; Lewis Merthyr Co. to do the same; Tylor & Co. now well on with new Cefn-nant-ddu colliery; Mardy Co. had started new shaft; Dowlais Co. is sinking 2 new shafts; Universal Colliery Co. to sink new pits north of Pontypridd. In Rhymney valley, Llandbradach Co. had found fresh coal; Rhymney Co. is sinking 2 new shafts at Pengam; Powell Duffryn Co. contemplated sinking in the same area. Universal Co. had started 2 pits at the top of Aber valley, a new pit is being sunk at Llanhilleth; E.V. Co. is sinking at Cwm and at Abertillery'. And all this was just around Cardiff area — leaving out developments in Ogmore and Garw valleys.

There remains the problem of the overall growth rate. To the extent that the above arguments undermine, or substantially modify, the notion of a decline in productivity, they dispose of an explanation, rather than of the fact, of a break in economic development. The notion of a downward shift in the pace of development seems to be much more firmly embedded in a lower growth rate. This, moreover, seems well-established for south Wales. The long-accepted view that there was a break in the 1880s in the growth of coal output of the United Kingdom has collapsed under close statistical scrutiny[16] (pounded from close range by the dreaded Boyns gun); but for south Wales this break has emerged from such treatment even more starkly. Whether the break is tested for 1883 or 1890 it still seems quite decisive; annual percentage growth rates of 5.5 and 2.6 before and after 1883, and 4.2 and 2.9 before and after 1890. Does this not demonstrate a significant deceleration in economic activity?

What it mostly demonstrates is the danger of using trends in the output of a single industry, albeit one of substantial dominance, as a growth indicator for the economy as a whole. It is almost unavoidable, unless the starting-point is at a very low level of absolute output, that a high growth rate for an individual industry cannot be sustained over time. An annual increase of 5 per cent per annum means that output is multiplied 130 times in the course of a century (10 per cent would multiply output 16,384 times!). All this is achieved through what Rostow called 'the magic of compound interest'. For the present purposes its significance is that, if the process is surveyed from a point where the absolute levels of output are already high, then the actual subsequent growth rate may not be the most appropriate criterion by which to assess the later development. Changes in the absolute levels of output, manpower, exports and so on may be better guides. If, for example, the pre-1883 growth rate had been maintained until 1913 the output of the south Wales coalfield would then have reached 125 million tons instead of the actual 57 million tons, i.e., five times the 1883 output of 25 million tons instead of just over twice that level. And even on the lower pre-1890 growth rate and the shorter time period for it to operate, output would have reached 75 million tons. Are we to consider that anything which falls short of these levels represents a 'failure'?

The contention is that if attention is focused upon the size of absolute changes attained in the decade or so before 1914, it is difficult to reconcile these with the implication of relative stagnation contained in the climacteric thesis. Thus in the decade and a half before 1913 the annual output of the coalfield increased by over 20 million tons; an *extra* 13 million tons a year were being exported from south Wales and an additional 100,000 men were employed.

The sheer scale of these increases necessarily spilled over into other sectors. One of the most dramatic and pervasive of these was — as Brinley Thomas taught us years ago — population change. The main outlines of the inter-censal findings for Wales in the first decade of the twentieth century are those most usually associated with thriving economies. The buoyancy was undoubtedly directly connected to the activity of the coal industry. In this decade alone the south Wales coalfield absorbed an additional seventy thousand miners. The impression of a *teeming* population can be caught in the accidental phrase of a newspaper reported at the time of a royal visit in 1912: '. . . all through Treorky the coal tips were black with people . . .' The overall population effect of the increase in the number of miners was substantially multiplied: the population of Glamorgan grew in this decade by 261,000 (an increase of 30 per cent), of Monmouthshire by 98,000 (33 per cent) and of Carmarthenshire by 25,000 (18 per cent). Although the birth rate in the coalfield (in common with that of the United Kingdom colliery districts generally) remained higher for longer than in other social and regional sectors, these represented growth rates that exceeded the rate of natural increase.

An additional feature of this decade was thus a substantial net gain by migration.[17] The Glamorgan–Monmouth colliery area gained 130,000 by migration in this decade and for Wales as a whole the gain was 98,000. In the context of the British experience since the middle of the nineteenth century such gains were exceptional. Indeed, they were unique. In each of the individual countries — England, Wales, Scotland, Ireland — in every decade from 1851 to 1911 there was a net loss through migration with this single exception for Wales from 1901 to 1911. The exception was, moreover, substantial. Proportional to its population, as Brinley Thomas has tellingly emphasized, Wales was for this brief period 'absorbing population at a rate not much less than the United States'. Moreover, this overall result was reached despite quite contrary trends in large tracts of Wales. Five of the (then) thirteen Welsh counties — the four in mid Wales plus Caernarvon in the north — actually suffered a decline in the absolute level of their population during this decade. It bears testimony to the extent to which the fundamental developments in the economy of Wales were influenced by the coal industry. Even in north Wales, where the number of coal-miners grew at a very sedate pace (an extra two thousand in this decade), the two coal counties of Flint and Denbigh were the only ones to show a population increase of over ten per cent for the decade — though the more important influence may have been the developing north Wales holiday coast.

House-building was another related sector which was influenced by the scale of the economic expansion. The broad pattern which emerges is that house-building in south Wales experienced a substantial boom in the 1890s and again in the 1900s.[18] In each case the level of activity was, proportional to population, comparable with the boom of the early 1870s. A few comments are required both to qualify and to emphasize the significance of this experience. Building is, of course, an industry in which fluctuations in activity are particularly marked. Thus it is not surprising to find that between the two post-1890 peaks there was a downturn around 1900 associated with the Boer War. The dip in activity at that time was common to the UK industry generally and was associated with the usual rising costs (especially interest rates) caused by the war, but the downturn was much sharper in south Wales than elsewhere. On the other hand, whilst building was generally active in the 1890s the resurgence in south Wales up to 1910 was contrary to the overall UK experience. Since the level of building activity is considered to be a major factor determining the general level of economic activity, the buoyancy of house-building in south Wales for much of the first decade of the century acts as an important indicator.

One further sector has been selected for comment, namely the degree to which continuing efforts were being made to extend and improve the capital infrastructure. Most of this consisted of either railway building or, more important, of dock construction. Already by 1890 south Wales had one of the world's most densely-developed rail networks, so the later activity was necessarily mostly of the nature of minor extensions and improvements. Thus in the period after 1890 the Barry Railway opened an additional 32 miles, the Cardiff Railway 23 miles, the Rhondda and Swansea Bay 17 miles, and the Port Talbot 21 miles. Elsewhere construction mostly took the form of light railways, like the Vale of Rheidol and the Lampeter to Aberaeron lines, although an additional 35 miles were also built for Cambrian Railways.[19] The provision of additional dock accommodation was on an altogether different scale. Indeed, captial expenditure on docks in Wales from the early 1890s to 1910 was higher than it had ever been.[20] The Barry No. 2 Dock, covering 34 acres, was opened in 1898. At Cardiff the Queen Alexandra Dock was opened in 1907 at a cost of £1.3 million. Its 52 acres increased the Bute Docks system by almost one-third.[21] At Newport a dock extension of 20 acres was opened in 1893 whilst the South Dock extension of 48 acres was finally completed in 1914. At Port Talbot a new dock was opened in 1898 the same year as a 28 acre extension to the Prince of Wales dock in Swansea. A decade later, in 1909, the King's Dock of 70 acres was also opened at Swansea and the Act which had authorized its construction had also provided for still further expansion, which eventually materialized when the Queen's Dock was opened in 1920. For the present purpose these substantial undertakings hold a double significance: they represented in themselves major works which would have large multiplier effects; and the readiness to build them is itself a telling indicator of a thriving economy with a confident future.

Most contemporary comment reflects this confidence. There are always instances of foreboding to be found and, with hindsight, they tend more readily to leap out of the page. Nevertheless, the more characteristic impression was the turn of the century assessment that 'in this year of grace 1901 it (Wales) is one of the brightest and most truly civilised spots in the Queen's dominions . . . with the black mineral pouring into the lap of Cardiff, Newport, Swansea and Llanelli, where the argosies of the nations await its arrival to convey it to the remotest parts of the earth . . . (with) the transformation of the Rhondda Valley from a sleepy hollow, into the most active and thriving community in Great Britain or the world . . .'[22] A less lyrical confirmation of the same buoyant judgement was delivered in the sober prose of Professor H. Stanley Jevons. Living in Cardiff and writing in 1914, just before the First World War he observed that 'A new and urgent demand for more dock accommodation at Cardiff is now being pressed . . . The South Wales coalfield is now producing at the rate of nearly 60 million tons per annum, and the rate of production is pretty sure to increase within 30 or 40 years to about 100 million tons per annum'.[23]

Whatever may be its validity for the UK as a whole, the 1890s climacteric hypothesis does not — in the end — correspond to the Welsh experience. The most convincing explanation of this contradiction is still contained within Brinley Thomas's perception of the working of an Atlantic economy. As a descriptive device for the Welsh economy, however, the notion of a climacteric need not be totally discarded. Instead, some would argue, it simply needs to be shifted. It is, perhaps, appropriately used, not for the 1890s, but for the 1920s. In 1907, reflecting the Edwardian confidence and high expectations, Lloyd George had rhetorically asked: 'Why should not South Wales and Cardiff' (this was Ministerial tact — he was in Cardiff at the time) 'develop into one of the greatest manufacturing centres in the whole Empire?'[24] It was not the kind of question that could have been posed with any sense of tact — or credibility — in, say, Merthyr or Blaenau Ffestiniog in the 1930s.

Section C
Twentieth Century

The First World War and Government Coal Control

GRAEME HOLMES

All historians are aware that the British coal industry in general and the south Wales coal industry in particular were marked by grave problems in the 1920s, especially in the field of labour relations. From the Sankey Commission's Report of 1919 onwards [1] the organization of the industry was the subject of keen debate. On the surface there is an apparent contrast between the relative industrial peace of 1913–14 and the hostile mood of 1919–21. Similarly, in political terms Kenneth Morgan stresses that down to 1914 'Lib–Labism' was the dominant and unifying creed in south Wales with Labour making limited progress. For Morgan the First World War introduced a totally new phase, the key to which was the dramatic expansion of the trade unions which more than doubled in membership between 1914 and 1920. [2]

Morgan echoes the assumption implicit in much writing, especially by political historians, that the war constituted a major turning-point. Political historiography, however, tends to present political action and discussion as paramount and to lose sight of the underlying economic and industrial factors. Economic historians would place more stress on such factors as the long strike of 1898; the vigorous debate over the equity of the sliding scale for wages; the Tonypandy riots of 1910; and the labour disturbances of 1911–12. From such a perspective it would be difficult to argue that there was an absence of discontent before 1914. To present too stark a contrast between the pre-war and post-war situations is untenable. None the less the magnitude of labour troubles in the 1920s implies that wartime circumstances led to a shift of emphasis which brought the pre-1914 arrangements for the industry into question to a degree which would not have been possible before the war. After all, the arrangements for determining wages and resolving labour disputes remained, albeit with significant modifications, much the same in 1914 as they had been in the 1880s. The war, however, produced a substantial change. Up to 1914 the Monmouthshire and South Wales Coalowners' Association considered itself to have the authority to resolve the major problems concerning the industry whereas between 1914 and 1926 the Government became a major influence on the situation with the Coalowners' Association often assuming a secondary role.

The increase in Government influence was associated above all with wartime control arrangements. It was the lifting of control on 31 March 1921 ('Black Friday') which was the occasion of the first of the major strikes in the 1920s. In 1915, 1917 and immediately after the war in 1919, there were threats of major stoppages, stoppages which were averted only by significant interventions by the Government. The main theme of this essay is to examine wartime control arrangements and to enquire how control might be linked with the aggravation of industrial difficulties. A major consideration is that the control mechanisms were rudimentary and were largely operated in the regional coalfields by local men who had long been associated with the coal industry. The south Wales coalfield bears examination because it posed many of the most serious problems confronting wartime administrators.

A crucial issue in the discussion is to define control. Control in the sense of Government intervention to deal with problems of producing, distributing and marketing coal was far from being a single coherent system. It is important to realize that control was a shifting series of overlapping and sometimes conflicting arrangements and can be found in no one document. For our purposes this can be illustrated and clarified by indicating the various phases through which control progressed. The first phase starts with the war itself. Such a view is in conflict with some previous expositions[3] which have tended simply to mention the position in 1914 as background before racing ahead to deal with what they see as the beginning of control with the Munition of War Act of 1915. They then shift rapidly to a situation described as total control. 'In 1917', states Lewis, 'Britain's coal industry was *completely reorganised* (my italics) and brought under government control'.[4] The point to be emphasized here, however, is that for south Wales the very declaration of war necessarily implied some control and thus requires examination as the first stage in a very long process. Why was this?

The declaration of war in August 1914 carried with it for south Wales a considerable expansion in the demand for steam-coal required for so-called Admiralty purposes. The *Colliery Guardian,* reviewing the year 1914 for south Wales, put the point directly: 'In fact all the collieries producing first quality seams were really controlled by the Government and the whole of the outputs reserved for the battleships. Exports were prohibited except to neutral countries . . .'.[5] In April 1915 Hugh Bramwell, a leading south Wales coalowner, said that the Admiralty normally bought about a million and a half tons per annum but on the outbreak of war they suddenly called for practically the whole output and during two months coal was being shipped at the rate of something like 15 million tons per annum.[6] Essentially the same point was being recognized when Lloyd George stressed the immense national importance of coal from south Wales during the wage dispute and threatened strike of June and July 1915.[7] Of course, there was no resistance from the coalowners to increased Admiralty demand, both because it was implicit in arrangements for supplying the Navy from south Wales which went back some four decades and because the supplies were made at favourable prices. 'Control' was thus more in the nature of a voluntary agreement about demand and supply arrangements for a particularly favoured customer.

The outbreak of war, then, introduced the first phase of 'control', the phase in which 'Admiralty coal' was given priority. The second and third phases overlapped with each other and both had significant repercussions for south Wales with its important steam-coal production for export markets. The second phase involved licensing for exports in order to ensure essential coal supplies for the home market. The requisite orders were made in May and August 1915. The third phase belonged to June and July 1915 with the threatened miners' strike in south Wales which resulted in Government determination of the wages issue on a national basis. Although there was some modification and tightening of export control in 1916 the fourth phase came in late 1916 and early 1917, involving once again the wages issue and resulting in the establishment of a formal coal control mechanism under the supervision of a full-time coal controller. The fifth, sixth and seventh phases all belong to the post-war period between late 1918 and the spring of 1921. The fifth phase involved some relaxation of export control and licensing between 1918 and early 1920, only for the pressures on supplies for the home market to reassert themselves resulting in a renewed tightening of export control in June 1920. The sixth phase overlapped with this and involved the questions of wages, management and the reorganization of the industry including the possibility of nationalization. The final phase came with the fall in prices which gathered pace from December 1920 enabling the Government to hasten the process of decontrol which was completed by the abolition of the formal coal control mechanism on 31 March 1921.

The foregoing summary helps to emphasize that Government control was a developing process. It should not, however, be taken to imply neat chronological compartments. The Admiralty demand, for example, remained an important component as long as war continued. Hugh Bramwell's admittedly approximate estimate of 15 million tons per annum for late 1914 can be compared with the estimate of Thomas that in 1918 nearly 14 million tons of coal were supplied by south Wales out of a total of nearly 20 million tons used by the Admiralty in that year. In 1920, by contrast, Admiralty requirements from south Wales ran at 1,088,017 tons out of a total regional production of 46,209,148 tons.[8] Although a goodly part of the apparently massive fall between 1918 and 1920 is explained by reclassification of coal destined for France, reclassification itself carried price implications which explained the reluctance of the French Bureau des Charbons to continue purchasing south Wales coal at relatively high prices after the middle of December 1920.[9] Admiralty demand tended to have an existence partly independent of any formal system of control, a feature explaining its destabilizing influence both in 1914–15 and again in the armistice period 1919–20.

Another feature exhibiting instability and independence from formal control was the labour supply. As with Admiralty coal, the outbreak of war had an immediate effect on the labour supply. The industry lost labour from the outset. By 1915 serious complaints were made about the effect of recruiting upon colliery manpower. Thus Sir Arthur Markham pointed out at the Tredegar company meeting in late June that the Government was sending recruiting officers to the collieries whilst at the same time they desired ouput to be increased.[10] Despite some counter-movement to the loss of men to the armed forces by the influx of new workers to the pits the general trend down to 1918 was for mining labour to be depleted. By contrast, the return of men from the armed forces provided a significant increase in manpower during the years of 1919–20. In 1920 employment in the south Wales coal industry reached its highest ever level:

Table 1
Employment: South Wales coal industry

1914	234,117
1915	202,655
1916	214,100
1917	219,718
1918	218,353
1919	257,613
1920	271,516
1921	232,043
1922	243,015[11]

The fluctuations in manpower show the partial nature of control over the labour supply. At first some colliery managers themselves encouraged enlisting in the armed forces. It was reported in the *Colliery Guardian* of 4 September 1914, that over 2,000 Rhondda colliers had already enlisted and nearly half of those came from the Cambrian combine collieries where the general manager, Mr Leonard Llewellyn, had been active in stimulating recruiting.[12] Within six months, however, a different tone was apparent. The *Colliery Guardian* complained that the younger men continued to dribble away from the Admiralty collieries where recruiting was supposed not to take place at all.[13] Although colliery courts were set up later, and even joint-pit committees towards the end of the war, they acted more as filtering mechanisms to release men considered at local level to have the lowest priority to remain in the mines. The effect on wages and wage costs, either of a shortage or of a plethora of men, does not seem to have entered very seriously into discussion, certainly not as an item of coal control. Even when the Coal Controller's Advisory Board first met in 1917 it assumed as one of its functions the assisting of recruitment. This view prevailed, rather than that of Robert Smillie who urged that the business of the Board was to safeguard the mining industry and to state whether any more men could be spared if and when they were demanded by the War Office, and not to devise methods in advance whereby they should be obtained.[14]

If labour supply and Admiralty demand provided two examples of instability which were difficult to regulate, especially at the beginning of the war and in its immediate aftermath, a third example lay in the fluctuations in shipping arrivals and in freight rates. The *Colliery Guardian* reported on 15 January 1915 that the all-absorbing topic in Cardiff was the exorbitant freight-rates and the great difficulty in providing sufficient tonnage for full work at the collieries.[15] Control in shipping rapidly became a major item of Government policy but, even so, the shipping problem for coal export from south Wales remained difficult simply because of the importance of neutral shipping which both influenced freight rates and was unreliable in its frequency of arrivals. Shipping shortages were a constant problem until the end of the war, but the situation was somewhat mitigated by the licensing system for coal, introduced on 13 May 1915 for exports to neutral countries and on 13 August 1915 for exports to Allied countries, the overall supervision of exports being under the aegis of the Coal Exports Committee. The licensing system acted as a restraint to the export of coal but it was a somewhat rough instrument having only a minor effect on exports once shipping returned to south Wales ports in large quantities after the end of the war. Already on 22 November 1918, less than two weeks after the armistice, the *Colliery Guardian* reported that: 'The abandonment of the convoy system has resulted in a considerable influx of tonnage, and there are now more vessels in the docks awaiting cargoes than for many months past.'[16] From then on shipping shortage was no longer a problem, and in an exceptional week reported on 9 May 1919, total Bristol Channel shipments were 523,666 tons, exclusive of shipments on Admiralty account, which exceeded by far anything that had been recorded since 1914.[17] Nevertheless, a licensing system still operated but less severely than between 1915 and 1918.[18]

In 1920 exports turned down again, a significant reason being the imposition of more severe export quotas in early June with a total of 20 million tons being allocated for the United Kingdom as a whole, of which 13½ million tons were allocated to south Wales. The effect of the quotas was that whereas south Wales exports for the first four months of 1920 averaged 2,590,416 tons per month, they would be limited to 1,700,000 tons per month for the rest of the year.[19] However, the restraint on exports — 1920 style — was short-lived, being removed by the lifting of controls in 1921.

The reason for licensing of exports was separate from the shipping problem and provided an illustration of the way in which direct controls were consequent upon the indirect controls operating virtually from the outset of war. Labour supply, Admiralty demand and the shipping problem were responsible both for a fall in production and for a structural change in export markets. South America was an obvious example of a problem market. Already in August 1914 it was reported that coal-exporters were naturally anxious about the prospects of American competition and could expect organized assaults upon Britain's South American markets in the future.[20] The question arose of the relationship between home and overseas markets and of the price at which coal should be sold in those markets. In spite of the normal peacetime importance of coal exports to the British economy and to the south Wales economy in particular, the fact was that even in peacetime home consumption of south Wales coal was still sizeable. In wartime, both supply and price to the home market became of paramount importance. 'Early in 1915 it became obvious that, if the most imperative demands were to be adequately met, there must be a curtailment of exports and also the haphazard distribution of the home supplies must be replaced by a more scientific organisation'.[21] The practical measures taken were the licensing of exports and the passing of the Price of Coal (limitation) Act on 29 July 1915 to limit the price of coal on the home market. Early in 1916 the question of inland distribution was tackled by the creation of a Central Coal and Coke Supplies Committee with district sub-committees, one of which was for south Wales and Monmouthshire.

Yet if home and Admiralty requirements were paramount, with a secondary priority being accorded to France (and later in 1916 to Italy), a subsidiary aim of the Coal Exports Committee was 'to encourage the free export of the surplus to neutral countries at the highest possible prices'.[22] The reason for encouragement of exports at high prices was simply to earn foreign exchange which in wartime conditions was all important. Hence control of supplies was a partial control only, creating in effect three markets: home, priority export, and free export. Clearly, the ability to sell in the free export market was to the profit advantage of coalowners who could take the opportunity to sell in that market. Quoted prices, however, were nominal since the ability to sell was dependent on shipping arrivals and on the expertise of the middleman who took his share of the profit. In a coalfield where exports accounted for something more than half normal production in peacetime the shifting relative balance operating between price-controlled home supplies, controlled export supplies and free export supplies was again a destabilizing influence, especially on colliery company profits.

It was, in fact, in the sphere of colliery company profits and wages that the most controversial items of wartime administration and control were to emerge. One example of net profit shifts is shown by the experience of the Cardiff Collieries Ltd., as follows:-

1913	52,471
1914	29,656
1915	52,565
1916	196,636
1917	81,242
1918	83,584
1919	169,928
1920	307,753
1921	− 53,471 (loss: first loss since 1896)[23]

There is in fact an alternative — and obviously less reliable — source for the same company's figures published by the Business Statistics Publishing Company at the time. Its figures tend to iron out the fluctuations by reducing profits in the years of high success (especially 1916–20). But even the Business Statistics Company's figures indicate for a number of south Wales coal firms that profits doubled during the war years.

One can emphasize only that all these sources need to be received with caution. The lack of knowledge about profits was primarily about their extent. It was at the time widely alleged that coalowners made excessively high profits, and it was primarily because of the unrest likely to arise if profits were high and wages relatively low that taxation of excess profits was introduced. Under Section 42 of the Finance (No.2) Act 1915 excess profits were taxed at 50 per cent and by the Coal Control Agreement of 1917 at 80 per cent. Financial control involved some degree of government audit but its perfunctory nature and the absence of any reliable published figures meant that the situation was uncertain. In addition any forecasts of sales and profit trends were highly conjectural. In such circumstances wage bargaining took on more of a short-term trial of negotiating strength than any serious attempt to create a long-term viable national wage structure.

The uncertainty and instability of wartime conditions was, of course, relative. The ebb and flow of the trade cycle was a well-known feature of the coal industry at any time between 1850 and 1914. Nevertheless, the instability experienced before 1914 occurred within reasonably well-known parameters which made it possible for attempts at reform of the industry's structure and organization to be contained, even if sometimes with difficulty, within existing arrangements for dealing with production, prices and wages. A key feature of pre-war arrangements was, of course, district bargaining over wages. It is arguable, if controversial, to suggest that a long-term viable wage structure has never been possible in the coal industry except on a district level because of the great differences in geological conditions and in custom and practice as between coalfields.

How to deal with those differences has long been the main difficulty confronting those who have tried to deal with the coal industry from a national viewpoint. It was a difficulty which had to be faced in 1915 when circumstances compelled national, as distinct from district, discussion of the industry to be a major item on the agenda. It was implicit in the arrangements being made that Government took key initiatives, with coalowners and trade unionists being brought together under the aegis of Government 'control'. The essential items for consideration early in 1915 were production, distribution, prices and wages. Yet in a world where long-cherished notions of economic thought dictated that the individual entrepreneur was free to make key decisions, it was clearly unthinkable that individual production units should undergo interference. In any event, the existence of some 1,500 separate colliery companies in Great Britain or 260 in south Wales in 1913[24] precluded any attempt at a 'railway solution' for the industry whereby Government effectively requested existing railway company managers to work together to organize railways as a national concern for the duration of the war. Hence the problems of 1915 which appeared capable of immediate solution were essentially about distribution, prices and wages.

In spite of the impracticable nature of a 'railway solution', the Government could scarcely resolve the problems imposed without some co-operation from both coalowners and trade unionists. The admission of the need to involve both sides of industry came with the appointment of the Coal Organisation Committee in February 1915[25] with three representatives each from the Mining Association and the Miners' Federation. The competence of the members concerned to undertake a review of the coal industry from a national viewpoint is best illustrated by 'the confession' of A.F. Pease, a member of the committee who was a coalowner from the north-east of England, that '. . . until he sat upon that Committee he had no idea how little he really knew about the coal trade. Nothing had so impressed him as the differences between the commercial and working conditions of the various coalfields in different parts of the United Kingdom. Regulations and arrangements which suited one district were absolutely inapplicable to another'.[26]

The humility of Pease was at variance with the ebullience of J.W. Beynon at the Ebbw Vale company meeting in late June. Commenting upon export restrictions Beynon said '. . . one would have thought it most desirable for the country to sell its exports at the highest possible figure in order to get the greatest amount of imports possible; but the government had set up in the House of Commons a Committee for limiting prices of coal, and had done it in order to pander to a few political cranks, who ought not to be allowed outside the confines of Bedlam'.[27] In other words, there was still in 1915 a twin problem, both of persuading coalowners to consider regarding the industry as a national entity and to arrive at solutions for national difficulties.

Distribution and prices, however, were not as important as the wage issue in compelling Government and the coalowners to consider the industry from a national viewpoint. In 1915 the Prime Minister, Asquith, wanted the wage issue to be settled on a district basis and in fact all districts reached agreement through their Conciliation Boards with the marked exception of south Wales. In spite of attempts by the Government to settle the situation, even by invoking the Munitions of War Act with its implied threat of compulsion, virtually all of the south Wales miners' demands were met. It is undeniable that the south Wales wages episode of 1915 roused extreme passions on a national scale: 'If it be necessary to proceed to extremes, this spurious trade unionism will have to be stamped out. We have no room for those who openly preach treason at the pithead . . . Failure to enforce the Munitions Act now will mean the downfall of the Government and chaos in the affairs of the nation'.[28]

There is little doubt that a number of coalowners felt that the Government had let them down. At a special meeting of the Monmouthshire and South Wales Coalowners' Association on 26 July 1915 Fred Davis said that before properly understanding the situation the Government had given away nine-tenths of the men's demands; the owners had placed themselves entirely in the hands of the Government but they had emphasized that every concession was a most serious matter to the trade.[29] It was to be the first in a long line of protests from the middle of 1915 to 1919, if not beyond, with the wage question looming large. Yet what emerges is that the key role in wage determination had shifted to the Government, and that south Wales miners had moved away rather rapidly from the 'Lib-Labism' of 1914, possibly encouraged in the expectation that they were dealing with a Government ill-equipped to resist wage claims in wartime conditions. The coalowners complained that miners had made considerable additions to their monetary wages by the time that the war came to an end. The significance of such a situation was that pre-war arrangements for wage bargaining, in themselves the subject of dissatisfaction from time to time before 1914, had broken down yet again in the absence of any stable arrangements for regulating wages. The Coalowners' Association, whose original major reason for existence had been precisely to regulate wages in the south Wales coalfield by way of a common overall bargaining procedure, now had one of its most notable functions emasculated.[30]

The wage dispute of 1915, therefore, was a significant turning-point. The resistance of south Wales miners to suggested district wage increases was as Woodhouse suggests, a relatively spontaneous and widespread show of discontent which miners' leaders did relatively little to initiate.[31] The solution was *ad hoc* and temporary, owing much to the intervention of Lloyd George who believed that it was necessary to concede the bulk of the miners' demands to bring wages into line with the cost of living. In effect, the pre-1914 arrangement by which miners' wages moved broadly in line with prices was discarded.

Yet, if the events of 1915 brought a neccesity to consider wages, prices and distribution on a national, as distinct from a district, basis it was far from clear what administrative mechanisms should be used to deal with the situation. This helps to explain why the various committees and control arrangements were brought into being in an improvized way. Not only in wage determination, but in export licensing and in home distribution arrangements, the coalowners were rather instruments of the Government than initiators of new mechanisms. The fact that coalowners' participation was a necessary ingredient of the operation of the Coal Exports Committee and of the Coal and Coke Supplies Committee might have coloured coalowners' attitudes in the sense that in general coalowners were not over-critical of Government actions. Government intervention was not yet seen as a major threat to the existing organization of the industry and until late in 1916 any note of alarm and suspicion of Government intentions was muted.

Nevertheless, the problems arising in 1915 were sufficiently important for the Government to be concerned that *ad hoc* arrangements were not enough. Those problems were coal shortages, rising prices of coal, inadequate distribution for wartime purposes, and wage determination under wartime conditions. Redmayne early in September 1915 prepared a memorandum on the subject of coal control for the Home Secretary which stated:-

> The main objects to be secured by government control of the collieries, a course only justified by the exigencies of war, are:
> 1. The regulation of the working of the collieries so as to secure the largest possible output of coal.
> 2. The more effective distribution of coal.
> 3. The regulation of the sellng price of coal.
> 4. The prevention of unrest amongst the workmen.[32]

It was the last feature which initiated the next phase of Government control. A new wage claim from the south Wales miners for a 15 per cent advance in wages was made in May 1916 and conceded by the Board of Trade; then in September the miners applied for a further 15 per cent and soon coupled their wage demand with a request for joint audit of the coalowners' account books, a request which the coalowners refused. With the threat of a strike looming, on 29 November a regulation was introduced (9G) 'enabling the government to take control of any coal mines; and they immediately applied this to the South Wales coalfield'.[33] Within a few days an inter-departmental committee appointed by the Board of Trade conceded the miners' claim for an advance of 15 per cent,[34] and a special meeting of the Coalowners' Association decided that 'a strong protest should be made against the government in upholding the workmen in terms of the Conciliation Board Agreement by refusing to allow the application to be proceeded within the usual way'.[35] The note of reservation and even of suspicion about the Government's intentions was unmistakable.

Yet the actual operation of control under a Coal Controller was a matter of agreement between the coalowners and the Government. The coalowners were not quite sure whether they were allowing themselves to be manipulated. Their ambivalence of attitude was shown by Evan Williams, emerging as their most powerful figure, at a special meeting of the Coalowners' Association held on 19 June 1917 to discuss the agreement with the Government by which the Coal Controller assumed control of the coalfields from 1 March 1917. (St David apparently favoured Government control!) Evan Williams, although he was a member of the drafting committee disassociated himself from any responsibility for the drafting of the Agreement and intimated that he intended only to explain the scheme and not to justify it.[36] His somewhat apologetic tone was suited to his audience. Other members of the Association would have preferred to see the matter settled in Parliament. A major criticism was that the scheme might be acceptable to the more successful collieries but was useless for the less fortunate ones. Sir Clifford Cory was not sure that members would lose anything by allowing the whole matter to be settled by Parliament, while Thomas E. Watson noted that since the outbreak of war the coalowners had been most patriotic supporting the Government in all coal trade matters with the result that the Government was taking advantage of them.[37]

Some of the coalowners, in fact, never ceased to dislike the implied *force majeure* of the Government actions nor did they cease to be wary of the Coal Controller. Thus at a special meeting of the Coalowners' Association of 15 October 1917, the question of the recent award of a war wage was discussed, particularly with reference to the compensatory increase in the price of coal by 2s. 6d. per ton. A major query was whether the Government was acting within the law, and Sir Clifford Cory maintained that the coalowners had submitted too long to the illegal procedures of the present Government.[38] A further special meeting on 29 October returned to the question of legality, and it was stated that 'Counsel had declined to give a written opinion as they considered it would be unwise to put into writing their opinion to the effect that the course adopted by the government in regard to the Collieries was "ultra vires". Counsel considered that the Compensation Agreement had been abrogated in consequence of the War Wage just granted'.[39] Equally startling was a special meeting of 29 July 1918 which called into question the legality of the Coal Controller's actions in regard to various matters, but especially in regard to an earlier order in Council by which the Board of Trade might authorize any person to take possession of a seam and get coal therefrom. At this meeting the note of hostility to, and wariness of, the Coal Controller was very clear.

The minutes of the coalowners' meetings scarcely encourage a belief that wicked coalowners were in league with a Government hostile to miners' aspirations. They were more concerned to protect coalowner interest (and power) from Government encroachment. In this they were often — and almost unavoidably — successful. The fact was that coal control — 1917 style — was far from being the 'complete re-organization' claimed by E.D. Lewis and in itself did little to alter the existing situation. Even the distinction between the period from 1917 as the period of 'Full Control' compared with the period of 'Partial Control' which preceded it is misleading.[40] The fact that not too much had changed was evident to many in the industry, the *Colliery Guardian* pointing out that the actual detailed management of the collieries must necessarily remain in the hands of experienced men then in charge.[41] Even in 1917 it was stated that: 'No matter how wide the extent of government control, the issue is not yet one of nationalisation. It is imperative that, as in the case of railways, the management remain as it is at present, and that the control be chiefly of sale, distribution, and price, rather than production, although it is to be hoped that the new system will facilitate production by ensuring a better supply of labour'.[42] Production was a key issue from the standpoint of the nation and it was the prospect of shortages due to diminished production which had prompted Government interference with the industry in the first place; but the actual control of the production process remained with the existing managements.

The 'new system', in fact, was very much a matter for improvisation, a feature which comes over strongly on a scrutiny of the Minutes of the Coal Controller's Advisory Board. At the very first meeting on 7 March 1917 there was a discussion of the Controller's functions, with the Controller explaining that the mine-owners would continue *for the present* to sell the coal and that the management of the mines, would *for the present* remain with the owners. The Controller would enforce the Price Limitation Act.[43] As for exports, Redmayne states that the Coal Exports Committee, though acting under the Coal Control, continued to be very much a self-contained body.[44] At no time did the multitude of collieries in existence have much more than a corresponding relationship with the Coal Controller in the form of providing returns about production and sales. Even those returns were provided very much on the coalowners' own terms since at a special meeting of the Coalowners' Association held on 18 April 1918 it was agreed that, in view of the depleted staffs of colliery companies, it was impossible to supply information every month. A quarterly return was agreed upon, but the prickliness expressed was one more instance of suspicion about coal control and its operation.

Indeed, the extent to which the Coal Controller could alter existing arrangements was questionable, especially in the management of the collieries themselves. The question of mine management was one about which coalowners were particularly sensitive. Perhaps the most forthright statement in this respect was that made at a Coalowners' Association meeting held on 29 March 1919 to the effect that it was quite impossible to allow any interference by the workmen with the management of the collieries.[45] Yet if the immediate background to that statement was the discussion occurring in the Sankey Commission, there were earlier indications of hostility to any possible erosion of managerial authority notably with the establishment of pit committees in 1918 whose duty was to stimulate output and to avoid unnecessary absenteeism. The *Colliery Guardian* reported on 16 August 1918 that employers in south Wales were understood to have a strong objection to workmen's representatives being granted power to investigate questions of management and equipment; and they intended to appoint a deputation to submit their views to the Coal Controller.[46] Pit committees were clearly a matter of contention since a later issue of 6 September stated: 'the difficulty which has arisen in forming joint committees at the pits . . . has led the Coal Controller to suggest a conference between the Coalowners' Association and the Miners' Federation in order that agreement may be reached'.

The discussion over pit committees could be viewed in several ways. Firstly, their establishment could show the potential power of the Coal Controller to investigate conditions in any individual pit; secondly, pit committees might show that some grievances in particular pits were justified; and, thirdly they might reinforce the belief that not all problems at pit level were of the miners' own creation. From a practical viewpoint pit committees were not of great consequence since the proposal to establish them came within three months of the armistice. Yet the relative paucity of information about their operation is paralleled for the historian by the relative lack of information about the functioning of individual colliery companies and about individual pits. Nevertheless from the individual miner's point of view and for an explanation of the demise of 'Lib–Labism' during the war some estimate of conditions at individual pits is unavoidable.

The evidence is scanty and disparate. The Minute Books of the Blaenavon Company, for example, show no great difference from pre-war functioning except in respect of the revival and expansion of iron- and steel-making, an activity which tended to have a higher priority in wartime than coal production. Not until 1921 in fact did labour problems in coal production take up much discussion among the Blaenavon directors.[47] Blaenavon shows the problem of analysing the vertically integrated company. Another company whose Minute Book for 1919–20 has survived, the Imperial Navigation Coal Co. Ltd., shows virtually no boardroom discussion of labour problems.[48] Other fragments of evidence show how wartime distortions tended to accentuate the diversity of operational conditions already existing in 1913. For example, the unevenness of demand in the anthracite coalfield led to short-time working by the Evan Bevan Company which reported to a meeting of the Coalowners' Association on 29 October 1917 that in consequence of not being able to work full-time, it had given notice to two hundred of the men employed at his collieries.[49] Another south Wales colliery stoppage to reach the Coal Controller was the Nine Mile Point colliery dispute.[50]

The Coal Controller's sympathies were by no means automatically in tune with the workmen's representatives, however. Yet, even if one or two disputes reached the Coal Controller most disputes were the subject of discussion by the Coalowners' Association itself, two notable examples being Gelli Colliery owned by Cory Brothers and South Duffryn Rhondda Colliery owned by Hill's Plymouth Company. Gelli Colliery provided a continuing saga of disputes from 1914 right down to 1918,[51] while Hill's Plymouth Company was granted permission at a special Cardiff District Board meeting on 10 November 1917 to give notice to workmen subject to Conciliation Board consideration.[52] These and other examples from the periodic Coalowners' Association indemnity lists provide evidence that at colliery level nothing very much had changed during wartime except that men were periodically being exhorted to work harder. The exhortations could ring rather hollow when bottle-necks occurred in supply with stockpiles occuring and with no obvious immediate need to increase output further. A poor colliery manager was more important as an immediate detrimental influence on men's morale than any exhortations from afar designed to stimulate motivation to work. Yet colliery managers, like so many other members of the labour force, could not be taken for granted. It is revealing that there was virtually no discussion about colliery managers by the Coalowners' Association until a special meeting of 12 January 1920 when there was a report of a meeting between colliery company representatives and representatives of the South Wales Colliery Managers' Association against a background of suggestions that a trade union of colliery managers was a possibility. The Coalowners' Association recommended appropriate minimum salaries but even then insisted that the resolution was sent out as a recommendation and not as an instruction. It was admitted that a number of companies had not treated their managers fairly with consequent resulting dissatisfaction and it was essential that managers should feel that they were being treated more in the way of colleagues than officials.[53]

By 1920, of course, colliery managers had become important against the background of discussion about the possibility of nationalization engendered by the Sankey Commission in 1919. Frank Hodges, indeed, recognized that one of the advantages to be derived from nationalization would be unification of management in districts so as to make provision for the quantum of coal required from the district as determined by the national co-ordinating authority.[54] This, of course, struck both at the authority of individual companies and their management and at the authority of the Coalowners' Association, and raises the question of the link between the nationalization debate of 1919–20 and coal control operating in 1917–18.

The major link between the two episodes was the opportunity for trade union representation on the Coal Controller's Advisory Board which could provide the occasion for fundamental questions to be posed by trade unionists about the industry. There was concern on the trade union side that the Advisory Board was merely a talking shop, Robert Smillie saying on 9 October 1918 that it was clear that the Board would never have any responsibility until it became executive.[55] On 6 November 1918 Robert Smillie handed in a document asking for information on eight points including pre-war profits, present profits and how profits were distributed; details as to costs of production showing (a) wages and (b) other items both pre-war and present; and ascertained prices of coal both pre-war and present. The opinion of the Law Officers of the Crown was then sought in view of certain sections of the Coal Mines Agreement (Confirmation) Act restricting the disclosure of information. They advised that there was no obligation on the part of the industry to disclose such information apart from 'a government purpose'.[56]

The dusty answer accorded to trade unionists, however, did not mean that the Coal Controller himself was satisfied with matters as they were. There is no evidence in the Advisory Board Minutes about the Controller's thought on the organization of the industry but there was an intriguing entry in the *Colliery Guardian* of 4 July 1919:-

The Yorkshire Post's London Correspondent gives a pretty story . . . He says: — Just before Christmas the Coal Control was getting ready for nationalization, and had a scheme prepared. It was held up because of illness and sudden death of Sir Guy Calthrop, who, however, had come to the conclusion that it was impossible to go on as we were going on and, being in virtual control, was seriously considering permanent control. This fact explains the evidence given by Sir Lowes Dickinson and other witnesses from the Control department in the early days of the Coal Commission, evidence which did much to give the Commission a bias towards nationalisation. Probably Mr Justice Sankey knew all about this scheme, but the other members of the Commission were not allowed to know it, or at all events were not told of it till after the report was complete.[57]

It is probable that Sir Guy Calthrop's dissatisfaction at the end of 1918 was due largely to the fact that the scheme of coal control as it existed provided a framework for jockeying for position between coalowners and trade unionists. That jockeying for position continued in the hearings of the Sankey Commission, a feature about which so many historians have commented. Yet, in retrospect, the holding of the Sankey Commission was itself remarkable when viewed from the perspective of 1914 and showed how much wartime circumstances, and especially coal control, had made the prospect of fundamental reorganization of the industry a feasible proposition. Of course, the cynic may argue that one recommendation of the Sankey Commission's First Stage Report was too extreme: 'Even upon the evidence already given, the present system of ownership and working in the coal industry stands condemned, and some other system must be substituted for it, either nationalisation or a method of unification by national purchase and/or by joint control'.[58] Yet he can hardly deny that the statement made by Evan Williams to a special meeting of the Coalowners' Association held on 16 April 1919 contained an important admission: ' . . . It is a very difficult matter to get the coal-owner's case put properly in Parliament. I must admit that, though the coalowners' members are full of zeal they do not command the ear of the House to the extent one would like them to . . .'.[59]

Indeed, the shift in emphasis brought about by coal control was shown by the terms of reference of the Sankey Commission where wages and hours of work were placed first on the list of items for enquiry.[60] The wages question brought into review not only the future arrangements for wage determination but the linkages between wages on the one hand and prices, production and distribution on the other. As we know the Sankey Commission recommended nationalization of the industry only on the casting vote of the Chairman himself but it must be remembered that the terms of reference included enquiry into any scheme for the future organization of the industry, showing that in the circumstances of 1919 the existing organization was subject to question. As Pigou said in his evidence to the Sankey Commission: ' . . . When an existing method of running an industry is up for trial as against a proposed new method, there is a tendency to exaggerate the advantages of change. Evidence of inefficiency in the present system is, of course, *pro tanto* an argument for change, but it is not a decisive argument'.[61] Pigou confessed to having only a limited knowledge of the coal industry. He was clear that nationalization might take different forms according to the inclination of whatever Government was in power but he was not clear that nationalization necessarily guaranteed higher standards in the industry.[62]

Even if nationalization was feasible the directors of the nationalized coal corporation would have intractable problems of reconciling the different levels of productivity and profitability in different districts in order to arrive at an appropriate sum for a national wage. Although a nationalized corporation might well overcome demand instability and of price fluctuations by using medium-term forecasting and by rationalizing the quantities distributed and the mechanisms appropriate to operate distribution, such an approach would be difficult to achieve. The whole approach of Victorian and Edwardian entrepreneurship had been to respond to the market and to adjust appropriately to the market on a short-term basis.

Indeed, the spectrum of opinions about the future organization of the industry from left to right of the political and economic scene was a feature not only of the Sankey Commission but of the situation from 1920 onwards. The operation of control, both in its direct and indirect operation, had merely provided a holding operation for limiting inland coal prices and for limiting excess profits for coalowners while the necessity for controlling prices remained. The novelty of the wartime situation was that key initiatives lay with either the Government or the trade unionists and the coalowners naturally wished to return to a situation where they felt themselves to have more influence on the course of events. In fact, the hesitancy of the Government to contemplate nationalization in 1919 limited the issue to one of deciding the alternatives to control in the form in which it existed and of deciding when existing control should end.

Even over those issues, the Government held considerable initiative. It is clear that the relative haste with which decontrol was announced to end on 31 March 1921 aroused as much embarrassment among coalowners as it aroused resentment among trade unionists. The issues were cogently put by Evan Williams in a printed document presented to the Coalowners' Association at a special meeting held on 22 February 1921. For him the consideration of any wages agreement was greatly complicated by the abnormal conditions and anomalies which had been introduced into the payment of miners' wages under Government control, there being no relation at present either between wages in the industry, and the ability to pay them, or between them and the price of coal. Hence entirely new bases should be determined. Yet the industry as a whole could not exist without a very great reduction in wages. In the absence of ascertained figures a scheme for determining wages, even if settled and accepted, could not operate so early as 1 April to bring wages into the proper relation to the industry to pay. It was a complicated situation which had developed so suddenly and the task was one of enormous difficulty especially when the available time was so short.[63] At the meeting in February 1921 Evan Williams did not emphasize a point made at a previous meeting on 22 March 1919 that, had the coal-owners been more open in the past in regard to the actual position of the collieries, possibly present difficulties would have been easier and existing misconceptions removed.[64]

Yet the Sankey Commission had dominated the attention of coalowners, a feature which explained the holding of another Coalowners' Association meeting only the next week, on 29 March 1919, when Evan Williams asked whether it was not in the coalowners' interest to try to devise a scheme whereby they could show that prevailing conditions could be improved. It was also suggested that the south Wales district could withdraw from the Mining Association but Williams retorted that the owners would put themselves in a very weak position if they confined their case to destructive criticism and that it would be very unwise to divide forces.[65] Indeed, the extent to which the coalowners were adjusting to the new situation by improving co-operation among themselves was shown by their alteration of their Deed of Association at a special meeting held on 2 June 1919. The new Deed provided for fixing of mimimum prices, fixing conditions for the marketing, disposal and distribution of output, restricting output at any colliery, pooling members' wagons and joint purchase of colliery requisites on behalf of members. There were provisions for disciplining non-compliance. The first major test whether members were willing to operate the new deed came at a special meeting on 5 February 1921 against the background of the sharp fall in the price of export coal. The proposal was to recommend fixed prices for coal sold for export. Even if W.D. Wight, speaking for Cory Brothers in the absence of Sir Clifford Cory, said that it would be better to allow matters to take their course and not to fix prices since the fixing of mimimum prices would be playing into the hands of workmen's representatives, even such a robust economic individualist as W. North Lewis said that in view of abnormal circumstances he was now of the opinion that something must be done to steady the market. There were only four members who voted against the proposal.[66]

The first three months of 1921, in fact, showed the coalowners uncertain how to proceed. The control agreement of 1917, by introducing the concept of a national compensation pool, had effectively penalized an exporting district like south Wales as long as export prices remained high. The uncertainty over demand engendered by excessive wartime fluctuations meant that there was no stable medium-term basis for determining future wage settlements. The control mechanism as such had left wage determination in the hands of the Government and politicians as always were moved by short-term considerations. The wage issue was the most important feature to reveal that coal control was a highly limited and imperfect instrument of co-ordination. Its limitations were a mirror of the lack of agreement about its role and functions. It is extraordinary that a recent study of British Government during the First World War contains virtually no mention of coal control.[67] Some form of control became a necessity but its very creation brought the lack of agreement about the organization of the industry more into the open. In that sense, the system of partial control which was actually established was an important factor in aggravating labour troubles within the industry and was an episode which had been unduly neglected.

The Development of the Electricity Supply Industry in South Wales to 1939

R.H. MORGAN

The group of industries called 'public utilities' has been generally neglected in accounts of the industrial development of south Wales. The present aim is to offer a broad general account of one such industry, that of electricity supply. The concern is essentially with the development of the supply industry itself, i.e., statutory undertakings. Those individuals and organizations generating electricity for their own needs and perhaps a limited number of local consumers, are not included. The discussion is also mostly confined to the industry in south Wales. Some consideration of the industry in Wales as a whole can be found in an article published in the *Welsh History Review* (June 1983).

This paper falls essentially into two parts. The first aims to give a general account of the development of the industry, the second presents what statistical information is available on the industry.

I

Electrical development in the area began when Cardiff Corporation granted a temporary licence to the Anglo–American Brush Company in the mid 1880s to supply direct current for all lighting in the Hayes, Wharton Street and the immediate neighbourhood. In 1892 a supply was started in Ogmore Vale and Nantymoel, and 1893 saw a supply in Pontypool. In the meantime, Cardiff had obtained powers and commenced supply in 1893 by means of a bulk supply from Cardiff Castle and in 1894 opened a station at Ninian Park. Generating stations started to operate at Gorseinon in 1894 and in Newport the following year. After this there was steady development of the supply in the area. In 1905 undertakings were established by Neath Corporation, Neath R.D.C. and Pontypridd U.D.C. The years 1910–11 saw the establishment of further statutory undertakings at Mountain Ash, Abertillery, Cardiff R.D.C., Aberdare, Gelligaer, Bedwellty and Mynyddislwyn.

The early development of the industry followed much the same pattern as elsewhere in Great Britain, which is hardly surprising as the nature of the industry was being determined essentially by parliamentary legislation. The first piece of legislation came in 1882 with the Electric Lighting Act, an Act which has often been blamed for putting a millstone around the neck of the industry, in that it favoured local authority ownership, stifling the more dynamic private sector.[1] True or not, there can be no doubt that the Act established the rights of municipalities to develop their own supplies. Byatt says in fact that the Board of Trade interpreted this Act as giving local authorities preference over private companies if both applied for powers at the same time.[2] The 1882 Act also contained a controversial compulsory purchase clause giving local authorities power of purchase after 21 years. This was strongly opposed by the companies which wanted perpetual concessions subject to Government control. This, however, they were not successful in obtaining, though in 1888 the period was extended to 42 years in a second piece of legislation.

The 1888 Act was also important in that it was to help establish an initial structure in the industry which, as we shall see, was to prove extremely difficult to change even though technical efficiency demanded it. Electricity generation came to be in the hands of a large number of small undertakings. Each undertaking had its own area of supply clearly laid down and could not go outside it. At the time this caused little difficulty. The principal system of supply was one of direct current generated by a slow speed horizontal engine. The effective radius of distribution of such a system was limited technically as well as being severely prescribed by law.

The favoured position given to municipalities meant that they came to dominate the industry in its early years. At the turn of the century, however, developments occurred which challenged this position. The development of alternating current distribution, economies of scale in generating, and ever-increasing uses of electricity, meant that the local small-scale undertaking was becoming increasingly inappropriate for future development. The Cross Committee,[3] reporting in 1898, recognized this and recommended that powers be granted to companies over large areas covering a number of local authorities. This started an important debate between the small-scale existing undertakings, mainly local authority owned, and those trying to put into effect the ethos of the 'power company' supplying a wide area.

South Wales figured prominently in this debate. In 1900 a proposal was put forward to set up a power company in the district. The scheme was to establish three power stations at Neath, Pontypridd and Pontypool to supply electricity over the whole county of Glamorgan and the industrial part of Monmouthshire. The promoters were influential people of the area and included representatives of the chief local industries. The first directors were Sir W.T. Lewis, Messrs. E.P. Martin, R. Forest, A. Hood, A. Walker, A. Keen, E.W. Richards and T.F. Brown.[4] These directors represented a strong coal and railway interest.

The movement, it was claimed, was a response to the small amount of progress made in the region regarding the use of electricity. In the whole of south Wales, only sixteen square miles were actually supplied by electricity.[5] The promoters contended that the establishment of a large central generating station just where abundant and regular supplies of coal were available, would mean a supply of electricity to consumers at low cost and an extension of supply to areas previously considered unprofitable. The idea of the promoters was to minimize the cost and expense of distribution by carrying their mains alongside the railways. They claimed that they could supply energy at a price three times as cheap as existing suppliers.[6] The promoters maintained that they were not seeking 'anything in the nature of a monopoly of supply in their area', but only 'the right to trade in the ordinary course of commercial competition in the business of electrical supply to wholesale consumers', that is, persons and undertakings who would not take less than 20,000 units per annum.[7]

The whole scheme, however, met with a hostile reception, most of the opposition coming from those local authorities which were likely to be affected by the scheme. A conference of the interested local authorities was held in Cardiff at which it was decided to oppose the bill in Parliament.[8] The issue of electricity supply was now firmly in the political arena as private interest attempted to wrest control of the industry from local authorities. Hannah sees the power company movement as an example of private entrepreneurs seizing the opportunity to 'choose the technical developments in the industry as a favourable background in their attempt to turn back the municipal tide'.[9] An influential contemporary of this movement also saw it as a political battle:

> The phrase 'organised opposition' is not a mere euphemism. Local authorities possess the equivalent of a trade union in the Association of Municipal Corporations, by means of which pressure can be brought to bear on every M.P. when desired, even though the question in issue concerns only one municipality. Many members find it difficult to resist this insidious local pressure and in this way decisions in favour of municipal ambitions are effectively produced.[10]

What were the motives of the protagonists in this battle? Was it, for example, a debate between the proponents of *laissez-faire* and capitalism, on the one hand, and the so-called 'gas and water socialists' on the other? The tone of some of the statements, at a superficial level, gives some weight to this interpretation. Councillor Jenkins, for example, speaking at a meeting in Cardiff arranged by the promoters to explain the scheme, stated:

> The gentlemen who were running this scheme were not philanthropists . . . They expected to get a return of 10%. They had tried to throw ridicule on the Corporation (Cardiff), machinery being idle 20 hours of the 24. Let people wanting power for works take the supply from the Corporation and prevent the machinery standing . . . they did not want capitalists to come in after they had spent so much in Cardiff. If the Dowlais or any other works wanted the power, the Cardiff Corporation would supply them at less than the maximum quoted by the promoters of the scheme . . . It was a question of whether they should allow the power to go out of the hands of the people. To allow these things was to set themselves back.[11]

Such a view, however, is too simplistic. As far as the supporters of the scheme were concerned, there were indeed grounds for complaint in terms of the efficiency of the municipal supplies, irrespective of any political hostility. During the parliamentary committee, for example, Mr Corbett, surveyor of the Bute Estate, stated that 'only the very large undertakings could afford to provide an electrical installation of their own . . .' He thought these works stood little chance of being supplied by the Corporation (Cardiff) with electric current, and that even if it were, it would not be as cheap as that supplied by the company.

Rees Jones of the Ocean Coal Company pointed to another problem. He stated that his company had to go to five different local authorities to get power in the different collieries. E.P. Martin, manager of the Dowlais ironworks, stated that 'it was of vital importance that the industries of South Wales should get this supply of electric power', and he did not think that they were likely to get it by means of the local authorities. Mr Butler of Messrs. Wright and Butler, iron and steel manufacturers, stated that 'the supply given by local authorities is hopelessly inadequate'.[12]

What of the motives of the local authorities opposing the scheme? As was hinted earlier, there is little substantial evidence to suggest that it resulted from a determination to defend a piece of self-conscious democratic socialism. It was, for the most part, a pragmatic response to something which threatened an established position. This is well illustrated by the statement issued by the Welsh Liberal MPs who had given their support to the local authorities. '. . . The main ground upon which the measure is opposed is that, Parliament having authorised the Corporations of Cardiff, Swansea and Newport to borrow money for establishing electrical supply undertakings on the security of the rates, special powers ought not, in the interest of the community, to be granted to a company trading for profit to execute work of a similar character within the areas controlled by these Corporations, or to enter into competition with them'.[13]

Related to this was the timing of the issue. The power company movement had followed a period of intense municipalization of certain sources of supply. Water, gas, eletricity and tramways had been swept up on powerful movements of municipal trading which had challenged many of the traditional ideas. The fight, however, had not been easy and so to expect the local authorities, which had come to regard companies operating utilities as natural monopolies and potential exploiters of the community, suddenly to revise their ideas, was perhaps expecting too much. The Bill establishing the company was in fact passed, but with its powers severely curtailed. Before the company could supply electricity, the consent of the relevant local authority was necessary. The company was to have no lighting power to ordinary consumers unless it had obtained a provisional order in the usual way. Any local authority which later obtained statutory powers to supply electricity was to have the option of taking over the company's supply in its area.[14] Concessions were also obtained by Cardiff Corporation. The company was prohibited from coming into the borough unless an unreasonable time had elapsed after an application had been made to the Corporation for a power supply. The Corporation also had the right to distribute power inside the borough, a clear reduction of 10 per cent being allowed by the new company on any power supplied by them and distributed by the Corporation. Barry Corporation secured similar rights.

A power scheme was also devised in 1904 for north Wales when the North Wales Electric Bill was passed. This Bill did not raise the kind of violent controversy of the South Wales Bill. There were two main reasons for this. Firstly, the main objective of the company was simply to supply power for traction. Secondly, and perhaps more significantly, the company was not impinging upon the supply areas of powerful Corporations, as the South Wales Power Company was doing in the south.

In fact the South Wales Power Company had to struggle for its very existence. In 1904, four years after the Bill had been passed, a further injection of capital had been needed to put 'a finishing touch upon the buildings and machinery so as to enable them to get to work and make the profits which were anticipated'.[15] An independent investigation of the prospects of the company was undertaken by E. Manville at the time and he reported favourable prospects. By May 1906, however, the available funds of the company had been exhausted and the original investors were asked to provide still more funds to keep the concern afloat. Another investigation took place, this time by C.H. Merz. He concluded that it was no use attempting to do anything with the business unless £500,000 could be found.[16] In response to this report, a debenture-holders' committee was formed which called a special meeting of colliery owners and power consumers in the district. The committee explained the situation and emphasized the need for funds to put the company on a sound financial footing. The committee, however, then put the onus on the consumers, saying that they would require a guarantee of 40,000 h.p. units in demand annually before they found the £500,000.

To consider this, the consumers formed their own committee in July 1906, and in November a meeting of both committees met in London. At this meeting the consumers' committee informed the debenture holders that there was no prospect of their being able to guarantee 40,000 h.p. The most they could get guarantees for was 14,387 h.p. Those who were not willing to bind themselves, but who may have required power, added 4,785 h.p.

The situation was set against a background of declining custom. The Cambrian Colliery Company, for example, was installing its own plant, which meant a loss of 1,103 h.p. The chairman of the South Wales Power Company, Mr Forest, was also a director of the Cambrian Colliery, but he could not persuade his fellow directors to continue taking all their supply from the company. The main reason for this was that they could not afford the possibility of the South Wales Power Company folding and ceasing to supply. The trend towards self-generation was increasing. Glamorgan Collieries, which were taking 1,000 h.p., put down separate installations. The Ferndale Company had been connected to the extent of 1,457 h.p. and were also putting down their own installations.

Given these trends, things did not look so well for the company. The largest creditors were called together and were told that the company was in a perilous condition and that it was impossible for any new money to be raised unless they could see their way to come not only behind the new money but behind the existing debentures and to take preference shares. Only creditors to the tune of £52,694 agreed to do so, however, and the company consequently found itself in serious trouble.

How, then, had the company reached this situation? South Wales was, after all, a highly industrialized area, which should have provided a secure market for a company supplying cheap power, and this had been the argument for setting up the company in the first place. There is evidence that bad management played its part. For example, the largest generating station of the concern was built at Treforest, near Pontypridd. Compulsory powers had been obtained to acquire the necessary land. In practice, however, no land had been acquired and the station was built on land which not only had not been paid for, but to which the company had no title. The site for the station at Neath had also been badly selected. There was no satisfactory road access and the cables were carried under terminable way-leaves. The contracts which had been entered into with the local authorities were also unsatisfactory. The Neath and Bridgend stations, for example, were to have only one consumer, the local authority.[17] In meeting these contracts the company lost £2,000 a year. The supply from these two centres was in fact taken over by the consumers.

Together with these blunders, of course, were the terms of the Company's Act, with its exclusion from the lucrative markets of Cardiff and Barry, and the need to seek the permission of the relevant local authority. Given these limitations, the possibility of success was slim from the outset. In the small local undertaking, works costs and management expenses were small, as was the capital expenditure compared with that needed for a generating station for general electricity supply. The whole power philosophy was to seek increased economy through the use of large-scale, technically efficient plant, the introduction of a diversity factor[18] and, consequently, a better load factor. The first years of a power company were thus likely to be hard, given its operation under increasing returns and low load. Co-operation between company and customer was, therefore, necessary in the form of fixed contracts so that the company could be sure of sufficient business to warrant the installation of large units at a low capital cost per unit. This should, of course, be backed up with a carefully thought out scale of prices. The latter point was very important and, unfortunately in the case of the Company, was not observed. A flat rate was charged, with the result that collieries utilized electricity for haulage and such intermittent work as was expensive to themselves, but continued to work by steam that machinery, such as pumps and fans, which had to run continuously. And of course many collieries installed their own generating plant.

The company, however, did not fold, due in the main to the consumers of the company. The four generating stations at Treforest, Bridgend, Neath and Cwmbran were at first kept going at the expense of the principal consumers. For this purpose the consumers formed a company called 'The Treforest Electrical Consumers Company Limited', with a nominal capital of £100,000. The stations at Neath and Bridgend were, as stated earlier, then sold to the local authorities.[19]

The story of the power company movement in south Wales has been told because of its importance in explaining the structure of the industry in the region before 1914. The proven technical superiority of large-scale generation and the establishment of such companies had done little to prevent the proliferation of local undertakings, small in size and supplying limited local markets. The 1914–1918 war emphasized, and made all too apparent, the structural weakness of the industry. All the committees which were set up, both during and after the war, were unanimous in their condemnation of the state of the industry and emphasized the need for reform.[20] Every report recognized the necessity for a national policy breaking away sharply from the trends of the previous thirty years, when development had been essentially local in character.

The first fruit of all this deliberation was the 1919 Act. A body of Electricity Commissioners was set up to supervise the industry. Co-ordination between the undertakings, however, was to be voluntary, the undertakings in particular districts putting forward their own schemes for what were to be called Joint Electricity Authorities. A Joint Authority was established in north Wales though no developments along these lines took place in the south.

It was becoming clear that voluntary reorganization would never take place. The result of this recognition was the 1926 legislation which established the National Grid. This legislation was based on the work of the Weir Committee.[21] The basic idea was to convert the whole of Britain into a single unified power-zone. Generation was to be in the hands of a Central Electricity Board. The task of this Board was to co-ordinate production by concentrating it in relatively few highly efficient stations which were to be interconnected. The output of these 'selected stations' was purchased by the C.E.B. at cost price. Authorized undertakers could then demand a supply from the C.E.B. and distribute it within their area. The 'national grid' was to be constructed by linking up regional systems through the erection of a high-tension mains transmission system. The responsibility of preparing each area scheme was to be the Electricity Commissioners.

South Wales came under the South West England and South Wales Electricity Scheme. The region was one of the largest. It included the whole of south Wales, the counties of Hereford, Monmouth, Somerset, Devon, Cornwall, Dorset and Wiltshire, and parts of the counties of Berkshire, Gloucester, Oxford and West Sussex together with the Isle of Wight. It was also a diverse area. It included the densely populated mining district of south Wales, the industrial centres of Bristol, Bath, Stroud, Swindon and large important ports like Southampton, Falmouth, Newport, Cardiff and Swansea. It also included a great deal of sparsely populated rural areas such as west and mid Wales, Devon and Cornwall. The scheme included the provision of 719 circuit miles of primary transmission lines. It was to be connected up through Reading with the system in south-east England and through Worcester with the system in central England.

The south Wales undertakers had argued for a separate scheme for the area itself including Bristol and the Bristol District, but nothing further west than Exeter. The motive here seems to have been to exclude sparsely populated areas of Devon and Cornwall. The C.E.B., however, was not convinced and argued that every area had to carry some development of rural areas and that this development would be met out of the savings which would be made by the scheme as a whole.[22] The area was to have six base load stations at Cardiff, Hayle, Newport, Portishead, Southampton and Upper Boat (S.W.E.P.D.). Back-up stations were at Bath, Exeter, Feeder Road, Llanelli, Lydney, Moredon, Newton Abbot, Oxford, Plymouth, Portsmouth and Swansea.

We can look at the effect of the construction of the grid on Wales in two ways. Firstly, there is the effect on the electricity industry itself. Consideration of this point is left to the next section. Secondly there is the broader effect of the construction of the system. It has been argued that the grid construction could not have been timed better in terms of its counter-cyclical effects on employment and investment.[23] Unfortunately it is not possible to quantify the effects of the grid construction on the Welsh economy, as the C.E.B. statistics do not give separate figures for Wales. It must be emphasized however, that whatever the effect, its timing was purely accidental. The C.E.B. did not see itself in the business of relieving unemployment. Its policy was the efficient production and distribution of electricity. This is well illustrated by the Board's reaction to a confidential memorandum by Lord Weir.[24] This suggested that to relieve unemployment in south Wales, generating stations be erected together with an auxiliary grid transmission system to export the electricity to mid and south England. It was claimed that this would help the mining industry and attract new industries.

The proposal, however, was rejected by the C.E.B. The Board concluded that the effect of actual construction on employment in the region would be trifling and the 'permanent employment of miners could be achieved equally well by a greater use of Welsh coal in generating stations situated elsewhere'. Technical efficiency would also suffer the Board claimed, '. . . the efficiency of large stations in South Wales which would have to use cooling towers, was likely to be less rather than more than that of stations placed on more suitable sites near the load centres, the cost of transporting Welsh coal to such centres would be much less than the cost of transmitting electricity . . .' The C.E.B. thus rejected the proposal on the grounds that it '. . . was economically unsound and that since it would not increase the use of either coal or electricity it could only benefit South Wales at the expense of other areas . . .'[25]

A sketch has been given of the experience of the electricity supply industry in south Wales up to 1939. It should be remembered, however, that we have referred only to statutory undertakings and there were important exceptions to this in terms of the non-statutory suppliers and private generation. The latter point was of extreme importance. For example, the chairman of the C.E.B., Sir Andrew Duncan, visited south Wales and found that about 56 per cent of generating was done by private plant.[26] Consideration of this aspect however must be the subject of further research. We now turn to look at the available statistics on the industry.

II

In trying to construct a statistical picture of the development of the industry, two sources of data are available. Firstly, there are the official statistics published by the *Electricity Commissioners*. Unfortunately, these only start in 1921. Secondly, for the years before 1921 there are the statistics which can be obtained from Garcke's *Manual of Electricity Undertakings* from 1897 onwards.[27]

The data supplied by Garcke's *Manual* is not very satisfactory due to lack of continuity. Information is not given for all the known undertakings. Also the data is quite often different in coverage for each undertaking. Furthermore, there are frequent gaps in the time sequence. Thus it is not really possible to build up a comprehensive and continuous statistical picture of the electrical supply industry in Wales before 1921. The best that can be done is to trace out the development of individual undertakings and try to pick out some general trends.

Surveying the growth of the industry first in terms of consumer numbers, the number of consumers connected in the first few years of operation appears to be small. Pontypool and Newport had only 64 and 204 consumers respectively in 1897, in 1900 Monmouth had 40 and Swansea only 122. Once established, however, growth did occur. Pontypool, for example, increased the number of consumers from 64 to 234 between 1897 and 1904, Cardiff from 599 to 3,726 between 1902 and 1914, Swansea from 122 to 3,686 between 1900 and 1917. It was in the larger urban areas, of course, that growth was most possible. This was due in large part to the physical limitations placed on expansion by the legislation on electricity supply. Each undertaking had its boundaries severely limited by its own Act and was not allowed to supply outside these limits. It followed, therefore, that the larger the population within a district the greater the possibilities for expansion.

The figures for electricity sold are rather more comprehensive, though still patchy. Again they illustrate that undertakings were able to expand and that the larger undertakings had the greatest scope for expansion. Between 1896 and 1905, for example, Pontypool increased its units sold from 35,011 B.T.U.'s to 75,014 B.T.U.'s. Cardiff, on the other hand, over the same period expanded from 308,430 B.T.U.'s sold to 2,767,606 B.T.U.'s sold. Similarly, Newport expanded from 91,557 units to 2,265,216 units over the same period. These larger urban areas, of course, such as Cardiff, Newport and Swansea also had the added advantage of running tramway systems. As these became electrified in the early part of the twentieth century, it provided a steadily increasing market.

The First World War saw a large increase in sales especially for the larger undertakings. Cardiff, Newport and Swansea all saw their sales expanding rapidly during the conflict. Cardiff increased its sales between 1913 and 1917 from 6,883,797 B.T.U.'s to 9,367,906 B.T.U.'s. Over the same period Newport and Swansea increased their sales from 4,929,633 B.T.U.'s to 7,429,206 B.T.U.'s and 3,440,350 to 5,301,956 B.T.U.'s respectively.

How typical these trends were is rather difficult to say because of the lack of data. There are factors, however, which might suggest that if these trends were present elsewhere, they were not as marked as in the large urban centres with a diversified industrial structure. In the mining valleys of south Wales, for example, with its typical one-industry town or village being supplied by the local undertaking, this trend was likely to be less marked because many of the collieries installed their own generating equipment. Thus, the small local undertakings had little scope to greatly increase its power sales to industrial customers.

One of the major arguments of the Cross Committee and the logic behind the power company movement, was that the small local undertaker was inefficient and supplied electricity at high cost because of the lack of scale economies. What is the evidence for this

IN SOUTH WALES TO 1939

argument? The only available data by which a judgement can be made is cost per unit sold figures for certain undertakings, again taken from Garcke's *Manual*. From this data it is possible to make two basic generalizations. First, generally speaking, the larger undertakings in the district tended to have lower costs per unit sold than the smaller ones, thereby supporting the 'power company' logic. Secondly, having said that, most undertakings saw their costs fall substantially as their sales grew. Table 1 illustrates these two points.

Table 1
Cost per unit sold for various undertakings 1896–1917 (d.)

Year	Cardiff	Newport	Pontypool	Swansea	Penarth
1896	—	2.76	4.28	—	—
1900	3.01	2.13	2.97	—	—
1904	1.79	1.81	3.04	1.40	4.01
1908	1.03	0.86	—	1.13	2.55
1911	0.91	0.74	—	1.03	1.53
1917	1.43	1.00	—	1.05	—

Source: Garcke's *Manual*

The large scale undertakings of Cardiff, Newport and Swansea clearly had lower costs than the smaller scale undertakings of Pontypool and Penarth, and seems to support the logic behind the power company argument and the belief that economies could be achieved by concentrating generation in larger undertakings. Short-run costs also seemed capable of reduction by undertakings increasing sales from their own generating plant. Most undertakings, irrespective of size, saw their costs per unit sold fall as their sales increased.

Although the data has been far from satisfactory, it has been possible to construct a rudimentary picture of the electricity industry in Wales up to 1919. As we have seen, it was a growing industry and an industry of increasing efficiency. The efficient low cost centres of supply, however, were confined to the larger urban areas, and though the smaller undertakings did see their costs falling the acceptance of the power company philosophy would have reduced costs even further.

This can be illustrated by comparing the Pontypridd undertaking with the South Wales Electric Power Distribution Company (S.W.E.P.D.C.) (Table 2), which as we have seen was not particularly successful. Pontypridd was in an ideal position to take full advantage of a supply from the S.W.E.P.D.C., whose costs of production were consistently beneath its own.

A more detailed statistical analysis of the industry is possible after 1920, with the publication of the Electricity Commissioners' statistics. Up to now it has only been possible to calculate statistics for the whole of Wales, but it can be said that south Wales

Table 2
Comparison of cost per unit between Pontypridd and S.W.E.P.D.C.

| Year | Cost per unit sold (d.) | |
	Pontypridd	S.W.E.P.D.C.
1908	1.40	1.26
1909	1.24	1.12
1910	0.96	0.89
1911	0.94	0.81

Source: Garcke's *Manual.*

was by far the most important area and the data available undoubtedly reflect the trends in this district.

The most obvious starting-point, is output. Table 3 presents figures on electricity generation. As can be seen, apart from the year 1926–7 there was rapid growth in electricity production, the growth being especially marked after 1935.

Table 3
Units of electricity generated by authorized undertakings in Wales 1920–38 (in thousands)

| Year | Electricity generated by | | Total |
	Companies	Local Authorities	
1920–21	79,924	63,269	143,193
1922–23	72,144	78,776	150,920
1924–25	103,532	108,535	212,067
1926–27	91,722	120,998	212,720
1928–29	126,774	148,313	275,087
1930–31	204,061	154,241	358,302
1932–33	214,704	186,797	401,701
1934–35	242,272	235,859	478,131
1936–37	359,539	381,446	740,985
1938–39	379,138	494,473	873,611

Source: *Electricity Commissioners Official Statistics*

Table 4 looks at electricity sales during this period. The table must be interpreted with some care. Column 6 refers to bulk sales to other authorized undertakings. Column 7 therefore contains an element of double counting. The important column is therefore

Table 4
Units of electricity sold in Wales by authorized undertakings 1922–1938

Year	Lighting & Domestic	Public lighting	Traction	Power	Bulk	Total including bulk	Total excluding bulk
			Units Sold (000's) for				
1922–23	23,084	3,128	7,790	92,124	4,972	131,098	126,126
1924–25	32,222	3,818	13,956	129,793	17,863	197,652	179,789
1926–27	44,428	4,708	13,921	135,263	17,090	215,410	198,320
1928–29	57,191	5,232	15,475	169,798	32,543	280,239	247,696
1930–31	72,780	7,255	15,504	206,669	44,656	346,864	302,208
1932–33	91,801	8,918	18,542	221,577	68,402	409,240	340,838
1934–35	119,298	10,559	15,775	306,690	100,236	552,558	452,322
1936–37	159,034	12,418	14,763	396,016	226,129	808,360	582,231
1938–39	214,783	14,536	9,126	521,204	329,486	1,089,135	759,649

Source: *Electricity Commissioners Official Statistics*

Column 8, with the bulk supplies taken out. Clearly it can be seen, using tables 5 and 6 that Wales was self-sufficient in electricity during the inter-war period. Table 4 also shows that all sectors except traction saw continuous growth throughout the inter-war period. The domestic load was gradually being won from the gas industry, and wider and wider industrial uses were being found for the fuel. This was being encouraged by the continuing fall in the price of electricity, as illustrated in Table 5.

Table 5
Revenue per unit sold (d.)
(a) Local Authorities

Year	Lighting & Domestic	Public lighting	Traction	Power	Bulk
1921–22	4.98	3.15	1.53	2.08	2.36
1924–25	4.31	3.31	1.23	1.17	0.70
1927–28	3.59	2.97	1.04	0.97	0.63
1930–31	3.09	2.32	0.83	0.87	0.79
1933–34	2.62	2.11	0.64	0.71	0.49
1936–37	2.20	1.83	0.61	0.57	0.16
1938–39	1.92	1.69	0.64	0.58	0.12

(b) Companies

Year	Lighting & Domestic	Public lighting	Traction	Power	Bulk
1921–22	5.85	2.86	0.77	1.34	1.10
1924–25	6.81	3.85	1.52	—	1.20
1927–28	6.13	4.17	1.51	0.97	1.09
1930–31	5.38	3.63	1.37	0.66	1.03
1933–34	4.18	3.12	0.76	0.63	0.93
1936–37	3.31	2.60	0.87	0.58	0.79
1938–39	2.95	2.66	0.94	0.60	0.78

Source: Calculated from *Electricity Commissioner Official Returns*

The figures do not refer to the actual prices charged. Many undertakings charged differential tariffs, allowances being made for large consumers. The data presented is a simple average. Clearly, however, the falling price of electricity had the effect of making it available to a far wider market.

Underlying all this inter-war development, of course, was the formation and construction of the National Grid. What effect did this then have on Wales? Unfortunately a detailed statistical analysis of expenditure on the grid in Wales is not really possible. This is because the published data refers to the schemes as a whole. South Wales and north Wales were parts of separate schemes and the data is not broken down into districts. It is possible, however, to look at the effects of the grid in terms of what it was meant to do, i.e., concentrate production in the hands of large efficient units. Is this what in fact happened?

To consider this the concept of the concentration ratio is useful. We use here the simple absolute ratio, i.e., the proportion of total sales controlled by the largest undertakings. The use and interpretation of concentration ratios is fraught with difficulties. Nevertheless they can be useful for our purposes of seeing if concentration of generation took place. The data is given in Table 6 and the concentration curves presented in Figure 1.

As can be seen from Table 6 and Figure 1 there was an increase in the concentration between 1927 (before the grid was constructed) and 1937, though the figures for 1934 show that during that year there was a decrease. In 1927 the two largest producers were supplying 49.12 per cent of the total electricity generated in Wales, whilst in 1937 this had increased to 63.01 per cent. The trend can also be seen in other ways. For example, in 1927 there were 60 statutory undertakings in Wales, 35 of which were involved in generating electricity (58.33 per cent). By 1937 the number of statutory undertakings had increased to 66, but the number of undertakings actually generating had declined to 29 (43.94 per

Table 6
Absolute concentration ratio for electricity generation in Wales 1927, 1934 and 1937

Number of firms cumulated from the largest size	Percentage of industry output		
	1927	1934	1937
1	30.23	27.65	32.14
2	49.12	43.52	63.01
3	64.83	59.28	74.60
4	79.22	73.60	84.09
5	88.56	87.78	93.13
6	92.17	93.84	97.35
7	94.51	95.18	98.16
8	95.64	96.02	98.70
9	96.39	96.77	99.00
10	97.10	97.48	99.25

Source: *Electricity Commissioners Official Statistics*

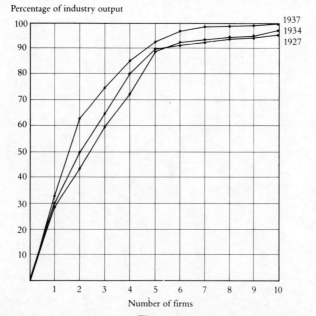

Figure 1
Concentration curves for electricity generation in Wales, 1927, 1934, 1937

cent). Undoubtedly then, over the period the grid was being constructed and operated there was a movement towards rationalization of the industry in Wales. The grid saw the concentration of generation in large units and this saw a subsequent fall in costs.

Not all the rationalization was due to the National Grid. The undertakings themselves quite often saw the advantage of combination. For example, in 1931 the West Cambrian Power Company purchased the majority of supply undertakings in Pembrokeshire (the major exception being Milford Haven Urban District Council) and also a number in south Cardiganshire and parts of Carmarthenshire. This was an important move as most of the undertakings were non-statutory, supplies usually being provided from small generating plants, often located in garages. Another example is provided by the Pontardawe Rural District Council which in 1931 acquired four non-statutory undertakings supplying Pontardawe, Clydach and Glais.

That then is the story of electricity supply in south Wales up to 1939. It is the story of how the problems of managing a complex and quickly changing technology were looked at and solved. It gradually came to be realized that the resolution of business policy in this public utility required political decisions. The early reforms were initially half-hearted compromises as the Government refused to grasp the nettle. Within a decade the limited experimentation of 1926 was generally accepted as being insufficient. It took another war to produce a more complete reform.

The Movement of Population from South Wales with Specific Reference to the Effects of the Industrial Transference Scheme, 1928–37

BRIAN STAINES

This paper intends to look at population movement from south Wales in the light of Government policy. In particular, the policy measure looked at is the Industrial Transference Scheme, which in many ways can be seen as a turning-point in Government policy, or at least in the way that the Government publicly viewed the problem of unemployment. However, it does not intend solely to consider the Industrial Transference Scheme but looks at population movement and migration in general largely for two reasons. Firstly, the problems that south Wales faced due to the Industrial Transference Scheme were very similar to those it faced due to migration, in that both involved a movement of population out of the region. Secondly, contemporary accounts frequently speak of the effects of the Industrial Transference Scheme when what in fact they are discussing is the effect of migration in general, and frequently the terms 'transference' and 'migration' are used interchangeably. Consequently, in some instances, it is difficult to isolate the effects of the transference scheme from that of migration.

In order to look at the significance of the Industrial Transference Scheme and to place it in its context it is necessary to look at Government policy in the immediate post-war period. Very generally speaking the immediate post-war view of unemployment was that it was transitory in nature, and would disappear (or return to pre-war levels) once the world economies had recovered from the disruption of the war and the pre-war 'system' was reintroduced. Hence the overriding aim of policy was to bring this 'return to normality' situation about, the centre-piece of this policy being the return to the gold standard at pre-war parity. Policy measures designed to give relief to unemployment were seen as deviations from policies attempting to restore the pre-war situation, especially if they involved financial expenditure. The measures undertaken were essentially short term, with authorization generally granted only for six months or one year, and relief works were designed as a mere holding operation. These measures were primarily administered by the Unemployment Grants Committee in terms of various types of financial assistance and loans.

If it is accepted that the Government's stated attitude in the immediate post-war period was that unemployment was transitory and would disappear on the return to normality, it had changed by the time of the formation of the Industrial Transference Board. The formation of the Board in itself is indicative of the change and this was spelt out clearly in its first report. 'But when we consider that since the armistice under a varied and comprehensive programme of works in relief of unemployment (not including Trade Facilities guaranteed schemes) works of a total estimated value of slightly under £190 million have been approved, and that, notwithstanding the magnitude of the undertakings, there have been at no one date more than 75,000 men employed on such works and of these many for short spells only, and that we still have to face a heavy volume of unemployment, we believe it would be clearly contrary to public policy to begin another cycle of such works. Begun under the conditions of today, they would be, in plain fact, relief works. A programme of relief works would, in our judgement, ignore the realities of the present situation'.[1]

It might be possible to argue over the extent of the 'varied and comprehensive' nature of the relief works but clearly the report indicates a shift in the attitude towards unemployment. However, in one other respect it could be argued that the policy is a continuation of past policy. Transference was always considered as a low cost solution (figures are given on page 241 as to cost of the scheme). With the increasing levels of unemployment the finance that would have had to have been made available to the Unemployment Grants Committee to make any appreciable impact would need to have increased substantially. The adoption of the policy of transference as a cure of unemployment allowed the Government to continue with their low financial commitment to policies designed to alleviate unemployment.

The Industrial Transference Board was finally brought into existence by the Ministry of Labour on 6 January 1928 and produced its first report on 26 June.[2] It was this report that formed the basis of the Government's approach towards unemployment until the passing of the Special Areas legislation in 1934 and transference continued to be pursued as a policy until the outbreak of the Second World War.

The Government's attitude in respect of south Wales is indicated in a memorandum circulated by the Ministry of Health shortly after the formation of the Industrial Transference Board. 'The only hope for the South Wales area is the redistribution of population which can be effected only by the economic pressure. Unemployment Benefit and poor relief have up to the present time tended to postpone the operation of this pressure, and it would be fatal especially in view of the establishment of the Industrial Transference Board to introduce special measures to the relief of distress in the area'.[3]

This memorandum epitomizes the Government's attitude to south Wales in the period after the formation of the Industrial Transference Board; and as such is different to the policies which dominated Government thinking at least until 1925.[4] It also meant that the small number of relief schemes operating within south Wales were brought to an end, and that, in order for the area to recover, a large-scale movement of population out of the region would be necessary. Although the precise meaning of 'economic pressure' is not stated, presumably it meant that market forces would be allowed to operate to their fullest extent so that as increased unemployment caused a drop in living standards the area would become progressively less attractive thus encouraging people to move from the region with the assistance of the transference scheme. In view of the fact that the Industrial Transference Board was set up '. . . to be a Board for the purpose of facilitating the transfer of workers, and in particular of miners, for whom opportunities of employment in their own district or occupation are no longer available . . .',[5] its applicability to south Wales was obvious, and it was hoped that it would provide a mechanism whereby this 'economic pressure' could be asserted more rapidly.

The transference scheme was basically administered by the employment exchanges. Areas of high unemployment were 'scheduled' which meant that the facilities available through the Industrial Transference Scheme were available to these areas. Briefly speaking, the main facilities available were: (i) help with or free payment of fares (generally in the form of a railway warrant) to the area to which a person was transferring; (ii) help with or payment of removal expenses; (iii) help with lodgings. A married man would receive the cost of lodgings in the area he moved to plus five shillings. His family at home would receive his income prior to transference less five shillings. For a single person their unemployment benefit would be increased so as to cover the cost of lodgings plus five shillings; (iv) additional facilities were also available under the family and juvenile transference scheme.

The criteria for scheduling areas were fairly vague with no hard and fast rules, and it was merely reflected upon after the scheme had operated for a decade that: 'It is understood that any area where the density and character of unemployment appears to justify this course can be scheduled for the purposes of the Industrial Transference Scheme'.[6] Generally speaking the formula normally applied was: 'that 40% of the insured adult population is normally employed in one or more of coal mining, iron and steel, shipbuilding and cotton industries; and that average unemployment among men is 15% or over'.[7] In addition, when at a later date the Special Areas Act was passed, areas within the scope of this fell within the scope of the transference scheme.

Obviously both these criteria had implications for south Wales, and the significance is all the more apparent when the statistical evidence is considered. As regards the 1928 figures the comparison is fairly outstanding, 41 per cent of all offices scheduled under the Industrial Transference Scheme were located in the south Wales area. Even by 1938 with the large expansion of the scheme, south Wales had the highest proportion of offices scheduled as depressed for transfer purposes. Consequently, whatever the effect of the scheme, it was likely to have a proportionately greater impact on south Wales than any other region. (Although at times reports quoted in this article talk of the effect of the scheme on Wales as a whole, virtually all of the scheduled areas were in south Wales).

This point is amplified by a consideration of further evidence related to provisional arrangements for the filling of vacancies in certain areas by applicants from other areas. This is supplied in Table 2 on page 240.

Not surprisingly Table 2 suggests that vacancies in Wales, the North-East, the Scottish Division and the North-West (all areas with high unemployment) are filled by people from the respective divisions (although it suggests the North-West could also draw people from Wales). What is more significant is that for the three prosperous (in relative

Table 1

Region	Local offices scheduled as depressed for transfer purposes May 1928		Local offices scheduled as depressed for transfer purposes May 1938	
		Approx % Figures		Approx % Figures
South West	2	2%	6	2%
Midland	7	6%	12	4%
North East	34	29%	10	4%
North West	14	12%	North 68	25%
			North West 57	21%
Scotland	10	10%	46	17%
Wales	48	41%	72	27%

Source: *Report of Enquiry into Industrial Transference Scheme* (May 1938), PRO LAB 8/218.

Table 2

Provisional arrangements regarding districts from which applicants will be supplied to fill vacancies occurring — 1928

Divisions in which vacancies occur		Districts from which applicants will be supplied
WALES	⟶	WALES
N.E. DIVISION	⟶	N.E. DIVISION
SCOTLAND	⟶	SCOTLAND
S.E. DIVISION	⟶	WALES AND DURHAM
S.W. DIVISION	⟶	SOUTH WESTERN DIVISION WALES AND N.E. DIVISION (mainly 2 latter)

Table 2 — continued

| MIDLAND DIVISION | ⟶ | WALES, NORTH EAST AND MIDLAND DIVISIONS |
| NORTH WEST DIVISION | ⟶ | NORTH WEST DIVISION AND WALES |

Source: PRO ED Circular 103/1 — ITB 151/2/1928

terms) regions, all were to be supplied with some transferees from Wales. Wales is unique in that respect and again it serves to illustrate the point that it is likely that the transference scheme would have had a far greater effect upon Wales than any other region.

Prior to a consideration of the effects of transference it is worth re-emphasizing the point briefly mentioned, that although in some ways transference is a departure from previous policy, it is also a continuation of that policy. Thus in its first report, the Board stated that: 'We have not excluded from our survey the possible creation by direct intervention in the employment market opportunities of employment through transfer. At the same time we have felt bound to have regard to the settled financial policy of the country and to follow the general lines of this policy in reviewing any of the more ambitious schemes, involving heavy outlays of money, which have been brought to our notice'.[8] Further it went on to say 'If a policy were to be adopted of artificially stimulating industrial activity generally with the object of absorbing surplus labour from the heavy industries, the scale on which the economic intervention by the state would have to take place would be unparalleled in any other age or country. Apart, therefore, from the doubt that exists as to the physical possibility of successful achievement on such lines, and the far reaching reactions upon the economic and industrial structure of the country resulting from such intervention in a sphere where failure would mean, at the least, a disastrous setback, we have felt that the implications of such schemes in their wider form clearly place them outside our province'.[9]

These two quotes illustrate the extent to which transference was a continuation of the policy advocating minimal financial intervention in creation of employment by the Government. Thus although transference was a departure in Government strategy, its roots and its rationale were firmly in the post-war, pre-Keynesian era. The limited financial provisions of the scheme are more clearly illustrated in a summary of the finances of the Industrial Transference Board. 'Rather more than 52,500 adults have been recorded as having transferred during the year (1937) and, on the basis of the estimates . . ., the average expenditure in respect of each of these transfers amounts to £3.13.0.[10] The significance of this seems to have been that the scheme was seen by Governments to be the only hope for the south Wales region, but the financial back-up for this 'only hope' was extremely limited.

Effects of the Industrial Transference Scheme and the problems associated with it

In considering the effects of the scheme attention is primarily focused on contemporary reports and commentaries. Although largely speaking they are contemporary comments on transference they should be seen in the majority of cases, as having been directed at migration in general. The complaints regarding the scheme can be generalized as follows: (i) the effects on the rates and social services when a person transferred from an area in that less people had to bear the burden for the upkeep of local services; (ii) the problem of per capita grants to a region with falling population, resulting in falling grants and the inevitable vicious circle of contraction; (iii) as a result of (i) and (ii) the local authorities had less money for the maintenance of services. Consequently an area became less attractive causing people and industry to move from it, revenue to decline, and it was argued, making the area more and more impoverished as time went on.

These problems are highlighted in the Merthyr region as the minutes of the council meetings clearly show. 'In the continuing discussion one member said that he did not want to prevent young men and women bettering themselves by securing employment outside Merthyr Tydfil, but what they did object to was the resultant effect on the rates and Social Services generally and the continuous depopulation of these parts'.[11] The predicament facing Merthyr was essentially a reflection of the situation as it affected the whole of south Wales as further extracts from the meeting illustrate. 'Several members spoke strongly against the government policy of transference of labour from the Special Areas. They urged that the only way to help Merthyr was to establish new industries in these areas'. Further, it was asserted that: 'The Commissioner suggested that this attitude was wrong. We could not get over economic facts and, rightly or wrongly, industry was moving away from these areas and it would seem that Merthyr was "off the map" in relation to present day Industrial Development. In these circumstances he thought it best that Merthyr Tydfil men should have the opportunity of getting work in other parts of the country'.[12] Essentially in this one exchange the whole problem of transference is encapsulated, local authorities arguing for positive Government action to attract industry, and the Government declining to do this, arguing instead that the population must move from the area.

Another major criticism of the transference scheme as it operated with south Wales was that it meant the area was gaining a more 'top heavy' population structure. It was feared that only certain elements of the population would be removed by the scheme leaving those least able to support themselves within the region. It is significant that this very point is admitted by the Government in the later years of the scheme. 'The proportion of unskilled workers who are suitable for, and willing to transfer is probably very small. In support of this suggestion an analysis of the live registers made at a number of depressed area local offices showed, in respect of 42,662 applicants covered by the analysis, that 28,996 (68% of the total registers examined) were over 35 years of age, and, as applicants in the "over 35" age group are more likely to have domestic ties than younger men, it is considered that only a small proportion of this group can be regarded as effective for transfer purposes. The analysis also showed that 6,937 (16% of the applicants included in the analysis) were suitable for light work only, or had to be compensated for injuries received during employment and, because of this, were probably unlikely to be suitable for the normal industrial vacancies which occur'.[13]

It would appear from this that the fears of the population were justified. The two significant points, that the Government statement brought to light, are firstly that transference could not be seen as a cure for unemployment for a large percentage of those unemployed (the survey of the registers indicated 84 per cent unsuitable for transference) and secondly that it was only young people who were considered suitable for transference. This raised the question as to the attractiveness of the remaining workforce to new employers coming into the area. In addition further points were raised regarding the operation of the scheme. In particular it was increasingly felt that the south Wales region was providing a subsidy to other regions of the UK. In the case of juveniles transferred, much of the costs of educating them was borne by the local ratepayers of south Wales, yet the benefits were accruing to regions to which they eventually transferred. Also the whole rationale of the Industrial Transference scheme presupposed the existence of vacancies in other areas. This issue was fully considered by the Commissioner for the Special Areas in 1935 who felt that: 'The next objection (to transference) is that even if they wanted to move the question is asked where can they move with the expectation of employment, in view of the widespread extent of existing unemployment. This objection is based upon a very deep rooted fallacy that there is only a certain amount of work to go round, and that if the population of a particular area increases there will be less opportunity of work for people in the area. The whole industrial history of the last 100 years refutes the fallacy. The population of London has increased rapidly in recent years, the proportion of persons in the London area who form the working population has increased still more rapidly, and yet unemployment in London on average has been lower than that found in any large area of this country. It is the population that makes the work, not work the population'.[14] But, of course, it was also felt that if population made the work why was there not more work available in south Wales with its unemployed population. Further, there was evidence of the 'prosperous areas' complaining about the fact that they had received too many transferees when they already had severe unemployment problems. Two issues raised at the time were firstly that much of the work to which people transferred was, especially in the later stages of the scheme, connected with the re-armament programme. Also some relief schemes were still in operation and these were deliberately sited in prosperous areas, again in an attempt to prevent people staying in south Wales. The latter meant that the areas least in need of Government assistance to provide employment were the only areas receiving that assistance. Further, a number of people who transferred under the scheme returned to south Wales, which again cast doubt on the efficacy of transference as a long-term solution.[15]

The objections listed are by no means exhaustive, but they serve to illustrate the fact that within south Wales there was much concern as to the operation of the Transference Scheme, basically centering around the fear it would lead to the ruination of the area.

Inter-regional comparison of the effects of the Industrial Transference Scheme and migration

The maps in Appendix 1 illustrate the areas which people transferred to from the different regions of the UK. They are based on the figures for transferees in 1936, this being the first year for which complete statistics for the scheme are available. The maps are fairly self-explanatory although a number of general observations can be made: (i) the strong pull of London and the South-East to transferees from all areas; (ii) the greater attraction for transferees from south Wales to the South-West partly due to geographical reasons (particularly true in the case of female transferees); (iii) the low number (in percentage terms) of males and females transferring to areas other than those listed; (iv) the most significant column is that headed 'transferred within the same area'. It was possible for people to get the assistance of the Industrial Transference Board even if they were transferring to a more prosperous part of the same region. In these cases they would be recorded as having transferred within the same area. The figure for males transferring within south Wales is negligible in contrast to other regions where the figures are at least 10 per cent and rise as high as 25 per cent. In all areas apart from south Wales more than half the females transferred within the same area — the figure for south Wales was only 14 per cent. This is a very telling indication as to the state of the south Wales economy in 1936. It would seem that the whole of the regional economy was depressed. It would also suggest that transference figures for south Wales should be seen in a slightly different light than other areas. The low numbers transferring within the same region indicate that most transferees were a net loss to south Wales, whereas in other areas the transferee was less likely to leave the region. Again this suggests that transference had a more significant impact on south Wales than is indicated by simple inter-regional comparisons of numbers transferring.

By way of comparison Table 3 gives the movement of unemployed men from south Wales on their own account, and includes the percentage figures for the Industrial Transference Scheme. The comparisons are self-evident, but perhaps it is the bottom line that is the most interesting. This indicates that 36 per cent of all men moving to take up employment, and 43 per cent of all men moving to look for employment came from a depressed part of Wales, yet only 31 per cent of the total number transferring came from this region. 'In percentage terms therefore the Industrial Transference Scheme was the least popular method of moving from South Wales in spite of the predominance of scheduled offices within the region, and the consequent assistance available'. There are a number of reasons stated for this proportionately lower uptake of the scheme within south Wales. But perhaps the most significant was public opinion: 'In some of the depressed areas notably SOUTH WALES and CUMBERLAND (my capitals) there is a considerable body of public opinion against the Industrial Transference Scheme. Its opponents allege that these areas are being denuded of their best types to such an extent as to make the areas unattractive to any employers who might consider the introduction of new industrial undertakings in those districts. They also state that the transference of

Table 3
The movement of unemployed men from depressed areas in Wales — 1936

Region moved to	Moving to take up assured employment		% by transference	Moving to look for employment	
	Nos.	% of total		Nos.	% of total
London	1312	24	20	3910	32
South-east	954	17	23	2639	22
South-west	1253	23	34	1469	12
Midlands	1213	22	22	3704	30
Other areas	329	6	1	215	2
Movement within same area	414	8	1	280	2
% from Wales as % of total		36	31		43

Source: PRO HLG 27/30.
Reproduced — Minutes of Evidence — *Royal Commission of Distribution of Industrial Population* — p. 328.

workers, and in a number of cases their families, has adversely affected the general conditions in the districts concerned . . . Protests have been made by Chambers of Trade that retailers have lost customers, by churches and schools that they have lost ratepayers. These bodies lose no opportunity of publicly expressing opposition to transference, and there is little doubt but that this publicity has had some adverse effect on the willingness of a number of applicants to consider transference to the more prosperous areas'.[16]

The second point raised queried why more people did not use the transference scheme. Given that the transference scheme was seen as the method by which the Government could 'equate supply with demand' it appeared that a large number of people did not make use of the facilities, and it was 'shown that nearly 76,000 (72%) of the men who transferred during the years 1936 and 1937 transferred on their own account'.[17] Although Government sources say the reasons are that some vacancies are not notified at employment exchanges and people get information on employment opportunities from friends, they seem totally unable to explain the low take-up of the scheme. It seems likely that at least part of the reason must be due to failings in the scheme itself, in particular the financial assistance available.

Appendix 2 is an attempt to combine together the details on transference and the movement of population in general. It should be emphasized that both the second and third graphs understate the position as there are no reliable statistics for women moving on their own account. The graphs illustrate three basic points: (i) in 1936 over 2 per cent of the insured population transferred through the Industrial Transference Scheme. This is far higher than those transferring from any other region. However, this 2 per cent does not explain the full significance of the transfer. When it is considered in respect of earlier comments about the age of men transferring, then the loss in active working population is significantly higher; (ii) over 4 per cent of the insured population transferred without the assistance of the scheme. This is far higher than for any other region and if the view is taken that only certain sections of the population are moving the impact is still greater; (iii) as can be seen the cumulative total is over 6 per cent of the insured population moving in one year, 1936. Even allowing for statistical abnormalities caused by the use of only one year's figures, the figure appears to be very large, especially in comparison with other regions.

Although little of substance is known of the return of workers to south Wales subsequent to a period of transfer, the following statement gives a rough outline of the situation. 'Reliable information about the return of applicants from non depressed areas is not available, but some indication of the volume of it can be obtained from the records kept during 1936 and 1937 in respect of men who returned to depressed areas after being placed in employment by local offices. These records show that approximately 29% of the men who had been placed returned to the depressed areas. In addition to this number it is known that 11.4% of the applicants sent forward to prospective employment also returned without obtaining employment. In the light of the available figures it is estimated that during the year 1936/37 about 33% of the total directed and undirected transfers returned to depressed areas. To this number must of course be added those men who returned direct to employment in the depressed areas and were not recorded in the local office records'.[18] The survey also estimated that 37 per cent of women returned to their home regions.

Two significant points seem to emerge from this: firstly that people transferring through the Industrial Transference Scheme are less likely to be removed permanently to other areas as a higher percentage return, and secondly that there was a net overall decline in insured persons in south Wales. Thus: 'Over the whole period from 1923–1937 the number of insured persons in employment decreased by 88,540 or 20.5%. this is the only one of the 7 areas in which a decline occurred'.[19]

It is difficult to pinpoint what impact the migration of population had on this, as one of the reasons for a decline in the insured population was an increase in unemployment. Also the transference scheme was only in operation for part of this period. However, with a decline of over 20 per cent it is likely that population movement was a significant factor.

Summary of conclusions

1. From its inception the terms of reference for the Industrial Transference Scheme and its method of operation meant it was likely to have a more significant effect on south Wales than most other regions.

2. Although a similar policy in some respects to that operating prior to 1928 which advocated minimum expenditure within the constraints of strict financial control, it was also a departure from previous policy as it dispelled the notion that unemployment was transitory and would disappear.

3. Throughout the operation of the scheme it met with considerable opposition, as it was seen as having a detrimental effect on the long-term prospects of the south Wales region.

4. Transference and migration were seen to be inextricably linked, with comments on transference frequently being comments on migration.

5. The Transference Scheme was not responsible for the movement of the majority of people who left south Wales. Transference was proportionately a less important factor in south Wales than other regions, and the majority of people moved without the assistance of the scheme.

By 1938 there had begun the development of a different type of approach to transference and unemployment and it was seen that: 'The special areas continue to present a serious problem of working population in excess of the present employment capacity in the areas; one cannot expect the problem to be solved by short term methods. Industry must be induced to go to these places or the people removed. The first is obviously the best solution'.[20] This is a total contrast to the quote by the Ministry of Health given earlier that: 'the only hope for the South Wales area is a redistribution of population which can be effected only by the economic pressure'.

Perhaps this illustrates the major result of the Industrial Transference Scheme in that its failure brought about a changed Government view of what to do in regions of high unemployment.

Appendix 1

Transferees (male/female) to various regions in 1936

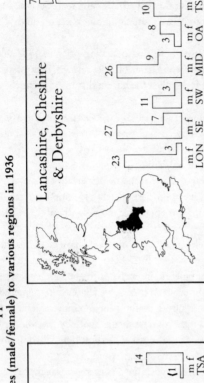

South Wales

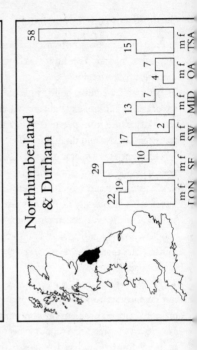

Lancashire, Cheshire & Derbyshire

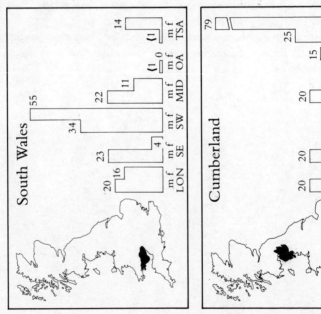

Cumberland

Northumberland & Durham

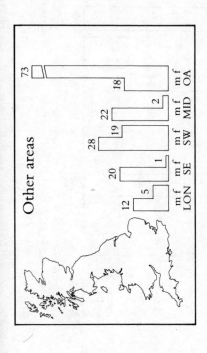

Other areas

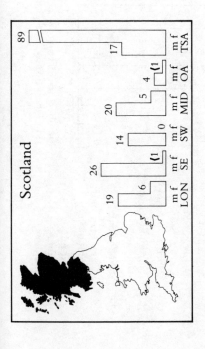

Scotland

MAPS SHOW REGION OF ORIGIN

LON = London

SE = South East

SW = South West

MID = Midlands

OA = Other Areas

TSA = Transferred within same area

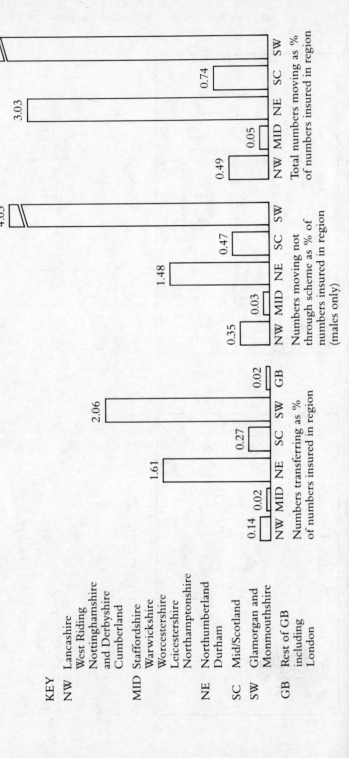

Appendix 2

Movements of people from various regions in 1936

KEY

NW   Lancashire
West Riding
Nottinghamshire
and Derbyshire
Cumberland

MID   Staffordshire
Warwickshire
Worcestershire
Leicestershire
Northamptonshire

NE   Northumberland
Durham

SC   Mid/Scotland

SW   Glamorgan and
Monmouthshire

GB   Rest of GB
including
London

Numbers transferring as %
of numbers insured in region

NW 0.14   MID 0.02   NE 1.61   SC 0.27   SW 2.06   GB 0.02

Numbers moving not
through scheme as % of
numbers insured in region
(males only)

NW 0.35   MID 0.03   NE 1.48   SC 0.47   SW 4.03

Total numbers moving as %
of numbers insured in region

NW 0.49   MID 0.05   NE 3.03   SC 0.74   SW 6.08

War and the Economy: The South Wales Experience

D.A. THOMAS

As far as south Wales[1] was concerned the Second World War acted as a stimulant and catalyst for change while providing a crucial discontinuity in the region's fortunes. The war imposed changes on the region, of a nature and extent, that could not have been otherwise achieved. It provided an obvious and dramatic halt to the pre-war trend and created the apparatus, the environment and the spring-board for future development, and the war 'was important not only for what it ended but for what it began'.[2] In his essay on the post-war expansion of the Welsh economy,[3] Brinley Thomas stated that: 'The war did three things which were to have an enduring effect on the Welsh economy: it eliminated unemployment, the core of a potentially strong manufacturing sector was established, and hitherto unknown employment opportunities for women were created'.[4] This paper attempts to elaborate on these features with respect to south Wales.

A 'Finished Place'

South Wales languished in a chronic industrial depression throughout the 1920s and 1930s.[5] The region's over-concentration on the staple industries of coal, steel and tinplate made it especially vulnerable to the most extreme effects of the coincidence of a downturn in the business cycle and a strong secular decline as well as to the vagaries of uncertain foreign markets. Although the depth of the depression varied between different parts of the region and over time, no part escaped completely unscathed. The percentage of insured persons unemployed in both Glamorgan and Monmouthshire reached a monthly average of over 40 per cent in 1932 and remained over 30 per cent until 1937. Within these counties there existed areas of extreme unemployment reaching, in some cases, over 70 per cent of the insured population. The suffering of most of the coalfield must be contrasted with the circumstances of areas with a more favoured industrial profile such as the coastal belt and the western anthracite area, but even in Carmarthenshire the unemployment rate reached 30 per cent in 1931 and averaged around 25 per cent throughout the 1930s, while actually attaining, in 1938, a higher level than that for Glamorgan and Monmouthshire.

The basic need of the region was an industrial restructuring with the introduction of new and growing industries recognized as a prime requirement 'not desirable on sentimental or compassionate grounds, but . . . justifiable as a sound measure of public economy'.[6] However the region's ability to self-generate such a solution was almost non-existent. South Wales possessed a variety of inherent disadvantages which were now aggravated and added to by the circumstances of the depression years.[7] A general air of decay which pervaded the region became itself a major factor repulsing the remedy.

The region's economic potential deteriorated with the combined effects of a heavy, and age-skewed migration flow and chronic unemployment. The decline in the quantity and quality of human capital was accompanied by the depreciation of the area's material equipment as services, social capital and general amenities, always deficient, also deteriorated. The region's internal market potential suffered from the reduction in income while the area remained cut off from the nation's major markets. Transportational difficulties made location costly, a fact not eased by the failure of the region to offer particularly cheap fuel and by the high rates which existed in many parts as a contrary effect of industrial decline. Fact and fiction intermingled to confirm the view of the region's remoteness and unsuitability for new industrial development and there seemed to exist an 'invisible line running across Mid-Glamorgan beyond which the industrialist is most reluctant to go'.[8]

The appreciation of the inability of south Wales, and similar regions, to achieve a natural rehabilitation eventually produced belated Government action. The Special Areas legislation, however, was too limited in scope to achieve any real impact.[9] The multi-sided activities of the Commissioner did produce some palliative effect, but in the crucial aspect of attracting new industry it was largely ineffective. The only policy which was effectively or energetically pursued was that of industrial transference. Between October 1937 and September 1938 8,306 persons were transferred from the Special Area of South Wales and Monmouthshire under various schemes. In addition 4,023 men were known to have found work for themselves elsewhere.[10] These migrants were the latest addition to an estimated figure of over 350,000 people who had moved out of south Wales since 1921.

The general paucity of new industrial development in south Wales is clearly shown by the figures recorded in the Board of Trade's 'Surveys of Industrial Development' for the years 1932–8.[11] During that period 42 new factories were opened in south Wales, only 24 of which were within the Special Area boundaries, including 13 located at the Treforest Trading Estate in 1937 and 1938. Of the 18 factories located outside the Special Area 10 were sited in the urban centres of Cardiff, Newport and Swansea.[12] Of the 6 factory extensions built during the period, 5 were located in Cardiff. Two of the factories opened were to close within a year and contributed to a total of 10 factory closures in the area during the period. About a quarter of the developments were closely related to the region's traditional activities.

The above figures refer to establishments employing 25 or more people and exclude those which were not engaged in manufacture or in the processing of new goods. They also exclude Government establishments set up in pursuance of rearmament programmes although similar establishments in private ownership are included. The figures thus give an indication of the scale of establishment of significant new manufacturing enterprises, including new branches in a few cases, which were largely unrelated to rearmament work and prior to the general influx of transferred and 'refugee' firms. In other words the figures indicate the scale of industrial development unaffected by war-related factors. They emphasize the failure to significantly modify the region's over-narrow industrial structure and also reaffirm the 'invisible line' influencing location.

The figures for Treforest suggest that it was the trading estate movement which provided south Wales with its most noteworthy benefit from the Special Areas legislation.[13] The limited employment opportunities provided, however, were inappropriate to deal with the region's basic problem of hard core male unemployment carrying, as they did, the involuntary motto of 'women and children first'. By the end of June 1939 of the 2,196 people employed at Treforest only 914 were men. At the other industrial sites connected with the Estate Company at Merthyr, in the Rhondda and in Monmouthshire a further 2,000 workers were employed in similar proportions.

New industrial development was thus insufficient to meet the region's needs. On the eve of the war south Wales remained the 'blackest of black spots'. It had shared little in the revival of the 1930s, a seemingly irreducible hard core of unemployment existed, and the region's economic structure remained an anachronism. In the South Wales Special Area in July 1938 the unemployment rate was 25 per cent. 70,892 men aged between 18 and 64 were wholly unemployed. Of these 31,356 had been unemployed for 12 months or more with 17,066 having been unemployed for at least 3 years.[14] In 1939, 35.1 per cent of all male employees in south Wales were involved in mining and quarrying and a further 13.5 per cent in metal manufacture.[15]

The situation in south Wales remained chronic. Extreme action was required to relieve, leave alone revitalize the region. That action came in the form of the war.

A violent upheaval

The initial effects of the Second World War were felt in the second half of the 1930s partly in the preamble of war preparedness and partly due to the arrival of refugee concerns. Initially the primary spin-off was indirect, a result of the expansion of iron and steel output to meet the needs of armament manufacture. Some iron- and steel-works were resurrected, or remodelled, and new plant introduced for the purpose of manufacturing such items as shells, bombs and mines. As the strategic factor in location became increasingly important a number of military establishments were sited in the presumed safety of the region, the construction and servicing of which produced a much needed injection of income. The siting of camps, aerodromes, storage depots, etc., together with the use of various docks and harbours by the Admiralty for the repairing and refitting of naval vessels and the increased activity at the ports meant that south Wales became the scene of intense military activity. This build-up was accompanied by the reception of evacuated civilians and government departments and a miscellany of national institutions.

All this activity, however, was ephemeral and the stimulus to the basic industries merely counteracted the recessive forces in tinplate and coal which set in during the latter part of 1937. In the absence of the advent of war it would have provided, at most, a temporary palliative. A development offering more permanent potential, however, was associated with the refugee movement.

The months preceding the outbreak of war saw the settling in south Wales of many foreign industrialists who in the main had fled the Nazi persecutions in Central Europe. Finance for these newcomers was made available by the Nuffield Trust and the Special Areas Reconstruction Association while their attraction was in some part due to the propaganda of the National Industrial Development Council of Wales and Monmouthshire.[16] The supply of such enterprises looking for a 'new home' was a major boon for an otherwise relatively unsuccessful policy of attracting new industry to south Wales. These foreign industrialists brought with them considerable skill and expertise together with the experience of world-wide trading connections. They introduced new products and processes and achieved great success in training the workforce in a variety of tasks. Of particular significance in this respect was the fact that the majority of employees were girls who were new to employment, quite unskilled and in most cases lacking in 'factory sense'. One contemporary observer wrote that it was 'no exaggeration to say that they have revolutionised the standard of technical education in their respective areas'.[17]

About 50 of these refugee concerns became domiciled in south Wales, with the majority being housed in otherwise vacant premises at the Treforest Trading Estate, employing around 2,000 workers at the outbreak of the war. The personnel at these factories, apart from a few key men, was recruited wholly from local workers and it was estimated that there was an average of 25 local workers for every immigrant worker. Although the scale of developments was thus limited, of crucial importance was the nature of the new enterprises and their role in 'priming the pump' in order to initiate a flow of new enterprises into south Wales. As far as the Treforest Trading Estate was concerned it may well be said that the success of the experiment was assured by an accident of history.

Away from Treforest typical examples of the combination of refugee enterprise and financial aid can be found in the Rhondda.[18] At Ynyswen, an industrial site associated with the Treforest Trading Estate, A. Polikoff Ltd. was settled as a branch of the parent firm located in London. It was financed partly by a Treasury loan of £40,000, the purchase of £55,000 in shares and a loan of £20,000 by the Nuffield Trust. Outside the management, all employees were local and the firm used 'green' labour to introduce new methods. At a similar site at Porth, Flex Fasteners Ltd. and its branch, Porth Textiles Ltd., were founded by German refugees with financial assistance by the Nuffield Trust. Basically involved in the manufacture of garments, slide fasteners and textiles respectively, all three firms were provided with Government contract work during the war to clothe and equip the civil defence and military forces and by the end of the war they had become well-established in the area.

The importance of these refugee industries for the post-war development of south Wales was stressed by the Welsh Reconstruction Advisory Council in its First Interim Report in 1944. It stated that 'the commercial successes already achieved, despite all obstacles, are remarkable . . . a growing stream of goods of small volume and high value, particularly suitable for export, could be made available from this source in the post-war period'.[19]

The impact of foreign refugee firms was largely a pre-war phenomenon but, just as their flow began to dry up, further impetus was provided by a flood of new enterprises generated by the need to tap unused sources of labour and to expand and disperse essential production away from vulnerable areas. The influence of the Ministries of Labour and Supply was progressively exerted to 'guide' industrialists to south Wales. In part the new enterprises settled in requisitioned premises but in many cases they established themselves in newly-converted Government factories.[20] Although the dispersal of activity in south Wales was widespread, a major centre of attraction was Treforest Trading Estate which became a microcosm of dispersed and diversified production.[21] A number of extensions were made and completely new factories were built and by the end of hostilities the Estate had grown to an industrial space of around 1,500,000 square feet — double that at the beginning of the war. In April 1944, employment at the Estate, with three-shift working, reached a peak of 16,300 compared with just over 2,500 in September 1939.

Wartime developments on the industrial front were not, however, limited to dispersed production. The war also revitalized and redirected existing activities as many enterprises obtained new, often different, contracts for war work. However, it should also be noted that for some firms the consequences of war were not so fortunate. Many suffered from the clamant need for premises for high priority service storage and for urgent categories of production. At Treforest for example, some 24 factories were requisitioned by the Ministry of Aircraft Production. In all, however, the bulk of the industries so affected, namely those concerned with the manufacture of consumer goods, were sparsely located in south Wales and the effect of these measures was, in consequence, relatively small.

The war also generated the widespread construction and operation of a variety of Government factories in south Wales. The most significant of these in terms of employment were the Royal Ordnance Factories (ROFs) which began to be located in the area during the pre-war rearmament programme.[22] South Wales was particularly favoured by the establishment of six such factories. The largest was that located at Bridgend. Started in 1938 it became the largest ammunition filling factory in Britain, and at its wartime peak, some 34,000 workers, mainly women and girls, daily converged on the factory from a wide radius. Another large ROF was built at Hirwaun where as many as 14,000 workers were engaged in the manufacture of small arms. Other ROFs in the east of the region were situated at Glascoed, Llanishen and Newport. The former was involved in shell-filling while the other two were basically engineering establishments. Also a Royal Naval Propellant factory was located at Caerwent in Gwent. In Carmarthenshire the ROF at Pembrey, near Llanelli, was the major supplier of TNT., tetryl and ammonium nitrate. Originally owned and operated by the Nobel firm, the factory had been taken over by the War Office in 1914 but during the inter-war years it had fallen into disuse. With the approach of the Second World War the factory, not without some local opposition, was once more taken over, reconditioned and largely rebuilt. War production began in December 1939. The peak employment was over 3,000 with many former coal-miners and tinplate workers employed.

The ROFs formed only a part of the Government-owned establishments located in south Wales. 'Agency Factories', were located at Kenfig and Dowlais, producing calcium carbide and ammonia respectively. These factories were the property of the State and provided and operated at public expense but under the management of commercial undertakings — factories such as British Industrial Solvents at Kenfig and ICI at Dowlais. The Grange Works at Cwmbran occupied by J. Lucas and Co. Ltd. and the Felinfoel premises of Morris Motors Ltd. were other examples of Government-owned but privately operated factories. Another development of particular significance for the future involved the siting of 'shadow' factories in the area. Suggested by the Ministry of Production in 1943, they were intended to meet the dual purpose of insurance against enemy action and as a provision for the future needs of peacetime industry. Built as blocks of around 50,000 square feet, each would provide ready-made factory space for post-war use. During 1944–5 such factories were located at Ammanford, Blackwood, Merthyr, Neath, Swansea and Ystradgynlais.

Apart from war production, buildings were also erected in the area as depots by the Ministries of Food and Supply. Such establishments were liberally scattered throughout south Wales and included those at Carmarthen, Ammanford, Cwmgors, Barry, Llantrisant, Caerphilly, St Mellons, Llantarnam, Chepstow, Monmouth and Abergavenny. A Government store for the Fleet Air Arm was located at Llangennech and a Ministry of Supply Experimental Station at Penclawdd.

In all, the war saw south Wales as the scene of heightened and varied activity. Many existing enterprises were stimulated and transformed, while there was also a substantial inflow of dispersed industry and a wealth of new industrial building. As far as the basic industries were concerned few emerged from the war with unmitigated and permanent benefits. At best, there was a welcome interlude of heightened activity, while for some there was drastic upheaval which merely drew their problems in more dramatic relief.

The situation of the coal industry had become steadily worse. A temporary boost to production during the early, 'phony', period of the war was followed by an abrupt end to the export trade in 1940. Collieries now closed by the dozen and the labour force declined dramatically. Some workers were swept into the forces, but many switched to other industries often leaving south Wales for jobs in England. This rundown was halted somewhat with the reopening of many mines, and the recognition of coal production as a priority, but it was impossible to correct the unbalanced position. In 1944 the number of persons employed in the coalfield was just over 112,000 while output stood at 22.4 million tons, representing a contraction since 1938 more rapid than the national average. There were, however, some favourable developments: open-cast working became a new feature: new products were derived from south Wales coal which was also put to new uses; and there was an increase in the area's share of the inland market. Nevertheless, it was a curtailed and run-down industry which emerged into the post-war world. By the spring of 1947 despite the fact that the contraction of manpower had been somewhat arrested there were some 25,000 fewer miners in the coalfield than there had been in 1938. Many mines were obsolete, most of the easily worked seams had been exhausted, while maintenance and development work had been virtually ignored during the emergency. Equipment was in a poor state and conditions were generally inadequate. These facts supplemented the traditional problems of relative lack of mechanization to produce a particularly low productivity level.

The tinplate industry was very much a war casualty. The export trade was abandoned completely and home consumption severely restricted. Official policy led to a concentration of production on a drastic scale, while further closures took place as a result of decisions by the firms themselves. The outcome was a sharp contraction in the number of mills in operation and the dispersal of a large percentage of the normal labour force to other parts of Wales and beyond. Many old works were requisitioned for storage and often converted in such a way as to make their return to peacetime production almost impossible. Most closures occurred in the period 1940–3 resulting in the loss of some 14,000 workers in the industry. After 1943 there was a general reluctance on the part of ex-millmen to return to their former employment, while the post-war years saw the reopening of only some of the mills.

By mid 1947 tinplate production was still below its pre-war level and insufficient to meet demand. The restoration of production was certainly hindered by the shortage of experienced mill crews and by fuel and raw material shortages, but the fundamental problem was the inefficient organization of the industry. The immediate post-war years now saw the instigation of a development programme designed to concentrate production at fewer, but larger, modernized sites. In this respect, it can be argued that the war enabled long-due reorganization to take place. The labour force was slimmed down to a more realistic size and an enforced rationalization had taken place by pruning the less-productive branches of the old hand-mill industry.

As regards steel sheets, the degree of concentration and loss of labour was not so marked. The older works in west Wales and the eastern valleys of Gwent had experienced a brief wartime boom in the production of air raid shelters and the rolling of billets and bars for armament work. But, whilst this was only a respite other areas of the steel industry greatly prospered: in particular, the continuous strip mill at Ebbw Vale, the large integrated works at Cardiff and Port Talbot, and the specialist re-rollers at Newport. In the immediate post-war period the steel industry managed to readjust quite well despite the problems of shortages in manpower, raw materials and fuel. The rate of production and the labour force in 1946 were not much below their pre-war levels.

In all, however, the future of the heavy industries in south Wales was in some doubt. To counteract further decline, reorganization was necessary in all sectors. In this connection the war had an important, if partly negative, influence. It highlighted the problems but also provided the opportunity for change and promoted the experience of centralized control and planning.[23]

If the traditional industries of south Wales were to remain, in a real sense, basic, it was also clear that the region's industrial recovery and the retention of the high wartime employment levels required the maintenance of the new activities introduced by the war and the further attraction of others. A significant 'black mark' in this respect, which had been highlighted during the war was the basic problem of the region's inadequate transport network. On the one hand the war years had given clear evidence of the potentiality and flexibility of rail transport which had also benefited from much improvement work. On the other hand, however, the war had emphasized the increasing east–west orientation of communications and transport within the region and beyond into England. This latter issue together with the increasing pre-eminence of road transport, itself a relative war casualty, ensured the continuation of the pre-war calls for a bridge, over the Severn Estuary. Against this and other 'black marks' which remained against the region's character, however, the war had provided a number of potentially rewarding legacies.

The legacy

As the war drew to a close south Wales began to have a foretaste of the transition problems to come. The curtailment of the Ministry of Supply programmes at the end of the war led to a reduction in the labour force of certain ROFs. Various service establishments were run down, and the decision to curtail the production of magnesium and aluminium was received with apprehension. The ultimate question was whether conditions would revert to those of pre-war. But more specifically and immediately the relevant issues concerned the future of wartime plants and evacuated firms.

As early as June 1942, awareness of the problems of post-war readjustment was given substance with the appointment of the Welsh Reconstruction Advisory Council 'to survey in conformity with the general examination of the reconstruction problems now being conducted by the government, those problems of reconstruction which are of special application to Wales and Monmouthshire, and to advise on them'.[24] The Council's First Interim Report, published in March 1944, specifically indicated what appeared to the Council to be the most obvious and striking weakness and also stressed three generally disquieting facts. Firstly, almost half the workers employed in new industries recently established were attached to concerns which were to close down or drastically curtail their activities at the end of the war. Secondly, the most that could be hoped for in the existing basic industries was that the downward trend be arrested. Finally, the pre-war trends which favoured the growth of luxury trades and services at the expense of the older basic trades, would, in the absence of very special measures to counteract them, continue to exert their influence after the war. The Report, by statement and implication, was not a cheerful document. Nevertheless, there were hopes that the process of 'industrial metabolism' would persist. The Report stressed that a new industrial structure could be developed out of the wartime changes while a favourable background to reconstruction could be assured in comparison with that which had prevailed in 1918. It was essential to avoid the mistakes of that earlier period, e.g., haphazard demobilization, scrapping of munition factory assets, and rapid abandonment of various wartime controls.

When the Report was issued it was assumed that the war against Japan would continue for a year or more after the end of the conflict in Europe, which was then in sight. Hostilities, it was generally supposed, would taper off rather than cease abruptly. This assumption of a 'cushion' effect was destroyed with the sudden ending of the war which immediately precipitated the problems of demobilization and readjustment in an aggravated form.

The months immediately following the war saw south Wales passing through a critical transition. There was a sudden cancellation of war contracts and many thousands of workers were made redundant overnight. The dislocation was particularly marked in the region because so much labour was concentrated in war factories. However, the run-down was not restricted to Government munitions factories. Thus by the end of 1945, employment at Treforest had fallen to 8,716. Unemployment began to rise sharply with the figures of some unemployment exchanges ominously approaching pre-war levels. In June 1946 the percentage unemployed at Ferndale stood at 35.6, 26.0 at Merthyr Tydfil and even as high as 11.2 per cent at Swansea.

Initial attempts to arrest the mounting unemployment took the form of public works schemes and the provision or continuation of Government contract work. There was, however, a certain lack of faith in these expedients manifested by the resort to a policy of industrial transference with a special Voluntary Temporary Transfer Scheme introduced in April 1946. Nevertheless, reconversion was gathering momentum, and was reinforced by direct long-term measures taken by the Government. In June 1945, the south Wales coalfield together with a part of Pembrokeshire was scheduled a Development Area. The Act empowered the Board of Trade to build factories in the 'development areas', and to provide finance for the creation and management of industrial estates. Provision was made for grants and loans to industrialists establishing themselves in the Development Areas and financial aid for the clearance of derelict sites. In addition a building programme was planned involving both new factories and extensions to existing buildings.

In its attempts to persuade the wartime firms to remain in south Wales and to attract new firms the Board of Trade was provided with a ready-made base of industrial building in the form of Government factories and 'war depots' which could now be converted to peacetime use.[25] As far as the large ordnance factories were concerned the policy was to release for industrial development those which could be spared. The Newport ROF was allocated to Standard Telephones and Cables Limited and those at Bridgend and Hirwaun were converted into trading estates. The conversion of premises at Bridgend presented many problems and proved an expensive task. Nevertheless, the establishment was soon transformed into a large number of units capable of meeting the needs of small- and medium-sized firms. By mid 1947, 74 firms of various sizes and covering a variety of light industries were in production, out of 80 which had been allocated space. The adaptation of Hirwaun told a similar tale, where by mid 1947 25 firms were in production out of 30 which had been allocated space. A variety of firms was represented but of particular significance was the estate's development as a centre of electrical equipment production. By June 1947 employment at the two converted factories totalled about 6,100 men and women, and more jobs were projected.

The ROFs at Glascoed, Pembrey and Cardiff were retained as reserve capacity for war material, and to some extent, as a source of current supply. By mid 1947, the employment situation at these establishments had stabilized at nearly 3,000 men and women at Glascoed, 1,000 at Cardiff and 1,000 at Pembrey. Alternative work which could be undertaken without serious prejudice to the munitions capacity of the factories was provided to maintain their level of employment. Glascoed was thus involved in making Airey concrete houses and in manufacturing concrete railway sleepers and like Cardiff was equipped to produce ceramics. Admiralty establishments which were retained included the stores at Llangennech and Bridgend while the RN propellant factory at Caerwent was also maintained.

Another example of peacetime conversion was that involving the wartime 'buffer depots' — sheds of about 25,000 square feet which were generally windowless, airless and without office and other necessary accommodation. For example, the depot at Ammanford was allocated to Pullman Spring-Filled Co. Ltd., that at Cadoxton Valley to J. Collis and Sons Ltd. for the manufacture of mechanical conveyors, and the one at Llantrisant to C.W.S. Ltd., as a milk depot. In addition to these conversions a number of factories which had become surplus to Government requirements were re-allocated. There was an early leasing of Government-owned factories to firms, some of which had been operating the same factories for the Government during the war. In January 1946 the list of such factories so transferred included those at Llanelli to Morris Motors Ltd., Cwmbran to J. Lucas and Co. Ltd., Cyfarthfa to Lines Bros. (toys), Treorchy to The Gramaphone Co. Ltd., Newport to Uskside Engineering Co., and Neath to Metalclad Ltd.

Another ready-to-use block of factory space was provided by the dual-purpose 'standard' factories. The tenants in each case had been chosen because their production would not only help in the war effort, but could be relied upon to continue post-war. They were allocated as follows: Ystradgynlais to Smiths English Clocks Ltd., Blackwood to South Wales Switchgear Ltd., Ammanford to Pullman Spring Filled Co. Ltd., Neath to the Midland Metal Spinning Co. Ltd., Merthyr to Kayser-Bondor Ltd. (underwear) and Swansea to Amalgamated Dental Laboratories and Mettoy Ltd. By mid 1947 around 3,000 workers had found new employment in these enterprises.

By July 1947 practically all Government-owned space in south Wales which was readily usable for industrial purposes had been allocated. This ensured that more new industry had gone to the South Wales Development Area since 1939 than anywhere else. The White Paper on Distribution of Industry published in 1948 clearly shows the value of this legacy of industrial building which would otherwise have had to be created from scratch.[26] The number employed at June 1948 in Government munitions factories converted to industrial estates, allocated, sold or otherwise disposed of in south Wales, was 24,151 involving 148 tenants. In comparison the numbers employed at the same time in *new* factories and extensions (financed by the Government or privately) of over 5,000 square feet completed since the end of the war in the Development Area was only 9,421.[27]

It is pointless to speculate how much of this existing building would have been otherwise undertaken and how quickly. One fact which is clear, as Brinley Thomas concluded using different figures, was that 'at that crucial stage the development area's programme of the new factory building was not digging into the country's scarce capital resources'.[28] This was especially significant because the progress of the new building programme was being hampered by shortage of materials, skilled workers of various grades in construction and civil engineering, and also in equipment and installations. In late 1947 a national decision was taken to cut capital investment. Thereafter, factories could only be built when they were deemed essential to export promotion or to the saving of imports, and in practice only extensions to firms already operating in south Wales were to receive approval. To emphasize the importance of the buildings which had been provided for war purposes we can quote an exception which seems to prove the rule in south Wales. In the Rhondda no Government munitions factories were located during the war. Thus post-1945 there was no available space for allocation to civilian production. Up to mid 1948 only 7 new enterprises were established in the Rhondda and only 3 were installed in new factories. The others occupied a mixture of existing buildings converted to meet requirements — an old chapel, a market hall, a disused colliery and a large house.[29]

In addition to the problem of maintaining and attracting new industry there was also the problem of the adaptation by individual firms to peacetime production. This was potentially very difficult for firms which had specifically transferred their attention to wartime needs or which had been set up during the war for a particular purpose. In most cases the adjustment, however, was made aided by interim assistance from various Government departments in the form of contract work.

An industry which underwent considerable readjustment was chemicals. During the war a massive increase in the numbers employed in the chemical industry had occurred. After the war there was a rapid reversion to the pre-1939 level of employment. None the less significant gains had been made and were retained. Thus factories at Dowlais and Kenfig were kept and operated, almost entirely for industrial purposes, by their wartime occupants. Similar developments also occurred in the light metallurgical sector with notable acquisitions being made at Waunarlwydd and Rogerstone, near Newport.

Other examples of readjustment abound, many obviously at Treforest where by 1947 employment had risen to over 11,000. At Cardiff a firm which made thousands of dinghies for the RAF during the war used the knowledge gained to develop further products such as rubberised cotton fabric inflatable rafts. At Hirwaun, two radio firms established for the production of radio and allied equipment were licensed to produce domestic radio receivers. At Chepstow an old-established works which in pre-war years had been specializing in bridge-building and had its outlook changed by war contracts began to pioneer welded all-steel mineral wagons. Treorchy and its environs witnessed the expansion of the Polikoff clothing factory and the conversion of the EMI wartime valve factory, evacuated from Middlesex in 1944, to electrical equipment and dry batteries. At Nantgarw an engineering unit, expanded during the war, passed to the Cardiff Lathe and Tool Works Ltd., while in the Neath valley, George Kent Ltd, established a successful engineering unit in a wartime munitions factory near Resolven, producing sheeting gear and water motors. At Cwmbran and Llanelli respectively, the firms of J. Lucas and Co. Ltd. and Morris Motors Ltd. settled down to their primary interests and provided a crucial foothold for the establishment of the motor vehicle industry in the region.

Thus it can be seen that the need for readjustment was widespread. Some enterprises had to undergo drastic changes, others merely built on the experiences brought about by war. In a large number of cases, firms continued to make use of premises which they had acquired during the war. Many enterprises, of course, returned to their pre-war location, and others were destined to close, but many more remained in existing or new premises. In addition, the release of requisitioned space and the conversion of a variety of Government concerns provided facilities to attract completely new enterprises. This complemented and boosted the new Government activity under the Distribution of Industry Act. Of course, the region's future prospects depended only partly on a satisfactory reconciliation of this issue. Of crucial importance were the circumstances of the basic industries which remained as a potential millstone. Nevertheless, a significant industrial restructuring had occurred and could be built upon. A more vigorous industrial and regional policy now had material to work with.

One particularly significant wartime development involved the dramatic increase in female employment. Apart from the coastal towns, opportunities for women had always been few in an area dependent on heavy, male-dominated industry. This situation was complemented by social traditions which did not encourage women going out to work. Thus, in the Rhymney valley and Tredegar area in 1938 there were only six insured females to each hundred males.[30] While the volume of female employment was particularly low it was also limited in character — basically involving domestic service but also commerce, public administration and retailing. Even these were overcrowded and many women, particularly domestic servants and teachers, left the region to work in England.

To a large extent, it was a question of 'non-employment' as far as most women were concerned rather than unemployment.[31] This seemed confirmed when the war brought into employment women who had hitherto not sought work or had not had the opportunity to gain employment: at least not within the region. Between July 1938 and July 1945 the number of insured females employed in the South Wales and Monmouthshire Development Area rose from 54,712 to 142,825 amounting to more than 80 per cent of the increase in total employment (Appendix Table 1). Nearly a half of the women were in chemicals, engineering, vehicles, metals and transport with the ROFs being a particularly significant employer. Much of this female employment was of a transient nature in the dual sense of being a substitute for males variously displaced and also directly related to specific war production. Many women who had tasted factory life, however, were to remain on the register if not in employment during the post-war years, attracted by the wages obtained, the social contacts enjoyed and the attendant independence.

The war thus realized the potentialities of female labour in south Wales, releasing a major source of virtually untapped labour. The ability to maintain the high wartime level of female participation was, however, crucially related to the increasingly diversified nature of industry in south Wales with the introduction of considerable light industrial employment during the war. But the relationship which existed was two-way. Many reports concluded that the availability of large supplies of unskilled female labour was a crucial attraction to the miscellaneous industry which arrived in the post-war period.[32] The figures for employment in existing and new building in south Wales quoted earlier show quite clearly the importance of female employees.[33] In June 1948, there were 8,981 females out of the 24,151 total employees in surplus Government factories. This represented a proportion of 37 per cent, similar to that in the new factories or extensions completed. The proportion of females in total employment estimated to be generated by all projects approved was 44 per cent. In general, the industries served by females were complementary to the male-dominated ones. They were aimed at different markets and were in the growth sectors of the economy.

This increase in the female portion of the labour force was supplemented by changes in its nature and quality. Before the war, precision and repetition work was almost non-existent in south Wales, but the requirements of wartime and of the new light industries encouraged the learning of new skills and a familiarity with new processes. The labour pool became more varied, and better equipped for the needs of new industries. This asset was reinforced by the experience of the refugee firms and other newcomers during the war. Their favourable reaction, manifested in the decision by many to stay after the cessation of hostilities, provided an invaluable advertisement encouraging others to follow suit and locate in the environment. These new enterprises had proved that 'jobs could be done' in south Wales. In addition, a host of prejudices and misconceptions concerning the lack of discipline of the workers, the incapability of the basic labour pool to adapt to modern refined production, and the incommodious environment, were broken down. The war had also displayed the willingness, albeit forced, of workers to 'bus' to work. This suggested that work could now be taken to south Wales anticipating that the workers would travel intra-regionally to work. In the words of one contemporary observer 'convoys of buses carrying middle-aged housewives, worn but thrilled from the high wages of their first factory experience, brought useful labour to old and new workplaces'.[34] This description, albeit colourful, does reflect a particularly significant impression which the war left on the region.

The above account of the impact of the war and its aftermath can be given perspective by comparing the post-war employment situation with what had existed pre-war.[35]

Discontinuity and diversification

The circumstances of wartime had seen the achievement and maintenance of a high level of employment together with an extremely low level of unemployment (3.4 per cent in July 1945 in the South Wales Development Area).[36] The latter condition, however, was not entirely the result of the former. The virtual disappearance of unemployment was only partly due to increased employment opportunities. It was also due to recruitment to the Armed Forces and the continuing movement of persons to other parts of the country to meet the labour shortage in key sectors. The increased employment level was the net result of additions to the workforce, the substitution of men displaced by females, and the re-entry of many older men who had, in the depression years, abandoned all hopes of again obtaining work. During the peak of wartime activity those persons who could be regarded as still out of work were largely immobile men and women with a limited capacity for normal industrial work. This category was not insignificant, however, as is indicated by the 6.5 per cent of the workforce still unemployed at Ferndale in July 1944. These were mainly old miners who had long been unemployed, suggesting that a basic problem remained. Nevertheless, the war had showed how low a proportion of the unemployed was completely unfit for work and retraining.

Although in the immediate post-war years the employment situation deteriorated rapidly, the trend was soon halted, and eventually reversed. By July 1948 readjustment to peacetime had been more or less completed providing us with an appropriate comparison with the pre-war situation.[37] (See Appendix Table 1). The total number of persons insured in the Development Area stood at 546,000, an increase of 6 per cent from the corresponding 1938 figure. The number of males insured had fallen slightly but the number of females insured had increased by nearly 85 per cent from 62,440 to 115,270. The number of females employed stood at 105,201 compared with 54,712 in 1938 — an increase of over 90 per cent. This contrasted with an increase of 32 per cent in total employment (from 387,069 to 512,575), and of 23 per cent in male employment. Females now represented 21 per cent of total employment in the area compared with 14 per cent in 1938. It should be noted that in July 1945, female employment had in fact accounted for 29 per cent of total employment.

At the same time unemployment had begun to stabilize at a long-forgotten peacetime rate. In June 1948 the percentage of insured unemployed in the counties of Glamorgan, Monmouthshire and Carmarthenshire was 5.1, 3.8 and 5.7 respectively. In the Development Area it was 6.1 per cent. Despite this dramatic break with the past, however, the region still retained its problem areas with some valley exchanges returning figures of over 20 per cent unemployed. These high rates can be largely explained by the area's topography making for the geographical immobility of the long-term unemployed while continuing to prevent factory sites being erected in the valleys.[38] The unemployment figures for the 6 December 1948[39] show that of the 21,759 males unemployed in the Development Area, 8,247 — i.e. 38 per cent — were aged 41 and over and had been unemployed for over 26 weeks. 80 per cent of those who had been unemployed for more than 26 weeks were in this age group. In total, 13,784 unemployed males were aged over 41, representing 63 per cent of total male unemployment compared with 54 per cent both for the Development Areas and for Great Britain as a whole.

Apart from these 'unemployables' the other significant feature of the unemployment figures was the increased importance of female registration. In July 1938 there had been 7,728 females registered as unemployed in the Development Area; in 1948 there were 10,069. Although the rate of female unemployment stood at 8.7 per cent compared with 12.4 per cent in 1938 the level of female unemployment had increased by over 30 per cent. Female unemployment now represented over 30 per cent of the total compared with only 6 per cent in 1938. (See Appendix Table 1). In December 1948 over 50 per cent of all females unemployed were aged between 21 and 41.[40]

The post-war unemployment figures must be interpreted in the light of the fact that disguised unemployment had been high amongst females in pre-war years, but given this qualification, it is clear that the employment situation at the end of the 1940s bore little resemblance to that which had existed in pre-war years. There now existed a surplus of labour for 'unskilled' and light industry work, especially female, alongside a shortage of skilled labour and workers suitable for heavy industry.[41] In July 1938, 126,881 insured persons had been unemployed in the Development Area. In July 1948 the figure was below 34,000. The fact that the unemployment rate was higher than in any other Development Area despite the significant employment increases testifies to the extent of the pre-war problem.

As well as providing a break with the past in the level of economic activity, the war also provided a significant break with respect to the composition of that activity. The net result of the expansion of some industries on the one hand and the introduction of new activities on the other hand, was to twist the economy into an 'unfamiliar mould' at the height of the war. Many of the changes were necessarily temporary and as soon as the war ended some parts of the region's economy again underwent rapid change. Nevertheless, the war clearly saw a radical alteration in the industrial distribution, involving a diversification of the industrial structure on a substantial scale. This is shown by a consideration of the mid 1948 figures of insured employees for the three south Wales counties in comparison with those of 1939. (See Appendix Table 2 and Table 3).

Over the period the total number of employees involved in mining and quarrying in the region fell from 158,229 to 124,527 and this category represented 18 per cent of total employment in 1948 compared with 30 per cent in 1939. The figure for male employment fell from 35 per cent to 24 per cent. In conjunction with this decrease there was an increase in the total number of employees in manufacturing industries from 128,882 to 201,010. This was an increase of 56 per cent — identical to that for Wales as a whole but compared with a rise of only 15 per cent for Great Britain. The percentage of employment in manufacturing industry rose from 25 per cent to 30 per cent of the region's total. The most significant feature was the increase in the female workforce in manufacturing of 156 per cent from 19,098 to 48,966. This compared with 146 per cent for Wales, but only 11 per cent in Great Britain. Females as a percentage of males in manufacturing rose from 17 per cent to 32 per cent. Some significant changes in terms of total employees and female participation occurred in chemicals and allied industries, engineering and electrical goods, vehicles, and clothing and footwear.

Despite the massive increase in the number of female employees in manufacturing, this sector accounted — at 30 per cent — for only a slightly greater proportion of all female employees than in 1939. The service sector remained the dominant source of employment accounting for 67 per cent of female employees compared with 70 per cent in 1939. The total workforce involved in the service sector rose by 52 per cent, from 221,591 to 335,995, and accounted for nearly 50 per cent of total employees compared with 52 per cent for Wales and Great Britain and only 43 per cent in 1939. The increase in female employees, from 47,629 to 108,733, represented an increase of 128 per cent. The percentage of females compared to males in the service sector rose from 27 to 48.

The numbers employed in 'all industries' rose from 518,521 in 1939 to 675,754 in 1948, i.e. an increase of 30 per cent. Female employment rose from 67,952 to 161,050, an increase of 137 per cent compared with 150 per cent in Wales and only 57 per cent in Great Britain. The increase in the number of male employees was a modest 14.2 per cent while the proportion of females to males rose from 15 per cent in 1939 to 31 per cent in 1948.

To obtain a fuller picture of the long-term transformation which occurred in the sex and industrial distribution of the workforce, we can refer to the occupation figures in the 1931 and 1951 Censuses, which reflect the permanent changes which the war brought. The years themselves are chosen for convenience but they do represent the 'two different worlds'. 1931 provides a still picture of the region prior to any war-related developments, while 1951 provides one of the region on a new plateau after readjustment. (See Appendix Tables 4, 5 and 6). As far as industrial diversification is concerned, the figures basically substantiate the employee statistics for the period 1939–48 and as such need not be laboured.[42] We can, however, obtain further information on the broader changes which occurred, especially with regards to increased female activity. (See Appendix Tables 7 and 8).

Between 1931 and 1951 the total numbers occupied in the three counties remained roughly the same, but the number of females increased by 37 per cent, while the number of males fell by 7 per cent. The increase in female occupation compared with an increase of 26 per cent in Wales as a whole and only 11 per cent in Great Britain. As far as the female to male ratio was concerned, there was a significant increase in south Wales compared with elsewhere. In 1931 only 21 women were occupied per 100 men compared with 24 in Wales as a whole and 42 for Great Britain. By 1951 the figure for south Wales had increased to 31, almost identical to that for Wales, and compared with 44 for Great Britain.

As far as the activity rates were concerned, the figure for females rose from 22 to 29.[43] This increase was similar to that experienced in Wales as a whole and very conspicuous compared with the meagre rise, from 39 to 41 in Great Britain. The overall activity ratio rose only slightly, from 62 to 63, because of a fall in male participation. To an unmeasurable extent the decline in male participation can be explained by fewer men remaining occupied after the age of 65 in 1951.[44] This point is amplified by the fact that the ratio of males occupied to total working age males in 1931 had exceeded 100 per cent.

The changes in female participation need to be placed in the context of the sex composition of the working-age population — the ultimate determinant of potential workforce. Working-age females as a percentage of working-age males rose from 97 to 104. The female group increased by 1.7 per cent but the male group fell by 5.1 per cent producing a net fall in the total working-age population — and hence in potential workforce. On this level of generalization an increase in female presence in the workforce could be expected — but it cannot explain the great increase achieved. The opportunity for employment had to exist for the potential to be transformed into effect.

It should be noted that despite the significant changes in female participation, in 1951 south Wales still possessed the lowest percentage of women in the total insured population of any region. This was partly due to the industrial structure which still involved the under-representation of industries which in the country as a whole employed more women. But to a large extent the relatively low proportion was due to the simple fact that an immense leeway had to be made up from exceptionally low pre-war figures. As in the case of the diversification of the region's industrial structure and the transformation of the unemployment situation, the increase in female participation was great and real. The three features were to remain an abiding legacy of wartime.

A new beginning?

In the absence of the war it is reasonable to assume that changes would have occurred in the governance and experience of the nation and its depressed regions. It is, however, unprofitable to conjecture on what the situation otherwise would have been in the late 1940s. In the event the war brought about a massive transformation at a national and regional level. It provided a level of heightened activity which was to spill over to the post-war world and created and conditioned future policy commitments. In sum it can be said that the exigencies of war 'forced immediate and large-scale action where study and propaganda might well have had little result'.[45] The war presented actualities as well as possibilities. This was particularly true as far as south Wales was concerned.

The war provided a sudden and immediate alleviation of the region's suffering. It had a profound influence upon the level and sex distribution of employment. The evil of high persistent unemployment was removed while industries were introduced on a variety and a scale which could not have been hoped for otherwise. An environment was created which encouraged industrial settlement and was more suited to house a more diversified industrial structure. In all, the war provided an inheritance of much that had been absent in the past. Industrial development in the late forties was to build on this legacy but a lot still had to be done.

South Wales lagged behind the rest of Great Britain on most indicators. The impact of the war had left the economy as a whole operating on a higher level and the regional pecking order was maintained but this would not matter overmuch if the level of activity could be maintained in absolute terms. The future of south Wales was thus a patchwork of hopes and fears. Progress, after a prompt and facilitated start, was to be slow. The regional problem was always to be a makeweight in post-war policy decisions while south Wales was to continue to be a poor relation in the national economy.

Appendix

Table 1
Employment and unemployment.
South Wales and Monmouth Development Area 1932, 1938, 1945 and 1948
(July of each year)

Total Persons	1932[a]	1938[b]	1945[c]	1948[c]
Number insured	494,600	513,950	512,950	546,000
Number employed	292,053	387,069	495,335	512,575
Number unemployed	202,547	126,881	17,595	33,425
% unemployed	40.9	24.7	3.4	6.1
Males				
Number insured	448,960	451,510	363,290	430,730
Number employed	254,251	332,357	352,530	407,374
Number unemployed	194,709	119,153	10,760	23,356
% unemployed	43.4	26.4	2.9	5.4
Females				
Number insured	45,640	62,440	149,660	115,270
Number employed	37,802	54,712	142,825	105,201
Number unemployed	7,838	7,728	6,835	10,069
% unemployed	17.2	12.4	4.5	8.7

Notes: [a] Insured persons between 16 and 64 years of age.

[b] Insured persons between 14 and 64 years of age, and including persons insured under the Agricultural Scheme introduced in 1937.

[c] Insured males between 14 and 64 years of age and insured females between 14 and 59 years of age.

Source: Ministry of Labour and National Service.

Table 2
Industrial distribution of employees[a] in Carmarthen, Glamorgan and Monmouth at June 1939 and 1948[b, c, d]

SIC Order[e]	Males		Females		Total aged 15 and over	
	1939	1948	1939	1948	1939	1948
I Agriculture, Forestry, Fishing	8,868	12,340	951	1,882	9,819	14,222
II Mining & Quarrying	157,955	123,058	274	1,469	158,229	124,527
TOTAL, All Extractive Industries	166,823	135,398	1,255	3,351	168,048	138,749
III Food, Drink & Tobacco	7,582	10,254	4,801	5,215	12,383	15,469
IV Chemicals & Allied Industries	3,721	12,865	218	2,695	3,939	15,560
V Metal Manufacture	60,801	61,277	3,108	7,077	63,909	68,354
VI Engineering & Electrical Goods	10,199	20,323	1,446	7,741	11,645	28,064
VII Shipbuilding & Marine Engineering	4,847	7,659	564	213	5,411	7,872
VIII Vehicles	4,694	9,448	557	3,350	5,251	12,798
IX Metal Goods not elsewhere specified	4,634	9,784	2,052	6,950	6,686	16,734
X Textiles	280	1,997	526	1,415	806	3,412
XI Leather, Leather Goods & Fur	247	616	143	634	390	1,250
XII Clothing & Footwear	1,156	1,590	3,505	7,889	4,661	9,479
XIII Bricks, Pottery, Glass, Cement, etc.	5,111	6,801	191	1,003	5,302	7,804
XIV Timber, Furniture, etc.	3,150	3,825	378	588	3,528	4,413
XV Paper, Printing & Publishing	3,089	3,494	1,408	1,682	4,497	5,176
XVI Other Manufacturing Industries	273	2,111	201	2,514	474	4,625

Table 2 — continued

SIC Order[e]	Males		Females		Total aged 15 and over	
	1939	1948	1939	1948	1939	1948
TOTAL, All Manufacturing Industries	109,784	152,044	19,098	48,966	128,882	201,010
XVII Construction	62,078	48,689	254	805	62,332	49,494
XVIII Gas, Electricity & Water	6,066	8,987	234	715	6,300	9,702
XIX Transport & Communication	37,603	66,909	671	5,409	38,274	72,318
XX Distributive Trades	36,963	35,082	26,839	31,406	63,802	66,488
XXI Insurance, Banking & Finance	1,468	5,127	559	2,228	2,027	7,355
XXII Professional & Scientific Services	4,060	13,743	3,252	22,201	7,312	35,944
XXIII Miscellaneous Services	8,714	16,881	12,292	34,036	21,006	50,917
XXIV Public Administration	17,010	31,844	3,528	11,933	20,538	43,777
TOTAL, Services	173,962	227,262	47,629	108,733	221,591	335,995
GRAND TOTAL	450,569	514,704	67,952	161,050	518,521	675,754

Notes: [a] Estimated number of employees (employed and unemployed) in the area of the employment exchanges.

[b] The figures are estimates based partly on the number of national insurance cards exchanged in the quarter beginning June, and partly on returns rendered by employers of five or more workpeople, showing the numbers of insurance cards held by them.

[c] Most civil servants have their contributions paid without the use of cards and are, therefore, excluded from the figures. The principal orders affected are XIX and XXIV. Also excluded are seafarers on foreign going ships whose contributions are paid in bulk.

[d] The figures are not sufficiently precise to enable detailed comparisons and no significance should be attached to relatively small changes.

[e] The industrial analysis is based on the 'Standard Industrial Classification'. (1958 edition).

Source: Figures provided by the Department of Employment and Productivity, Employment Record II, Order Totals.

Table 3

Industrial distribution of employees in Carmarthen, Glamorgan and Monmouth 1939 and 1948 (percentage form)[a]

As percentage total (M/F/T) employees

SIC Order	MALES		FEMALES		TOTAL		FEMALES as % MALES	
	1939	1948	1939	1948	1939	1948	1939	1948
I Agriculture, Forestry, Fishing	2.0	2.4	1.4	1.2	1.9	2.1	10.7	15.3
II Mining & Quarrying	35.1	23.9	0.4	0.9	30.5	18.4	0.2	1.2
TOTAL, All Extractive Industries	37.0	26.3	1.8	2.1	32.4	20.5	0.7	2.5
III Food, Drink & Tobacco	1.7	2.0	7.1	3.2	2.4	2.3	63.3	50.9
IV Chemicals & Allied Industries	0.8	2.5	0.3	1.7	0.8	2.3	5.9	20.9
V Metal Manufacture	13.5	11.9	4.6	4.4	12.3	10.1	5.1	11.5
VI Engineering & Electrical Goods	2.3	3.9	2.1	4.8	2.2	4.2	14.2	38.1
VII Shipbuilding & Marine Engineering	1.1	1.5	0.8	0.1	1.0	1.2	11.6	2.8
VIII Vehicles	1.0	1.8	0.8	2.1	1.0	1.9	11.9	35.5
IX Metal Goods not elsewhere specified	1.0	1.9	3.0	4.3	1.3	2.5	44.3	71.0
X Textiles	0.1	0.4	0.8	0.9	0.2	0.5	187.9	70.9
XI Leather, Leather Goods & Fur	0.1	0.1	0.2	0.4	0.1	0.2	57.9	102.9
XII Clothing & Footwear	0.3	0.3	5.2	4.9	0.9	1.4	303.2	496.2

XIII Bricks, Pottery, Glass, Cement, etc.	1.1	1.3	0.3	0.6	1.0	1.2	3.7	14.7
XIV Timber, Furniture, etc.	0.7	0.7	0.6	0.4	0.7	0.7	12.0	15.4
XV Paper, Printing & Publishing	0.7	0.7	2.1	1.0	0.9	0.8	45.6	48.1
XVI Other Manufacturing Industries	0.1	0.4	0.3	1.6	0.1	0.7	73.6	119.1
TOTAL, All Manufacturing Industries	24.4	29.5	28.1	30.4	24.9	29.7	17.4	32.2
XVII Construction	13.8	9.5	0.4	0.5	12.0	7.3	0.4	1.7
XVIII Gas, Electricity & Water	1.3	1.7	0.3	0.4	1.2	1.4	3.9	8.0
XIX Transport & Communication	8.3	13.0	1.0	3.4	7.4	10.7	1.8	8.1
XX Distributive Trades	8.2	6.8	39.5	19.5	12.3	9.8	72.6	89.5
XXI Insurance, Banking & Finance	0.3	1.0	0.8	1.4	0.4	1.1	38.1	43.5
XXII Professional & Scientific Services	0.9	2.7	4.8	13.8	1.4	5.3	80.1	161.5
XXIII Miscellaneous Services	1.9	3.3	18.1	21.1	4.1	7.5	41.1	201.6
XXIV Public Administration	3.8	6.2	5.2	7.4	4.0	6.5	20.7	37.5
TOTAL, Services	38.6	44.2	70.1	67.5	42.7	49.7	27.4	47.8

Notes: [a] Calculated from figures in Table 2.

Occupational distribution of the population in

	MALES				1931ᶜ	
	1931ᶜ	as % total occ.	1951ᵈ	as % total occ.		a f
1 Fishing	560	0.1	334	0.1	14	
2 Agriculture	28,724	4.6	24,605	4.2	2,972	
3 Gas, Coke & Chemicals	1,839	0.3	5,546	1.0	25	
4 Metal Manuf. & Engineering	67,793	10.8	89,754	15.5	1,518	
5 Mining & Quarrying	203,020	32.5	93,183	16.0	25	
6 Woodworkers etc	10,975	1.8	13,186	2.3	50	
7 Leather workers etc.	2,937	0.5	2,094	0.4	68	
8 Textile workers	538	0.1	1,344	0.2	333	
9 Clothing workers	3,111	0.5	2,468	0.4	7,495	
10 Food, Drink & Tobacco	5,951	1.0	4,979	0.9	1,405	
11 Paper & Printing	2,507	0.4	2,336	0.4	865	
12 Building etc.	25,324	4.0	42,006	7.2	22	
13 Makers of other products	3,213	0.5	2,179	0.4	137	
14 Painters & Decorators	5,885	0.9	8,425	1.5	50	
15 Stationary Engine Drivers etc	18,298	2.9	18,529	3.2	23	
16 Labourers (n.e.c.)	27,711	4.4	53,442	9.2	96	
17 Transport & Communications	70,896	11.3	62,639	10.8	1,657	
18 Warehousemen etc	5,492	0.9	10,117	1.7	1,349	
19 Clerical Workers	20,018	3.2	27,428	4.7	10,275	
20 Sales Workers	54,432	8.7	42,034	7.2	24,778	
21 Services etc.	17,873	2.9	20,652	3.6	57,486	
22 Admin. & Managers	3,153	0.5	11,294	1.9	134	
23 Prof., Tech. Workers Artists	15,777	2.5	25,311	4.4	15,711	
24 Armed Forces	877	0.1	8,926	1.5	—	
25 Inadequately described occ.	27,747	4.4	6,051	1.0	4,787	
26 Glass, Ceramics, Cement	986	0.2	1,935	0.3	96	
Total Occupied	625,637	99.9	580,797	100	131,371	10
27 Retired & Unoccupiedᵉ	63,053		90,080		544,268	
	688,695		670,877		675,639	

Notes: ᵃ Persons out of work are included in the tabulation of persons by occupation.

ᵇ The classification is that adopted for the 1971 census.

ᶜ Persons aged 14 and over.

ᵈ Persons aged 15 and over.

ᵉ Much higher proportions of persons, especially men, retired at or soon after 65 in 1951 than in 1931. (See footnote 44).

Source: Census of Population, 1931, 1951.

en, Glamorgan and Monmouth 1931 and 1951[a, b]

| | MALES & FEMALES | | | | FEMALES as % M & F | | FEMALES as % MALES | |
| 1951[d] as % total occ. | 1931[c] | as % total occ. | 1951[d] | as % total occ. | in each class | | in each class | |
					1931	1951	1931	1951
0.0	574	0.1	335	0.0	2.4	0.3	2.5	0.3
1.9	31,696	4.2	28,110	3.7	9.4	12.5	10.3	14.2
0.4	1,864	0.2	6,206	0.8	1.3	10.6	1.4	11.9
3.6	69,311	9.2	96,256	12.7	2.2	6.8	2.2	7.2
0.0	203,045	26.8	93,210	12.3	0.0	0.0	0.0	0.0
0.1	11,025	1.5	13,338	1.8	0.5	1.1	0.5	1.2
0.5	3,005	0.4	2,916	0.4	2.3	28.2	2.3	39.3
0.6	871	0.1	2,339	0.3	38.2	42.5	61.9	74.0
6.1	10,606	1.4	13,450	1.8	70.7	81.7	240.9	445.0
1.0	7,356	1.0	6,844	0.9	19.1	27.3	23.6	37.5
0.6	3,372	0.4	3,365	0.4	25.7	30.6	34.5	44.0
0.0	25,346	3.3	42,058	5.5	0.1	0.1	0.1	0.1
0.7	3,350	0.4	3,497	0.5	4.1	37.7	4.3	60.5
0.2	5,935	0.8	8,704	1.1	0.8	3.2	0.8	3.3
0.1	18,321	2.4	18,657	2.5	0.1	0.7	0.1	0.7
8.7	27,807	3.7	69,043	9.1	0.3	22.6	0.3	29.2
2.0	72,553	9.6	66,254	8.7	2.3	5.5	2.3	5.8
2.0	6,841	0.9	13,677	1.8	19.7	26.0	24.6	35.2
19.2	30,293	4.0	62,000	8.1	33.9	55.8	51.3	126.0
16.6	79,210	10.5	71,870	9.4	31.3	41.5	45.5	71.0
22.8	75,359	10.0	61,710	8.1	76.3	66.5	321.6	198.8
0.6	3,287	0.4	12,289	1.6	4.1	8.1	4.2	8.8
11.2	31,488	4.2	45,488	6.0	49.9	44.4	99.6	79.7
0.1	877	0.1	9,195	1.2	0.0	2.9	—	3.0
0.9	32,534	4.3	7,716	1.0	14.7	21.6	17.3	27.5
0.2	1,082	0.1	2,352	0.3	8.9	17.7	9.7	21.6
100.1	757,008	100	760,879	100	17.4	23.7	21.0	31.0
	607,326		623,163					
	1,364,334		1,384,042				98.1	106.3

Table 5
Numbers occupied in Carmarthen, Glamorgan, Monmouth, Wales and G.B. 1931 and 1951[a]

	Males		Females		Totals	
	1931	1951	1931	1951	1931	1951
CARMARTHEN	60,791	56,750	14,111	16,074	74,902	72,824
GLAMORGAN[b]	415,371	386,040	89,529	124,121	504,900	510,161
MONMOUTH[b]	149,475	138,007	27,731	39,887	177,206	177,894
SOUTH WALES	625,637	580,797	131,371	180,082	757,008	760,879
WALES	872,672	833,523	206,139	259,361	1,078,811	1,092,884
G.B.	14,772,544	15,648,877	6,250,690	6,961,169	21,023,234	22,610,046

Notes:　[a] As for Table 4.

　　　　[b] 1931 figures for counties as constituted at the time.

Source:　Census of Population, 1931, 1951.

Table 6
Working age populations in Carmarthen, Glamorgan, Monmouth, Wales and G.B. 1931 and 1951[a]

	Males		Females		Totals	
	1931	1951	1931	1951	1931	1951
CARMARTHEN	60,317	57,687	60,732	60,137	121,049	117,815
GLAMORGAN[b]	413,044	392,451	405,634	412,950	818,687	805,401
MONMOUTH[b]	147,210	138,798	138,268	141,561	285,478	280,359
SOUTH WALES	620,571	588,927	604,634	614,648	1,225,205	1,203,575
WALES	863,276	843,957	864,938	882,665	1,728,214	1,726,622
G.B.	14,567,602	15,675,206	16,086,070	16,899,787	30,653,672	32,574,993

Notes:　[a] 14–64 age group.

　　　　[b] 1931 figures for counties as constituted at the time.

Source:　Census of Population, 1931, 1951.

Table 7
Percentage changes in numbers occupied in Carmarthen, Glamorgan, Monmouth, Wales and G.B. 1931 and 1951[a]

	Males	Females	Totals
CARMARTHEN	− 6.65	+ 13.91	− 2.77
GLAMORGAN	− 7.06	+ 38.64	+ 1.04
MONMOUTH	− 7.67	+ 43.84	+ 0.39
SOUTH WALES	− 7.17	+ 37.08	+ 0.51
WALES	− 4.49	+ 25.82	+ 1.30
G.B.	+ 5.9	+ 11.37	+ 7.55

Notes: [a] Calculated from figures in Table 5.

Table 8
Female participation in Carmarthen, Glamorgan, Monmouth, Wales and G.B. 1931 and 1951. Some Calculations[a]

	Females as % of total occupied		Females as % of males occupied		Activity rate[b]	
	1931	1951	1931	1951	1931	1951
CARMARTHEN	18.84	22.07	23.21	28.32	23.23	26.73
GLAMORGAN	17.73	24.33	21.55	32.15	22.07	30.06
MONMOUTH	15.65	22.42	18.55	28.90	20.06	28.18
SOUTH WALES	17.35	23.67	21.00	31.00	21.73	29.30
WALES	19.11	23.73	23.62	31.12	23.83	29.38
G.B.	29.73	30.79	42.31	44.48	38.86	41.19

Notes: [a] Calculated from figures in Tables 5 and 6.

[b]
$$\text{Activity Rate} = \frac{\text{Number occupied}}{\text{Working age group}}$$

See Footnote 43.

Notes

Introduction

1 A.H. John, *Industrial Development of South Wales* (Cardiff, 1950).

2 Glanmor Williams and A.H. John, eds., *Industrial Glamorgan*, Vol. V, *Glamorgan County History* (Cardiff, 1980).

3 J.H. Morris and L.J. Williams, *The South Wales Coal Industry, 1841–1875* (Cardiff, 1958).

4 A.H. Conrad and J.R. Meyer, 'The Economics of Slavery in the Ante-bellum South', *Journal of Political Economy*, LXVI (April 1958), 95–130.

5 See especially Brinley Thomas, *Migration and Economic Growth* (Cambridge, 1954), (2nd edition, 1973). *Migration and Urban Development: A Reappraisal of British and American Long Cycles* (London, 1972).

6 Brinley Thomas: 'The Migration of Labour into the Glamorganshire Coalfield, (1861–1911)', *Economica*, (1930), 275–94; 'Labour Mobility in the South Wales and Monmouthshire Coal Industry 1920–30', *The Economic Journal*, XLI (June 1931), 216–66; 'The Movement of Labour into South-East England, 1920–32', *Economica* (New Series), I (May 1934), 220–41; 'The Influx of Labour into London and the South-East, 1920–36', *Economica* (New Series), IV (August 1937), 323–36; 'The Influx of Labour into the Midlands, 1920–37', *Economica* (New Series), V (November 1938), 410–38.

7 *The Welsh Economy: Studies in Expansion* (Cardiff, 1962).

8 'Wales and the Atlantic Economy', *Scottish Journal of Political Economy*, VI (September 1959), 169–92.

9 A.H. John, op. cit., Chapter 1.

10 See especially R.O. Roberts, 'The Development and Decline of the Non-ferrous Metal Smelting Industries in South Wales', *Transactions of the Honourable Society of Cymmrodorion*, (1956), 78–115.

11 Below, p. 31.

The Industrial Revolution and the Welsh Language

1 *Scottish Journal of Political Economy*, VI (November 1959), 169–92. See also Brinley Thomas, ed., *The Welsh Economy: Studies in Expansion* (University of Wales Press, 1962), pp. 26–9. In writing the present paper I received much assistance over materials from Brian James of the library staff of University College, Cardiff.

2 Ibid., p. 29.

3 See E.A. Wrigley, 'The Supply of Raw Materials in the Industrial Revolution', *The Economic History Review* (2nd series), 15 (1962), 1–16; and Brinley Thomas, 'Towards an Energy Interpretation of the Industrial Revolution', *Atlantic Economic Journal*, 8 (March 1980), 1–15. This challenge was more profound than the timber shortages of the sixteenth and seventeenth centuries. John U. Nef (in *The Rise of the British Coal Industry*, 2 vols., Routledge, 1932) argued that those shortages constituted a national crisis necessitating a large-scale switch to coal. Most economic historians now agree that the processes using coal in the sixteenth and seventeenth centuries did not alter the mainly agrarian character of that society and do not justify the term 'first industrial revolution'.

4 See Brinley Thomas, 'Feeding England During the Industrial Revolution: A View from the Celtic Fringe', *Agricultural History*, 56 (January 1982), 329–35.

5 Charles K. Hyde, *Technological Change and the British Iron Industry 1700–1870* (Princeton University Press, 1977), p. 81.

6 Brinley Thomas, 'The Rhythm of Growth in the Atlantic Economy of the Eighteenth Century', in Paul Uselding, ed., *Research in Economic History*, 3 (J.A.I. Press, 1978), 18.

7 *Reports of the Commissioners appointed to inquire into the State and Conditions of the Woods, Forests and Land Revenues of the Crown, 11th Report, Naval Timber, House of Commons Journal*, Appendix 11 (1792), pp. 314–27.

8 Ralph Davis, *The Rise of the English Shipping Industry in the Seventeenth and Eighteenth Centuries* (David and Charles, 1972), pp. 184–5.

9 C.H. Feinstein, 'Capital Formation in Great Britain', in P. Mathias and M.M. Postan, eds., *The Cambridge Economic History of Europe*, vol. VII, *The Industrial Economies: Capital, Labour and Enterprise*, Part I (Cambridge University Press, 1978), p. 40.

10 See C.R. Morton and N. Mutton, 'The Transition to Cort's Puddling Process', *Journal of the Iron and Steel Institute*, (July 1967), 722–8.

11 J. Russell Smith, *The Story of Iron and Steel* (New York, Appleton, 1913), p. 75.

12 Philip Riden, 'The Output of the British Iron Industry before 1870', *The Economic History Review* (2nd series), 30 (August 1977), 448 and 455.

13 See Brinley Thomas, *Migration and Economic Growth: a Study of Great Britain and the Atlantic Economy* (Cambridge University Press, 1973), (2nd edition), chapter XV.

14 W. Stanley Jevons, *The Coal Question* (1865) (3rd edition ed. by A.W. Flux, New York, A. Kelley, 1965), pp. 199–200.

15 B.R. Mitchell and Phyllis Deane, *Abstract of British Historical Statistics* (Cambridge University Press, 1962), p. 131.

16 Sidney Pollard, 'A New Estimate of British Coal Production, 1750–1850', *The Economic History Review* (2nd series), 33 (May 1980), 229.

17 A.H. John, *The Industrial Development of South Wales 1750–1850* (University of Wales Press, 1950), Chapter III.

18 Ibid., pp. 63–4.

19 G.S. Kenrick, 'Statistics of Merthyr Tydfil', *Journal of the Statistical Society of London*, IX (March 1846), 14–21.

20 Ibid., p. 14.

21 Ibid.

22 Ibid., p. 15.

23 For an illuminating analysis of Caernarfonshire and Swansea and District see Ieuan Gwynedd Jones, *Explorations and Explanations: Essays in the Social History of Victorian Wales* (Llandysul, Gwasg Gomer, 1981), Chapters 1 and 2.

24 The South Wales Railway was opened between 1850 and 1859. In 1862 the total mileage of the Great Western and West Midland Railways was 1,104. E.T. MacDermot, *History of the Great Western Railway* (1927), pp. 863–5.

25 W.T.R. Pryce, 'Migration and the evolution of culture areas: Cultural and linguistic frontiers in north-east Wales', *Transactions of the Institute of British Geographers* (June 1975), 79–107.

26 Ibid., Table 1, p. 82.

27 Ibid., p. 103.

28 Philip N. Jones, art. cit. (in text), p. 87. Italics in the original.

29 Ibid., p. 88.

30 See Brinley Thomas, 'The Migration of Labour into the Glamorganshire Coalfield, 1861–1911', *Economica*, 10 (November 1930), reprinted in W.E. Minchinton, ed., *Industrial South Wales 1750–1914, Essays in Welsh Economic History* (F. Cass & Co., 1969), 51–3.

31 R.I. Aaron, 'The Struggle for the Welsh Language: Some Pre-Census Reflections', *Transactions of the Honourable Society of Cymmrodorion* (1969, Part II), 230.

32 Philip N. Jones, art. cit., p. 93.

33 *Commission of Inquiry into Industrial Unrest, Report for Wales including Monmouthshire*, P.P. (1917–18), XV, 8668, pp. 12–13.

34 Philip N. Jones, art. cit., p. 93. Italics in the original.

35 See footnote 30.

36 See Brinley Thomas, 'The Migration of Labour into the Glamorganshire Coalfield . . . ', loc. cit.

37 John E. Southall, *Wales and her Language,* Newport, Mon., J.E. Southall, 149 Dock Street, London: E. Hicks Jun., 2 Amen Corner, Paternoster Row (1892), p. 356. Italics in the original.

38 See Brian Ll. James, 'The Welsh Language in the Vale of Glamorgan', *Morgannwg*, XVI (1972), 26–30.

39 See John Parry Lewis, 'The Anglicisation of Glamorgan', *Morgannwg*, IX (1960), 28–49.

40 D. Isaac Davies, *Yr Iaith Gymraeg 1785, 1885, 1985!* (Dinbych, T. Gee a'i Fab, 1886), pp. 22–3.

41 E.G. Ravenstein, 'On the Celtic Languages in the British Isles: a Statistical Survey', *Journal of the Statistical Society*, 42, Part III (September 1879), 579–643.

42 Ibid., p. 580.

43 Ibid.

44 Brinley Thomas, 'Wales and the Atlantic Economy', in Brinley Thomas, ed., *The Welsh Economy: Studies in Expansion* (1962), p. 11.

45 Ieuan Gwynedd Jones, op. cit., p. 292.

46 The source for these figures is the admirable survey by D. Lleufer Thomas, 'Bibliographical, statistical, and other miscellaneous memoranda', *Report of the Royal Commission on Land in Wales and Monmouthshire (1896)*, Appendix C, pp. 195–7.

47 Ibid., p. 197.

48 D. Isaac Davies, op. cit.

Canals and the Economic Development of South Wales

1 Phyllis Deane, *The First Industrial Revolution* (Cambridge, 1965), p. 73.

2 W.T. Jackman, *The Development of Transportation in Modern England,* Vol. 1 (Toronto, 1916), pp. 363–4.

3 J.H. Clapham, *The Economic History of Modern Britain,* Vol. 1 (Cambridge, 1932), p. 78.

4 Charles Hadfield, *The Canals of South Wales and the Border* (Newton Abbot, 1967), p. 15.

5 Archdeacon Coxe, *Tour through Monmouthshire* (London, 1801), p. 35.

6 H.J. Dyos and D.H. Aldcroft, *British Transport: An Economic Survey from the Seventeenth Century to the Twentieth* (London, 1974), pp. 67–71.

7 4 Geo. III, *Local and Personal,* c. 88.

8 Walter Davies, *General View of the Agriculture and Domestic Economy of South Wales,* II (1814), 395.

9 C. Hadfield, op. cit., pp. 30–1.

10 M.V. Symons, *Coal Mining in the Llanelli Area,* Vol. 1, (Sixteenth Century to 1829) (Llanelli, 1979), 74–82.

11 C. Hadfield, op. cit., pp. 45–6.

12 T. Boyns, D. Thomas and C. Baber, 'The Iron, Steel and Tinplate Industries 1750–1914', Chapter III in Glanmor Williams and A.H. John, eds., *Industrial Glamorgan,* Vol. V, *Glamorgan County History* (Cardiff, 1980), 101–3.

13 A.H. John, *Industrial Development of South Wales* (Cardiff, 1950), pp. 24–5.

14 T.S. Ashton, *Iron and Steel Industry in the Industrial Revolution* (Cambridge, 1924), p. 37.

15 P. Deane, op. cit., p. 81.

16 There were few exceptions. The only two of any real importance were the extension of the Glamorgan Canal's catchment area into the Aberdare valley and the northern reaches of the Neath valley via the Aberdare Canal, and the Tennant Canal which linked the lower Neath part of the Neath Canal with Swansea.

17 30 Geo. III c. 82.

18 36 Geo III c. 69.

19 Enid A. Walker, *The Development of Communications in Glamorgan with Special Reference to the Growth of Industry between 1760 and 1830* (M.A. thesis, University College Swansea, 1947), p. 146.

20 Gary R. Hawke, *Railways and Economic Growth in England and Wales* (Oxford, 1970), p. 79.

21 Enid Walker, op. cit., p. 148.

22 The Dowlais Company was usually the main adversary of Cyfarthfa, and the two works vied for the position of major iron producer in Britain throughout this period.

23 Permissable rates for canal charges were laid down in the enabling Act, and could only be changed through legal petition.

24 Enid Walker, op. cit., p. 153.

25 C. Hadfield, op. cit., pp. 99–100.

26 32 Geo. III c. 102 (March 1793).

27 37 Geo. III c. 100 (July 1797).

28 C. Baber and G. Price, 'The Construction and Operation of the Monmouthshire Canal and its Tramroads', *Journal of the Railway and Canal Historical Society,* 19, No. 1 (1973), 9–16.

29 D.R. Phillips, *History of the Vale of Neath* (Neath, 1925), p. 330.

30 H. Pollins, 'The Swansea Canal', *Journal of Transport History,* I (1954), 150.

31 Aldcroft and Dyos, op. cit., p. 103.

32 The advantages of the early canals, although becoming more widely appreciated, often depended upon firsthand experience before being put into practice.

33 H. Pollins, art. cit., p. 138.

34 This was the case of almost all the canals built in Britain. See Aldcroft and Dyos, op. cit., p. 107.

35 Baber and Price, art. cit., p. 12.

36 Ibid., p. 14.

37 C. Hadfield, op. cit., pp. 50, 64, 95, 130.

38 Ibid., p. 219.

39 R.O. Roberts, 'Banking and Financial Organisation', Chapter VIII in Glanmor Williams and A.H. John, eds., *Industrial Glamorgan,* Vol. V, *Glamorgan County History* (Cardiff, 1980), p. 383.

40 Baber and Price, art. cit., p. 13.

41 Hadfield, op. cit., pp. 17, 19.

42 T. Boyns and C. Baber, 'The Supply of Labour 1750–1914', Chapter VII in Glanmor Williams and A.H. John, eds., *Industrial Glamorgan,* Vol. V, *Glamorgan County History* (Cardiff, 1980), 316–20.

43 See W.T. Jackman, op. cit., p. 359.

44 J.H. Clapham, op. cit., p. 80.

45 Harry Scrivenor, *History of the Iron Trade* (London, 1854), pp. 124 and 257. See also Appendix 1, pp. 39–42.

46 Cf. esp. Document M000625Acc (Newport Public Library) with Scrivenor.

47 M.J. Daunton, 'The Dowlais Iron Company in the Iron Industry 1800–50', *Welsh History Review,* 6 (1972), 21–4.

48 B.R. Mitchell and P. Deane, *Abstract of British Historical Statistics* (Cambridge, 1962), pp. 131–3.

49 H. Pollins, art. cit., p. 145.

50 D.R. Phillips, op. cit., p. 338.

51 C. Hadfield, ibid., p. 53.

52 These are derived from Document M000625Acc p. 6, which seems to be based upon information from various issues of the *Mining Journal.* (Newport Public Library).

53 Alun C. Davies, *Aberdare: 1750–1850. A Study in the Growth of an Industrial Community.* (M.A. thesis, Aberystwyth 1950).

54 J.H. Clapham, op. cit., pp. 81–2.

55 See below M. Atkinson, 'The Supply of Raw Materials to the South Wales Iron Industry, 1800–60,' p. 47.

56 C. Hadfield, op. cit., p. 27.

57 Ibid., p. 23.

58 C. Baber, 'The Subsidiary Industries of Glamorgan 1760–1914', Chapter V in Glanmor Williams and A.H. John, eds., *Industrial Glamorgan,* Vol. V, *Glamorgan County History* (Cardiff, 1980), 214.

59 J. H. Morris, 'Evan Evans and the Vale of Neath Brewery', *Morgannwg,* (1965), 52.

60 J. H. Clapham, op. cit., p. 78.

61 W.T. Jackman, op. cit., p. 449.

62 *Cambridge Chronicle and Journal* (10 September 1813).

63 Enid Walker, op. cit., p. 146.

The Supply of Raw Materials to the South Wales Iron Industry 1800–60

1 James Stephen Jeans, *The Iron Trade of Great Britain* (London, Methuen, 1906), pp. 8–9.

2 Charles K. Hyde, *Technological Change and the British Iron Industry 1700–1870* (Princeton U.P., Princeton, 1977), p. 237. Figures for the Abersychan ironworks for 1827–51 agree very closely with the 1.5:1 ratio — see Gwent R.O., E.133.46 and Reading R.O., D/Efe E2 (1827–39).

3 Bute MSS, Cardiff Central Library, Bute XIV.13, XIV.34, XIV.35.

4 William Needham's Report on the Plymouth Iron Works 1839. Newport Reference Library, document px M220.012.

5 Presidential address of William Menelaus. *Proceedings of the South Wales Institute of Engineers,* 1 (1857–9), 4.

6 Isaac Lowthian Bell, *The American Iron Trade* (Special volume of the *Journal of the Iron and Steel Institute,* 1890), 184.

7 Jeans, *Iron Trade,* p. 45.

8 R.C. Riley, *Industrial Geography* (London, Chatto and Windus, 1973), p. 85.

9 *Second Report of the Royal Commission on Depression on Trade and Industry,* P.P. (1886), (4715) XXI Appendix A(1), p. 337.

10 See below p. 48.

11 Howard G. Roepke, 'Movements of the British Iron and Steel Industry 1720–1951', *Illinois Studies in Social Sciences,* 36 (1956), 27.

12 Alan Birch, *The Economic History of the British Iron and Steel Industry 1784–1879* (London, Cass, 1967), p. 181.

13 See *Mineral Statistics of the United Kingdom* (HMSO annually) and Furnace Accounts for Plymouth and Duffryn Works for December 1862, NLW MS 1154DC. The amount of fuel used varied between works and it is difficult to generalize on this point, but reference to various furnace records, e.g., Rhymney, Abersychan, Dowlais etc. shows the downward trend.

14 Birch, op. cit., p. 187, and W.K.V. Gale, *The British Iron and Steel Industry* (David and Charles, 1967), p. 68.

15 Birch, op. cit. p. 170; M.J. Daunton, 'The Dowlais Iron Company in the Iron Industry 1800–1850', *Welsh History Review,* 6 (1972), 22; Walter Isard, 'Some Locational Factors in the

Iron and Steel Industry since the early Nineteenth Century,' *Journal of Political Economy,* 56 (1948), 212; and Roepke, art. cit., 41.

16 Evan J. Jones, *Some Contributions to the Economic History of Wales* (London, P.S. King and Son, 1928), p. 55.

17 Richard Meade, *The Coal and Iron Industries of the United Kingdom* (London, Crosby Lockwood, 1882), p. 698.

18 Cyfarthfa MSS, NLW, Box XII.1.

19 Barrow-in-Furness R.O., Box 38.

20 Buccleuch MSS, Barrow-in-Furness R.O., Bd/Buc Box 25. There is a complete series of figures of ore shipments from Furness from 1824 to 1845.

21 Cyfarthfa MSS, NLW, Box XII.1.

22 Leconfield MSS, Carlisle R.O., D/Lec/2. Main series leases 18/1.

23 Thomas Sopwith, *The Award of the Dean Forest Mining Commissioners as to the Coal and Iron Mines in Her Majesty's Forest of Dean* (London, Weale, 1841), p. 179.

24 Ibid., pp. 80, 182.

25 Clement le Neve Foster, 'Notes on Haytor Iron Mine,' *Quarterly Journal of the Geological Society,* XXXI (1875), 628.

26 David Mushet, *Papers on Iron and Steel* (London, Weale, 1840), p. 150.

27 Dowlais MSS, G.R.O., Main series letters 1847(1) GW–G f.773; 1848 C–H f.329; 1849 A–H f.408, 410; 1849 J–W f.617–8, 671–2.

28 In a discussion of William Fairbairn, 'Experimental researches into the properties of the iron ores of Samakoff in Turkey, and of the haematite ores of Cumberland', *Journal of the Institution of Civil Engineers,* III (1844), 245.

29 *Mining Journal* for 6 February and 30 April 1836.

30 Cyfarthfa MSS, NLW, Box XII.3.

31 Dowlais MSS, Main series letters, D/DG 1827(1) no. 105.

32 Dowlais MSS, Main series letters, D/DG 1833(1) nos. 31–2, 53–5, 69–71, 189–91.

33 Dowlais MSS, Main series letters, D/DG 1838(1) no. 256.

34 Dowlais MSS, D/DG Section E, Box 3.

35 Dowlais MSS, Main series letters, D/DG 1836(1) f.51.

36 Dowlais MSS, D/DG Section C, Box 4.

37 Dowlais MSS, Main series letters, D/DG 1847 f.804.

38 Dowlais MSS, D/DG Section C, Box 3.

39 Leconfield MSS, Carlisle R.O., Box 94.

40 Maybery MSS, NLW, no. 3600.

41 Supplement to the *Mining Journal* for 1837, p. 100. See also T. Mitchell, *The Monmouthshire Iron and Steel Trade* (Newport, 1906), p. 6.

42 Rhymney MSS, G.R.O., D/D Rh.53.

43 Cyfarthfa MSS, NLW, Box XII.3.

44 *Mining Journal* for 1836, p. 76.

45 G.R.O., D/D Xqk2. See also Parliamentary Papers 1844–8 (937) 1XIII, Railway Traffic Returns.

46 Braithwaite Poole, *Statistics of Commerce* (London, 1852), pp. 201–2.

47 There is little evidence of ores from south-west England being sent to other areas than south Wales. Only when railways rendered long-distance movement of ore viable did small amounts go to Staffordshire, notably from the Torbay mines. See *Mineral Statistics* — notes to iron ore production tables.

48 Evidence of William Menelaus to the *SC on the Rating of Mines,* P.P. (1857) (241 Sess. 2) XI, q. 1768–70.

49 Evidence of William Llewellin to the *SC on the Rating of Mines,* q. 1342.

50 Leconfield MSS, Carlisle R.O., D/Lec Box 92.

51 Evidence of Menelaus to the *SC on the Rating of Mines,* q. 1853.

52 Evidence of Llewellin to the *SC on the Rating of Mines,* q. 1471.

53 *Mining Journal* for 1853, p. 555.

54 Rhymney MSS, G.R.O., D/D Rh.151. Letters of 31 July and 3 August 1858.

55 Wentsland and Bryngwyn MSS, Gwent R.O., D.38.370. Produce Book of the Abersychan works.

56 John Percy, *Metallurgy: Iron and Steel* (London, John Murray, 1864), p. 202.

57 Cecil S. Orwin, *The Reclamation of Exmoor Forest* (London, Oxford University Press, 1929), pp. 128, 135.

58 Between 1876 and 1882, the Ebbw Vale Company's Abersychan furnaces were almost exclusively used for the production of 'speigeleisen'. See Gwent R.O., D38.369 and D454.2005.

59 See Arthur H. John, *The Industrial Development of South Wales 1750–1850* (Cardiff, University of Wales Press, 1950), p. 78; Bute MSS, Cardiff Central Library, Bute XIV.5; and Dowlais MSS, D/DG Section C, Box 8 — report by Menelaus on the general state of Dowlais Works 1857.

60 Dowlais MSS, D/DG Section E. Annual Balance Sheets.

61 Cyfarthfa MSS, NLW, Box XII.3.

62 Dowlais MSS, D/DG Section C, Box 3.

63 Fairbairn, 'Experimental Researches' p. 245 and Dowlais MSS, D/DG Section C, Box 3.

64 Cyfarthfa MSS, NLW, Box XII.3.

65 Evidence of Thomas Powell to the *SC on the Rating of Mines,* q. 1729.

66 Dowlais MSS, D/DG Section C, Box 8..

67 Evidence of Samuel Dobson to the *SC on the Rating of Mines,* q. 1544.

68 W. Needham, *On the Manufacture of Iron* (1830), p. 26.

69 *Mining Journal,* 17 August 1850.

70 Mushet, op. cit., p. 141.

71 Mushet, op. cit., pp. 151, 153.

72 William Truran, *The Iron Manufacture of Great Britain* (London, Spon, 1855), p. 53.

73 J. Percy, *Metallurgy,* pp. 548–9.

74 Mushet, op. cit., p. 166.

75 Evidence of J.T. Smith to the *Royal Commission on Depression of Trade and Industry,* P.P. (1886), (4715) XXI, p. 56 q. 2186.

76 See Board of Trade returns for ore imports in the annual *Mineral Statistics.*

Coal-mining in the Llanelli Area — Years of Growth 1800–64

1 *Coal Mining in the Llanelli Area,* Vol. 1, (Sixteenth century to 1829), by M.V. Symons, (Llanelli Borough Council, 1979), gives details of Llanelli's pre-nineteenth century coal industry.

2 This statement is based on the assumption that coals composed of less than 91 per cent carbon are bituminous coals.

3 'Steam-coals' were so called because they proved particularly suitable for firing the boilers and raising steam to power the nineteenth-century steam engines.

4 Local Collection 37 (11 May 1824) at Llanelli Public Library and *Report from the Select Committee of the House of Commons on Steam Navigation to India* (14 July 1834) confirm that steam-coal from the Llangennech region of Llanelli was well known and in demand before 1830.

5 In the absence of full output figures, coal exports have been taken as a good indicator of total coal production. As late as 1864, coal exports from Llanelli accounted for virtually three-quarters of the area's total coal production — evidence of: *Returns to the House of Commons of exports of coal, cinders and culm* (1864); Hunt's *Mineral Statistics* (1864); *Report of the Commissioners appointed to inquire into the several matters relating to coal in the United Kingdom* (1871), Vol. III.

6 The population of Llanelli Borough Hamlet increased from approximately 2,000 in 1800 (J.L. Bowen, *History of Llanelly* (1886)) to 4,173 in 1831 (*Census Enumeration Abstracts* (1831)). Reliable statistics are not available to estimate the population growth within the entire area of this study.

7 Estimates of coal exports from 1551 to 1880 have been obtained from the following sources: 1551–61 — J.U. Nef, *The Rise of the British Coal Industry* (1932); 1566–1603 — E.A. Lewis, *Welsh Port Books 1550–1603* (1927); 1604–1709 — B. M. Evans, *The Welsh Coal Trade during the Stuart Period 1603–1709* (M.A. thesis, University of Wales, 1928); 1744–46, 1772–77, 1788–91 — Cawdor (Vaughan) 21/614 (Carmarthen Record Office); 1793–1800 — D. Bowen, *Hanes Llanelli* (1856), (Llanelli Public Library); 1804–15 — 'Ship News' in *The Cambrian* newspaper (this entails the allocation of average tonnages in the coal-ships frequenting Llanelli); 1816–80 — interpretation of the sometimes contradictory returns in the *Report of the Commissioners appointed to enquire into the several matters relating to coal in the United Kingdon* (1871), *Returns to the House of Commons,* and Hunt's *Mineral Statistics.* Estimates of population from 1800 to 1881 have been obtained from J.L. Bowen, op. cit., and from *Census Enumeration Abstracts,* 1801 to 1881.

8 The name 'Llanelly Copperworks Company', although commonly used, was not the Company's official title. It operated under the seven following titles during its lifetime: — 1805–17, Daniell, Savill, Guest and Nevill; 1817–19, Daniell, Savill, Sons and Nevill; 1819–24, Daniell, Son and Nevill; 1824–35, Daniell, Nevill and Co.; 1835–37, Nevill, Sims, Druce and Co.; 1837–73, Sims, Williams, Nevill, Druce and Co.; 1873 onwards, Nevill, Druce and Co.

9 See M.V. Symons, op. cit. for details of Llanelli's early nineteenth-century industrialists.

10 Ibid., for an account of the successes and failures of Llanelli's early nineteenth-century industrialists.

11 *The Cambrian* (1804–25). Detailed listings of sailings with their destinations were given for these years.

12 *The Cambrian* (1804–29). Detailed listings of vessels entering Llanelli were given until 1846.

13 Nevill 16 (1 January 1830) at Carmarthen Record Office; Thomas Mainwaring's *Commonplace Book* at Llanelli Public Library.

14 Thomas Mainwaring, op. cit.; Museum Collection 181 (1827–34) at Carmarthen Record Office.

15 *The Cambrian* (16 June 1832).

16 9 Geo. IV c91 (19 June 1828).

17 *The Cambrian* (19 July 1834).

18 5 and 6 Will. IV c96 (21 August 1835).

19 Nevill MS XVIII (January 1836) at National Library of Wales.

20 Nevill MSS XLVIII (1837–50), XIII (1850–61), XIV (1862–74), XVI (1874–80).

21 Children's Employment Commission, Appendix to First Report, Mines Part II (1842) p. 713.

22 Local Collection 1789 — Letter books of the Llanelly Railway and Dock Company — copy letter dated 14 October 1842.

23 Nevill MS VII, loose copy letter 154 (17 December 1844).

24 Details of the smaller concerns have been built up from numerous primary documentary sources. These sources show the listings in Hunt's *Mineral Statistics* to be incomplete and unreliable in terms of updating.

25 Hunt's *Mineral Statistics* (1860), p. xvi.

26 Ibid. (1866) p. v; (1868) p. ii.

27 Evidence of: *The Cambrian* (5 March 1858, 8 March 1861, 12 July 1861, 11 April 1862); The *Llanelly Guardian* (19 March 1874, 10 June 1875, 21 September 1876).

28 *Inspector of Mines Reports* (1864 onwards).

29 *The Cambrian* (11 November 1859).

30 Ibid. (12 December 1862).

31 'Non-ferrous smelting' by R.O. Roberts, in *Industrial South Wales 1750–1914*, (1969).

32 J.H. Morris and L.J. Williams, *The South Wales Coal Industry 1841–1875* (Cardiff, 1958).

33 *The Cambrian* (18 January 1856).

34 Nevill MSS XLVIII, XIII, XIV and XVI.

35 Nevill MS XIV; *Report of the Commissioners* (1871), op. cit.

36 Coal exports for 1800 have been estimated as 12,000 tons (M.V. Symons, op. cit.). It is unlikely that local consumption would have exceeded 8,000 tons.

37 *Report of the Commissioners* (1871), op. cit.

Banks and the Economic Development of South Wales before 1914

REFERENCES

Sources to which a number of references are made in the notes, preceded by the abbreviations used for them.

L.B. (L.–S.) (S.–L.)   Bank of England, Swansea 'Branch Bank' Letter Books, London to Swansea (L.–S.) and Swansea to London (S.–L.). — studied by kind courtesy of the Governor and Company of the Bank.

W.Q.   Evidence of John Parry Wilkins in June 1832 to the *Committee . . . on the Charter of the Bank of England* (P. P., (1831–2), VI). References, Q, are given to the questions answered.

The following are written by the author of this chapter

R.a.   'Bank of England Branch discounting, 1826–1859', *Economica*, XXV No. 99 (August 1958), 230–45 (reprinted in *Industrial South Wales, 1750–1914*, ed. W.E. Minchinton; London, 1969, pp. 173–89). The pagination in *Economica* is given because this version contains the detailed references to the Bank records.

R.b.   'Bank advances for Welsh drovers in the early nineteenth century', *The Bankers' Magazine*, 187 No. 1383 (June 1958), 483–6.

R.c.   'Financial crisis and the Swansea "Branch Bank" of England', *The National Library of Wales Journal*, XI No. 1 (Summer 1959), 76–85.

R.d.   'The operations of the Brecon Old Bank of Wilkins & Co., 1778–1890', *Business History*, I No. 1 (December 1958), 35–51.

R.e.   'The Brecon Old Bank and the economic development of Breconshire', *Brycheiniog*, VII (1961), 56–69.

R.f.   'The Bank of England, the Company of Copper Miners and the Cwmavon Works', *Welsh History Review*, 4 No. 3 (June 1969), 219–34.

R.g.   'Banking', *Neath and District–Symposium* (ed. Elis Jenkins, Neath, 1974), Chapter 13, pp. 252–65.

R.h.   'Banking and Financial Organization, 1770–1914', Chapter VIII in Glanmor Williams and A H. John, eds., *Industrial Glamorgan*, Vol. V, *Glamorgan County History* (Cardiff, 1980), pp. 363–420.

NOTES

1 On Lancashire see papers by T.S. Ashton, *Economic History Review*, XV (1945); S. Checkland, *Economica*, (New Series), XXI (May 1954); B.L. Anderson, *Business History*, X (1969) and XII (1970), and with P.L. Cottrell, *Economic History Review*, XXVIII (1975); M. Collins, *Business History*, XIV (1972). On Birmingham see D.J. Moss, *Economic History Review*, XXXIV (1981) and *Business History*, XXIV (1982).

2 R.S. Sayers, *Modern Banking* (London, 1939), pp. 1,17,18.

3 B. of E. (S.–L.), Bundle–Private No. 188, 9 June 1835.

4 Daniel Hardcastle Jnr. (pseud. of Richard Page) *Banks and Bankers* (London, 2nd edition, 1834), p. 1; *Greal y Bedyddwyr*, III (1829), 210–11 (excerpt kindly given by the late Professor David Williams).

5 J.F. Jones, 'The Union Bank of Haverfordwest', *Carmarthen Antiquary*, III, 2 (1960), 107; Ivor Walters, *Chepstow Miscellany* (Chepstow Society, 1958), p. 63; R.e., p. 57.

6 R.d., p. 42.

7 Ibid., p. 42.

8 W.F. Crick and J.E. Wadsworth, *A Hundred Years of Joint Stock Banking* (London, 3rd edition, 1958), p. 187 fn.

9 Cf. D.J. Moss, 'The private banks of Birmingham 1800–1827', *Business History*, XXIV, 1 (March 1982), 80–1.

10 B.G. Owens, 'Trenewydd deeds and documents', *National Library of Wales Journal*, IX (1956), 489.

11 W.Q., 1788–9, 1795–7, 1801–4; R.d., p. 42.

12 R.d., pp. 41–2.

13 B. of E., S.–L. (parcel), 9 June 1835.

14 R.d., p. 39; R.a., p. 244.

15 G. Wilkins, *History of Merthyr Tydfil* (1st edition, 1867), p. 369; W.Q., 1691–4; cf. R.S. Sayers, *Lloyds Bank in the History of English Banking* (Oxford, 1957), pp. 110, 116–17; cf. NLW, Nevill Papers, A4, 24 December 1804, 10 January 1805.

16 W.Q., 1652, 1756; R.d., p. 40.

17 R.b., p. 485; R.d., p. 42; W.Q., 1675.

18 W.Q. 1615–7, 1625–6, 1688–9, 1698–1703, 1734–7, 1786–7; R.d. pp. 43–4; Moss, op.cit., p. 33.

19 R.d., p. 44; *Report on the Operation of the Bank Act, 1844*, P.P. (1857), Appendix 39, 324; Checkland, op.cit., p. 130.

20 R.a., pp. 233–4; R.d., p. 44; R.h., pp. 366, 374; W.Q., 1718, 1721; Moss, op.cit., p. 84.

21 R.a., pp. 233–4; B. of E., L.B. II (L.–S.), 11 October 1831; B. of E., L.B. I (S.–L.), 21 January 1840.

22 A.H. John, *The Industrial Development of South Wales, 1750–1850* (Cardiff, 1950), pp. 43, 46; NLW, Nevill Papers, V and XXI.

23 B. of E., L.B. II (L.–S.), 10 February 1834; R.d., pp. 49–50.

24 P. L. Cottrell, *Industrial Finance 1830–1914* (London and New York, 1980), p. 15.

25 A.H. John, op.cit., p. 48.

26 R.d., pp. 46–7; R.e., p. 68.

27 Information kindly given by R. Craig.

28 NLW, Nevill Papers, A4, letters October–December 1804.

29 Monmouthshire Canal Co. Minutes — information generously provided by P.G. Rattenbury, whose typescript is deposited in the University College Swansea Library Archives.

30 G.R.O., Tennant Papers, D/DT/987/1, f. 170, per R. Craig.

31 A.H. John, op.cit., p. 48; M.V. Symons, *Coal Mining in the Llanelli Area to 1829* (Llanelli, 1979), p. 137.

32 T.M. Hodges, 'Early banking in Cardiff', *Economic History Review*, XVII, 1 and 2 (1948), (reprinted in *Industrial South Wales*, ed. W.E. Minchinton); Bute Papers, John Bird to 2nd Marquess of Bute, 21 September 1823 — excerpt kindly supplied by Dr John Davies; R.h. pp. 370–2.

33 R.g., p. 257.

34 B. of E., L.B. I (S.–L.), 19 June 1841.

35 Cf. A.H. John, op.cit., p. 47; L.S. Pressnell, *Country Banking in the Industrial Revolution* (Oxford, 1956), p. 28; R.h., pp. 416–17.

36 T.M. Hodges, op.cit., p. 89.

37 Information by P.G. Rattenbury (see note 29) respectively from Gwent R.O., D.751/328; *Hereford Journal*, 16 August 1815; id., 7 November 1810; Gwent R.O., D43/2313.

38 B. of E., L.B. I (S.–L.) 24 August 1840; E.H. Brooks, *Chronology of the Tinplate Works of Great Britain* (Cardiff, 1944), p. 8; R.d., p. 47.

39 Cf. R.S. Sayers, op.cit., pp. 187–8.

40 B. of E., L.B. II (S.–L.), 7 October 1845.

41 See R.a., R.c., and R.h., pp. 372–8.

42 R.h., pp. 372, 379–80, 418–20; L.S. Pressnell, op. cit. pp. 129–30; J.E. Wadsworth, *Joint-Stock Banking*, pp. 167, 193.
   The North and South Wales Bank extended southwards only as far as Aberystwyth and Knighton.

43 R.h., pp. 381, 394; P.L. Cottrell, op.cit., p. 206.

44 Cottrell, ibid., pp. 201–2, 204, 220–1; R.h., p. 391.

45 R.h., p. 381.

46 This paragraph is based on a draft written by P.G. Watkin in the late 1940s and kindly made available by him.

47 *Mining Journal*, 31 May 1845.

48 R.h., pp. 388, 393–8.

49 Except where otherwise stated the information is derived from R.h., pp. 382–3, 393–5.

50 E.D. Lewis, *The Rhondda Valleys* (London, 1952), p. 47.

51 Monmouthshire Canal Company Minutes, 6 February 1852, 22 December 1852, 6 October 1854 (notes by P.G. Rattenbury).

52 Unpublished draft by P.G. Watkin.

53 B. of E., L.B. II (S.–L.), 9 October 1847.

54 R.R. Toomey, 'Vivian & Sons, 1809–1924', (Ph.D. thesis, University College Swansea, 1979; Garland Publishing Inc., New York and London, 1985), pp. 200–1.

55 Cf. R.h., pp. 370, 380–1.

56 Monmonthshire Canal Company Minutes, 1 December 1802, per P.G. Rattenbury.

57 A.H. John, op.cit., p. 48; R.R. Toomey, op.cit., p. 197.

58 NLW, Nevill Papers, A4, October–December 1804; XXI, Annual Reports; V, 12 December 1823, 6 February 1824; VII, 9 September 1836; VIII, 20 January and 16, 25, 27, 28 February 1837.

59 R.h., p. 377; cf. J.P. Addis, *The Crawshay Dynasty* (Cardiff, 1957), p. 162; NLW, Crawshay Papers, Box I, 125, 16 February 1822.

60 John Davies, *Cardiff and the Marquesses of Bute* (Cardiff, 1981), pp. 59, 66 fn.; Bute Papers, excerpts on business with banks, generously provided by Dr John Davies.

61 B. of E., L.B. II (S.–L.), 13 September 1845.

62 Gwent R.O., D751–57, per P.G. Rattenbury.

63 Monmouthshire Canal Company Minutes, 1 December 1802, per P.G. Rattenbury.

64 NLW, Nevill Papers, V, 1 November 1824.

65 R.R. Toomey, op.cit., p. 197.

292   NOTES

66 NLW, Nevill Papers, VII, 9 September 1836; id. VIII, 20 January and 16, 25–28 February 1837.

67 A.H. John, op.cit. p. 44.

68 P.R. Reynolds, *Brecon Forest Tramroad* (Swansea, 1981), pp. 46ff.

69 B. of E., L.B. I (S.–L.), 10 March 1841.

70 J. Morris, 'Evan Evans and the Vale of Neath Brewery', *Morgannwg*, IX (1965), 47.

71 R.h., p. 383.

72 R.h., p. 382; cf. R.f., p. 224.

73 R.f., pp. 225–8.

74 R.h., p. 383; cf. D. Morier Evans, *Facts, Failures and Frauds* (London, 1859), pp. 293–4, 360–1.

75 John Davies, op.cit. p. 273.

76 R.R. Toomey, op.cit., p. 201.

77 John Davies, op.cit. p. 274.

78 Unpublished work by P.J. Watkin; see Table 2 above.

79 A.L. Cramp, review in *Economic Journal*, LXXVIII (June 1968), 426; summary of a paper by P.L. Cottrell, *Business History*, XXIV, 1 (March 1982), 109.

80 P.L. Cottrell, *Industrial Finance, 1830–1914*, p. 241; and summary of a paper by P.L. Cottrell, *Business History*, XXIV, 1 (March 1982), 109.

81 D.J. Moss, art. cit., p. 99.

82 A.K. Cairncross, review in *Economic History Review*, XXIX, 1 (February 1976), 157; on north Wales see A.H. Dodd in *Economica*, (Old Series), VI, 16 (March 1926), 18.

83 P. Hudson, 'The role of banks . . . in West Yorkshire', *Business History Reveiw*, LV (1981), 379.

84 Summary of a paper by Charles Munn, *Business History*, XXIV, 1 (March 1982), 107.

85 L.S. Pressnell, op.cit., p. 301.

86 P.J. Watkin, unpublished draft.

87 A.H. John, 'The industrial development of South Wales, 1750–1914', *Colloques Internationaux de C.N.R.S.*, no. 540 (Uppsala, 1972), 521.

88 P.L. Cottrell, op.cit., p. 15; cf A.K. Cairncross, review in *Economic History Review*, XXIX, 1 (February 1976), 158–9.

89 P. Hudson, art. cit., pp. 379, 387, 397, 400.

90 Summary of Cottrell's paper, cit., p. 110.

91 A.H. John, *The Industrial Development of South Wales, 1750–1850*, p. 49.

Farming in South-East Wales c. 1840–80

* I am indebted to Colin Baber and R.O. Roberts for the helpful comments they made on the conference draft of this paper.

1 Many of the ideas expressed in this paragraph owe much to the late Professor A.H. John.

2 D.W. Howell, *Land and People in Nineteenth-Century Wales* (London, 1978), pp. 88–9.

3 The term is used by Professor Hobsbawm in his *Industry and Empire* (Penguin, 1970), ch. 15.

4 Cited in D.W. Howell, op. cit., p. 88.

5 D.W. Howell, op. cit., p. 91.

6 J. Davies and G.E. Mingay, 'Agriculture in an Industrial Environment', Chapter VI in Glanmor Williams and A.H. John, eds., *Industrial Glamorgan*, Vol. 5, *Glamorgan County History* (Cardiff, 1980), p. 298.

7 S(elect) C(ommittee) into the State of Agriculture, P(arliamentary) P(apers), (1836), VIII, part I, q. 4, 319; *Report from the S.C. of the House of Lords into the State of Agriculture in England and Wales*, P.P., V (1837), q. 1, 317. We should note, however, the evidence of J. Buckland in H(ouse) (of) L(ords) R(ecord) O(ffice), Minutes of Evidence, H. of L., 1845, Vol. 13 concerning the South Wales Railway Bill, which stated that very great amounts of provisions shipped from southern Ireland to Bristol were resold there by Bristol middlemen to south Wales merchants and then trans-shipped to Cardiff and Newport in order to reach the mining districts by the canals. Buckland claimed (H. of L. 1845, Vol. 80) that most Irish produce entering Cardiff was imported first into Bristol. Even so, Irish corn was produced more cheaply than corn could be produced in Glamorgan.

8 P.P. (1837), V, qs. 1,317, 2,471, 2,473–2,475.

9 H.L.R.O., Minutes of Evidence, H. of C., Vol. 73 concerning the Vale of Neath Railway Bill.

10 S. Lewis, *A Topographcial Dictionary of Wales* (4th edition, London, 1849), p. 376.

11 H.L.R.O., Minutes of Evidence, H. of C., 1846, Vol. 52 concerning the South Wales Railway Bill.

12 H.L.R.O., Minutes of Evidence, H. of C., Vol. 23, 1862.

13 H.L.R.O., H. of C., Select Committee on Llantrisant and Taff Vale Junction, Vol. 42, 1861.

14 J. Richards, *The Cowbridge Story* (Bridgend, 1956), p. 99; B. Ll. James and D.J. Francis, *Cowbridge and Llanblethian Past and Present* (Barry, 1979), p. 101.

15 *Railways, General Returns*, P.P. (1866), LXIII; P.P. (1867), LXII; P.P. (1867–8), LXII; P.P. (1868–9), LIV; P.P. (1870), LIX; P.P. (1871), LX; P.P. (1874), LIX.

16 T. Bowstead, 'Report on the Farm-Prize Competition of 1872', *Journal of the Royal Agricultural Society of England*, (Second series), VIII (1872), 313.

17 W. Little 'The Agriculture of Glamorganshire', *Journal of the Royal Agricultural Society*, (Second series), XXI (1885), 181.

18 *Report of the R(oyal) C(ommission) on Land in Wales and Monmouthshire*, P.P. (1896), XXXIV, p. 483.

19 Cited in Anon., *Letters from Wales* (London, 1889), p. 199. For a more favourable view as to the usefulness of English Customs see F.M.L. Thompson, 'The Second Agricultural Revolution, 1815–1880', *Economic History Review* (Second series), XXI, no. I (1968), 72.

20 J. Howells, 'The Land Question from a Tenant Farmer's Point of View', *Red Dragon*, II (1882), 81; J. Davies, *Cardiff and the Marquesses of Bute* (Cardiff, 1981), 161–2; A.W. Jones, 'Glamorgan Custom and Tenant Right', *The Agricultural History Review*, 31, part 1 (1983), 13; Id., 'Agriculture and the Rural Community of Glamorgan, *circa* 1830–1896' (Unpublished Ph.D. thesis, University of Wales, 1980), I, p. 327.

21 J. Howells, op. cit., pp. 81, 73.

22 W. Little, op. cit., pp. 181–3; J. Darby, 'On Agriculture of Glamorganshire', *Journal of the Bath and West of England Society* (Third series), XVII (1885–6), 135–7.

23 A.W. Jones, 'Glamorgan Custom and Tenant Right', *The Agricultural History Review,* 31, part 1 (1983), p. 3.

24 P.P. (1896), XXXIV, p. 484; W.Little, op. cit., p. 183.

25 Ibid.

26 J. Darby, op. cit., p. 135. For a comparison between Lincolnshire and Glamorgan Customs, see A.W. Jones, op. cit., pp. 5–6.

27 J. Darby, op. cit., p. 137.

28 Anon., *Letters from Wales,* p. 194.

29 B. Ll. James, 'The "Great Landowners" of Wales in 1873', *National Library of Wales Journal,* XIV, no. 3 (1966), pp. 301–20.

30 Anon., *Letters from Wales,* pp. pp. 195–7. The author of these *Letters* has been correctly identified as J.E. Vincent.

31 D.W. Howell, op. cit., pp. 51, 53.

32 J. Davies, op. cit., pp. 171–3, 168–9.

33 Anon., *Letters from Wales,* p. 196; J. Darby op. cit., p. 137. For rents on large estates in Wales generally see Howell, *op cit.,* pp. 81–2.

34 W. Little, op. cit., p. 172; J. Darby, op. cit., p. 141.

35 P.P., (1870), XIII, p. 22.

36 J. Darby, op. cit., p. 135.

37 J. Davies and G.E. Mingay, op. cit., p. 301.

38 J. Davies, op. cit., pp. 177–8.

39 W. Little, op. cit., p. 176.

40 Cited in Howell, op. cit., p. 76.

41 R.C. on Land in Wales and Monmouthshire, Evidence, P.P., (1894), XXXVI, qs. 170–1.

42 A.W. Jones, 'Agriculture and the Rural Community of Glamorgan, *circa* 1830–1896', (Unpublished Ph.D. thesis, University of Wales, 1980), vol I, p. 298.

43 J. Davies, op. cit., pp. 180–1.

44 W. Little, op. cit., pp. 171–2.

45 C.S. Read, 'On the Farming of South Wales', *Journal of the Royal Agricultural Society of England,* X (1849), 153–4.

46 A.W. Jones, op. cit., p. 58.

47 T. Bowstead, op. cit., pp. 304–12; W. Little op. cit., p. 176.

48 T. Bowstead, op. cit., pp. 304–12; W. Little, op. cit., p. 173.

49 A.W. Jones, op. cit., p. 58 citing H.L.R.O., Minutes of Evidence, H. of C., 1846, vol. 52 concerning the South Wales Railway Bill.

50 Thompson, op. cit., pp. 62–77.

51 P.R.O., Customs 23/2, 23/3, 23/4, 23/5, 23/6.

52 A.W. Jones, op. cit., p. 52: R.E. Prothero, 'Landmarks in British Farming', *Journal of the Royal Agricultural Society of England,* (Third series), III (1892), 30.

53 J.D. Chambers and G.E. Mingay, *The Agricultural Revolution 1750–1880* (London, 1966), p. 176; C.S. Orwin and E.H. Whetham, *History of British Agriculture, 1846–1914* (Newton

Abbot, 1964), pp. 194–200; D.W. Howell 'Welsh Agriculture 1815–1914' (unpublished Ph.D. thesis, University of London, 1970), pp. 315–16; P.P., (1896), XXXIV, pp. 246–8.

54 R.C. on Land in Wales and Monmouthshire, Evidence, P.P., (1896), XXXV, pp. 688–93; Davies and Mingay, op. cit., p. 300.

55 P.R.O., I.R. 3/3, 3/4, M.A.F. 66.

56 A.W. Jones, op. cit., p. 262.

57 J. Davies, op.cit., p. 174, I have found no evidence to support Davies' statement (p. 174) that 'Glamorgan landowners borrowed considerable sums of money under the Improvement of Land Act to undertake drainage schemes'; Davies and Mingay, op. cit., pp. 300–1.

58 W. Little, op. cit., p. 174.

59 D.W. Howell, Land and People in Nineteenth–century Wales, p. 143; J. Darby, op. cit., p. 140.

60 Cited in A.W. Jones, op. cit., p. 55.

61 T. Bowstead, op. cit., pp. 306, 312, 313.

62 J. Darby, op. cit., p. 140; W. Little, op. cit., pp. 179–80.

63 C.S. Read, op. cit., p. 154.

64 T. Bowstead, op. cit., pp. 306, 311; W. Little, op. cit., pp. 177–8.

65 T. Bowstead, op. cit., p. 320.

66 W. Little, op. cit., p. 176.

67 A.W. Jones, op. cit., p. 70.

68 J.D. Chambers and G.E. Mingay, op. cit., pp. 183–4.

69 J. Darby, op. cit., p. 141.

70 E.L. Jones, 'The Changing Basis of English Agricultural Prosperity, 1853–73', Agricultural History Review, XXI (1962), 104–8.

71 A.W. Jones, 'Agriculture and the Rural Community of Glamorgan, circa 1830–1896', op. cit., pp. 71–2.

72 T. Bowstead, op. cit., p. 313.

73 A.W. Jones, op. cit., p. 86.

74 J. Darby, op. cit., p. 137.

75 W. Little, op. cit., p. 182.

76 W. Fothergill, 'The Farming of Monmouthshire', Journal of the Royal Agricultural Society of England, (Second series), VI (1870), 290–6; T. Bowstead, op. cit., pp. 312–15.

77 NLW, Tredegar Park MS. 72/139–41: cattle show bills, 1842 and 1851.

78 T. Bowstead, op. cit., pp. 280, 291–300.

79 W. Fothergill op. cit., p. 297.

80 P.P., (1896), XXXV, pp. 688–93.

81 P.R.O., I.R. 3/3, 3/4.

82 W. Fothergill, op. cit., pp. 290–1, 295.

83 Ibid., pp. 290–3; T. Bowstead, op. cit., p. 291.

84 A.W. Jones, op. cit., pp. 76–7.

85 C.S. Read, op. cit., pp. 152–3.

86 Ibid.; C.R.M. Talbot, *Remarks on the Advantages of the East Lothian System of Farming as Compared with the System Pursued in the Vicinity of Swansea* (London, 1850).

87 W. Little, op. cit., p. 184.

88 J. Darby, op. cit., p. 158.

89 W. Little, op. cit., p. 184; C.S. Read, op. cit., p. 152. Read was informed that there was a movement on foot among the better class of farmers to introduce better breeds of cattle and sheep.

90 J. Darby, op. cit., pp. 155–6.

91 D.W. Howell, op. cit., pp. 119–20.

92 Ibid., pp. 124–7, 142, 144.

93 J. Darby, op. cit., pp. 161–4.

94 J. Davies and G.E. Mingay, op. cit., p. 305.

95 H.L.R.O., Minutes of Evidence of H. of C., 1845, vol. 80 concerning the South Wales Railway Bill: evidence of James Buckland; J. Williams, 'On the Connection between the West of England and South Wales', *Journal of the Bath and West of England Society*, VIII (1860), 56.

96 Robin Craig and R.O. Roberts both made helpful comments relating to this point. Robin Craig also directed my attention to the 'railway' material at the House of Lords Record Office.

Capital Formation by Railways in South Wales 1836–1914

1 In some areas, and south Wales was easily the most important, the apparently trivial change of preposition from 'by' to 'in', could have significant consequences in that it would bring within the scope of the enquiry the private traders' wagon. See *Report on the Number Capacity and Construction of Private Traders' Railway Wagons in Great Britain at 1st August, 1918*, Statistical Department, Board of Trade (1919).

2 The series are found in A.K. Cairncross, *Home and Foreign Investment, 1870–1913* (Cambridge, 1953), pp. 135–41; R.C.O. Matthews, *A Study in Trade-Cycle History: Economic Fluctuations in Great Britain, 1833–1842*, (Cambridge, 1954), pp. 106–13, 120–6; C.H. Feinstein, 'Income and Investment in the United Kingdom, 1856–1914', *Economic Journal*, LXXI (1961), 370. Also B.R. Mitchell and Phyllis Deane, *Abstract of British Historical Statistics* (Cambridge, 1962), pp. 373–4; B.R. Mitchell, 'The Coming of the Railway and United Kingdom Economic Growth', *Journal of Economic History*, XXIV (1964), 315–36; A.G. Kenwood, 'Railway Investment in Britain, 1825–1875', *Economica*, (New Series) XXXII (1965), 313–22; G.R. Hawke, *Railways and Economic Growth in England and Wales 1840–1870* (Oxford, 1970) pp. 197–212; C.H. Feinstein, *National Income, Expenditure and Output of the United Kingdom, 1855–1965* (Cambridge, 1972), pp. 186–7, 189, 201, 291–3. These are variously for the United Kingdom, Great Britain and England and Wales.

3 Especially useful are: E.T. MacDermot, *History of the Great Western Railway* (1927), revised C.R. Clinker (1964); and D.S.M. Barrie, 'South Wales'; Peter E. Baughan, 'North and Mid Wales'; Rex Christiansen, 'Thames and Severn', being vols. XII, XI and XIII, *A Regional History of Railways of Great Britain* (Newton Abbot, 1980 and 1981)..

4 Hawke, op. cit., p. 1; A.G. Kenwood, 'Fixed Capital Formation on Merseyside, 1800–1913', *Economic History Review*, (Second series), XXXI (1978), 214–37. The same author provides a series of railway capital formation in north-eastern England in, 'Capital Investment in North Eastern England, 1820–1913' (unpublished Ph.D. thesis, University of London, 1962). I owe a

debt of gratitude to Dr Kenwood, for his helpful comments, assistance and his generosity in providing me with information on north-east England and south Wales.

5 Before reorganization in 1974, the counties of Monmouth, Glamorgan, Carmarthen and Pembroke. As the total area is nearly the same, the old names will be used to avoid confusion.

6 E.g., South Wales Railway; Brecon and Merthyr Railway.

7 C.E. Lee, *The Evolution of Railways* (Second edition, 1943), p. 104; and *The First Passenger Railway* (1942), p. 3; Michael Robbins, *The Railway Age* (Harmondsworth, 1965), p. 12.

8 To see that it is quite the opposite, see 'ibid' pp. 11–17; Jack Simmons, *The Railway in England and Wales, 1830–1914* (Leicester, 1978), I, pp. 17–21.

9 Robbins, op. cit., p. 12.

10 C.H. Newton, *Railway Accounts* (1930), p. 3.

11 D.S. Barrie, *The Barry Railway* (Lingfield, Surrey, 1962), pp. 176–8.

12 C.H. Newton, op. cit., pp. 3, 8.

13 E.g., The Cardiff Railway.

14 E.g., The Taff Vale Railway.

15 E.g., The Barry Railway; in the original incorporation of 1884, most appropriately the Barry Docks and Railway Company.

16 E.g., Alexandra (Newport and South Wales) Docks and Railway Company.

17 N.H. Appleby and G.W.R., *Great Western Ports* (1925).

18 W.E. Simnett, *Railway Amalgamation in Great Britain,* (1923), pp. 50–4.

19 C.H. Newton, op. cit., p. 10.

20 Hence the permanent way, but for the estimates of the life of assets used by the LNER (London and North Eastern Railway) in the 1920s, see Newton, op. cit., p. 185. Interestingly, the figure for the permanent way is 21 and one-half years, for steam locomotives 33 and one-third, and dock buildings, 100 years. Many of these assets exceeded their estimated lives in practice.

21 P.R.O. RAIL 1110 — until transfer to P.R.O. these were B.T.H.R. RAC 1.

22 P.R.O. PER 3; PER 2; PER 7; RAIL 1038; 1040–56, 1140–4.

23 Simnett, *Railway Amalgamation,* p. 5. The number of railways in south Wales which survived to come under the scope of the Railways Act was 8 constituent and 12 subsidiary companies.

24 Railway accounting practice and malpractice have been particularly well assessed by Harold Pollins, 'Aspects of Railway Accounting before 1868', in A.C. Littleton and B.S. Yamey, eds. *Studies in the History of Accounting* (1956), pp. 138–61; Seymour Broadbridge, *Studies in Railway Expansion and the Capital Market in England 1825–1873* (1970), pp. 176–95.

25 For the distinction between the different categories of Parliamentary enactments, see T.I. Jeffreys Jones, *Acts of Parliament Concerning Wales* (Cardiff, 1959), pp. ix–xii. The term 'Special' is used throughout to describe those Acts by which railways gained incorporation and further powers. This follows the practice of the Railway Companies (Accounts and Returns) Act, 1911. Under the Regulation of Railways Act, 1868, capital powers were described simply under the heading of Acts of Parliament. The term 'General' requires no comment.

26 Railway Regulation Act (1844, c. 85); Companies Clauses Consolidation Act (1845, c. 16); Railways Clauses Consolidation Act (1845, c. 20); Pollins, op. cit., 142; C.H. Newton, op. cit., p. 1.

27 C.H. Newton, op. cit., p. 2.

28 Ibid.

29 Pollins, op. cit., pp. 138–9; C.H. Newton, op. cit., p. 3.

30 For a classic treatment not only of railway accounts but also of finance, see C.C. Wang, *Legislative Regulation of Railway Finance in England* (Urbana, Illinois, 1918); G.A. Lee, 'The Concept of Profit in British Accounting, 1760–1900', *Business History Review,* XLIX 1 (1975), 187–25.

31 Pollins, op. cit., p. 138.

32 Pollins, op. cit., pp. 149–55.

33 R. Price Williams, 'The Maintenance and Renewal of Railway Rolling Stock', *Minutes of Proceedings of the Institution of Civil Engineers* XXX (1869–70), pp. 136–214; 'The Maintenance and Renewal of Waterworks', *Proceedings,* CXLVIII, II (1901–2), 305–25 (quotation is from p. 311); 'On the Serviceable Life and Average Annual Cost of Locomotives in Great Britain', *Proceedings,* CLXXV, I, (1908–9), 252–75.

34 B.R. Mitchell, 'The Coming of the Railway and United Kingdom Growth', *Journal of Economic History,* XXIV (1964), 336.

35 Central Statistical Office, *National Income Statistics, Sources and Methods,* (1965), pp. 281–2.

36 R. Price Williams, 'The Maintenance and Renewal of Railway Rolling Stock', *Minutes of Proceedings of the Institution of Civil Engineers,* XXV (1869–70), 136–48.

37 P.A. Stone, 'A Survey of the Annual Costs of Contractors' Mechanical Plant', *Journal of Industrial Economics,* IV (1956), 129–50.

38 A.K. Cairncross, op. cit., pp. 136–7: Kenwood, 'Railway Investment in Britain', 1825–1875, *Economica* (New Series), XXXII (1965), 313–14.

39 Harold Pollins, 'A Note on Railway Constructional Costs, 1825–50', *Economica,* (New Series), XIX (1952), 407, shows the importance of the cost of land for railways in Great Britain in the early period. For example, it cost the Taff Vale 10.5 per cent (a low figure) of its total expenditure, up to 1841, and the South Wales 13.0 per cent (about average) up to 1854. The corresponding figure for the Great Western up to 1841 was 12.7 per cent.

40 Anual depreciation figures used by the LNER before 1930 support 2 per cent as not out of line. See C.H. Newton, op. cit., p. 185. Buildings, brick and stone 1 per cent; swing bridges 2 per cent; machinery and plant 4 per cent; jetties 3 per cent; dock gates 2 per cent; timber structures 3 per cent; floating craft 3 per cent.

41 C.S. Howells, *Transport Facilities in South Wales and Monmouthshire* (Cardiff, 1911), pp. 30–1.

42 The South Wales Railway Act, (1845, CXC L. and P.), clause 19. In fact the South Wales Railway was from the outset very much a creature of the Great Western Railway Its prospectus was issued in 1844 from the Great Western's London office, the Great Western subscribed 20 per cent of the capital, the Great Western's chairman was the new company's chairman, the Great Western nominated six directors and had the powers to make agreements. The leasing powers in the Act were not fully exercised and gave rise to two arbitration awards in 1854 (P.R.O. RAIL, 640/642. B.T.H.R. SOW 3/3) and 1859 (R.R.O. RAIL 640/643. B.T.H.R. 50W 3/4).

43 Correspondence between Frederick Saunders and Sir Daniel Gooch, 1859. P.R.O. RAIL 640/53 (B.T.H.R. SOW 5/1); R. Price Willians, art. cit., p. 151; and Great Western Railway, Reports and Accounts, P.R.O. RAIL 1110/421 (B.T.H.R. RAC 1/385).

44 South Wales Railway, Reports and Accounts, half-year ended 31 December 1850. P.R.O RAIL 1110/431 (B.T.H.R. RAC 1/385).

45 E.T. MacDermot, *History,* Appendix I.

Fixed Capital Formation in the Ports of the South Wales Coalfield, 1850–1913

1 Significant changes had also taken place in the relative importance of the different south Wales' ports before 1850. By 1841 Swansea had lost its pre-eminence in the sea-coal trade to Newport and Cardiff. At first the increase of coal shipments was most marked from Newport, but following the opening of the West Bute dock in Cardiff in 1839 and the completion of the construction of the Taff Vale railway to Cardiff in 1842, the shipment of coal through Cardiff forged ahead of that of Newport, reaching 750,000 tons in 1850 compared to 600,000 tons for Newport. See J.H. Morris and L.J. Williams, *The South Wales Coal Industry 1841–1875* (University of Wales Press, 1958), pp. 11, 26–32.

2 A private dock company had begun constructing the South Dock at Swansea in opposition to the town council and the Harbour Trust in 1852. It soon ran into financial difficulties and in 1857 the dock was transferred to the Harbour Trustees. It was completed and opened in 1859. See R.H. Edwards, 'Some Historical Notes on the Docks in South Wales', *Proceedings of the South Wales and Monmouthshire Railways and Docks Literary and Debating Society,* Session 1956–57, No. 14.

3 Gross fixed capital formation in the docks and harbours of south Wales totalled £23.8million in current prices between 1850 and 1913. For the Welsh economy as a whole it totalled just over £26million.

4 The occupational data in the decennial census returns give a rough guide as to the numbers employed in the ports of south Wales. The numbers of males and females aged 10 years and above employed as dock and wharf labourers, and as officials and servants of harbour, dock, wharf, and lighthouse authorities was 1,468 in 1871, 3,471 in 1891, and 10,767 in 1911.

5 We have not included the net series in figure 1 because it overlaps the gross series in the early years covered by the data. However, the major turning-points in the net capital formation series fall in the same years as those for the gross series throughout the whole period covered by the two sets of statistics. This can be checked by referring to the table in the Appendix.

6 The previous burst of dock construction in south Wales had occurred in Cardiff and Newport during the late 1830s and early 1840s.

7 In the following brief description of dock and harbour construction in south Wales between 1850 and 1913, the details are taken from the following works: *A History of the Alexandra (Newport) Dock Company from AD1864 to AD1877* (Newport, 1882); J.H. Bird, *The Major Seaports of the United Kingdom* (1963); E.L. Chappell, *History of the Port of Cardiff* (Cardiff, 1939); J.W. Dawson, *Commerce and Customs. A History of the Ports of Newport and Caerleon* (Newport, 1932); R.H. Edwards, op. cit; J.H. Morris and L.J. Williams, op. cit; *Newport Harbour Commission 1836–1936* (Newport, 1936); Sir D.J. Owen, *The Origin and Development of the Ports of the United Kingdom* (1939); 'The Alexandra (Newport and South Wales) Docks and Railway', *Great Western Railway Magazine,* (June 1922).

8 L.S. Higgins, 'The Porthcawl Dock', *The Glamorgan Gazette,* (8 July, 1966).

9 L.F.V. Harcourt, *Harbours and Docks, their Physical Features, History, Construction, Equipment and Maintenance, with Statistics as to their Commercial Development* (Oxford, 1885), Vol. 1, p. 475. The technical nature of the changeover from steam-driven machinery to hydraulic machinery is described in W.H. Hunter, *Dock and Lock Machinery* (1921). See also Harcourt, op. cit., pp. 483–4.

10 See S. Kuznets, 'Long Swings in Population Growth and Related Economic Variables', *Proceedings of the American Philosophical Society,* 102, 1 (February, 1958), 25–52. Reprinted in S. Kuznets, *Economic Growth and Structure: Selected Essays* (1966), pp. 328–78.

11 The figures of net capital expenditure on the railways of south Wales are taken from T.W. Taylor, op. cit., Table, Appendix 1 (see pp. 110–11).

12 The housing index for the south Wales coalfield is taken from J. Parry Lewis, *Building Cycles and Britain's Growth* (1965), Col. (1), Table, Appendix 4, pp. 316–7. See also J. Hamish Richards and J. Parry Lewis, 'House-Building in the South Wales Coalfield, 1851–1913', *The Manchester School,* XXIV (1956), 289–300.

13 B.R. Mitchell and P. Deane, *Abstract of British Historical Statistics* (Cambridge, 1962), Table, p. 373. The dock and harbour investment figures for Great Britain are taken from an unpublished paper by B.R. Mitchell which were used in the construction of the Feinstein estimates.

14 For estimates of gross fixed capital formation in residential building it would be necessary to have estimates of capital expenditures on additions and alterations to existing properties as well as expenditures on the repair and upkeep of the existing housing stock.

15 B. Thomas, 'Wales and the Atlantic Economy', in B. Thomas, (ed.), *The Welsh Economy. Studies in Expansion* (Cardiff, 1962), pp. 1–29; B. Thomas, *Migration and Urban Development* (1972), pp. 170–8; J. Hamish Richards and J. Parry Lewis, op. cit., p. 295.

16 The link between transport developments and building has been analysed by W. Isard. See, for example, W. Isard, 'A Neglected Cycle: the Transport-Building Cycle', *Review of Economic Statistics,* (November 1942); and W. Isard, 'Transport Development and Building Cycles', *Quarterly Journal of Economics,* (November 1942).

17 Labour migration into the south Wales coalfield was first dealt with by B. Thomas in his article 'Labour Migration into Glamorganshire, 1861–1911', *Economica,* (November 1930). He subsequently expanded this analysis in his later works. See footnote 16 above.

18 J. Parry Lewis, op. cit., p. 97. See also, Hamish Richards, 'The Deomgraphic Factor in the Demand for Housing', in Hamish Richards, (ed.), *Population, Factor Movements and Economic Development. Studies presented to Brinley Thomas* (Cardiff, 1976), pp. 196–208. The demand for housing is also discussed at length in M.J. Daunton, *Coal Metropolis: Cardiff 1870–1914* (Leicester, 1977).

Labour and Technology in South Wales, 1870–1914

1 R. Price, *Masters, Unions and Men. Work Control in Building and the Rise of Labour 1830–1914* (Cambridge, 1980).

2 D. Montgomery, *Workers' Control in America* (Cambridge, 1979) and R. Harrison, ed., *Independent Collier. The Coal Miner as Archetypal Proletarian Reconsidered* (Hassocks, 1978). The phrase is, of course, from Carter Goodrich's *The Frontier of Control. A Study in British Workshop Politics* (New York, 1920).

3 Price, op. cit., p. 4.

4 This view is most obviously associated with the work of D.N. McCloskey: see *Economic Maturity and Entrepreneurial Decline: British Iron and Steel 1870–1913* (Cambridge, Mass., 1973); *Enterprise and Trade in Victorian Britain. Essays in Historical Economics* (London, 1981); and, with L. Sandberg, 'From damnation to redemption: judgements on the late Victorian entrepreneur', *Explorations in Economic History,* IX (1971).

5 H.J. Habakkuk, *American and British Technology in the Nineteenth Century* (Cambridge, 1962); P.A. David, *Technical Choice, Innovation and Economic Growth. Essays on American and British Experience in the Nineteenth Century* (London, 1975); N. Rosenberg, *Perspectives on Technology* (Cambridge, 1976); C.K. Harley, 'Skilled labour and the choice of technique in Edwardian industry', *Explorations in Economic History*, XI (1974).

6 These comments are based upon C.R. Littler, *The Development of the Labour Process in Capitalist Societies. A Comparative Study of Work Organisation in Britain, Japan and the USA* (London, 1982); R.C. Edwards, *The Contested Terrain. The Transformation of the Workplace in the Twentieth Century* (London, 1979); H.A. Turner, *Trade Union Growth, Structure and Policy. A Comparative Study of the Cotton Unions* (London, 1962); W.H. Lazonick, 'Production relations, labor productivity, and choice and technique: British and U.S. cotton spinning', *Journal of Economic History*, XLI (1981); R.C. Edwards, M. Reich, D.M. Gordon, eds., *Labor Market Segmentation* (London, 1975).

7 Lazonick, loc. cit. and 'Industrial relations and technical change: the case of the self-acting mule', *Cambridge Journal of Economics*, III (1979): for the neo-classical view see L. Sandberg, *Lancashire in Decline. A Study in Entrepreneurship, Technology, and International Trade* (Columbia, Ohio, 1974).

8 This section is based upon my 'Cardiff Coal Trimmers Union, 1888–1914', *Llafur*, II (1978).

9 N.B. Dearle, *Industrial Training, with Special Reference to the Conditions prevailing in London* (London, 1914), Chapters II, III–VI.

10 This appears clearly in Lazonick's comparison of mule-spinning in the cotton industry of Lancashire and Massachusetts; again, plumbers in London were recruited by mateship, and in the provinces as apprentices.

11 This and other variations in the labour system in south Wales and the north-east of England are discussed in my paper 'Down the pit: work in the Great Northern and south Wales coalfields, 1870–1914', *Economic History Review*, (2nd series),XXXIV (1981).

12 C. More, *Skill and the English Working Class 1870–1914* (London, 1980), p. 119.

13 Ibid., pp. 119–20; see also K. Stone., 'The origins of job structures in the steel industry', in Edwards, Reich and Gordon, eds., *Labor Market Segmentation*.

14 The comments which follow are based upon a number of readily available sources, and do not claim any originality: J.H. Jones, *The Tinplate Industry, with Special Reference to its Relations with the Iron and Steel Industries. A Study in Economic Organisation* (London, 1914); W.E. Minchinton, *The British Tinplate Industry. A History* (Oxford, 1957); P.S. Thomas, *Industrial Relations. A Short Study of the Relations between Employers and Employed in Swansea and Neighbourhood, from about 1800 to Recent Times* (Cardiff, 1940); W. Robson Brown, *Tinplate* (Swansea, 1936); P.P. 1912–13 XXVI, *Report on the Conditions of Employment in the Manufacture of Tinplate with Special Reference to the Process of Tinning: Report of an Inquiry by the Board of Trade into the Conditions of Apprenticeship and Industrial Training in Various Trades and Occupations of the United Kingdom* (1915); J. Percy, *Metallurgy. The Art of Extracting Metals from their Ores and Adapting them to Various Purposes of Manufacture* (London, 1864); R. Hunt, *Ure's Dictionary of Arts, Manufactures and Mines, containing a Clear Exposition of their Principles and Practices* (London, 1875); British Library of Political and Economic Science. Webb Trade Union Collection E, Section A, Volume XX.

15 C. More, op. cit., pp. 127–8.

16 See my 'Jack ashore. Seaman in Cardiff before 1914', *Welsh History Review*, IX (1978).

Growth in the Coal Industry: the Cases of Powell Duffryn and the Ocean Coal Company, 1864–1913

1 L.J. Williams, 'The Coal Industry, 1750–1914', Chapter IV in Glanmor Williams and A.H. John, eds., *Industrial Glamorgan*, Vol. V, *Glamorgan County History* (Cardiff, 1980), p. 194.

2 Each separate owner listed is considered to be a separate undertaking. This may understate the number of large undertakings where subsidiary companies still retained a separate legal identity.

3. L.J. Williams, op. cit., pp. 193–5.

4 This was the valuation placed on the Aberdare and Tredegar collieries of the Powells by T.E. Forster, William Armstrong and George Elliot in 1863.

5 Glamorgan Record Office (GRO), D/D NCB 23 — Powell Duffryn Cost Book July 1864–June 1866. Output figures prior to 1872 were given in tons of 2520 lbs. (i.e., 21 cwts. of 120 lbs. each), and have therefore been converted to statute tons to make them comparable with later figures.

6 E.M. Hann, *A Brief History of the Powell Duffryn Steam Coal Company 1864–1921* (no information), pp. 5–6.

7 The five collieries and their output levels were as follows: New Tredegar No. 2 Pit — 185,548 tons; Elliot (West) — 184,171; Aberaman — 182,038; Fforchaman — 163,610; and Cwmneol — 162,015.

8 The output of the Aberdare and Rhymney collieries varied over the period as follows: (output and as per cent of total):

	Aberdare Collieries	Rhymney Collieries
1885	1,073,317 tons (78.5%)	294,370 tons (21.5%)
1900	1,076,469 tons (55.6%)	861,437 tons (44.4%)
1913	1,362,240 tons (35.2%)	2,511,540 tons (64.8%)

9 *The Powell Duffryn Steam Coal Co. Ltd., 1864–1914* (Published by the company, c.1914), p. 20.

10 Note that in the period 1899–1906, the dividend of 7 per cent on ordinary shares was the maximum allowed whilst the debentures were still outstanding. These debentures were paid off at the beginning of 1907 when the company's share capital was rearranged and increased.

11 J.H. Morris & L.J. Williams, *The South Wales Coal Industry 1841–1875* (Cardiff, 1958), p. 161.

12 The original purchase price for the Powell collieries was reduced by £52,020 after a court case, due to the yearly operating cost of the collieries being understated at the time of purchase by over £11,000 (see Morris & Williams, ibid., pp. 161–2). Further, only £120,000 of the original £125,000 purchase price for the Aberaman estate was actually paid, due to the removal of timber and other items by Crawshay Bailey, and the purchase price for Cwmneol and Fforchaman was reduced by £10,000 when it was found that the Cwmneol workings had trespassed into part of the Abergwawr property (E.M. Hann, op. cit., p. 6). Thus it would appear that the actual amount paid for these collieries was £512,730, though R. Walters, 'Capital Formation in the South Wales Coal Industry, 1840–1914', *Welsh History Review*, 10 (1980), 74, gives the total purchase price at £533,625.

13 According to Walters, art. cit., all of the original share capital of £500,000 had been called up by 1872. However, the Summary of Capital & Shares for the 10 March 1874 records that only £4,800 had been called up on each £5,000 share. Further, fifteen preference shares, value £1,500 had been returned making the paid-up capital at this date £578,500 compared to the authorized capital of £600,000. (See PRO, BT31 30728/1487c).

14 By a Special resolution of 30 September 1875 the directors were empowered to borrow this sum (see PRO BT31 30728/1478c). According to Walters, art. cit., p. 76, the Aberaman Estate had previously been mortgaged in 1868 for £60,000 and the £70,000 mortgage was renewed in 1883, and finally paid off by an issue of debentures in 1889.

15 E.M. Hann, op. cit., pp. 7–10.

16 Ibid., p. 10. Note that Walters, art. cit., p. 82, states that Powell Duffryn 'had overdrafts of up to £30,000 at Glyn Mills, Currie & Co., from time to time for most of the period 1864–93'.

17 E.M. Hann, op. cit., p. 11.

18 Ibid., op. cit., p. 6.

19 Ibid., p. 12 and Powell Duffryn Cost Books (GRO).

20 E.M. Hann, op. cit., p. 12.

21 R. Walters, art. cit., p. 90.

22 E.M. Hann, op. cit., p. 17, gives the cost of these operations as £35,000 for the period 1890–3. However, the company's cost books give figures for the years 1892–6 amounting in total to £32,756 (GRO D/D NCB 23).

23 E.M. Hann, op. cit., p. 16.

24 GRO D/D Ra 11/476–513 — Subscription List for issue of £50,000 of 5 per cent debentures — Powell Duffryn Steam Coal Co. Ltd., November 1897.

25 The information contained in this section is based mainly on I. Thomas, *Top Sawyer* (1938), pp. 145–57, and the output records of the Ocean collieries held at the Glamorgan Record Office.

26 The five original partners were J. Osborne Riches (coal exporter), Thomas Webb, Morgan Joseph (engineer), Benjamin Howell and Ezra Roberts.

27 I. Thomas, op. cit., p. 147.

28 R. Walters, art. cit., p. 72.

29 Advertisement for 'Ocean (Merthyr) Steam Coal' in *South Wales Coal Annual for 1916* (Cardiff), p. xxxix.

30 *Royal Commission on the Coal Industry* (Sankey Commission) 1919, (Cmd. 360), q. 9,864.

31 A.P. Barnett & D. Willson-Lloyd, eds., *The South Wales Coalfield* (Cardiff, c.1921), p. 33.

Trade and Shipping in South Wales — the Radcliffe Company, 1882–1921

1 *Rebirth of a Nation: Wales 1880–1980* (Oxford, 1981).

2 L.H. Jenks, *The Migration of British Capital to 1875* (London, 1963), p. 334.

3 Gwyn A. Williams, 'Dic Penderyn: The making of a Welsh working class martyr', *Llafur*, II, 3 (1978), 110.

4 H.S. Appleyard and P.M. Heaton, *The Baron Glanely of St Fagan's and W.J. Tatem Ltd.* (Kendal, no date), p. 3.

5 L.S. Higgins, 'The rise and decline of Porthcawl Dock', *Mariner's Mirror*, 50, No. 4 (November 1964), 319–27.

6 A. & R. Long, *A Shipping Venture: Turnbull Scott & Company, 1872–1972* (London, 1974), p. 103.

7 For an early authoritative endorsement of limited liability in the shipping industry, see *The Economist* (2 April 1864), p. 415.

8 On single ship companies, see J.B. Jeffreys, 'The denomination and character of shares, 1855–1885', *Economic History Review*, XVI (1946), 53–4; P.L. Cottrell, 'The Steamship on the Mersey, 1815–1880: investment and ownership', *Shipping, Trade and Commerce: essays in memory of Ralph Davis*, edited by D.H. Aldcroft and P.L. Cottrell, (Leicester, 1981), pp. 137–63; and P.L. Payne, *The Early Scottish Limited Companies, 1856–1895: an historical and analytical survey* (Edinburgh, 1980), pp. 66–72.

9 On '64thers' see *Maritime Review*, (13 April 1904), p. 186.

10 Brokerages, both on ships and bunkers, accrued to the partners rather than the shareholders and formed an important element in Radcliffe revenue, as can be seen in Table 3, columns (f) and (h) (see pp. 188–9). Moreover, when new ships were ordered payments to shipbuilders were normally by instalments often extending over several years, so that the firm enjoyed an accession of liquidity between the time when shares in a new company were fully subscribed, and the last instalment of the cost of the ship was paid. Additionally, shipbuilders often gave commission to those who placed orders with them for new tonnage. Such commission payments accrued to the partners, not the shareholders.

11 There were striking similarities in the pattern of investment in shipping and coal-mining in south Wales. See J.H. Morris and L.J. Williams, *The South Wales Coal Industry 1841–1875* (Cardiff, 1958), pp. 152–62. Morris and Williams stress the importance of capital which flowed into Wales from outside the Principality, pp. 153–4.

12 See, for example, the evidence given by Cardiff Chamber of Commerce to *Royal Commission on Depression in Trade and Industry*, P.P. XXI (1886), p. 79.

13 An editorial in *Maritime Review*, (24 February 1904), p. 42, comments upon how few shipping investors there were in Cardiff, apart from ship repairers, ships' stores' purveyors, and the owners of small collieries, who might 'have a little flutter'. Indeed, the *Review* suggests that investment was, by this time 'extremely unpopular' in the district, whereas some towns 'up North could be painted red with their faith in the dividend-paying capacity of Cardiff's leviathans'.

14 Including Edward Nicholl destined to become a leading Cardiff shipowner, and Captain Thomas Hesketh who gave evidence to the *Select Committee on the Manning of Merchant Ships*, P.P. XL–XLI (1896).

15 On Radcliffe's treatment of apprentices, see, for example, Captain H.C. Fellingham's letter in *Sea Breezes*, 57, No. 445 (January 1983), 73.

16 On trimming at Cardiff, see Martin Daunton, 'The Cardiff Coal Trimmer's Union, 1888–1914', *Llafur*, II, 3 (1978), 10–23.

17 On the development of this trade see L. Siegelbaum, 'The Odessa grain trade: a case study in urban growth and development in Tsarist Russia', *Journal of European Economic History*, IX (Spring, 1980), 113–51.

18 S.B. Saul, *The Myth of the Great Depression 1873–1906* (London, 1969), passim.

19 The incidence of Excess Profit Duty hit shipowners especially hard and the legislation expressly discriminated against them. On this, see C.E. Fayle, *The War and the Shipping Industry* (London, 1927), pp. 305–6, who pointed out that shipowners alone had to pay the full percentage due without adjustments. See also J.S. Boswell & B.R. Jones, 'Patriots or Profiteers? British Businessmen and the First World War', *Journal of European Economic History*, XI (1982), 423–45.

20 Radcliffe's activities included 'regular lines running from Odessa to Rotterdam, and from New Orleans to Rotterdam', according to an article in Daniel Radcliffe on *Cardiff Commercially Considered* (London, 1889), p. 73.

21 From a schedule of investments at the date of Henry Radcliffe's death on 16 December 1921, prepared by Richard Leyshon & Co., accountants and auditors, Cardiff in January 1922, the deceased held 912 shares in twelve active shipping companies managed by Evan Thomas, Radcliffe & Co., valued at £63,420, and 1481 shares valued at £704,192 in nineteen shipping companies managed by the firm which were then in liquidation.

22 I am most grateful to Dr J. Geraint Jenkins and his helpful staff at the Welsh Industrial and Maritime Museum, Cardiff, for their generous assistance. Mr Peter Frank and Dr S. Jones are also thanked for making available the printed accounts and circulars preserved by a Whitby investor in Radcliffe shipping companies.

The Climacteric of the 1890s

1 E.H. Phelps Brown and S.H. Handfield-Jones, 'The Climacteric of the 1890s', *Oxford Economic Papers*, IV (1952).

2 D.H. Aldcroft, 'The Entrepreneur and the British economy, 1870–1914', *Economic History Review*, XVII (1964).

3 D.J. Coppock, 'The Climacteric of the 1870s', *Manchester School*, XXIV (1956).

4 D.N. McCloskey and L.G. Sandberg, 'From Damnation to redemption: Judgements on the late Victorian Entrepreneur', *Explorations in Economic History*, IX (1971); Some recent manifestations of a large and growing literature can be seen in the section on Victorian Britain in *Journal of Economic History*, XLII (March 1982) 87–118.

5 R.H. Hayes and D.A. Garvin, 'Managing as if tomorrow mattered', *Harvard Business Review*, 60, 3 (1982).

6 C. Wilson, 'Economy and Society in late Victorian Britain', *Economic History Review*, XVII (1965).

7 Ibid., p. 198.

8 D.H. Aldcroft and H.W. Richardson, *The British Economy, 1870–1939* (London, 1969), tables on pp. 4, 11 and the sources given for them.

9 K.O. Morgan, *Rebirth of a Nation, Wales, 1880–1980*, (Oxford, 1981), Chapter 4.

10 The most recent comprehensive attempt has been the C.H. Feinstein, *Statistical Tables of National Income, Expenditure and Ouput of the U.K., 1855–1965* (Cambridge, 1976).

11 Trevor Boyns, *Labour Productivity in the British Coal Industry, 1874–1913* (U. of Wales, Ph.D. 1982).

12 A.J. Taylor, 'Labour Productivity and Technological Innovation in the British Coal Industry, 1850–1914', *Economic History Review*, XIV (August 1961).

13 Ibid., pp. 48–51.

14 Rhodri Walters, 'Labour Productivity in the South Wales Steam-coal Industry, 1870–1914', *Economic History Review*, XXVIII, 2 (May 1975), 281–2.

15 The following draws heavily on Trevor Boyns, op. cit..

16 Trevor Boyns, op. cit., Chapter 1.

17 This paragraph is based on B. Thomas, 'Wales and the Atlantic Economy' as reprinted in Brinley Thomas, *The Welsh Economy* (Cardiff, 1962).

18 J. Hamish Richards and J. Parry Lewis, 'House Building in the South Wales Coalfield, 1851–1913', *Manchester School*, XXIV (1956), 289–300; J. Parry Lewis, *Building Cycles and British Growth* (1956), esp. Appendix 4 and Chapter 8..

19 Ernest Carter, *An Historical Geography of the Railways of the British Isles* (1959), Chapters 14 and 15.

20 Tom Taylor, 'Capital Formation by Railways in South Wales, 1836–1914', Appendix 1 (see pp. 110–13).

21 M.J. Daunton, *Coal Metropolis: Cardiff, 1870–1914* (Leicester, 1977), p. 28.

22 *Western Mail* (1 January 1901).

23 H.S. Jevons, *The British Coal Trade* (1915), pp. 109, 111.

24 Quoted in M.J. Daunton, op. cit., p. 37.

The First World War and Government Coal Control

1 Coal Industry Commission. Command 359, 360, 361 (1919).

2 K.O. Morgan, 'The New Liberalism and the Challenge of Labour: the Welsh experience 1885–1929'. *Welsh History Review*, 6, No. 3 (June 1973), 304.

3 J. Thomas, 'The South Wales Coalfield during Government control'. (M.A. thesis, University College Cardiff, 1925).

4 E.D. Lewis, *The Rhondda Valleys* (London, 1959), p. 249.

5 CG, Vol. 109, 20.

6 CG, Vol. 109, 873.

7 C.J. Wrigley, 'Lloyd George and the Labour Movement', (Ph.D. thesis, University of London, 1974), pp. 194–6.

8 J. Thomas, op. cit., pp. 19, 63.

9 CG, Vol. 120, 1611, 1614.

10 CG, Vol. 110, 32.

11 *South Wales Coal Annual* (1924), p. 169.

12 CG, Vol. 108, 532.

13 CG , Vol. 109, p. 817.

14 PRO, BT 189/1 (28 March 1917).

15 CG, Vol. 109, 135.

16 CG, Vol. 116, 1033.

17 CG, Vol. 117, 1094.

18 D. Willson Lloyd, 'The Coal Export Trade of the United Kingsom, 1910–1921', (M.A. thesis, University College Cardiff, 1922), p. 106.

19 CG, Vol. 119, 1582.

20 CG, Vol. 108, 423.

21 R.A.S. Redmayne, *The British Coal Mining Industry during the War* (Oxford, 1923), p. 23.

22 Ibid., p. 25.

23 GRO, NCB Collection. Notebook D/D CC21.

24 G.M. Holmes, 'The South Wales Coal Industry 1850–1914', *Transactions of the Honourable Society of Cynmrodorion,* (1976), p. 183.

25 R.A.S. Redmayne, op. cit., p. 13.

26 CG, Vol. 110, 268.

27 CG, Vol. 110, 32.

28 R. Page Arnot, *South Wales Miners. A History of the South Wales Miners' Federation (1914–1926)* (Cardiff, 1975), pp. 62, 78; CG, Vol. 110, 123.

29 MSWCA. General Minute Book MG13, p. 230.

30 L.J. Williams, 'Monmouthshire and South Wales Coalowners' Association 1873–1914', (M.A. thesis, University College of Wales, 1957).

31 C.M. Woodhouse, 'Rank and file movements among the miners of South Wales', (Ph.D. thesis, Oxford, 1969), pp. 121–33, esp. 129–30.

32 R.A.S. Redmayne, op. cit., p. 88; M.W. Kirby, *The British Coalmining Industry 1870–1946: a political and economic history* (Macmillan, 1977), p. 223, note 28.

33 R. Page Arnot, op. cit., pp. 123–4; R.A.S. Redmayne, op. cit., pp. 60–4. Redmayne has a printing error on page 62: 29th October should read 29th November.

34 R. Page Arnot, op. cit. pp. 123–4.

35 MSWCA. MG13, pp. 288–91.

36 MSWCA. MG14, p. 15.

37 MSWCA. MG14, pp. 15–16.

38 MSWCA. MG14, p. 24.

39 MSWCA. MG14, p. 26.

40 E.D. Lewis, op. cit. p. 249; J. Thomas, op. cit. passim.

41 CG, Vol. 112, 1123.

42 CG, Vol. 113, 393.

43 PRO. BT189/1 (7 March 1917).

44 R.A.S. Redmayne, op. cit., p. 125.

45 MSWCA, MG14, p. 93A.

46 CG, Vol. 116, 374.

47 Gwent Record Office, Blaenavon Company Minute Books D480, passim.

48 GRO, NCB Collection, D/D NCB 22/11.

49 PRO, BT 189/1, 9 May 1917.

50 Ibid., (9 May 1917).

51 MSWCA,, MG13, p. 257; MG14, p. 74, Cardiff District Board Minutes MC6, passim.

52 MSWCA, MG14, pp. 29, 32. Cardiff District Board Minute Book MC6, pp. 246–7.

53 MSCWA, MG14, pp. 142–4.

54 Frank Hodges, *Nationalisation of the Mines* (London, 1920), p. 93.

55 PRO, BT 189/2 (9 October 1918).

56 Ibid. 6 November 1918; 20 November 1918; 24 December 1918.

57 CG, Vol. 118, 33.

58 Coal Industry Commission, Vol. I, Cmd. 359 (1919), p. iv.

59 MSWCA, MG14, Printed Report (16 April 1919), p. 24.

60 Coal Industry Commission, Vol. I. Cmd. 359 (1919), p. viii.

61 Ibid., Vol. II, Cmd. 360, p. 416.

62 Ibid., pp. 416–7.

63 MSWCA, MG15, p. 96.

64 MSWCA, MG14, p. 87.

65 MSWCA, MG14, pp. 94–5A.

66 MSWCA, MG15, p. 91.

67 Kathleen Burk, ed., *War and the State. The Transformation of British Government: 1914–1919* (London 1982).

The Development of the Electricity Supply Industry in South Wales to 1939

1 For a fuller discussion see L. Hannah, *Electricity Before Nationalisation* (1979), pp. 5–10.

2 I.C.R. Byatt, 'The British Electrical Industry 1875–1914', (unpublished D.Phil. Thesis, Oxford, 1962).

3 *Report of Joint Select Committee of the House of Lords and House of Commons on Electrical Energy (Generating and Supply)* (1898), (Cross Report).

4 *South Wales Daily News,* (26 February 1900).

5 *Electrical Review,* 46 (9 March 1900), 317.

6 *South Wales Daily News,* (26 February 1900).

7 *Electrician,* 46 (26 October 1900), 17.

8 *South Wales Echo,* (8 February 1900).

9 L. Hannah, op. cit., p. 24.

10 E. Garcke, *The Progress of Electrical Enterprise* (1907), p. 123.

11 *South Wales Echo* (22 March 1900).

12 *Electrical Review,* 47 (6 July 1900), 8.

13 *Electrical Review,* 46 (23 January 1900), 9.

14 *South Wales Echo,* (4 July 1900).

15 *Electrician,* 58 (11 January 1907), 509–510.

16 Ibid.

17 *Electrical Review,* 62 (3 April 1908), 64.

18 Diversity factor is obtained by dividing the sum of the maximum demands of individual consumers during a given period by the actual maximum demand during the same period.

19 *Electrical Review,* 64 (26 March 1909), 325.

20 The Committees set up were:

Ministry of Reconstruction, *Interim Report of the Coal Sub-Committee* (1917), Cmd. 8880 (Haldane Report).

Report of the Committee Appointed by the Board of Trade to consider the Question of Electric Power Supply (1918), Cmd. 9062 (Williamson Report).

Ministry of Reconstruction, Advisory Council, *Report of the Committee of Chairmen on Electric Power Supply* (1919), Cmd. 93 (Birchenough Report).

21 Ministry of Transport, *Report of the Committee Appointed to Review the National Problem of the Supply of Electrical Energy* (1926) (Weir Report).

22 *Central Electricity Board,* Minutes, (28 February 1930).

23 R.F. Betherton, F.A. Birchandt, R.S.G. Rutherford, *Public Investment and the Trade Cycle in Great Britain* (Oxford, 1941).

24 *Central Electricity Board,* Minutes, (18 December 1936).

25 Ibid., (18 December 1936).

26 Ibid., (14 March 1930).

27 Electricity Commissioners, *Engineering and Financial Returns,* Annual and Garcke's Manual (E. Garcke, *Manual of Electrical Undertakings,* Annual).

The Movement of Population from South Wales with Specific Reference to the Effects of the Industrial Transference Scheme 1928–1937

1 Cmd. 3156: *First Report of the Industrial Transference Board* (26 June 1928), p. 53, para. 1412.

2 Cmd. 3156: *First Report of the Industrial Transference Board.*

3 Memorandum by Ministry of Health — 23 January 1928, PRO HLG 30/47.

4 See PRO CAB 27/389. Letter sent by the Unemployment Grants Committee on 15 December 1925 generally indicating substantial limitations on work that would qualify for assistance from UGC.

5 Minute by the Minister of Labour 6 January 1928 — produced in Cmd. 3156.

6 *Report of Enquiry into the Industrial Transference Scheme* (May 1938) p. 4, para. 16.

7 *Report of Enquiry into the Industrial Transference Scheme* (May 1938), p. 4, para. 16.

8 Cmd. 3156: *First report of the Industrial Transference Board,* p. 5, para. 8.

9 Ibid., p. 6, para. 10.

10 *Report of Enquiry into the Industrial Transference Scheme* (May 1938), p. 16, para. 75, PRO LAB 8/218.

11 Minutes of report of Meeting of Commissioner Special Areas with Mayor and Special Sub-Committee of County Borough of Merthyr (20 March 1935), PRO LAB 23/75.

12 Ibid.

13 *Report of Enquiry into Industrial Transference Scheme* (May 1938), p. 13, para. 60, PRO LAB 8/218.

14 Cmd. 49587: *First Report of the Commissioner for the Special Areas* (July 1935), p. 66, para. 167.

15 For evidence of these points consult PRO References LAB 2/493, LAB 2/1298.

16 *Report of Enquiry into the Industrial Transference Scheme* (May 1938), p. 6, para 27, PRO LAB 8/218.

17 Ibid., p.7, para 35.

18 *Reports of Enquiry into the Industrial Transference Scheme* (May 1938), p. 9, para. 45.

19 Minutes of Evidence — *Royal Commission on Distribution of the Industrial Population* (February 1938), p. 280, para. 17.

20 *Report of the Commissioner for Special Areas* (1938), p. 3, para. 10.

21 Memorandum by Minister of Health, — 23rd June 1928, PRO HLG 30/47.

War and the Economy: the South Wales Experience

1 For the purpose of the essay south Wales is described as the three counties of Carmarthen, Glamorgan and Monmouth. Frequent reference is made to the South Wales and Monmouthshire Special Area and the Development Area and appropriate statistics are quoted.

2 W. E. Minchinton, 'The Evolution of the Regional Economy', in G. Manners, ed., *South Wales in the Sixties* (Pergamon, London, 1965), p. 26.

3 B. Thomas, 'Post-War Expansion', in B. Thomas, ed., *The Welsh Economy* (Cardiff, University of Wales Press, 1962), 30–54.

4 Ibid., pp. 32–3.

5 For a contemporary account of south Wales in the 1930s see B. Thomas, 'The Changing Face of South Wales', *The Listener,* (23 March 1938), 611–18.

6 Board of Trade, *Industrial Survey of South Wales* (London, 1932), p. 153.

7 See G. Manners, 'A Profile of New South Wales', in G. Manners, ed., op. cit., pp. 37–40; C. Baber and D. Thomas, 'The Glamorgan Economy, 1914–45', Chapter XI in Glanmor Williams and A.H. John, eds., *Industrial Glamorgan,* Vol. V, *Glamorgan County History* (Cardiff, University of Wales Press, 1980), pp. 536–51.

8 Nuffield College Social Reconstruction Survey. Quoted in M.P. Fogarty, *Plan Your Own Industries* (Blackwell, Oxford, 1947), p. 15.

9 See C. Baber and D. Thomas, op. cit., pp. 551–62.

10 These figures are derived from the *Fifth Report of the Commissioner for the Special Areas in England and Wales* (1938), H.M.S.O. Cmd. 5896, Appendix VIII.

11 Board of Trade, *Surveys of Industrial Development* (H.M.S.O., London, 1933–8).

12 The Special Area did not come into existence until 1935. It should be noted that the boundary of the area was structured with little regard to the essential unity of the industrial area.

13 For details of pre-war developments at the Treforest Trading Estate see *Wales and Monmouthshire* — the official handbook of the National Industrial Development Council of Wales and Monmouthshire, published quarterly between 1935 and 1939. Also see G. Percival, 'Industrial Estates in Wales', *International Labour Review,* 90, No. 2 (August 1964), 130–49.

14 Cmd. 5896, op. cit.

15 Ministry of Labour.

16 See R.O. Roberts, 'Special Financial Facilities for Industries in the Depressed Areas with

Particular Reference to the Experience of South Wales', *The Manchester School*, 21, No. 1 (January 1953), 39–61.

17 C.C. Salway, *Refugees and Industry* (Christian Council for Refugees from Germany and Central Europe, London, 1942), p. 18.

Another source is the P.E.P. pamphlet no. 4, *Are Refugees an Asset?* (September 1939).

18 See G. Llewellyn, *Industrial Location Policy in England and Wales since 1934* (unpublished M.A. thesis, Wales 1953), Statistical Appendix, Tables 30, 31. Also E.D. Lewis, *The Rhondda Valleys* (Phoenix House, London 1959), p. 260.

19 Office of the Minister of Reconstruction, *Welsh Reconstruction Advisory Council — First Interim Report* (H.M.S.O. 1944), p. 57, henceforth referred to as WRAC.

20 The following information on wartime developments is obtained from a number of sources including various editions of the Board of Trade Journal in the late 1940s. For a review of wartime and post-war developments also see various editions of *Wales and Monmouthshire* — the National Industrial Development Council for Wales and Monmouthshire (1947, 1951 and 1955).

21 G. Percival, op. cit., pp. 140–1.

22 See I. May, *The Story of the Royal Ordnance Factories, 1939–48* (H.M.S.O., London, 1949).

23 See E. Pride, 'The Economic Province of Wales', *Transactions of the Honourable Society of Cymmrodorion*, (1969), Part 1, 70–81.

24 WRAC, op. cit., p. 5.

WRAC was only a part of the programme of studies and plans being undertaken at a national and regional level. 1943 onwards saw the increasing involvement of the Board of Trade and WRAC was to be left behind by events. See E. Pride, op. cit., and M.P. Fogarty, op. cit.

25 Much of the following information again comes from various editions of the Board of Trade Journal and *Wales and Monmouthshire*, op. cit. in note 13. Also see *Wales and Monmouthshire. A Summary of Government Action 1st August, 1945 — 31st July, 1946*. Cmd. 6938, H.M.S.O., Appendix 7.

26 Board of Trade (1948), *Distribution of Industry*, Cmd. 7540, H.M.S.O., London, paras. 73–5, Appendices 6, 7 and 8.

27 It should be noted that in the 96 new factories already completed the *estimated* total employment was to be 18,990. In addition there were 145 projects which were under construction or proceeding with an *estimated* employment of 36,820. Cmd. 7540, op. cit.

28 B. Thomas, op. cit., p. 35.

29 G. Llewellyn, op. cit., pp. 169–70.

30 M.P. Fogarty, *The Prospects of the Industrial Areas of Great Britain* (Methuen, London, 1945), p. 100.

31 P. Massey, *Industrial South Wales: A Social and Political Survey* (Gollancz, London, 1940), pp. 71–2.

32 See for instance two studies published by the National Institute of Economic and Social Research in 1952: W.F. Luttrell, *The Cost of Industrial Movement*, and O.C. Hague and P.K. Newman, *Costs of Alternative Locations: the Clothing Industry*.

33 Cmd. 7540, op. cit.

34 E. Pride, op. cit., p. 74.

35 Precise comparisons of the pre-war and post-war periods cannot be made on the basis of statistics

relating to the aggregate insured population or its industrial distribution for two basic reasons: i) the coverage of the insurance scheme was changed in 1948 with the introduction of the National Health Service Act; ii) the system of industrial classification employed by the Ministry of Labour was replaced by the Standard Industrial classification. The figures used have been adjusted to provide some consistency. (See notes to tables in the Appendix).

36 For example, at Merthyr Tydfil in July 1944 the unemployment rate had fallen to 3.5 from 47.7 in July 1939, while the Rhondda displayed figures of 1.3 at Pontypridd, 1.0 at Treorchy and 1.7 at Porth.

37 It should be noted that the number of insured females for 1945 and 1948 refer to those between 14 and 59 years of age compared to the 14 and 64 group in 1938. This does not dramatically alter the picture of increased female participation.

38 J.H. Dunning, 'The Development Areas. A Further Note', *The Manchester School*, 24, No. 1 (January, 1956), p. 88.

39 *The Ministry of Labour Gazette*, (February 1949), pp. 45–6.

40 Ibid.

41 Cmd. 6938, op. cit., para. 11.

42 References can be made here to the diversification indices calculated for the South Wales region by E.C. Conkling for 1931 and 1951 using employment data and adopting the boundaries established for the Development Area. The diversification index for south Wales increased from 35.0 to 51.5 compared with a rise from 55.8 to 61.8 in Great Britain. Conkling also showed that the region was far from uniform in the distribution of economic activity by calculating local indices. See E.C. Conkling, 'South Wales: A Case Study in Industrial Diversification', *Economic Geography*, 39, No. 3 (July 1963), 258–76.

43 An *activity rate* should express the number of economically active persons in a population group as a percentage of that group as a whole. Care must be taken when using and interpreting such rates. In this case the activity rate is calculated as the ratio of occupied persons/working age population. For 1931 and 1951 the working age population has been taken as 14–64 but figures for occupied refer to 14 and over for 1931 and 15 and over for 1951. The activity rates calculated then do not give us the number of persons per 100 of the working age population group who are economically active.

44 See *Census of Population, General Report and Tables,* (H.M.S.O., 1951), p. 129.

45 National Council of Social Service, *Dispersal* (Oxford University Press, London, 1944), p. 16.

Index

iron ore 3, 43–4, 45–9, 59, 171
ironmasters 25, 29–30, 32, 36, 47–50, 56, 76
ironstone 3, 26, 30, 36, 37, 43–5, 48–9
ironworks 26, 37, 56
 Aberdare 46
 Abersychan 37, 40–1, 48, 49
 Beaufort 37, 40–1
 Blaenavon 26, 32, 34, 37, 40–1, 71
 Blaina 40–1
 Blakemore 42
 Broseley 32
 Brown & Co. 42
 Bute 40–1, 42
 Clydach 40–1
 Coalbrook Vale 40–1
 Cyfarthfa 9, 26, 29, 42, 46–8, 49, 51, 282
  n.22
 Dowlais 26, 30, 33, 44, 47, 48, 49, 51, 85,
  96, 225, 282 n.22
 Ebbw Vale 26, 32, 37, 40–1, 49, 51
 Gadlys 42
 Garnddyrris 40–1
 Glamorganshire 35
 Hirwaun 26, 42, 48
 Melingriffith 32
 Monmouthshire 35
 Nantyglo 37, 40–1
 Penydarren 9, 26, 30, 32, 33, 42
 Pentwyn 40–1
 Plymouth 26, 29, 30, 33, 42, 47, 49
 Rhymney 40–1, 48, 49, 51
 Sirhowy 26
 Taff Vale 42
 Tredegar 40–1
 Varteg 12, 40–1, 44, 71
 Ynyscedwyn 31, 35
 Ystalyfera 35
 Ystradgynlais 35
Isard, Walter 46

Jeans, James Stephen 44
Jenkins, Mr (coal company director) 167
Jenkins, Dr Geraint 172, 175, 179, 185
Jenkins, Williams 168
Jesus College, Oxford 136
Jevons, Professor H. Stanley 203
John, Professor A.H. 1, 2, 10, 80
 Industrial Development of S. Wales 1
Joint Electricity Authorities 228
Jones, A.W. 87, 92

Jones, Alfred 172
Jones, Gruffydd 21
Jones, Rev. J. Cynddylan 179, 180, 186
Jones, J.H. 148, 149, 151
Jones, Phillip 71
Jones, W. & C.T. Co. Ltd. 179
Joslin, David 1

Kayser-Bondor Ltd. 260
Keen, A. 223
Kenfig 256, 261
Kenrick, G.S. 12
Kent, George Ltd. 262
Kidwelly 26
Knighton 66
Kylsant, Lord (Owen Philipps) 172
Kymmer, Thomas 26

Labour, Ministry of 238, 255
Labour Party 140
labour relations 206
 see also strikes, employment
Lady Windsor Colliery 163, 164, 167
Lampeter 13
Lancashire 46, 48, 50, 65, 142, 153
landowners 28, 32, 43, 66, 82, 84, 88, 90, 94
lead ore 59
Leconfield, Lord 48
Lewis, Sir W.T. 223
'Lib-Labism' 206, 213, 217
life-expectancy 128–9, 132
Lighthouse, The 178, 179
lime 30, 35, 36
limestone 26, 36, 37, 43, 44, 85
Limited Owners' Residences Act 93
Lines Bros. (toys) 260
Little W. 86, 88, 90, 91, 94
Liverpool 73, 134
Llandaff Railway Station 84
Llanelli 3, 26, 46, 117, 152, 260, 261
 coal industry **53–64**, 287 n.5, 288 n.36
 docks 61, 120
Llanelli Railway and Dock Co. 61
Llanelly Copperworks Co. 55–64, 287 n.8
Llangennech 256, 260
Llangennech Coal Co. 55, 58, 60–1, 62
Llansamlet 26
Llantrisant 84, 85, 94, 256, 260
Llantrisant and Taff Vale Junction, Select
 Committee on 85